ANTONY WILD worked for thirteen years as a buying director for the country's foremost speciality coffee roaster, and is widely credited with having introduced speciality coffees into the United Kingdom. He subsequently worked as a consultant, journalist and writer, specialising in colonialism and its history. He has written several books, including *The East India Company* and *Remains of the Raj*.

By the same author

The East India Company
Remains of the Raj

BLACK GOLD

THE DARK HISTORY OF COFFEE

Antony Wild

4th ESTATE • London

4th Estate
An imprint of HarperCollins*Publishers*
1 London Bridge Street
London
SE1 9GF

www.4thestate.co.uk

This edition published by 4th Estate 2019
1

Previously published by Harper Perennial 2005

First published as *Coffee: A Dark History*
by 4th Estate 2004

'The Importance of Cupping Protocol' by
Mike Riley, courtesy of the author

PS™ is a trademark of HarperCollins*Publishers*

A catalogue record for this book
is available from the British Library

ISBN 9780008353438
Printed and bound by CPI Group (UK) Ltd, Croydon, CR0 4YY
Set in Sabon

MIX
Paper from
responsible sources
FSC® C007454

This book is produced from independently certified FSC™ paper
to ensure responsible forest management.

For more information visit: www.harpercollins.co.uk/green

CONTENTS

PREFACE

Dark history lifts lids and turns over stones. This onerous task can be accomplished only with the help of many who might wish for lids to remain unlifted, and stones to remain unturned. Many of my friends and colleagues from my former incarnation in the coffee trade who contributed their time, opinions, and expertise to this book do not deserve to have their names associated with such a disreputable work. They are not thus individually acknowledged, although collectively I am greatly in their debt. Myriad other sources have been ruthlessly quarried in order that this edifice might be erected: inasmuch as the book covers a wide variety of topics, I have been deeply dependent on work already done in these areas. Again, each unwitting contributor was unaware that their work would be hijacked to my particular purpose, and they remain unacknowledged, as their individual contributions to the shape of a specific stone cannot be acknowledged without unfairly implicating them in the design of the entire structure.

A note on notes, or rather the lack of them. Facts, figures, and dates are to the best of my knowledge independently verifiable by those who care so to do. My decision not to include notes or a bibliography is largely stylistic: a dark history spangled with pinpoints of objective illumination ceases to be dark at all.

One acknowledgement must be made. Over lunch in Hammersmith I expressed my desire to write about the gloomier side of coffee's history to Clive Priddle, then commissioning editor at Fourth Estate. It was he who, with deceptive casualness, suggested this book's title, which unleashed the daemons that inform every word I have written.

Normandy, October 2003

PROLOGUE

On 21 May 1502, a Portuguese fleet under Admiral João da Nova was making its way northwards from the Cape of Good Hope across the vast emptiness of the South Atlantic Ocean when the lookout unexpectedly spotted land. The ships later put in opposite a small valley with fresh water that was the only breach in the otherwise sheer cliffs of a previously unknown 47-square-mile island. Da Nova named the discovery St Helena, after the mother of the Emperor Constantine whose Saint's Day it was. The sailors briefly explored the island, finding an unpopulated Garden of Eden free of all predators and poisonous insects, the rich volcanic soil of its steep mountains luxuriantly wooded with ebony, gum-wood, and fruit trees. Following the traditional mariners' practice of the time, they put some goats ashore for the benefit of future visitors before they left for home.

In about the same year, in Yemen in southern Arabia, a new drink made from the fruit of a plant of Ethiopian origin had made its first appearance. Coffee's popularity expanded rapidly throughout the Islamic world, and it was in fairly wide use by the time its consumption first attracted controversy in Mecca in 1511. By the end of the sixteenth century, European merchants and travellers began to venture warily into the confines of Ottoman Empire and reports of the 'Wine of Araby' began to reach the West, soon followed by the drink itself, which became very popular in seventeenth-century Europe, especially in

England, France, and Holland. The European maritime powers realized that the virtual monopoly the Yemeni port of Mocha held on the coffee trade could be circumvented if they themselves started coffee plantations in their new tropical colonies. First the Dutch, then the French, managed to obtain coffee seedlings from Yemen. The English East India Company likewise managed to take some seeds from Mocha to St Helena in 1732, where, neglected, they grew virtually in the wild until their recent rediscovery.

By the middle of the eighteenth century European colonies dominated the world coffee trade, meeting the demands of eager consumers at home from plantations frequently worked in conditions of slavery or near-slavery. In the meantime, St Helena – the world's most isolated island – played a role of great strategic importance in the maintenance of British power in the East. For all its remoteness, the island was visited by many of the luminaries of the Raj as they returned from India and beyond, and was chosen by the British Government as the only suitably secure location for the exile of Napoleon after his defeat at Waterloo in 1815.

Today, one of the world's rarest and most expensive coffees comes from St Helena, grown from plants directly descended from those introduced by the East India Company in 1732. The island is still a British Overseas Territory, an anachronistic remnant of the Empire upon which the sun never set. Whilst its coffee may be admired by connoisseurs, the environment of the island itself has degraded enormously since its discovery: descendants of da Nova's goats ravaged the trees, its endemic ebony was made virtually extinct, and other man-made disasters stripped the island of its rich topsoil, exposing the forbidding volcanic rock that now forms most of its surface. The island lost its strategic significance with the opening of the Suez Canal: it has no airport and can be reached only by one heavily subsidized ship.

Many of the momentous events and grand personages of world history have scratched ghostly messages on the black basalt of

St Helena, and deciphering them in this isolated context conveys a curious sense of the underlying connectedness of the island with the pivotal phenomena of that larger world. Thus da Nova's fleet was returning from India, where the Portuguese were starting to build a trading empire that was to dominate the Indian Ocean for the next century; the East India Company was threatening to usurp that empire by the time it took possession of the island in 1659; the Dutch and French success with growing coffee in their colonies outshone that of the Company, whose neglected seedlings were buffeted by the southern trade winds; Napoleon had introduced to Europe the drinking of chicory as a coffee substitute under his 'Continental System' and, during his exile, he planted a coffee tree in his garden that died from exposure to those same winds; the island became a refuge for captured slave ships after abolition and one such was on its way to Brazil, where slavery was the cornerstone of that country's coffee industry . . .

The 5000-strong population of St Helena has been used recently as a kind of Petri dish by sociologists wishing to study the effects of television – introduced only in the last few years – on everything from crime rates to Girl Guide membership. In this book, the island will also be used as a Petri dish: we will return to it repeatedly to study how the history of coffee and colonialism evolved together over the last five hundred years to forge an unholy alliance that still exists for the benefit of Western coffee consumers at the expense of the people of the Third World countries – more often than not former colonies – that produce it, and of the planet itself.

INTRODUCTION

In 1991 I bought a small one-kilo bag of coffee, and the press coverage that generated was phenomenal.

'He's a pioneer among coffee traders', the then-young tyro journalist Nigel Slater wrote, moderately enough; 'The Indiana Jones of the coffee world', campaigning food writer Joanna Blythman said, upping the ante – I could scarcely complain about that flattering comparison; but then . . . 'The Christopher Columbus of coffee . . .' I'd had an inkling that introducing the now infamous *kopi luwak* to the Western world would sprinkle a bit of magic PR dust, but I'd hardly expected to be compared to the leading light of the Golden Age of Exploration.

During my time as the Coffee Director for Taylors of Harrogate in the 1980s and early 90s, most of my suppliers in Europe used to look at me with quizzical amusement when I kept asking them to source me bizarre coffees they'd never heard of. Usually I had to jump on a plane to Yemen or Cuba or wherever to track down my quarry myself. But in the case of kopi luwak . . .

It happened like this. I'd spent most of 1981 in London serving my coffee taster's apprenticeship with various City merchants, and I passed some of my spare time researching in the library of the International Coffee Organization. One day I pulled a back copy of *National Geographic* magazine off the shelf. In it I found a full-length feature about Sumatran coffee, and one paragraph caught my eye – a reference to the author being served a sublime coffee made from beans that had been digested in the stomach of a small weasel-like wild animal called a luwak. These luwaks prowled the plantations at night selecting to eat, in time-honoured fashion, 'only the finest, ripest coffee cherries', which were then digested by the animal, evacuated, collected, washed and roasted. I mentally filed this curious tale and forgot about it, until nearly ten years later when I was on the phone with a particularly persistent Swiss coffee trader who was trying as usual to sell me some coffee that I didn't need. 'Get me some kopi luwak,' I said to distract him, 'I'll buy that . . .!' I explained to him exactly what it was, and where it was to be found: he had been duly amazed and amused, and I had thought no more about it. Three months had passed when he called to announce, 'Mr Wild! I have a kilo of kopi luwak for you!'

Of all the remarkable coffees I had ever bought, this small bag of kopi luwak generated the most interest by far. The press and public couldn't get enough of the story. I found out, to my amazement and shock, that what had been once an almost unheard-of delicacy that I had introduced more or less on a whim had become the must-have coffee on the books of many aspiring specialist green coffee trading companies both in Europe and the United States. It had even made an appearance in a Hollywood film; in *The Bucket List,* a terminally ailing Morgan Freeman brings some for a similarly ailing Jack Nicholson to taste.

As a consequence of all this attention, demand for kopi luwak had soared, and to meet it, wild luwaks were being coaxed onto Sumatran coffee farms to gorge themselves on coffee cherries and produce more crap. An American company had artificially synthesised the flavour imparted by this unorthodox 'processing' and licensed a roaster to use it. Far from recoiling in horror, discerning consumers at that time were falling over themselves to taste kopi luwak. A long way from the days when I was the only one willing to drink it, I thought almost fondly, dazzled by the success of my protégé, and wondering idly how this demand was met by the 500 kilos the roasters still proclaimed were collected in the wild each year.

Many other aspects of today's speciality coffee market amaze me, too. The coffees that I introduced to the startled British public for the first time twenty-five years ago – St Helena Island, Yemeni Mocha Matari, Jamaica Blue Mountain Peaberry, Cuba Crystal Mountain and Harrar Longberry – would now appear really quite run-of-the-mill to the so-called 'Third Wave' coffee traders and roasters, focused as they are on individual plantations and plant varietals, along with exceptional husbandry and processing. And they have developed a range of coffee vocabulary far beyond that with which I was apprenticed, to go with their expertise.

But in one respect little has changed since this book was first published: the myths about the history of the coffee trade that are endlessly repeated and recycled by the trade itself are as flawed and derivative as they ever were. When this book was first published in 2003, one of my aims was, as far as possible, to set the historical record straight. The first edition of this book was published in the UK and USA, and translated into Chinese, Japanese, French, Turkish and Vietnamese, so it was hardly an obscure tome. Yet it is still possible to read abject nonsense about the history of coffee on a million coffee trade websites as though its true heritage had never existed. It seems that all the care and attention to detail that is lavished on the other aspects of the coffee trade goes out of the window when it comes to discussing its roots in our past. No one, for example, even seems to have noticed the significance of the find at Kush mentioned in the last chapter.

The book also concerns the economic, environmental and

political aspects of the coffee trade. When I was first writing it in 2001/2, world coffee prices were at an all-time low and the human suffering this caused to those working at the most basic level of the trade was immense. Some critics called the approach I took in this book anti-corporate and anti-capitalist, and back then, when economies in the developed world were booming, such an approach was distinctly unfashionable. We live in a very different world to that following the economic crash of 2008, and since then the capitalist model has been under question in a way it has rarely been before. In my pioneering coffee days I was said to be ahead of my time: unfortunately it seems that, with regard this book, my time has finally come, and what I forecasted back then with some fore-boding is actually happening now.

So what happened next to my pet rarity cum superstar, kopi luwak? When looking into this coffee and its origins, I quickly came to realise that I had inadvertently created a monster. An article in the *Guardian* had appeared, exposing, to my horror, the horrendous practice of caging wild luwaks in racks of crude metal cages, where they were force-fed coffee cherries simply to make the prized beans. The journalist claimed that the produc-tion of kopi luwak in this intensive, battery fashion was not just confined to Indonesia, but had also been adopted by other South East Asian coffee origins too, such as the Philippines, India, Vietnam and Thailand.

Then out of the blue I received an email from my literary agent. The BBC had come across this book when they were looking for a coffee expert for a programme they were thinking of making, she wrote. What's the programme about? I replied. *Something called kopi luwak,* came the reply. *Have you heard of it?*

So it was that, five months later, in June 2013, I found myself in Medan, Sumatra, in the utterly unfamiliar role of undercover reporter alongside the experienced BBC investigative journalist Guy Lynn, secretly recording interviews with coffee exporters as part of the BBC World *Our World* investigation into the truth about the kopi luwak trade. I was there in the guise of a director of a (virtual, i.e. non-existent) UK coffee company to provide specialist knowledge of the coffee trade, so that we'd appear to know what we were talking about. After expressing an interest in buying large quantities of genuine wild kopi luwak, we accompanied one trader to Takengon, in Aceh Province, a supposed centre of kopi luwak production. He wanted to demonstrate to us how the coffee he was proposing to sell us was all sourced from wild luwaks living in the virgin forests of the nearby Gayo Highlands. It was a gruelling fifteen hours' drive from Medan, and when we arrived, we were supposed to go to our hotel to meet up with Chris Rogers, another BBC reporter who would be presenting the finished programme. He had already been there for a few days, secretly filming caged luwaks. As we arrived in the Takengon centre, our driver was flagged down by a man standing in the deserted midnight street. Curiously, he seemed to be expecting us, and after a hasty conversation in Indonesian, we were told that we needed to go to a different hotel to the one we had booked. We went along with the change of plan: the proposed hotel looked OK, and even though Chris was for some unexplained reason still at the original hotel, I was past caring about the whys and wherefores. I collapsed exhausted into bed – only to be woken by a phone call about ten minutes later.

'Pack your bags and meet me in the lobby!' Guy's voice whispered. 'Our guy has threatened to shoot Chris's driver. He waved a gun at him!'

He added that I had to destroy the notes that I had made (he'd seen me writing on my iPad non-stop) and I obeyed, grumpily, mourning the tragic loss to travel literature. I was also to give him the recording and camera equipment. This was the same equipment I had been asked to carry all the way from London and smuggle through Medan customs to avoid the attention of the Indonesian authorities who weren't too keen on unauthorised journalists roaming around their country, apparently. That's why I had to destroy my notes, incidentally: they were potentially evidence of our nefarious activities.

'Have we been rumbled?' I asked Guy five minutes later when I met him in the lobby. He didn't seem to hear me. He was too busy talking in full-on emergency mode on a satellite phone to some senior producer at the BBC in London. I'd signed all the BBC Health and Safety Compliance forms before we left, but none of them mentioned what the appropriate response to armed threats should be. It was all a far cry from my coffee-buying trips for Taylors, where I'd disappear to far-off lands with nothing more than a cheery wave. I could have been captured by Danakil tribesmen and sold into white slavery – or worse – for all the company knew. Different days.

The long and the short of the matter was that it turned out we'd become enmeshed in some kopi luwak mafia turf war, and far from being rumbled, we had been treated as potentially serious buyers. Chris's driver's unexplained presence had been interpreted by our guy as a threat from a commercial rival, and the gun routine was designed to force him to leave the town. In the end it was decided by the faceless voice back in London that we should act as if nothing untoward had taken place, and invent a reason for returning to Medan urgently. So we ended up making a swift exit in our gun-toting trader friend's 4X4 via a token visit to some entirely spurious wild kopi luwak collecting 'farm' which appeared to have been hired for the day as set dressing by our friend, for whom I had by now conceived a distinct loathing.

I finally caught a glimpse of the ravishing, almost Alpine

lakeside setting of Takengon as we left to drive the fifteen hours back to Medan. The trader's choice of a particularly ear-piercing, mind-frazzling, boom-boom Indonesian electro music to play on his CD player seemed designed to add torture to the excitement of the previous night. Even the back of his head (I was seated behind him) assumed a vile aspect. What did I think of kopi luwak at this point? That it was just coffee's dark history run amok.

The programme was finally screened in September 2013 (you can still watch it on YouTube. WARNING: some of the footage is distressing) and made waves across the kopi luwak as well as the wider coffee trade.

During the months before we left for Indonesia that we spent researching the programme, I'd quickly come to realise that the *Guardian* report was broadly correct and that the fiction that kopi luwak is a wild-sourced, incredibly rare coffee is maintained even after the coffee arrives in the consuming markets. Some exporters provide certificates of origin to support their claims, but if you examine them closely, they provide no reassurance that the coffee originates from wild animals, only from a certain plantation or district. In turn these certificates can often be used by importing companies to persuade their roaster and retailer clients that they are buying the real deal. I can't count the number of times I heard the term 'trusted supplier' from people in the trade, knowing in some cases that beyond a shadow of doubt the supplier in question was buying coffee from caged luwaks. Retailers, importers, exporters all passed the buck back down the line, but in the actual place where the buck stops, at origin, nine times out of ten I suspected that the coffee was coming from caged luwaks. But even if you visit a plantation, you can't be sure that what you're being told is true – just watch the BBC programme and you'll see that one particular estate I visited producing so-called wild kopi luwak later reluctantly admitted that they had luwaks in cages, although only when faced with incontrovertible evidence from the BBC. There was neither sight nor sound of the luwaks while I was actually there – and I was actively looking for them. That's the key problem faced by buyers trying to source genuine wild kopi luwak: producers know the process of production is controversial, so they conceal the ugly truth. And the buyers, whether in the know or not, prefer not to look too hard.

Once back in the UK, I timed the launch of my Facebook campaign, which I had titled 'Kopi Luwak: Cut the Crap', to coincide with the programme, created to encourage an independent certification for genuine wild kopi luwak. This is the only way it seemed to me that all links in the supply chain could guarantee authenticity, and might eventually lead to a falling off in consumption of kopi luwak.

The super-premium price that kopi luwak commands is sustained by two myths: one, that the coffee comes from the digestive tract of a wild animal freely roaming the plantations at night and selecting only the finest, ripest cherries; and secondly, that only 500 kilos of this rarest of coffees are collected annually.

Both claims are demonstrably false.

If the second isn't true, it makes the first irrelevant. Estimates of the real annual crop vary wildly, but I know for sure that the UK trade alone accounts for over two tonnes annually, and one kopi luwak farm I visited proudly boasted that it produced 1.6 tonnes per annum from a hundred enclosed animals. One UK roaster that claimed to be incredibly scrupulous about only sourcing genuine wild kopi luwak and carried the usual 'Only 500 kilos . . .' claim on its packaging, grudgingly admitted to me they were selling over a tonne of their kopi luwak a year.

Now that the fact that much of the coffee comes from caged or enclosed luwaks has been exposed, those suppliers who unwillingly admit this have started to claim that it doesn't matter, because their luwaks are well looked after, their cages are clean and suchlike. Animal welfare experts, however, say that there is no such thing as a well looked-after luwak: they are solitary, nocturnal wild animals that become immensely stressed when kept in the company of others. To my surprise, no one seemed to mention anything about the effect of caffeine on the creatures, nor could I find any research on the matter. So using the tried-and-tested scientific technique known technically as a 'back of an envelope' calculation, I started to work it out myself. I knew that the usual amount of coffee cherry that luwaks are fed daily on a farm is about 1.5 kilos. Although the bean itself passes through their system, I worked out that the flesh of the cherry alone contains the caffeine equivalent of 120 espressos a day. That's consumed by a luwak, a small mammal. Imagine the effect of 120 espressos on a fully grown adult human – it hardly bears considering. In addition, anecdotal evidence suggests that luwaks suffer from caffeine-induced calcium deficiency, and blood in their scats, frequently dying within a year or so of captivity. And I've even seen for myself one wretched animal in a half-hectare enclosure with a hundred other luwaks so distressed that it had gnawed off its own foot. I repeat: gnawed off its own foot. Correct me if I'm wrong, but not even your most hyped-up, caffeine-addicted office colleague has ever been driven to such gruesome excess.

There are genuine producers of wild kopi luwak, though. They are mostly smallholders in remoter districts, and for them – given world coffee prices at the moment – the popularity of kopi luwak is a valuable source of income. Inevitably this has led to fraud and corruption, but if a genuine independent certification scheme were available to these genuine producers, it would not only protect their source of income but would help protect the wild luwaks and their forest habitat, too. Frequently jungle areas bordering remote coffee-growing districts are under threat of illegal logging, precisely because they are far away from the not-very-watchful eye.

That's why as well as exposing the cruelty of caged coffee production, my 'Kopi Luwak: Cut the Crap' campaign lobbied for the creation of such a scheme. I was supported in this by the World Animal Protection organisation in the UK. We had our first break when we mounted a petition on Change.org, which resulted in Harrods being forced to abandon one of their suppliers who had in turn been supplied by an Indonesian company that had been exposed on the BBC programme. Harvey Nichols and Selfridges soon followed suit, as did other major retailers internationally. After that we shifted our attention to the major coffee certifiers – UTZ and Rainforest Alliance – which were in danger of inadvertently altering their code of practice in such a way that would allow caged kopi luwak to be produced on estates that they had certified sustainable. To our relief, we managed to successfully lobby these bodies against this potentially disastrous move.

Meanwhile, the Indonesian government said that it regarded genuine wild kopi luwak as 'a national treasure' and was working towards the creation of certification – conveniently failing to note that the government's own estates in East Java were a major promoter of caged kopi luwak. At the time, I did another back-of-an-envelope exercise with a trader familiar with these large estates. We worked out that when coffee prices were low, their kopi luwak sales were worth more to the government than all the top-quality, much sought-after coffee produced on its hundreds of hectares. He also told me that if a certification problem arose, the government would simply move the caged kopi luwak production off the estate in question.

The sheer amount of money to be made in this cruel trade of a coffee whose price is bolstered by the deliberate perpetuation of the myths about it – principally that it is wild and scarce – mean effectively it is worth too much economically to suppress. And that's not just at producer level, but all the way down the supply chain.

Go online today, and you'll see that plenty of vendors of kopi luwak have taken on board the raging controversy about this particular coffee. Taken on board, not in terms of changing their production practices (perish the thought . . .), but by changing their marketing. A whole new generation of false and fraudulent claims has arisen, the general gist of which is that, acutely aware of false and fraudulent claims, the vendors have declared that they have gone out of their way just for their lucky clients to source the absolute genuine article. These same traders wave their 'Genuine Wild Kopi Luwak with Official Indonesian Government Certificate' credentials to lend them credibility, some even posting detailed documents on their websites that are supposed to substantiate their claims. Are these certificates themselves genuine, or knocked up on a laptop on some Takengon back-street? Who knows? To adapt the translation of the famous Latin quote *'Quis custodiet ipsos custodes?'*, for this modern coffee context, 'Who certifies the certifiers?'.

One thing is sure: if there is anything this Kopi Luwak fiasco has amply demonstrated, it is that if there is any room for fraudulent and deceitful practice in the trade, there will be.

How might a watertight certification work? I've met one source of genuine wild kopi luwak who has convinced me that his product is bona fide precisely because of the protocols that he has in place to ensure there is no forgery or adulteration. These include strict observation of the freshness and dietary mixture of the luwak's scats, strict quotas (maximum sustainable production ceiling) and significant financial incentives – if you, as a smallholder, are accepted as a supplier, you'll have long-term rewards that you'll lose immediately and irrevocably if you attempt to cheat. And cheating may eventually become easy to prove: a Japanese scientist is currently working on a method to distinguish between wild and caged kopi luwak, which would give the certification of this product a solid foundation.

It's interesting not only to see how modern methods can be used to tackle such animal welfare issues, but also how the same issues can have unexpected resonances with the past. One aspect of certification has an uncanny echo of the learned debates about coffee itself in the sixteenth- and seventeenth-century Islamic courts of Mecca and Cairo that we'll encounter later in this book. As befits the government of the world's largest Muslim population, when they felt that they were ready to ramp up the production of caged civet coffee through the creation of a civet-breeding programme, in 2010 the plantations in East Java applied to the Indonesian Ulema Council of Islamic clerics for a fatwa (juridical opinion) to determine whether kopi luwak was halal or haram (forbidden). In the final fatwa, it was declared that as long as certain production protocols were met (none of which mentioned the provenance of the coffee, as we've seen), it was judged halal, presumably to some relief.

It's been a long road since my initial impulse purchase in Yorkshire back in 1991, and the end is not yet in sight, but consciousness about kopi luwak has certainly been raised, and that can only be for the good – eventually. In the meantime, this coffee has acquired a new name in academic circles: apparently, it's an 'excremental commodity'. So at least it can now be talked about without embarrassment at polite dinner parties.

A month or two ago I met an Australian coffee planter in Sri Lanka who has a hundred hectares under cultivation, high in the central mountains adjoining a forest. I told him about my involvement with kopi luwak. 'Luwaks?' he said, 'Got hundreds of those little blighters running around my plantation. My guys have gathered up 40 kilos of their droppings. Dunno what to do with them!'

'Do nothing,' I advised him. 'The game ain't worth the candle.'

NOTE ON THIS NEW EDITION:

The opening chapter of this book concerns the deep coffee crisis of the early noughties. While this dire phase has thankfully passed, the wider observations made remain relevant today, and there is nothing to prevent such a crisis arising again, as indeed appears to be happening right at this moment, in a less severe incarnation. I therefore have not attempted to update the statistics I used previously to reflect current market conditions.

1

THE WAY WE LIVE NOW

I see I have been bitter. But what would you think of
someone who could write such things without bitterness?

'MULTATULI', *Max Havelaar, or the Coffee Auctions of*
the Dutch Trading Company (1860)

The catastrophically low price currently paid to the producers of coffee is leading to the largest enforced global lay-off of workers in history. Nonetheless, it is remarkable how little agreement there is concerning the numbers of people who are dependent on coffee growing for their livelihood. The *Wall Street Journal*, a newspaper not given to exaggeration in matters of business, estimated that some 125 million people depended on coffee in 2002. ActionAid claimed 60 million, Fair Trade 100 million. The World Bank has calculated that there are 25 million small producers in developing countries who depend on coffee as their sole source of income, each supporting an average of five family members: this is the equivalent of the entire population of Japan, the world's eighth most populous country. Furthermore, the Bank estimates that a staggering 500 million people globally are involved directly or indirectly in the coffee trade. This figure is echoed by Dow Jones Commodity Services, which also assesses the importance of coffee to developed countries too: they have calculated, *inter alia,* that 300,000 people work in Italy's 110,000 coffee shops, serving 70 million cups of espresso per day.

The coffee market in the USA is worth $19 billion annually, with 161 million consumers directly serviced by 150,000 full- or part-time workers. The Specialty Association of America estimates that if everyone from coffee machine mechanics to styrofoam cup makers were accounted for, the figure for those involved in the business would leap to 1.5 million. In Japan, a leading roaster has claimed that over 3 million jobs – 4.5 per cent of the workforce – are directly or indirectly related to coffee. While the industry is keen to stress the importance of coffee, if only to alert politicians to the gravity of the problems affecting it, clearly there is huge international dependence on the trade.

As long as the price that coffee fetches on the world market continues to be lower than the cost of production, smallholders and farmers must subsidize coffee consumers. They cannot do this indefinitely. The result is unemployment and the loss of livelihood on the vast scale commensurate with the numbers previously employed. Thus the World Bank estimates that between the years 2000 and 2002 some 600,000 workers in the coffee industry lost their jobs in Central America alone. This is the equivalent of the entire population of the city of Bristol becoming unemployed. With no sign of a meaningful price recovery, this employment crisis is getting much worse, rapidly and globally. It has started to cause political and social disruption, poverty and privation on an unprecedented level in countries where the national economies are frequently already extremely fragile. There has also been a fundamental shift in the recipients of the coffee trade's largesse. In 1991 the global coffee market was worth around $30 billion, of which producing countries received $12 billion, or 40 per cent. Current figures suggest that the global revenues from coffee sales are in the region of $55 billion, of which only $7 billion (13 per cent) goes to the exporting nations. Coffee is the world's most valuable trading commodity after oil, but the share of the coffee trade enjoyed by producers has fallen by two-thirds in ten years, whilst transnational coffee companies have reaped huge windfall profits from the low price that they now need to pay for the commodity. The average price paid to producers of coffee internationally has fallen 80 per cent since their last high in 1997: over the same period, the average retail price of the keenly competitive major US brands has fallen to $2.75 per pound, only 27 per cent less than its peak. The price of instant coffee in the UK, which represents 85 per cent of that market, has fallen by a paltry 5 per cent since the same date. The four multinational roasters that dominate the world coffee trade – Procter & Gamble, Nestlé, Sara Lee, and Phillip Morris account for 40 per cent between them – report record sales and record profits, although all except Sara Lee ($495 million in reported profits from their coffee and tea division) are under-standably chary of stating exactly how much is attributable to coffee. Nestlé attributed a significant proportion of its 5.5 per cent half-year growth in sales to August 2003 to its 'star performers', instant coffee and bottled water.

Starbucks, a relative newcomer to the international coffee trade, is likewise reaping a huge profit harvest, up 19 per cent in 2003, and adding to its 6000 existing stores worldwide almost daily. The business is regarded as that rare breed, a 'tastemaker', a company that successfully creates a new market. Starbucks has repositioned coffee as an 'affordable luxury', and has provided a suitably mellow environment for people to indulge in it. The company's Chairman and Chief Global Strategist, Howard Schultz, is a lean corporate colossus fêted by stock analysts and the business press. He is the 'author' of the soft-focus New Age autohagiography entitled *Pour Your Heart Into It* in which he writes that 'My ultimate aim . . . is to reassure people to have the courage to persevere, to keep following their hearts even when others scoff. Don't be beaten down by naysayers.' It is unlikely that the smallholder abandoning his coffee plantation in Guatemala for a dismally uncertain future in a city shanty-town would derive any comfort from Schultz's inspirational message. The price that his coffee achieves in the branded coffee shops of the developed world clearly spells out imbalance and inequity. Starbucks generally buys better coffee than many companies, and consequently pays the higher price by which its Public Relations division sets great store; but it is no coincidence that the company has become one of the prime targets of the anti-globalization movement. It has come to represent the unacceptable face of unfettered capitalism with its combination of modern aspirational marketing techniques and an attritional strategy towards its independent competitors. Crucially, in the eyes of activists, it also has a lead product that is effectively subsidized by the suffering of Third World farmers.

The widening gap between the haves and the have-nots in our globalized economy is brutally exemplified by the growing inequalities in the coffee trade, and, just as politicians in wealthy Western nations respond to popular concerns about Third World poverty with spin rather than substance, so the major corporations that have benefited from the current world coffee crisis have demonstrated a notable lack of commitment to doing anything about it beyond window dressing. Procter & Gamble, makers of Folgers, maintain that they contributed $10 million to community programmes in Mexico, Brazil, and Venezuela. Kraft, Sara Lee, and Nestlé claim that they go out of their way to help small producers, 'ensuring that they receive the full value of their crop', according to a Nestlé spokesman. Presumably this comment is designed to reassure concerned consumers that the transnationals do not actually steal the coffee at gunpoint.

The poverty of the world's coffee farmers contrasts with the coffee trade's wealth of statistics. Most of these emanate from an unremarkable 1960s office block in Berners Street, just north of Oxford Street in London, in which can be found the down-at-heel remnants of the once globally powerful International Coffee Organization (ICO). Funded by coffee-producing nations (invariably tropical and undeveloped), as well as consuming nations (generally Western and developed), in its heyday the ICO, with all its undoubted flaws, was a pragmatic attempt by the world coffee trade to mitigate the effects of wilder fluctuations in coffee prices. These arose from a combination of over-supply punctuated by periodic crop failures in Brazil. Although the motivation for the creation of the ICO was primarily commercial rather than philanthropic – chronic instability in a market is bad for business – the net effect was to impose limits on the gap between poverty and privilege in the coffee trade. Mandated by the International Coffee Agreement (ICA), which was signed under the auspices of the United Nations, the ICO promoted, regulated, monitored, and administered the ICA, which worked through an elaborate quota system permitting the pre-agreed restriction or expansion of coffee supplies to keep prices within certain thresholds. However, the full functioning of the ICO required the active participation of the USA, consumer of 25 per cent of the world's coffee. Whilst there was a perceived threat of creeping Communism in the coffee-producing countries of Central America, it was in the best interests of the USA to support the ICA in order to help defuse social unrest in its backyard; but with the break-up of the Soviet Union this *raison d'être* evaporated and the ideologically driven policies of laissez-faire capitalism were given full rein. An international commodity-price control agreement had no place at the neo-liberal economic table, and the USA withdrew its support for the ICA in the late 1980s, and from the ICO itself six years later. The importance of the Berners Street headquarters of the ICO thus diminished; the research laboratory, lecture theatre and other facilities were closed down, and the promotional budget was slashed. The organization still hosts meetings of the member nations, and still compiles statistics with commendable zeal, but is a shadow of its former self.

The problems resulting from the market free-for-all unleashed by the US withdrawal from the ICA were exacerbated by the World Bank and its cousin, the Asian Development Bank. Both of these institutions had lent heavily to Vietnam in the mid 1990s in line with their mandate to stimulate low-cost production and end market inefficiencies. Having massively defoliated the nation with Agent Orange during the Vietnam War, the USA promoted – through the World Bank, in which it has a controlling stake – the refoliation of Vietnam with low-grade Robusta coffee bushes, with a devastating effect on the other Third World economies dependent on coffee. From its previous position as a very minor producer of coffee, by the year 2000 Vietnam had become the world's second largest coffee producer after Brazil, exporting 9 million bags of 60 kilos each – still of low-quality Robusta – which, along with Brazilian coffees harvested by machines, were produced at a labour cost of one-third of that required for the higher-quality Arabicas of many other producing countries.

The result of the Vietnamese expansion was a catastrophic fall in prices, as well as a considerable falling-off in the quality of coffee blends internationally. Robusta is a coarse-flavoured strain of the coffee plant that is more resistant to disease than its refined cousin, Arabica. It is also considerably cheaper and, despite its low quality, represents an opportunity for roasters to improve their margins. The flood of Vietnamese Robusta on to the market depressed the price of all coffees, and thus the smallholders elsewhere who tended to the plantations producing high-quality Arabicas found their margins inexorably squeezed. Good coffee comes at a price, and for many that price could not be obtained on the world's markets any more. The situation was sufficiently serious for the usually conservative coffee trade magazines to produce hand-wringing editorials: 'Vietnam is now the Number Two world producer of coffee – plenty of Robusta for all and more. Yet roasters claim there's little if any Robusta in their blends. Well, who is buying it all then – the man in the moon?' The men in the moon in the form of traders in Germany, Italy, and Poland devised a new method of steaming Robusta coffee to remove the worst of its harsh flavours, allowing roasters to use even more in their blends. Junk retailers sold junk coffee to junk consumers at the lowest price point. The World Bank remained unrepentant. 'Vietnam has become a successful producer,' said Don Mitchell, principal economist at the Bank. 'In general, we consider it to be a huge success.' However, fulfilling the dire predictions concerning the 'race for the bottom' (the tendency for export markets for Third World products to migrate to whichever country has the cheapest labour) made by many international NGOs and aid organizations, one of the victims of Vietnam's success recently has been Vietnam itself. The price of coffee has tumbled so far that farmers there are starting to tear up the newly maturing coffee bushes because they cannot cover the costs of production. The unsubstantiated rumours that China, with its vast low-paid labour force, has started to gear up for the creation of a large-scale coffee industry, assisted by Nestlé, may mean that Vietnamese coffee will be further priced out of the market and that the country's brief moment in the sun will be over.

While coffee-producing countries fight over the diminishing scraps falling from the consuming countries' table, a separate coffee futures industry flourishes in London and New York. Coffee futures were originally designed as a financial instrument to enable coffee traders to hedge against windfall gains or losses resulting from movements in coffee prices over time. The creation of a futures market depends upon there being an acceptable set standard of coffee that forms the basic unit of contract – the New

York 'C' market uses contracts based on 'Other Milds' (including Colombian, Kenyan, and Tanzanian Arabica), the London market uses Robusta coffees. The creation of these standards has been possible because of the relatively predictable nature of coffee production: tea, a commodity that varies much more by the year, the season, the weather, and the day of picking, has yet to evolve a futures market because it has not been possible for traders to find, let alone agree upon, a homogeneous type to form the unit of contract.

The coffee futures market is a financial instrument that has now assumed a life of its own largely abstracted from the real trade in coffee. Speculators and investment funds trade on the market with no intention of ever seeing a single coffee bean delivered. It is grimly ironic that, whilst coffee farmers struggle for survival, the capitalist institutions based on the same commodity flourish, and it is no coincidence that when the vast trading floor of the New York Coffee, Sugar & Cocoa Exchange, formerly housed in the World Trade Center, was destroyed on 11 September 2001, it was able to resume business almost seamlessly in contingency premises prepared after the previous bomb attack in 1993 and maintained at a cost of $350,000 a year. The Third World, in the meantime, has neither the financial resources nor the political infrastructure to be able to respond meaningfully to the crisis it faces. The only international organization of coffee growers, the Association of Coffee Producing Countries, shut its doors in January 2002. Although speaking for over 70 per cent of the world's production, it was unable to find unanimity amongst its member countries, never mind amongst those outside the organization. Colombia's Federation of Coffee Growers, a central buying and marketing organization which for over seventy-five years had successfully helped its smallholder members to absorb the worst of global coffee price cycles, is now straining under additional pressure from the increasing violence and instability of that country. The membership is sometimes turning to illegal coca cultivation in desperation. 'Colombia is facing a deep internal crisis related very much to the situation of drugs and coffee,' the Secretary General of the association of producers reported. Similar national marketing organizations in other producing countries have collapsed over the last ten years, defeated by the World Bank and the IMF's insistence on placing stringent conditions on loans to countries operating any constraint over the free market. The Nicaraguan Government, for instance, had to drop proposals to delay foreclosures on loans to coffee growers after intensive pressure from the IMF and the Inter-American Bank.

The large-scale social unrest forecasted as a result of the poverty and displacement caused by the near-collapse of the coffee industry continues to grow. New Guinea highlanders are reported to be abandoning their plantations; Indian and African smallholders have uprooted their worthless coffee plants; Nicaraguan coffee workers marched on Managua and fourteen of their counterparts from the oppressed state of Chiapas in Mexico were found dead of starvation and dehydration in the Arizona desert, where they had been dumped by the people they had paid to smuggle them into the USA. By 2001, Oxfam had reported that, in real terms, 'coffee prices are lower than they have ever been' and that a minimum price mechanism of $1 a pound should be installed – roughly double the prevailing price. The newly formed British Coffee Association of leading roasters dismissed the report's findings as 'too short term', although they conveniently neglected to come up with a long-term alternative.

While there is evidence that 'Fair Trade' coffees have had a significant impact on a minority of consumers, the four transnational roasters that dominate the world coffee trade and the six multinational exporters that control 40 per cent of the export trade are unlikely to turn into corporate do-gooders overnight. The central concept of Fair Trade coffee – that the price paid for coffee allows growers to receive a living wage – has also remained of marginal interest to cut-price retailers and bargain-hunting consumers alike. Similarly, 'shade grown' and 'bird-friendly' coffees – those grown in a more environmentally sensitive way that helps to preserve the local ecosystem and migratory bird life – have found their way onto the shelves in the USA, but the industry as a whole continues to back technologies that bring down the costs of production with scant regard for the social or environmental costs.

The most recent manifestation of this tendency was the announcement that a new Genetically Modified coffee is in development that would allow the ripening of coffee beans on the bushes to be triggered chemically, obviating the need for the labour-intensive process of harvesting the bushes repeatedly by hand as they produce a mixture of flowers, unripe cherries and ripe cherries. By cutting back on labour requirements, the new GM technology threatens primarily the livelihood of producers of high-quality Arabicas. In Brazil, where quality standards are less demanding, one pass with a vast coffee-harvesting machine already does the trick for over half of the coffee grown there. The producers of quality Arabicas are precisely the ones suffering most from the current crisis in the industry, so the prospect of GM coffee is a particularly cruel blow. Those who back the technology say that it will enable poor coffee farmers to control the timing of the harvest and enable them to grow other crops. Detractors point out that it will also enslave them to the use of specific – and expensive – proprietary seeds and chemicals, with no guarantee that they will receive higher prices for their coffee.

The development of GM coffee – which will probably be ready for the market within five years – has been possible because coffee is the single most scientifically scrutinized of foodstuffs. Coffee science is in part research and development, in part a concerted attempt by the industry to combat the attacks made by the medical profession on coffee, and particularly caffeine, its most active ingredient. Funded largely by the transnationals, bulletins extolling the health properties of coffee issue forth from apparently independent scientific bodies, while anti-caffeine scientists and campaigners fight battles for legislation to curb the widespread, unregulated use of the drug, not just in coffee, but also increasingly in soft drinks and 'energy' drinks.

The world consumes the equivalent of 120,000 tonnes of pure caffeine per annum, just over half in the form of coffee. Caffeine itself is a white alkaloid with a sufficiently pronounced bitter taste to make its absence noticeable in decaffeinated coffees. It is possible to kill oneself with a caffeine overdose: about ten grams, or the equivalent of a hundred cups of coffee rapidly consumed, will do the trick for an adult, making Balzac's daily consumption of sixty cups of coffee decidedly risky. Less than 3.5 grams is lethal for children, and early researchers showed that 'a $\frac{1}{67}$ of a grain of caffeine will kill a frog of moderate size', should you happen to have such a frog that you have ceased to be fond of. Smoking increases the rate at which caffeine is metabolized by the body (smokers therefore experience less effect), whereas drinking decreases it. Caffeine does not counteract the debilitating effect of alcohol although it may give the illusion of so doing. Caffeine intoxication has its own entry in the USA's *Diagnostic and Statistical Manual of Mental Disorders*. The diagnostic criteria assume the recent consumption of more than 250mg (50mg less than the daily recommended safe dose), and as well as the usual suspects include gastrointestinal disturbance, muscle twitching, rambling flow of thought and speech, tachycardia or cardiac arrhythmia (palpitations), and psychomotor agitation. They do not include the 'bilateral burning feet' and 'restless leg' syndromes that have been clinically noted elsewhere. Caffeine intoxication can tip over into caffeine psychosis, which can produce hallucinations: truck drivers in the USA have reported being pursued by balls of white light, which suggests that caffeine psychosis could explain the widespread belief in UFOs in that country. It is also claimed that caffeine 'is capable of undermining psychological well-being', although there are individual variations in sensitivity – 'patients with anxiety disorders may find the normal effects distressing, whilst the non-anxious find them pleasant and stimulating'. Long-term caffeine intoxication, which is called 'caffeinism', is more common in psychiatric patients, who in general consume more caffeine than the rest of the population. Caffeine is believed to cause urinary incontinence in the elderly, and has been found (with unknown effects) in the systems of new-born infants who do not have the necessary liver enzyme to metabolize it. There is also evidence to suggest that caffeine can cause osteoporosis as it increases the rate of calcium elimination from the body. On the plus side, caffeine is used to treat neonatal apnoea (cessation of the spontaneous breathing of an infant) and to increase sperm mobility.

It is remarkable that we voluntarily introduce this powerful drug into our systems knowing so little about what it might be doing to us. While the producing countries face ruin, the West, so the gainsayers maintain, has become a dangerously caffeinated society. The cheap, coarse-flavoured Robusta coffees that are dragging world prices down contain twice as much caffeine as higher quality Arabicas. There are the first signs that the effect of the increased use of these Robusta coffees in blends is causing a slowdown in consumption, as coffee drinkers, consciously or unconsciously troubled by the stronger caffeine hit of their usual brew, are drinking less coffee. The impact of health and quality issues on coffee consumption may yet add another problematic dimension to a coffee trade that is already in turmoil.

The explosive growth of the 'specialty' coffee market, led by the USA, may represent the only future survival mechanism for a few fortunate farmers. This market maintains its upward momentum largely through the ability of the coffee roasters' buyers to single out distinguished, high-quality coffee producers in countries of origin. Since the price of 'commodity' coffee has been so low for so long, there is a real prospect that even producers of quality Arabicas may be unable to continue in the trade. However, a few coffees may rise from their ranks to become specialty coffees, their historical and gustatory qualities nurtured by buyers and thus be capable of fetching viable prices. Many are called but few are chosen; as a result, the discrepancy between the price that a specialty buyer is willing to pay for such a coffee and the more run-of-the-mill types is increasing. It is feared by many in the trade that this will quickly lead to a two-tier coffee market for producers and consumers alike, one in which the vast majority of coffee is of a low quality – probably Brazilian and Vietnamese – sold competitively to cost-conscious consumers, and a small amount is marketed as a refined, luxury item for the true *aficionado*. This polarization will weigh particularly heavily on the producers of good-quality but not necessarily very distinguished Arabicas. Thus mainstream Arabica coffees from countries such as Honduras, Ethiopia, or El Salvador are largely ignored by the specialty market because they lack distinction either of flavour or pedigree, and as a result they are forced to compete with Brazil and Vietnam.

Coffee has always marched hand in hand with colonialism through the pages of history. It was once known as the 'Wine of Araby', and the trade in coffee was an important component in the creation and consolidation of the Ottoman Empire in the sixteenth century. It was first consumed in the late fifteenth century as a sacred ritual amongst the Sufis in Yemen, whence it quickly spread through Islam. In that religion, despite some initial opposition, it was considered an acceptable stimulant because, unlike the reviled alcohol, it never left the drinker 'incapable of distinguishing a man from a woman or the earth from the heavens'. The popular coffee houses of Cairo and Constantinople attracted the attention of the first European visitors to the Orient, and eventually coffee itself appeared in most of Europe at the same time as merchants, sailors, and adventurers from that continent were starting to establish, largely through superiority of arms and technology, their fledgling trading empires. Coffee was amongst a number of valuable and desirable oriental goods that they sought, but its supply was effectively under the monopolistic control of Ottomans. By the early eighteenth century the Dutch, the French, and the British had managed to obtain coffee seedlings to take to their own tropical colonial possessions, there to be cultivated under the plantation system worked by slave or near-slave labour. Slavery, with its attendant horrors, persisted as the preferred method of coffee production in many colonies until abolition, or in the case of Brazil until as recently as 1888, by which time coffee had become a thoroughly globalized commodity. The so-called benefits of the colonial plantation system were mainly experienced by the consumers in the home countries of these various European empires, who responded with alacrity to the low price and ready availability of what had formerly been a rare luxury.

Coffee had become universally consumed in the nations of Europe and in the USA, much of it in coffee houses that became meeting places for men of commerce, politics, and culture. The effect of caffeine itself ensured that there were always likely to be lively, well-informed debates and intense, original exchanges, in contrast to the only other public meeting places of the time, the tavern or the church. The coffee house played a pivotal role in the creation of many of the financial institutions that in turn supported the expansionist trading empires that had led to the growth of coffee consumption in the first place. Lloyds of London, the maritime insurance company, emerged from the interests of the clientele of Lloyds Coffee House who gathered there to exchange news and gossip concerning the movement of ships. Coffee was an important commodity shipped from afar, and thus the fledgling insurance business conducted at Lloyds in part provided the financial structure whereby the risks of the coffee trade itself could be mitigated. This feedback loop of cause-and-effect, fuelled by caffeine, underpinned the dramatic rise of capitalism and its most successful offspring, globalization. Coffee lay at the very heart of the triumph of free-market economics in our times: that it is now suffering the awful consequences of that same ethos is ironic, but horribly apt.

With the dieback of former European imperialism, and the increasing assertion of the hegemony of the USA over the western hemisphere, the many coffee-producing countries of Central and South America have found themselves overtaken by US neo-colonialism. Many of those countries are deeply dependent on coffee for export income, and because their northern neighbour consumes 25 per cent of the world's supplies but chooses to buy 75 per cent of its needs from their southern neighbours, inevitably coffee became a significant factor in hemispherical geopolitics. Economies that are historically coffee-based have created the ground rules by which a ruling oligarchy can impose its will on the unrepresented masses. The sweatshop economies of much of Central America and the Caribbean depend upon the political élite's control of the media and the military apparatus, and the structure of the coffee trade provided the working model. El Salvador, for example, a country which until recently was dependent on coffee for over half its export income, now derives 57 per cent of that from the 'garment industry'. Arguably, along with the world economy as a whole, the coffee trade has reverted to a paradigm that more closely resembles the height of the European colonialism, albeit now under US domination, than the protectionism that prevailed during the era when strong, liberal, democratic Western nation states allied against the threat of Communism. The fact that the date of the dissolution of the International Coffee Agreement broadly coincided with that of the fall of the Berlin Wall is by no means coincidental: the USA, having vanquished its most serious rival, no longer saw the need to humour its more liberal allies.

The catalytic effect of coffee-house culture on the emergence of those financial and cultural institutions that underpinned the rise of Western capitalism should not be underestimated. The coffee houses of the City of London were the progenitors of such global institutions as the Stock Exchange and Lloyds, and those of Covent Garden and St James's were the seedbeds of the Royal Society and the Enlightenment. Coffee gradually gave way to tea in England, but the imposition of taxes on tea in the American colonies precipitated the Boston Tea Party, the actual as well as the ideological rejection of tea, and the triumph of coffee in America, where coffee houses became the foremost meeting places for merchants, politicians, and businessmen. The Declaration of Independence was first read publicly outside the Merchant's Coffee House in Philadelphia, and President-elect George Washington was ceremonially welcomed to New York in front of (another) Merchant's Coffee House – which had, amongst other things, formerly hosted slave auctions – a week before his inauguration. If he had been able to walk from there but a few hundred yards and a couple of centuries in time he would have come to the Coffee, Sugar and Cocoa Exchange in 4, World Trade Center, which was to be destroyed in the 9/11 attacks masterminded by Osama bin Laden, whose forbears came from Yemen, itself the original home of the coffee trade. One of the purported reasons why the World Trade Center was targeted was because the towers were a symbol of the Western financial institutions that were accused of destroying traditional Islam: coffee played a significant role in the evolution of both.

Coffee is now falling victim to globalization: then, it played an intimate part in its rise.

2

ORIGINS

All theory is grey. Green is the golden tree of life.

GOETHE

Although it is enjoyed daily by a good proportion of the world's population, very little is generally known about the origins of coffee. There are a number of myths that are ritually aired by the coffee trade to keep the curious at bay, but nothing in the way of substantiated fact is usually presented to the public. To build a satisfactory picture of what happened in the time before coffee bursts upon the historical stage in the sixteenth century requires piecing together disparate elements of anthropology, archaeology, and even theology. Indeed, the search for coffee's roots takes us back to the roots of man himself.

In 1974, at Hadar in the Afar desert of northern Ethiopia, palaeontologists unearthed the fossil remains of a group of *Australopithecus afarensis*, mankind's oldest known ancestor. Despite earlier discoveries of Java Man, Peking Man and others, it seems that Ethiopia is mankind's original location; genetic research suggests that all modern humans are directly descended from a group of about a hundred and fifty *Homo sapiens sapiens* who lived in the Ethiopian Highlands some 120,000 years ago. Even the Holy Grail of anthropology, the so-called Missing Link, may well have been found there, for the recent discovery of a fossilized toe of *Ardipithecus ramidus kadabba* offers the first tentative evidence of the species' separation from the chimpanzee some six million years ago. Despite its highland forest environment, *Ardipethecus ramidus kadabba* appears to have walked upright. Previously it had been conjectured that man's need to stand upright was forced upon him by the evolutionary process to enable him to peer over the high grass of the plains in pursuit of prey. The fact that he appears to have stood upright whilst still confined to the forest has fatally undermined this theory.

One of the other abiding mysteries of anthropology is the so-called brain explosion that probably took place about 500,000 years ago, the result of which was that man's brain size increased by 30 per cent, principally in the cerebrum, the upper brain where most conscious thinking purportedly takes place. Various theories have been put forward for this, but the development of language would seem to provide the most credible explanation, as language requires a great deal of thought and in turn generates a great deal to think about. Its arrival put mankind in a position, at least in part, to determine the course of his own evolution, allowing him to develop and communicate concepts that had been hitherto literally unthinkable, and to begin to adapt his environment to his needs. It is tempting to wonder whether the proliferation of wild coffee trees in the same Ethiopian highland forests could also have had a hand in the process. Coffee has always been associated with speed of cognition and expression, and the sudden dawn of self-awareness in the Genesis story concerning the forbidden fruit of the 'Tree of Knowledge' is something that could have been prompted by a psychoactive substance such as caffeine. Such awareness (or, perhaps, gnosis) is also an attribute of language and thought, without which it is quiescent. To place the bright red coffee cherry centre stage in the story of the Fall is altogether a more inspired piece of casting than the choice of a lowly Golden Delicious; imagine coffee berries driving their eaters into a caffeine-fuelled frenzy of quick-fire contention and ingenious thinking, engines of brain evolution. The previously docile brains of *Homo sapiens sapiens* would have been ill prepared for such an assault. Likewise the Ethiopian Highlands, with their sumptuous vegetation and spectacular scenery, are a properly marvellous setting for the mythical Garden of Eden. Even today the wild coffee trees grow under the forest canopy on the escarpments of the Rift Valley, their white flowers heavy with a scent close to that of jasmine. The coffee cherries, the stones of which make two coffee beans, ripen in clusters as they grow from green through gold to a rich red colour, which stands out in bold contrast to the smooth, luscious dark green leaves of the tree. They were doubtless suitably tempting to our early ancestors. The description of the Tree of Knowledge contained in the rediscovered Old Testament Book of Enoch could easily suggest the coffee tree, with its depiction of delicious fragrance and clusters of fruit – and that previously missing book, supposedly suppressed because of its salacious content, was unearthed by the eighteenth-century explorer James Bruce in, strange to say, Ethiopia.

At this point it would seem appropriate to introduce this native of Ethiopia, the species *Coffea arabica* of the sub-genus *Eucoffea* of the genus *Coffea* of the family Rubiaceae of the order Rubiales of the sub-class Sympetalae of the class Dicotyledonae of the sub-kingdom *Angiospermae* from the kingdom of Vegetables. Left to its own devices the Arabica coffee plant can grow up to twenty feet high; its lush, dark-green, ovoid leaves are about six inches long, and it produces small white flowers with the characteristic heady jasmine-like fragrance. The coffee tree usually flowers once in a season, but in some countries where it has been transplanted from its homeland, such as Colombia, it may blossom and produce cherries at various stages of ripeness throughout the year. The flowers are pollinated by insects and the wind, and go on to form 'drupes', which are infant coffee berries, and which grow over a period of six months to form bunches of cherries that in many respects resemble the bright red domestic eating cherry.

As perhaps was the case with our putative Adam and Eve, ripe coffee cherries are a tempting proposition to some animals and birds, giving rise to some esoteric practices. Kopi luak is a fine Sumatran coffee, much valued in Japan, made from beans gathered from the dung of *Paradoxurus hermaphroditus*, the common palm civet, which skulks around the plantations at night selecting only the finest, ripest cherries. The beast digests the skin and the pulp of the cherry, the mucillage and the parchment surrounding the bean, and even the final obstacle, the thin 'silverskin'. In so doing it achieves exactly what modern 'wet' and 'dry' processing technology seeks to emulate – that is, the complete separation of the core coffee bean from all its protective layers. The civet cannot digest the hard beans, however, and they pass through its system: they are picked out of the civet's dung because the flavour imparted by the digestive process is highly prized once the beans are cleaned and roasted. Indian monkeys, parrots, and mongooses are also supposed to subscribe to this recondite method of coffee processing, and their coffee byproducts likewise are said to attract local enthusiasts. Not all such coffees pass entirely through an animal's system: the spread of coffee cultivation in the Spanish Philippine Islands in the nineteenth century was evidently greatly assisted by *Pardasciurus musanga*, a small mammal which ate the flesh of the cherries but spat out the bean, which was then ready for germination.

Insects, however, find their enjoyment of the coffee cherry considerably lessened by its caffeine content. While the leaves and flowers of a coffee plant contain slightly less than 1 per cent caffeine by dry weight, the pulp of the cherry contains a little more, and the bean itself around 3 per cent. Nature has so ordered things that the highest levels of caffeine are to be found in the most important part of the plant, its seed. This is because caffeine is nothing more than a natural insecticide, and the high caffeine levels protect the seed from unwanted attention. Hapless insects who ingest too much find that their nervous systems go into overdrive. By the miracle of international trade, the same symptoms can be observed in office workers the world over.

The other species of coffee grown commercially around the world is *C. canephora*, the best-known variety of which is Robusta. The plant was first spotted by explorers in Uganda in 1862, where it was then used by the native Buganda tribe in a blood-brother ceremony. However, it was not until its rediscovery in the Belgian Congo in 1898 that it was thought worth cultivating. This was after outbreaks of *hemileia vastatrix* or 'coffee rust' had devastated the Arabica coffee plantations of Ceylon and the Dutch East Indies. Robusta coffee is, as the name implies, more robust than its Arabica cousin. It grows at lower altitude (and contains as much as double the amount of caffeine, perhaps in order to deal with the more persistent insects of the tropical lowlands), it tastes coarse and rubbery, and has very little to recommend it other than resistance to disease, which is in itself a recommendation only to planters. It was initially banned from the New York Coffee Exchange as a 'practically worthless bean'. Being considerably cheaper than Arabica, it can be found in all sorts of less salubrious locations: instant coffee, cheap blends, vending machine coffee and the like. Its harsh flavour and heavy caffeine kick are easily identified. Introduced only a century ago, with the sudden rise to prominence of Vietnam (see chapter 18), it threatens to become a major force in the market, replacing the subtle refined flavours and aromas of Arabica coffee with its pestilential presence. It has some uses in espresso blending, but otherwise it is Arabica coffee's crude, boorish, sour, uncivilized, black-hearted cousin, and true coffee *aficionados* rightly give it a very wide berth. No coffee-taster worth his or her salt would seek to maintain that a Robusta coffee was better in flavour terms than all but the worst-produced Arabica: its only merit is its price. Nonetheless, nearly half of the coffee sold in the UK is Robusta, and even in Italy, a country which celebrates its coffee culture like no other, a third of the coffee drunk is Robusta, whilst nearly a quarter of the coffee drunk in the USA is Robusta. The country that has thus far remained most immune to its pernicious influence is Norway, where it is still virtually unknown. Of global coffee consumption today, one-third is of a low-quality coffee variety that scarcely existed a century ago, and the proportion is growing. We are witnessing the triumph of the 'practically worthless bean' in our coffee cups. At the same time, ironically, with prices at their current levels of 35 cents per pound, Robusta coffee is even more practically worthless than its Arabica cousin.

Despite its widespread use, this black sheep in the coffee family receives an almost total informational blackout when coffee companies come to describe their wares. There are no illustrated pamphlets extolling the virtues of Togolese Robustas over those of Uganda, no analyses of the typical flavour characteristics of the Cameroon variety. Whereas many companies might draw attention to the fact that their blends are '100 per cent Arabica', few would proudly point out that they use 50 per cent Robusta. This is simply because all coffee professionals know that Robusta coffee is a cheaper, inferior type and are unwilling to admit that they have any association with it. Arguably, if consumers really understood the extent to which their coffee has become tainted by this parvenu coffee bean, they would turn away in droves. Even so the creeping infiltration of cheap Robustas into mainstream blends is noticeable. What might once have been a reasonable coffee from a vending machine has changed over the last few years into an unpalatable, caffeine-kicking monstrosity. It seems, however, that many consumers are largely unaware of the change, although there is some evidence to suggest that the additional caffeine content of coffee with a higher proportion of Robusta is leading to a drop in consumption.

If proto-humans had experienced Arabica coffee in their highland fastness it would have been in its raw form, whereas today it is used almost exclusively after roasting – so much so that most people outside the coffee trade would be hard pressed to say what a green (raw) coffee bean looks like. The almost miraculous, quasi-alchemical transformation of coffee in the roasting process can be created easily enough in the home: all that is required is a large handful of unroasted green coffee beans and a large cast-iron frying pan preheated (but not oiled) on a hot ring. Stirred constantly with a wooden spatula, within minutes the beans acquire a golden hue. Occasionally, sputterings of complaint can be heard, an odd explosion like that of corn popping, caused by steam expanding within the cell structure of the bean. The heat starts to transform the unpromising, torpid vegetable matter into that wonderful substance, roasted coffee. Some smoke, heavy with oil and moisture, clambers limply from the pan, and the beans patchily break past their golden threshold and acquire a brownish tinge. The explosions become more frequent, and the occasional bean flies out of the pan. The dull brown beans now turn rich brown and oily, and the aroma of the smoke that pours from them is like incense for the gods themselves. Finally, amidst a profusion of popping and smoke, the process has to be stopped quickly to prevent the oily beans blackening into worthless soot. This is best accomplished by pouring the coffee between two metal colanders outside in fresh cool air. Clouds of white chaff (the detached remains of the silverskin) waft into the breeze. The sound of the roasted beans will strike the ear, brittle but curiously strong. After a few minutes, the beans will cool, and *voilà*! – roasted coffee, perhaps one of the most dramatic transformations of a natural plant product that human intervention has yet devised solely for its pleasure. After ten minutes or so the beans are ready to be ground; the aroma then released is extraordinary, rich and sublime. Roasted coffee contains over eight hundred separate flavour and aroma components, most of which form in the crucible of the roaster. This strange alchemy accounts in part for the hold that coffee exerts over our imagination.

As well as being uniquely endowed with early men and early coffee, Ethiopia was home to another drug, namely *qat* or *khat* (*Catha edulis*), a psychoactive plant containing cathinone and cathine, which is greatly appreciated on both sides of the Red Sea today, but particularly in Yemen, where it represents a third of that country's Gross Domestic Product. *Qat* induces a mild euphoria, alertness, and tranquillity, and is widely consumed in convivial communal *qat* chewing sessions which frequently take all afternoon, meandering conversations punctuated by poetry and hypnotic pauses. While it is interesting that Ethiopia should offer two notable drugs amongst its indigenous plants, judging by its effects, *qat* would seem the less likely cause of the 'brain explosion'. It is also less exportable, as the active ingredients are susceptible to rapid decay, and only fresh leaves produce good results. Caffeine is, by contrast, almost indestructible, surviving the ordeal by fire, pulverization and oxygen deprivation which the coffee industry routinely inflicts on it for prolonged periods with no apparent diminution of its powers.

Setting aside the tempting but unproven image of coffee as an evolutionary catalyst, it nonetheless needs to be explained how coffee came into common use. Remains of many of the plants that were domesticated by mankind early in prehistory turn up in archaeological digs, allowing a plausible timescale and map for the spread of many plants to be developed. It can be asserted with some confidence that the domestication of plants – that is, the selective breeding of plants from their wild forbears to encourage characteristics most useful to man – began with cereals in about 8500 BC in the so-called Fertile Crescent, an area that encompassed the modern-day Mediterranean Near East, southern Turkey, and northern Iraq. The techniques and practice of cultivation quickly spread to areas with a comparable climate, and gave rise to the earliest civilizations – ancient Egyptians, for example, cultivated wheat, grapes, peas, beans, and barley, all of which depended on winter's rains and shorter daylight hours.

In the Ethiopian Highlands specific indigenous plant species flourished that were used to summer rains, and even daylight hours throughout the year, as well as the lower temperatures that came with altitude. While coffee and *qat* remained wild, some of these other plants were domesticated, including *teff* (a tiny-seeded cereal used for *enjera* bread), *noog* (used for seed oils), *ensete* (a banana-like plant used for bread), and finger millet used for beer. Remarkably, for a plant that is now cultivated throughout the tropical world, coffee has not been shown by archaeology to have been domesticated before the sixteenth century. In fact, history is almost silent on all aspects of coffee cultivation and consumption in Ethiopia, with the exception of anthropologists' reports of coffee being used, as already noted, for 'chewing and blood-brotherhood ceremonies' by the Buganda tribes, and in the 'slaughtering of the coffee' ceremony, in which the Oromo celebrated the birth of cattle or children. The Oromo, the tribes who inhabit the corner of south-west Ethiopia where coffee originated, considered coffee to be the *buna qala* – the tears of Waqa, the supreme sky god. It was believed that coffee destroyed cattle, so in the ceremony coffee was roasted, along with barley, in butter: the symbolic union of coffee and cow thus propitiating the guardian spirits, reaffirming life, stimulating procreation and all manner of useful things. It has been reported anecdotally that coffee mixed this way with butter was also eaten by soldiers, farmers, and merchants faced with hard work or long journeys.

The anthropological supposition has been that if a tribe practised coffee consumption in certain ways in recent history, there is a chance that it may have done so in ancient times.

If hard evidence of ancient coffee trading or use has remained elusive, written sources are no more helpful. The Greek historian Herodotus reported that cinnamon originated in African swamps guarded by bats and was used by giant birds to build their nests, that fat-tailed sheep in Arabia needed wheeled wooden carts to carry their fat tails, and that cannabis was used as a ritual purifier; but on the subject of coffee he was overwhelmingly reticent. Opium was used extensively in religious ceremonies in Minoan Crete, but not coffee. The *Periplus of the Erythraen Sea,* a first-century AD Greek compendium of the Red Sea trade, makes no mention of it amongst the contemporary Ethiopian exports of ivory, tortoiseshell, ostrich feathers, spices, aromatics, and ebony. Although there have been extensive excavations in the city of Aksum, the centre of an Ethiopian empire that reached its zenith in the fourth and fifth centuries AD, it has not been shown that coffee was either consumed or traded from there. This is despite frequent mentions of Aksum and its activities in Graeco-Roman and Byzantine texts, and rather undermines the common contention that it was the Aksumites who introduced coffee to Yemen, which they ruled at intervals between the third and sixth centuries. Fragmentary archaeological evidence of Aksumite trade with distant China in the third century AD has been found, but, of trade in coffee grown a few hundred miles away, none.

While the record is thin concerning coffee in Ethiopia, it is bafflingly obscure elsewhere in the ancient world. If coffee were to be found there, Egypt would be the first place to look, being just downstream (albeit 1500 miles and four cataracts of the Nile) from coffee's highland home. When the first humans originally migrated from Ethiopia in about 100,000 BC, they ventured north into Egypt and thence to the Near East. This pioneering band died out, and it is only when a second batch left the Highlands in 80,000 BC and crossed the lower Red Sea into Yemen that the common ancestry of all non-African humans was established. The fact that over a period of the next 5000 years humans made their way from Yemen, first to India and thence to Java and Sumatra, describing in slow time coffee's later onward march, is a compelling prehistorical curiosity.

If there had been coffee use in early Ethiopia, it is highly probable that the Egyptians would have learnt about it. They were frequently supplied with slaves from that area, along with gold and cattle, by their southern neighbours, the Nubians, and the 25th Dynasty, around 600 BC, was the result of the Ethiopian conquest of Egypt. That the knowledge of coffee somehow failed to make it down the Nile would suggest that, despite its availability, coffee was not in use in Ethiopia at that time. Recent analysis of mummy remains has tended to confuse matters further. It would appear that while caffeine is not to be found in the hair of the deceased, traces of cocaine and nicotine are. The idea of the ancient Egyptian aristocracy tooting and toking may come as something of a shock to an orthodox view of life on the banks of the Nile, but the real mystery is that both coca and tobacco are native bushes of the New World, and in ancient times the Americas supposedly remained to be discovered for another two thousand years. The competition to identify the earliest Old World travellers to the New is certainly hotting up and the ancient Egyptians make a distinguished addition to the roster; but from the point of view of this study, if they were prepared to travel across the Atlantic for cocaine and nicotine, one wonders why they ignored the caffeine that could be found up the Nile?

It may be the case that knowledge of coffee travelled to ancient Greece. Some classicists have maintained that *nepenthe*, which Homer tells us Helen brought with her out of Egypt and used to alleviate her sufferings, was coffee: 'She mingled with the wine the wondrous juice of a plant which banishes sadness and wrath from the heart and brings with it forgetfulness of every woe.' However, this seems a somewhat inadequate description of the effects of caffeine, which in excess can make its consumers edgy and irritable. Others identify coffee with the 'black broth of the Lacedaemonians' – a position maintained by a welter of seventeenth-century scholars including George Sandys (the poet and explorer), Robert Burton (author of *The Anatomy of Melancholy*), and Sir Henry Blount (the traveller). Their notion remained in general currency until one Gustav Gilbert determined with great conviction in 1895 that the 'black broth' was 'pork, cooked in blood, and seasoned with salt and vinegar'. This sounds a concoction far more suited to the Lacedaemonians, better known as the Spartans.

There have been claimed sightings of coffee in the Old Testament, including in the presents Abigail made to David, the red pottage for which Esau sold his birthright, and in the parched grain that Boaz ordered to be given to Ruth. Some have suggested that Pythagoras' prohibition on the consumption of beans was aimed at coffee, but it seems more likely to have been the result of his dislike of wind, of both bodily and mental origin. In conclusion, while speculating on the subject has provided hours of harmless amusement to many, there is no confirmed reference to coffee in the Egyptian, biblical, or classical literatures.

Given the fact that the coffee tree produces tempting red cherries, it is easy to imagine that some pioneering individuals attempted to eat them raw. The flesh of the cherry is pleasant to eat, but humans would find chewing the two green beans that make up the stone of the cherry hard work. It is unlikely that early man, with a reasonable selection of foods available, would have been bothered. Although the cherries contain some caffeine, most is to be found in the bean, which would probably have been spat out, and the full effects would have gone relatively unnoticed.

The spread of farming, however, introduced to Ethiopia a more determined masticator. By about 8000 BC the early Fertile Crescent farmers had domesticated a number of the tractable animals that surrounded them, including the goat. These spread within a few thousand years from their Fertile Crescent roots to Egypt and thence up the Nile to the Ethiopian Highlands. While sheep and cattle are contentedly pastoral in their eating habits, goats are notoriously destructive eaters and tend to range wider for their foraging. Unlike birds, which plants use to spread their seeds via their digestive systems, woolly-haired animals spread seeds that adhere to their coats, leaving them free to chew into oblivion any plant, fruit, or seed that comes their way. Goats' stomachs are fully equipped chemically to deal with vegetable matter that other mammals would simply pass. Thus it is quite possible that it was the domesticated goat, observed perhaps by an accompanying human, that first experienced the raw caffeine hit of a chewed green coffee bean. This is purely conjecture, however.

If Egyptologists, classicists, and biblical scholars have failed to pinpoint the use of coffee in their respective literatures, neither have Arabists fared any better, despite the fact that coffee drinking first arose amongst the Sufis in Arabia Felix, now Yemen. Until the use of coffee became fairly widespread in the sixteenth century, the references to it remain obscure, and no material evidence exists alongside the texts to help prove that coffee was the substance referred to. For example, the renowned Persian physician Abu Muhammad ibn Zakiriya El Razi (known more commonly as Rhazes), who lived between AD 865 and 922, describes a beverage he calls *bunchum* as being 'hot and dry and very good for the stomach'. Although it is difficult to resist the obvious suggestion that *bunchum* is the same as *bun*, the Arabian and Persian word for coffee berry, other scholars have identified it as some sort of root. Nonetheless, the reference to *bunchum* in the works of Ibn Sina ('Avicenna'), the influential Bokharan physician (AD 980–1037), is sometimes held to be a description of coffee: 'It is hot and dry in the first degree, and according to others, cold in the first degree. It fortifies the members, it cleans the skin, and dries up the humidities that are under it, and gives an excellent smell to all the body.' Many scholars dispute the attribution, however, and there is no supporting archaeological evidence whatever to show that coffee was prepared or consumed at the time. Neither does the description make mention of the most obvious feature of coffee – the effect of the caffeine upon the nervous system.

However, this does not mean that the obscure terms used in these early descriptions should be lightly dismissed. While European culture had, since the sack of Rome in AD 455, gone into the dramatic decline known to history as the Dark Ages, Middle Eastern culture, by contrast, was flowering, with an added impetus provided by the new religion of Islam. In the fields of medicine, astronomy, mathematics, architecture, and astrology, as well as the arts, the Muslim world was significantly in advance of its European contemporaries. The description used by Avicenna may seem fanciful, but the terms made sense within a coherent, applied medico-scientific structure, derived, at least in part, from knowledge of the ancient world that had been lost to the Western purview with the destruction of the Library at Alexandria in AD 391. The remains of what was known as Alexandrian syncretism – the holistic amalgam of ancient Egyptian, Zoroastrian, Kabbalistic, and Roman and Greek esotericism alongside pre-Socratic and Neoplatonic philosophy and that of early Christianity – had been preserved by scholars at the sacred town of Harran in southern Turkey. The Hermetic school at Harran became a strong influence on emerging Islamic science and mathematics, as well as alchemy. Rhazes was a noted exponent, and both he and Avicenna exhibited the polymathic traits that characterized the alchemist through the ages – in equal measures poet, astronomer, philosopher, musician and physician. Alchemy was only superficially the search for a way to turn base metals into gold: it was, more importantly, a spiritual quest for the transmutation of the human soul. Science, art, and philosophy were brought equally into the service of this perfectionism.

The Sufis, a mystical branch of Islam who came to prominence in the second century after its foundation, were influenced by alchemy. 'The Sufi master operates upon the base metal of the soul of the disciple and with the help of the spiritual methods of Sufism transforms this base metal into gold', it was recorded. The word 'sufi' derives from the Arabic for wool, reflecting their simplicity of dress. Although the sect came about as a reaction to the perceived worldliness of early Islam, members did not believe that a practitioner should withdraw from human society. Sufi 'orders' were not like the closed monastic orders of Christendom; adherents continued to work and enjoy family life, and, as a result, most of their prayers and rituals took place at night. The general character of Sufi practice involved the communal singing of poetry; the ritual repetition of the divine name; a veneration for saints, many of whom were *shaykhs*, or former leaders of Sufi orders; and the ritual visits to the tombs of such saints.

Spread by proselytising *shaykhs*, by the twelfth century Sufism had reached Yemen. There, in the late fifteenth century, it would appear that the Sufis were the first to adopt coffee drinking. Not only did coffee assist in enabling devotees to stay awake during their night rituals, but the transformation of the coffee bean during roasting reflected the alchemical beliefs in the transformation of the human soul which lay at the heart of Sufism. Coffee worked both at a spiritual and a physical level.

The arrival of Sufism in Yemen is a matter of historical record. The same cannot be said about the arrival of coffee. By the end of the sixteenth century the mountains of Yemen were producing a significant proportion of the world's coffee, and it would be natural to assume that it had been introduced from Ethiopia across the Red Sea in earlier times. This is not the case.

Pre-Islamic Yemen was a wine-growing area, and alcohol thus appears to have been tolerated. Its diversity and wealth of crops and cultures made Yemen a society that was highly cultivated in both senses, and even after the introduction of Islam it remained a dominant cultural force in Arabia. However, despite the ebbing and flowing of power and religious influence from across the Red Sea, and despite archaeological evidence of the introduction of crops such as sorghum from Africa into Yemen in the pre-Islamic period, there is nothing to suggest that coffee had found its way from Ethiopia at this early stage. Rather as Aksum itself seems to have been unfamiliar with either the plant or the beverage, the regions into which the Ethiopian empire periodically expanded remained in caffeine-free ignorance.

Islam was quickly embraced by the Yemenis, but the country later became fragmented into a number of states and kingdoms that periodically waxed and waned: only the rule of the Shi'a Imams was sufficiently stable to forge an enduring dynasty, the Zaydis, which lasted over a thousand years until the revolution of 1962, at which time their rule extended over the whole of what is modern day Yemen. However, throughout the Zaydi epoch, independent states flourished that were influential in their time. The most significant of the independent dynasties was that founded in 1228 AD by 'Umar Ibn 'Ali Ibn Rasul. His kingdom was centred on Ta'izz in the south of the country, and there, for two hundred years, the arts, sciences, and trade flourished and Sufis first made their appearance in Yemen. It is during this Rasulid period that the first tantalizing rumours of coffee and its handmaiden *qat* can be heard from behind the purdah screen of history.

The town of Ta'izz is situated on the northern slopes of Jabal Sabir – at 3006 metres, one of Yemen's highest mountains – on the road that leads up from the southern end of sweltering

Tihama, where the port of Mocha is found, to the airy highlands and Sana'a, the capital, to the north. The town was the capital of the Rasulids until their demise in 1454. Their interest in science, astronomy, poetry, and architecture made the kingdom a natural haven for Sufism, and early in their rule a number of important *shaykhs* such as Shadhili came to the city. Sufism had an important proselytic dimension, and missionaries passed through Ta'izz on their way to Mocha and Aden, and thence to Africa. One noted Sufi missionary, Abu Zarbay, is credited by legend, in the confusing way that legends have when it comes to such matters, either with having introduced *qat* to Yemen in 1430 from the town of Harar in Ethiopia, or with having founded Harar itself, where what are considered amongst the very best *qat* bushes still grow. There is an anecdotal story that the Rasulid kings' interest in botany led to the introduction of *qat* and coffee plants in the environs of Ta'izz. It is true that they imported fruit trees and flowers from places as far away as India, and compiled detailed astronomical data to help farmers determine the correct seasons for planting and harvesting. However, a register of plants compiled for the Rasulid King himself in 1271 lists interlopers such as cannabis and asparagus, but there is no sign of imported coffee or *qat*. Ibn Battuta, the renowned Moroccan explorer whose traveller's feats far eclipse those of the Polos, visited Ta'izz, and this usually meticulous chronicler fails to mention either coffee or *qat* in dispatches from the city in 1330. Thus whilst in the Rasulid era the association of Sufis with these stimulating plants had acquired some additional folkloric momentum, our struggle to find actual coffee stains on the tablecloth of history remains frustrated.

3

ENTER THE DRAGON

potus niger et garrulus
('the black and tongue-loosening drink')

ANON.

By the end of the fifteenth century, the archaeological evidence shows that ritual coffee drinking was widespread amongst the Sufis in Yemen. What caused them to adopt a drink derived from a hitherto unknown plant from neighbouring Ethiopia? Curiously, to understand the genesis of coffee drinking, it is necessary first to look at tea; at China, where it originated; and at the trade links between China and the Middle East.

Before the fall of Rome, the Arabian Sea played an enormous role in world history, and once the Romans and Greeks sufficiently mastered the Red Sea and the monsoon (a word derived from the Arabic *mawsim*, meaning season) they were able to trade with India and Ceylon. After the fall of their respective empires, and with the rise of a hostile Islamic Turkish empire, which effectively blocked all the sea routes from the West to the Orient, Europeans were rarely seen east of the Red Sea. Nonetheless, the Arabian Sea was awash with trading and colonizing activity, some conducted in boats like those which, as Herodotus had observed, were made with planks sewn together with coir, and oiled with whale blubber to soften the wood in case of unforeseen encounters with coral reefs. From further afield came *wakas* – double outrigger canoes – in which the Waqwaqs of Indonesia braved the ocean voyage from Indonesia to Zanj ('Land of the Negroes' or East Africa) laden with cinnamon, and thence sailed to the previously uninhabited island of Madagascar, where they settled from the fifth century onwards. Arabian and Persian ships frequently visited Sirandib – the 'Isle of Rubies', now known as Sri Lanka or then known as Ceylon – and convoys sailed to China, the 'Land of Silk'. This was the longest sea voyage then regularly undertaken by man: one Persian captain famously made the round trip seven times. The city of Chang'an on the Yellow River had two million residents by the seventh century, and was a great market for 'western' goods such as sandalwood from India, Persian dates, saffron and pistachios, Burmese pepper, and frankincense and myrrh from Arabia. Slaves from Africa could also be bought, and the Chinese even at this early stage had a good understanding of the peoples of Zanj, even being aware of the Somali herdsmen's habit of drawing blood from their cattle and mixing it with milk to drink. The principal Chinese exports were silks and porcelain, the latter by this time being shipped by Persians from the southern Chinese port of Guangzhou (Canton). A maritime Porcelain Route evolved that vied in importance with the better-known Silk Route across Central Asia – porcelain, for obvious reasons, being less suited to overland freight. Ports along the Porcelain Route were valued according to their use of standard weights and measures, their safety and their non-interference in commerce: a maverick sultan could jeopardize this fragile web of trading links that spanned the East. The spread of trade went hand-in-hand with the spread of Islam, which underpinned a faith-based commercial network that guaranteed probity of dealings and a community of interests. The legacy of this can be traced today in the Hawali banking system, whereby large sums of money can be 'transferred' internationally by no more than a letter of authority. A comparable system did not evolve in Europe until the rise of the Knights Templar. As Islam spread, Indonesia, the Spice Islands, and the Philippines fell under its sway. Only the Chinese remained completely unconverted, although substantial Muslim populations settled in Chinese cities – Guangzhou had 200,000 Arabs, Persians and other Muslim residents in the seventh century.

A little-recognized incentive to the creation of this maritime empire of faith lay in the fact that Muslims had to pray three times a day in the direction of Mecca, a prayer which for its proper execution depended, of course, on the sure knowledge of the whereabouts of that sacred city. When the first Arab traders tentatively colonized parts of the coast of Zanj, they built unsophisticated wooden mosques which frequently can be shown to have been misaligned: only later, when the ports and their trade were more secure, were stone mosques built in the Arab style with the required alignment to Mecca, achieved by use of the magnetic compass and the astrolabe and an understanding of the stars. Thus the fundamental ritual of Islam was a significant encouragement to the science of navigation, and the concomitant spread of faith and commerce. This was reinforced by the necessity for the faithful to make the Haj pilgrimage to Mecca at least once in their lives, with the result that the Muslims were highly motivated and experienced travellers over long distances. Had Christianity evolved similar rituals in connection with Rome or Jerusalem, the necessary navigational skills and equipment might have been developed earlier. Ironically, Jerusalem had been the geospiritual target of early Islamic prayer until Mohammed made the former pagan site of Mecca (the Ka'ba having been worshipped there previously for many centuries) into the proper focus of Islamic prayers by decree in AD 624. As it was, the compass had been originally invented by the Chinese but discovered again by the Arabs: the astrolabe was their original invention, along with early clocks, theodolites, and instruments for measuring the apparent movement of a star by an observer who had himself changed position. Islam was structured in such a way that it not only encouraged science, but positively required it. By contrast it took the rise of sea-borne mercantilism in Europe in the seventeenth century to provoke intense interest in astronomy and navigation: the observatories of Paris and London were set up with the principal aim of solving the problem of longitude.

Islam having established a bridgehead in China, it was inevitable that the Sufis should also turn up there. Indeed the Emperor invited a group of Sufi astronomers to Peking in the 1270s to assist in the setting up of an observatory. The presence of Sufis in south China seems to have influenced Japanese Buddhism, leading to Zen Buddhism, which, like Sufism, focuses on 'masters' and illustrative tales from their lives. The Sufis, and the Muslim population in general, would have been widely exposed to the Chinese habit of drinking tea, which had been established for at least a thousand years – it is recorded that there were over a hundred water-powered tea mills in the first century AD. Surprisingly, there is no mention of tea consumption in Middle Eastern sources until a reference in Giovanni Ramusio's *Delle navigationi et viaggi* (1550–9), citing Hajji Muhammed, a traveller in the Caspian region, who thought that if the Franks and Persians had known about tea they would have given up rhubarb. Marco Polo, usually an inveterate chronicler, made no mention of tea at all. Nonetheless, it is tempting to suppose that the Sufis, who were inclined to embrace enthusiastically anything that could bring them closer to God, would have experimented with tea drinking in China, and may have adopted it as part of their rituals.

What is certain is that the celebrated Treasure Fleets sent out by the Ming dynasty Yongle Emperor into the Indian Ocean contained, amongst silks and porcelain and other trading goods, tea. The fleets were the most impressive ever seen, with hundreds of vessels of which the largest were nine-masted, 400-feet long and 160-feet wide juggernauts. Their ostensible mission was to extract tribute and assert the hegemony of the Middle Kingdom over the known world, principally the lands bordering the Indian Ocean. Envoys were brought back to Peking to pay their obeisance to the Emperor, accompanied by exotic animals such as the giraffe brought from Malindi and presented to the Emperor in 1414 and which was believed by the Chinese to be the legendary *qilin*, a sacred animal that would appear only in times of great prosperity. As well as putting on an awesome display of the might of the Dragon Throne and trading in Chinese goods, the Treasure Fleets (there were seven voyages between 1405 and 1433) were missions of discovery that prompted a sudden increase in the Chinese knowledge of plants and medicines, and of the lands from where they came. It seems that from the Chinese understanding of tea, which had initially been valued for its medicinal effects, the notion of infusion – the steeping of plant matter in boiling water to extract the desired essence – had developed. This deceptively simple discovery was spread through the popularization of tea.

The Treasure Fleets were led by the Admiral Zheng He, the 'Three Jewelled Eunuch'. His father had been a Muslim soldier from Yunnan province who was caught up in the fighting at the break-up of the Mongol Empire. In 1381 he was killed, and his son was taken into captivity and castrated in the Chinese manner, an excruciating variant that also involved the removal of the penis. Eunuchs were highly prized at court, being considered not only immune to the charms of the imperial harem but also particularly loyal to the ruling Emperor. Zheng He rose rapidly to prominence in the service of the prince of Yan, Zhu Di, who was campaigning against the Mongols in the northern steppes. An able commander and an imposing figure, Zheng He stood by Zhu Di when he usurped the Dragon Throne from his nephew, and was the natural choice for leader of the Treasure Fleets, upon which most of the highest positions were held by eunuchs. Both his father and grandfather were 'Hajji', meaning that they had made the pilgrimage to Mecca, and Zheng He's religion was an asset in the Indian Ocean.

The fifth voyage under Zheng He called at Aden in 1417, then part of the Rasulid kingdom of Yemen. It was an extremely wealthy port, and the sultan grandly ordered that only those with 'precious things' could trade with the Chinese. Whether tea was sold to the Arabs is not recorded, but it can be reasonably assumed that Zheng He and his officers would have drunk tea either with or in the presence of visiting merchants and dignitaries. The awesome majesty of the Treasure Fleet would have given the visitors particular reason to note the customs and behaviour of their distinguished company, and the concept of infusion to create a beverage would have been dignified by association. The stimulatory effects caused by the caffeine in tea may likewise have been noted and discussed. After the sultan had presented lions, zebras, ostriches, and another *qilin* for the Emperor's collection, the voyage then went on to Malindi and the coast of Zanj. It is almost certain that the Rasulid monarch in Ta'izz, having great interest in exotic plants and Chinese porcelain, would have paid attention to any reports of the Chinese drinking tea.

The seventh and last voyage in 1432 had a more extensive impact in the Red Sea: Zheng He, ill and exhausted, eschewed the opportunity to make the Haj and instead sent the fleet of more than 100 ships and 27,000 men to Hormuz and beyond with his deputy, the eunuch Hong Bao. Unable to land at Aden as a result of local fighting, he secured the permission of the Emir of Mecca to sail up the Red Sea to the port of Jiddah, where the Chinese were received with due honour. As well as their usual interest in trading, a translation of an Arab text *Hut yaw fang*

('The pharmaceutical prescriptions of the Muslims') had appeared in China to intense interest there, and particular attention was paid to the acquisition of Arab drugs and medicines. The use of aloes (a purgative and tonic), myrrh (for the circulation), benzoin (a gum that aids respiration), storax (an anti-inflammatory), and momocordia seeds (for ulcers and wounds) was recorded. It is significant that at this stage there is no mention of coffee: both the Chinese and Arabs would have had good cause to have analysed its properties if it had been a known substance at the time. It seems that knowledge of coffee was still confined to the Ethiopian Highlands. *Qat* is likewise absent from the pharmacopoeia.

Although there are Chinese reports of Mecca and Medina, they are surprisingly cursory: with Zheng He at Calicut and in failing health, the precision of purpose seems to have left the voyage. He died on the way back to China in 1433 at the age of 63, and was buried at sea. The returning fleet carried an ambassador from Aden, and yet another giraffe, and although pleased with the outcome, Zhu Zhanj, the Emperor since 1426, who was of a more introspective Confucian turn of mind than his grandfather, never subsequently authorized another voyage. Confucius believed that a healthy Chinese state should be able to provide for all its own needs, and that active involvement in foreign trade was beneath the divinely ordained dignity of the Middle Kingdom. It was for this reason that China had remained a relatively closed nation throughout its history, and why the Treasure Fleets were such a dramatic aberration. Once Confucianism regained the high-ground, the shipyards closed down, and the country turned in on itself again.

A Sufi missionary, Shahkh Shadomer Shadhili, is reported to have introduced *qat* to Ta'izz in 1429, and, whether or not it is true, the date is significant, as it is at around that time that the Chinese were present in the Arabian and Red Seas – the fifth and seventh Treasure Fleets of Zheng He. If the Yemenis had been introduced to tea as a result of these visits, either by experience, by report, or possibly by purchase, and if the emerging Sufi community was already familiar with its stimulating properties by repute, then the scene is set for the necessary discovery of infusions based on dried leaf material with similar properties to tea. The Sufis were eager to embrace chemical assistance in order to get closer to God, and help was at hand.

Tea leaves in China were made in a number of ways: the three most common, green, oolong, and black teas, were produced by differing combinations of sun-drying, pan firing, rolling, fermenting, and final firing. The coffee industry today is curiously coy about the fact that the current way of preparation is one of only many ways, and that coffee can also be a tisane or tea: an infusion of dried vegetable matter in hot water. Ethiopians, as we have seen, still sometimes drink a coffee made from the leaves (as opposed to cherry or bean) of the coffee plant. For one, *amertassa*, green coffee leaves are allowed to dry naturally in the shade, then infused. The other, *kati*, is made from leaves that have been pan fired. The use of dried leaf material in this way is very similar to tea, and *kafta*, a drink made from the dried leaves of the *qat* plant, is likewise related. Furthermore, in Yemen and other parts of Arabia today it is common to find *kish'r*, which is an infusion of the dried coffee cherry from which the beans have been removed. These cherries are sold in the markets in open sacks alongside green coffee beans, and are as much in demand. *Kish'r* has a pleasant, light fruity flavour with hints of its smoky coffee origins, but has more in common with a herbal infusion such as verbena or melise. Coffee cherry has also been detected in the manufacture of a cheap instant coffee. The evolution of these coffee teas through the use of the roasted bean into the beverage we now know as coffee was slow, and these varieties continued in parallel, as indeed they still do. Coffee did not spring into the world as a fully-fledged double espresso to go.

At the time of the visits of the Treasure Fleets, the Ethiopian Highlands were within the trading range of the merchants of Aden and Mocha, and Sufi missionaries also ventured across the Red Sea. It would seem perfectly plausible for a Sufi, inspired by what he had seen of tea drinking amongst the Chinese visitors, to learn what he could of the manufacturing process from them. Aware from his own learning that none of the plants in the conventional Arab pharmacopoeia had the characteristics he sought, he may have taken the opportunity of a missionary trip to Ethiopia to experiment with various endemic plant types there, and settled on coffee and *qat* as the most interesting. At this stage, in imitation of the Chinese, only the leaves of the coffee plant were used for the infusion, but as they contain less than 1 per cent caffeine, they might not have been sufficient for his ecstatic purpose. However, these things vary considerably according to brewing method and quantities used. Weight for weight, tea contains twice the quantity of caffeine as Arabica coffee, but as the volume of vegetable matter used is much less than half, the net effect is less caffeine in the final beverage. Coffee leaves could thus have been brewed 'strong' to provide a high caffeine yield, but this would have made the drink itself unpalatable. It is significant that *qat* loses much of its potency when its leaves are dried; thus as a tea it does not have a particularly interesting effect. This is why Yemenis today favour the chewing of the fresh green leaves, and perhaps also explains why *qat* has only recently started to find a wider public with the invention of airfreight.

It is at this point in coffee's history that a number of real people finally begin to peer from behind the purdah screen. When the first European merchants came to Yemen in the early seventeenth century, they were naturally very curious about the origins of the coffee that they had come so far to buy. Amongst the stories they were told by the local traders were many that were obviously fantastic, including those of fabulous multi-coloured coffee birds and plague-ravaged princesses. Interestingly, the story of Kaldi and his dancing goats was not amongst the stories recorded by the Europeans. This tale of the discovery of coffee is so favoured in our times that it has assumed the status of established fact. It involves a goatherd, Kaldi, who sees his flock eating coffee cherries and then dancing. Kaldi likewise eats and dances, and then tells the abbot of a nearby monastery of his discovery. Angered by what he regards as a diabolical substance, the abbot throws some cherries on a fire; the resulting aroma, however, convinces him that they must be of divine origin, and he makes an infusion of the beans which he gives to his monks to help to keep them awake during night prayers. The omission of the Kaldi story from those told to the earliest Europeans is a clear indication that it was probably the later invention of a coffee house storyteller. Some of the stories, however, concerned genuine historical Sufi leaders, of whom sufficient is known to be able to evaluate whether they could have instigated the hypothetical scenario of the Sufi missionary in Ethiopia outlined above.

The first candidate is one dear to the heart of the coffee trade, 'Ali Ibn 'Umar al-Shadhili, patron saint of the coffee port of Mocha. As an English sailor named William Revett reported in 1609: 'Shaomer Shadli was the fyrst inventour for drynking of coffe, and therefore had in esteemation'. It is understandable that the town which owed much of its wealth in the late sixteenth and seventeenth centuries to coffee should seek to associate its prosperity with its pet saint, whose tomb is one of the few fine buildings that remains there. However, he died in 1418, and while it is conceivable that he may have been in Aden when Zheng He visited the year before, it is unlikely that he would have been able to make a trip to Ethiopia, returning with the newly invented tea substitute, before he died. In addition, the earliest descriptions by the historians Abu al-'Abbas Ahmad al-Shardji and Mohammed al-

Sakhawi of the life of Shaykh 'Umar fail to mention his discovery of coffee, which after all would have been a very distinguished addition to his curriculum vitae. Finally the Shadhilaya Sufi order from which he derived his name was founded in the thirteenth century and was known for its orthodoxy and sobriety, and the writings of the order make no mention of coffee.

The second contestant is Mohammed bin Sa'id al-Dhabhani, also known as Gemaleddin, who was both a Sufi and a mufti (religious leader) in Aden. Although he died in 1470, somewhat late to have met Zheng He in 1417, he would have been alive in 1433 when the seventh voyage picked up an envoy from Aden who, upon his return from China, may have furnished the necessary details concerning tea production. Alternatively, tea drinking may have been a recognized practice in Arabia using precisely the tea which it is recorded that the Treasure Fleet carried for trading purposes. Upon the cessation of the Chinese visits after 1433, tea would have been impossible to obtain, and a substitute could have been sought. The most intriguing thing about the al-Dhabhani story as recorded by al-Djaziri is that it specifically refers to the fact that he had visited Ethiopia as a missionary and had learnt about the benefits of coffee drinking there. As well as being a religious leader, Gemaleddin was also a renowned man of science. There is some speculation in early European writings, unsupported by primary sources, that Gemaleddin gave coffee his mufti's seal of approval in 1454, and that his endorsement led to the rapid spread of coffee drinking in the Sufi community.

The third candidate is Abu Bakr al-'Aydarus, another Sufi who was patron saint of Aden. However, he died in 1508, which would appear to be quite long after coffee drinking had become established amongst the Sufis, as can safely be determined from the historical and archaeological record.

The persistence of such legends identifying the first coffee drinker as a Sufi master in the era shortly after the arrival of the Chinese Treasure Fleet bearing tea, the mutual interest in the *materia medica* of the Arabs and the Chinese, and the active presence of Sufism in the region all suggest that there may be a new, compelling version of the tale of the discovery of coffee to replace the time-worn myth of Kaldi. Although it is conjecture, the story is extrapolated from known facts and involves historical figures, all of which is a distinct improvement on that of the goatherd. Its hero is the Mufti of Aden, Gemaleddin, to whom we will ascribe the not unreasonable age of three score years and ten at his death in 1470.

As a young man, Gemaleddin was in Aden when the Treasure Fleet of Zhe Heng arrived at the port in 1417. He was struck by the description of the Chinese drinking an infusion they found refreshing called tea, made with dried leaves mixed with hot water. Gemaleddin later became a Sufi and a scholar respected in matters of both science and religion. In his early thirties he made the pilgrimage to Mecca, where he met a Sufi who described how he had seen the Sufis drink tea in China to help them stay awake during night prayers. Gemaleddin heard that another Treasure Fleet from China was at that moment on its way to Jiddah, the nearest port to Mecca, and so he hurried to meet it. As he was by now a man of great distinction, he was welcomed aboard the flagship by the fleet's commander, Hong Bao, where he drank tea with the dignitaries, noted its stimulating effect, and questioned them closely about the origins of the tea plant and the methods of drying the leaves. The description of the tea plant did not correspond with that of any plant he knew of in Arabia, and it appeared that the growing conditions required for tea would make it ill suited to the region. Gemaleddin wondered whether he might somewhere find a plant with similar properties if it could be infused in the same way. Having previously decided to go on a missionary expedition to Abyssinia, he began to look out for any as yet undiscovered plants which might have the desired effect. From Arab slave traders bringing captives from the Oromo tribe in the west of Abyssinia he learnt of a plant there called *bun*, which was supposed to make goats very lively when they ate it. He went to the Oromo, discovered coffee, and tasted infusions of the leaves, which he dried in the manner described to him by the Chinese. He noted that the stimulatory effect of the drink was very similar to that of Chinese tea. He also took samples of the cherries of the coffee bush back with him to Aden. The flesh of the cherry made a more palatable and stimulating drink than the leaves, and so Gemaleddin developed the drink called *qish'r*, which is still widely drunk in Yemen today, often flavoured with ginger. Gemaleddin encouraged his disciples to drink *qish'r* and it became a part of Sufi ritual; but, versed as he was in the mysterious science of alchemy, he continued to experiment and was struck by the enormous changes that took place in the rejected stones at the heart of the coffee cherry when they were roasted on a pan. These pale green, tasteless, and unpromising beans transformed into brown polished nuggets with an overwhelmingly delicious aroma and a bitter but alluring flavour when ground and boiled. The change to the coffee bean represented on a physical level the transformations that Sufism wrought upon the human soul, and the fact that coffee enabled adherents to remain awake during their night prayers was further proof of its spiritual qualities. The drink was also as black as the Ka'ba, the sacred black stone at Mecca to which all Muslims must make the Haj. Gemaleddin's learning and piety had uncovered a mysterious substance that assisted the Sufis in their communion with God.

Hence coffee stands before us finally unveiled, discovered by an alchemist who identified in its transformation the means of bringing men closer to God, in the same way that the use of communion wine, which is variously forbidden and allowed in different branches of the Christian ritual, has underlying it much of the same transformational thinking. That the Sufis should

have adopted a similar ritual use of a communal drink is not surprising, and the fact that coffee is known as the 'Wine of Araby'
also takes on another dimension of meaning in this context.

The way in which coffee was eagerly adopted by Sufism
illumines the alchemical element in the new myth. We have seen
that 'The Sufi master operates upon the base metal of the soul of
the disciple and with the help of the spiritual methods of Sufism
transforms this base metal into gold.' Even those who do not like
the flavour of coffee usually concede that it has a peculiarly
seductive aroma when freshly roasted, and when the beans are
broken up by grinding or pulverizing they release a new set of
aromas that are if anything even more beguiling. The transformation of coffee from dull, sublunary vegetable matter into a substance of almost divine aroma and extraordinary flavour is a
compelling symbol of what alchemy and its Sufi followers wished
to achieve with their spiritual quest. In every sense, then, coffee
brought them closer to God and it became a vital component of
their communal prayers.

The ritual use of coffee is itself a hypothesis, but one supported
by archaeological evidence, the first that we have come across in
our peregrinations around coffee's prehistory. Excavations at Zabid
have shown that initially (c.1450) coffee was almost certainly
served amongst the Sufi community at their *dhikrs* (communal
worship, usually at night) from a ladle dipped into a glazed bowl
named a *majdur*. Previously, this sort of pottery had not been
glazed, which suggests that coffee was deemed of higher importance than other liquids. Shortly afterwards, smaller glazed
bowls started to be produced at Haysi, a nearby town. These
would have been passed around from person to person, replacing the ladle. Significantly, these small bowls bear striking resemblance in shape to the Chinese porcelain tea-drinking bowls of
the same era, and some have rudimentary imitations of the
classic blue and white Chinese patterns. The passing around of

coffee was one of the reasons why it was banned in Mecca in 1511 as sharing was associated with alcohol consumption. Some Sufi sects today still pass around a drinking bowl of coffee in connection with events of particular importance such as the funerals of members.

Sufis did not live a cloistered existence, and the reason why their *dhikrs* tended to take place at night was that many of their numbers followed a normal life of work and family during the day – hence the value ascribed to coffee as a means of staying awake during prayers. As they lived amongst the community it would seem that the new habit of coffee drinking was rapidly disseminated amongst the population as a whole. Again the best evidence for this comes from archaeology; within a hundred years the Haysi potteries had evolved an individual coffee cup of the size and shape of a modern demitasse, or the smaller Turkish *findjan*. This would suggest that coffee consumption had spread from ritual to individual domestic consumption. Its wildfire spread through Islam, however, was the result of geopolitics: the growth of the coffee trade depended upon the relative security of the Red Sea and its ports, and a unified political and spiritual rule that allowed coffee to be quickly adopted.

It happened that the late fifteenth and early sixteenth centuries, when coffee drinking was first becoming established in Yemen both ritually and domestically, coincided with the first flush of the Ottoman empire. In 1517 at Cairo, having already conquered Constantinople and most of the Balkans in the previous century, the Ottomans under Selim I finally defeated the Mamelukes, who had been the rulers of Egypt and the Levant for the previous 250 years. The Ottomans had thus acquired, along with the holy Islamic cities of Mecca and Medina, the Caliphate – the spiritual leadership of Islam. The Mamelukes were originally a soldier-slave élite from southern Russia and the Caucasus. Driven from Egypt by the advancing Ottomans, a large number made their way to Yemen in 1516 where they settled in the Tihama, the desert coastal plain – it is said that they chose Yemen because they knew that *qat* was plentiful there. They finally succumbed to the Ottomans, who had taken Aden in 1538 and themselves started to occupy the Tihama, although they did not take inland San'a for another ten years.

It was during the Mameluke rule in Mecca that the spread of coffee attracted its first serious obstacle, in the form of the ban imposed on it by Kha'ir Bey, who was the Pasha of the city as well as the *muhtasib*, the inspector of markets. On 20 June 1511, outside the mosque, he spotted a number of men drinking what appeared to him to be alcohol in buildings resembling taverns; he made enquiries and found that it was in fact a new beverage, coffee, being drunk in rudimentary coffee houses. To confuse matters, there are some indications that it was actually *qish'r* coffee that had reached Mecca, not yet the roasted bean form, *bun*. Additionally, the dry coffee cherries which made *qish'r* could be lightly roasted before brewing, producing *sultana* coffee, and the word *kafta*, by which coffee was sometimes known, was applied as much to a decoction made of the leaves of *qat* as to one made of coffee beans. It can be seen that there was probably a reasonable requirement for an authoritative clarification of exactly what was what, and what was permissible. Clearly the habit of drinking some form of coffee-based decoction had moved up the Red Sea coast in the thirty years or so since it had become established in Yemen, but it had not until this time been subjected to the catechism, and its novelty represented something of a puzzle to Islamic orthodoxy. Because of the strict prohibition on any form of intoxication, coffee was a genuinely sticky issue which required a ruling. Kha'ir Bey was the first man to attempt to provide it.

He rapidly assembled a team of learned men, doctors, clerics and 'men on the street'. The issues they were called upon to consider, which are reported in the *mahdaf'* or minutes of the meeting of jurists at Mecca, were the application of core Islamic concepts to coffee; regarding things not expressly forbidden (*sunna*) in the Qur'an that were permissible unless harmful to the body; regarding *khamr* (wine) and the idea that 'every intoxicant is *khamr* and every intoxicant is forbidden' as it rendered men 'incapable of distinguishing a man from a woman or the earth from the heavens'; regarding *jaziri ta' assub* or a fanatical non-textual conviction based on an exaggerated sense of piety; regarding *ijima*, or communal acceptance; and regarding *marqaha*, the specific intoxication brought about by coffee. The coffee houses themselves also needed to be considered: were they, as had been suggested, centres of music, gambling, and mixing of the sexes? The fact that coffee was passed around, although ritually in a *dhikr*, evidently evoked the alehouse. There were many issues for discussion: even its most virulent detractors could hardly claim that the result of drinking coffee met the def-inition of intoxication, yet it undoubtedly had some effect. The inherent moderating influences of Islam demanded that it should not be banned on the basis of an exaggerated sense of piety, yet perhaps coffee was harmful to the body? Medical opinion was sought on the basis of the humour system and its degrees – the first representing food; the second, food and medicine; the third medicine; and the fourth, poison. Coffee, it was found, was 'cold and dry' and heightened melancholia.

The debate and the people who took part are usually charac-terized in Western coffee histories as superstitious and irrational, whereas the Western heroes of the coffee saga (de Clieu, Franz Georg Kolschitsky, and Francisco de Mello Palheta, amongst others, whom we shall meet in these pages) are treated as roman-tic, swashbuckling figures. We have seen that Islam had been the torch-bearer of science and culture during the European Dark Ages, but as soon as the West started to overtake it in the last five hundred years of the second millennium, history, as much as any other field of endeavour, was skewed to represent the natural superiority of European, Christian ways over those of the benighted unbelievers. Many popular historians view the genuine issues and debate surrounding the introduction of the new beverage in Islam with, at best, levity and at worst an underlying contempt. It is easy to forget that coffee is a powerful drug, and that its cultural assimilation was by no means preordained. Islam, by virtue of geography, was at the forefront of the process of weighing up its advantages and disadvantages. The intellectual approach involved theology, science, polemic, and even poetry – in Yemen a literary genre emerged that pitched coffee and *qat* against each other in imaginary dialogue:

> *Qat* says: They take off your husk and crush you. They force you in the fire and pound you. I seek refuge in God from people created by fire!
>
> Coffee says: A prize can be hidden in a trial. The diamond comes clear after fire. And fire does not alter gold. The people throw most of you away and step on you. And the bits they eat, they spit out. And the spittoon is emptied down the toilet!
>
> *Qat* scoffs: You say I come out of the mouth into a spittoon. It is a better place than the one you will come out!

Hashish and tobacco were similarly scrutinized when they arrived in the Middle East at the end of the sixteenth century. Alcohol had long before been the subject of controversy: the Qur'an refers (47: 15) to 'rivers of wine . . . delicious to the drinkers' but its prohibition is based on verses 5: 90–1. The continuation of that prohibition into the present day is a recognition of the weight of the authority of the initial debate. Western laws that today license alcohol and tobacco consumption but prohibit hashish and opium use have likewise emerged from a cultural consensus, a combination of science, social pragmatism, and superstition. If coffee were to be introduced to the West today, it is hard to imagine that it would get the approval of the regulatory authorities – as it was, coffee caused fierce controversy when it was introduced to Europe during the seventeenth century, and there were doubts about its suitability in Christendom. Unsubstantiated reports have Pope Clement VIII giving coffee his blessing on the basis that such a delicious drink should not be the exclusive preserve of Muslims.

The result of the Mecca debate was that Kha'ir Bey banned the consumption of coffee in that city, and reported his action to the Mameluke Sultan in Cairo, where it appears that coffee was already well established, inevitably, amongst the Sufi community. The Sultan ordered Kha'ir Bey to rescind the ban, and eventually the hapless Pasha lost his job for unrelated reasons. The Mameluke Sultans had waged a constant battle against taverns, but for the time being the coffee house was not tainted by association. After the Ottomans took Cairo in 1517, the two doctors who had given evidence in support of the ban in Mecca were arrested and cut in two at the waist on the orders of Selim I, who died in 1520. Coffee, from being an ecstatic in the service of the Sufis, rapidly spread throughout the newly united territories, acting both as an engine of social cohesion and a valued internal trading commodity. It was adopted by the Khalwatiyya, confrères of the élite bodyguard of the Sultan, and the approval of coffee by the Court Physician to Suleiman in 1522 further secured its position. Ottoman support for coffee drinking was by no means unwavering, however: a succession of prohibitions ebbed and flowed around the Empire. Banned again at Mecca in 1526, coffee houses in Cairo were smashed up in 1535 as a result of the preachings of al-Sunbati and reinstated by the judge Ibn Ilyas. In 1539, again in Cairo, night watchmen imprisoned any coffee house customers they found, and a prohibition order arrived in Cairo from Istanbul in 1544, but was enforced only for a day.

The intense controversy provoked by the growth of coffee consumption throughout the Ottoman Empire became one of the intellectual and literary obsessions of the sixteenth century. Coffee, increasingly secularized, became a powerful social force, in that people now had a reason to be out at night other than the performance of their religious duties. Traditional patterns of hospitality were broken as the coffee house started to replace the home as a place of entertainment; strangers could meet and converse, and men of different stations in life could be found sharing the beverage. In addition, of course, coffee by its nature was a powerful aid to intellectual dispute and clarity of thought, as well as providing the means whereby debate could be prolonged into the night. These factors combined to make coffee potentially subversive in the eyes of not only the religious authorities, but the secular ones as well. The increasing assertiveness of the Ottomans in the Red Sea trade, their possession of Yemen and, in 1555, parts of coastal Ethiopia, gave them greater access to the coffee entrepôts that sustained the coffee habit that had spread throughout the empire and beyond to Persia and the Moghul empire. Coffee had truly been adopted as the drink of Islam. But it was Constantinople, capital of Suleiman the Magnificent's eponymous empire, that witnessed the great flowering of Ottoman coffee culture.

Introduced by two Syrian merchants, Hakim and Shams, in 1555, coffee drinking in Constantinople took off so quickly that by 1566 there were six hundred establishments selling coffee, from splendid coffee houses to the humblest kiosk. The best were located in tree-shaded gardens overlooking the Bosporus, with fountains and plentiful flowers, and provided with divans, hookahs, carpets, women singers hidden behind screens, storytellers, and conspicuously beautiful 'boyes to serve as stales [prostitutes] to procure them customers'. The coffee was brewed in large cauldrons, and might be flavoured with saffron, cardamom, opium, hashish, or ambergris, or combinations thereof. Opium and hash were also smoked widely, along with tobacco. As there was no restaurant culture at the time in 'unhospitall Turkie', the coffee house was, other than the reviled tavern, the only place to meet friends outside the home, discuss politics and literature, play backgammon or chess and perhaps gamble. Foreign merchants seeking trade, newlyqualified lawyers seeking clients, and provincial politicians seeking advancement would all congregate there. The coffee house was an integral part of the imperial system, providing a forum for the coming together and dissemination of news and ideas, just as it was to do later in Europe. On the domestic level, the Sultan and other wealthy householders employed a special official, the *kaveghi*, to take care of all coffee matters. The Sultan's coffee service (both animate and inanimate) was naturally the most sumptuous: golden pots on golden braziers were held on golden chains by slave girls, one of whom gracefully passed the finest porcelain cup of coffee to the Sultan's lips. While the cares of state were thus soothed in the seraglio, wives of lesser mortals could legitimately claim that the lack of coffee in the household was grounds for divorce.

Other cities of the empire did not necessarily emulate the splendid coffee houses of the capital. Those of Cairo quickly attracted a low-life reputation, as they were filled with 'dissolute persons and opium eaters', and were used for the procurement of boys. Which is to say that they were in essence very similar to the coffee houses of Constantinople, but less beautiful and the clientele more conspicuously seedy. Because of their vicious reputation, the knives came out for the Constantinople coffee houses in 1570, with the clerics taking the lead role, spurred on by the fact that the mosques were emptying. The same issues were dusted down: whether coffee was an intoxicant, whether it was charcoal and thus forbidden, and whether the coffee houses were dens of iniquity. As it happened, the coffee houses were prohibited, but merely went underground. In the meantime, street coffee vendors continued to ply their trade. The interplay between secular laws imposed by the Sultan and the religious law of Shariah left scope for intervention by both sides in the coffee debate according to their particular needs at any time. Even when it was classed with wine by decree in 1580, its consumption was so widespread that there was no alternative but for the authorities to turn a blind eye, and eventually religious opposition was countermanded.

More serious was the secular threat under Amurath IV. The Grand Vizier Kuprili determined that the coffee houses were hotbeds of sedition, hosting political opponents to his unpopular war with Candia. He banned them outright, with offenders punished first by a severe beating and then, if caught again, by being sewn up in a leather bag and thrown into the Bosporus. Even this picturesque fate was not enough to deter hardened coffee drinkers, and eventually Kuprili was forced to relent. It is noteworthy that the taverns, which technically were forbidden under Islam, were allowed to remain open during the time of Kuprili's ban. This underlines the very different nature of the effect of wine and coffee on the human mind. On the face of it, taverns and coffee houses were both potentially places where political dissent could arise, being meeting places where open debate between strangers was inevitable. However, it is in the nature of coffee to clarify and order thought, and in the nature of alcohol to blur and confuse it. A tavern might generate heated discussions, but it is likely that the content of that debate would have been forgotten by the following day. The violence and disorderliness that frequently accompanies communal alcohol consumption is of an anti-social, rather than an anti-establishment, nature and represents no real threat to the status quo. Coffee house discussions could, and frequently did, lead to tangible results, whether commercial, intellectual, or political. Kuprili was the first to identify the revolutionary threat posed by the very nature of the substance imbibed combined with the location where it was consumed.

Under Suleiman – who, later in life, decided to throw himself into the soft bosom of the seraglio instead of the viper's nest of statecraft – the Grand Vizier became the foremost officer of the Ottoman Empire, with the absolute authority of the Sultan. However, the harem, full of machinating wives and jealous princelings, became the power behind the throne, and the result was the onset of the lengthy decline of the Ottoman Empire, a process only completed after the First World War. Under Murad IV, who ruled from 1623 until 1640, power was returned to the Sultan's hands. He achieved this through a ruthless force of personality, and amongst the many who attracted his ire were coffee drinkers and tobacco smokers. The old leather-sack-into-the-Bosporus routine for recidivists was reinstated and, if he found any of his soldiers smoking or drinking coffee on the eve of battle, he would execute them or have their limbs crushed.

Considering the widespread use of coffee throughout the Ottoman empire from the sixteenth century onwards, it is surprising how slowly the habit caught on in Europe. Even in Venice, a city that had every reason to be familiar with the customs of the Levant, coffee was initially sold in small quantities for medicinal purposes, and the first coffee house opened as late as 1683. It has been suggested that the city's *aquacedratajo* or lemonade-sellers traditionally included coffee in their portfolio of refreshing drinks, but there is no concrete evidence that this was the case. The more or less continuous enmity between Christian and Muslim could explain the slow transfer of new habits between the near East and Europe, but the dilatoriness of the Venetians is less comprehensible, as the city, even when at war with the Turks, was the vital commercial link between East and West. That the first coffee house in Venice opened some thirty years after the first one opened in England is an unexplained historical anomaly.

Coffee was introduced into Europe by the Ottomans during the seventeenth century via two channels: diplomacy and war. In the former case, it was the Turkish ambassador who brought coffee to the attention of the French, and in a manner befitting a meeting of the most powerful empires of East and West. In 1669, the Court of the Sun King, Louis XIV, at Versailles was nearing its magnificent zenith when news arrived that Sultan Muhammed IV had sent Soliman Aga to Paris for an audience with the young King. Whilst the prospect of an alliance between the Christian monarch and the Muslim Sultan seemed remote, both were concerned that the ambitions of the Habsburgs be kept in check. Statecraft aside, the chance to impress the ambassador from the orient was not one that Louis could easily ignore, and so he commissioned a new suit of clothes specifically for the audience, encrusted with diamonds and precious stones and costing 14 million livres. It was topped by a feather head-dress of surpassing beauty. The other noblemen of the Court were fitted out to complement Louis's suit.

Evidently the costumes took some time to make, for although Soliman Aga came to Paris in July, he was not received by the King at Versailles until December. Leaving his attendants behind, he presented himself in the audience hall dressed in a plain woollen robe – itself an interesting echo of the origins of Sufism – and seemed not the slightest dazzled by the magnificence that surrounded him, which was not unduly surprising considering the style that the Sultans themselves maintained. He further put the King's nose out of joint by failing to prostrate himself in a suitably abject manner before the throne, contenting himself with a slight bow and handing Louis a letter from the Sultan. It was then the turn of Soliman Aga to be mortified when the King glanced at the letter and suggested that, as it was rather long, he would look at it later. Soliman protested when Louis did not rise to his feet when he saw the Sultan's name at the foot of the letter. Louis replied that His Majesty would do as He chose. Impasse. The ambassador was dismissed, both parties seething with indignation. When his interpreter finally got around to reading the letter, Louis discovered that Soliman was not given the title 'ambassador' by the Sultan, and thus felt further insulted that he had gone to all this trouble for a man of doubtful status. To turn the tables, he ordered the Court composer, Lully, to write 'un ballet Turc ridicule', with a scenario by Molière. The 'Cérémonie des Turcs' received its première in front of the King at Chambord the following October. Evidently the humiliation still rankled, for the King did not congratulate Molière after the performance, and the courtiers were universal in their condemnation – which swiftly turned to praise when Louis saw it again a few days later and told Molière that he had been seduced into silence on the previous occasion.

While these elaborate insults were being devised, Soliman Aga himself was not idle. If plain wool had been his style for his first encounter with the King, his diplomatic offensive continued in an altogether more voluptuous vein. He had rented one of Paris's finest palaces and proceeded to remodel it *à la Turque*. Fountains trilled in courtyards, recesses were filled with emerald and turquoise Iznik tiles, and domes were softly illuminated by stained glass. Divans, carpets, and cushions were spread sumptuously about. Soliman Aga did not need to go again to Court, for the Court, intrigued, came to him – particularly the women, countless countesses and duchesses, who lolled in oriental luxury and were served unfamiliar coffee by Nubian slave girls. The coffee was bitter to their taste, and Soliman Aga quickly realized that the addition of sugar made the new beverage more palatable to his visitors – a simple addition to the recipe that has proved remarkably enduring. While he regaled them with innocuous stories concerning the origins of the drink, the coffee unlocked their tongues, and soon Soliman knew what he needed to know: that the King was really concerned only that his border with the Habsburg Empire remained intact, and what happened to the east was of no concern to him.

In the meantime, Paris society became besotted with the Ottoman style, and coffee was the fashionable beverage that accompanied it. One of Soliman Aga's retinue, Pascal, remained in Paris after his master had left and opened a stall selling coffee at the market of Saint-Germain. The bourgeoisie, drawn by the aroma wafting through the air, flocked to try what the aristocracy had endorsed, and thus coffee slowly became established in France. When the market closed, Pascal opened the first coffee house decorated in an oriental manner on the Quai de l'École near the Pont Neuf, and other immigrants from Crete, Armenia, and the Levant followed his lead. However, the vogue for all things Ottoman was short lived, and it was not until the establishment of the Café de Procope in 1689 that coffee found a truly Parisian expression.

While, on the face of it, Soliman Aga's diplomatic mission may have been a failure, the intelligence that he had gleaned concerning French attitudes to their eastern frontier certainly influenced subsequent Ottoman policy. Evidently feeling the need to counterbalance their indulgence in the coffee houses of Istanbul with expansionist militarism, the Ottomans decided to conquer Europe. Sultan Muhammed IV put his Grand Vizier, Kara Mustapha, in charge of an army of 300,000 men with strict instructions not to return until the infidel had been utterly annihilated; he further suggested that Vienna would make a suitable starting point, since that was where his illustrious forbear, Suleiman the Magnificent, had been halted in 1529. The resultant

Siege of Vienna in 1683 is regarded as a critical event in the history of Europe – for most people because it was the high-water mark of Islamic expansion, but for coffee historians because the dark stain left by its retreat was that of coffee. In common with much of coffee's history, a hero had to be found in whom these momentous events could be personified; and so it is that one Franz Georg Kolschitsky is the acknowledged man of the hour, saviour of the city, honoured with statutes and credited with being the first man to open a coffee house in Vienna. That the man who saved Vienna from the Muslim hordes also made coffee the favourite beverage of the city makes a romantic tale, and one that is exploited to the full by Vienna's Guild of Coffee Makers. It has in turn been further embroidered by Ukrainian nationalists, who claim Kolschitsky as one of that country's more illustrious sons and who clearly like the idea that enfeebled Western Europeans required the intervention of a Ukrainian Cossack to save them from the ravages of the Muslim hordes.

According to a loose amalgam of the stories put around by these special interest groups, the Emperor, Leopold, having fled the city, left a mere 17,000 citizens to face the Grand Vizier's vast army. It was evident that without the help of the small army of the Prince of Lorraine, camped near the city on Mount Kahlenburg, Vienna must surely fall. The Turks were already digging 'workings, trenchings and minings' by the city walls, and preparing to swarm through the breaches that subsequent explosions would make. Only one man in Vienna could save the day – Kolschitsky, who had been a coffee house keeper in Istanbul and knew the customs and language of the Turks well. He volunteered to slip through the Turkish lines in disguise to carry messages to and from the Prince of Lorraine. This, in the more elaborate versions of the tale, also involved heroically swimming across four channels of the Danube. He managed the round trip four times, doing much to boost the morale of the beleaguered city. On his final outing, when he took the alarming news that the Turks were about to blow a significant breach in the city walls, Kolschitsky found that the Prince of Lorraine had been joined by the warrior-king Jan Sobieski of Poland, at the head of an army of 30,000 men. Kolschitsky was given crucial information about the attack signal, which would enable the Viennese garrison to make a diversionary sortie. On his way back through the Turkish lines, Kolschitsky joined a group of soldiers drinking coffee around a campfire. He listened as they spoke wistfully of their Anatolian homes, of their Fatimas and little Mohammeds, and was so convinced that the morale of the Turks was at an all-time low that, when he regained the city, he rushed unannounced into the chamber of the garrison commander, Count Rudiger von Staremburgh. The Count awoke to find what appeared to be a Turk gabbling excitedly at him, and understandably summoned the guard. They were about to kill the assassin when the Count recognized Kolschitsky. Had the sword fallen, it is said, then so too would have Europe, for the diversionary sortie from Vienna proved crucial to the success of the joint army of Poland and Lorraine in the battle the following day, 12 September 1683.

The Turks were routed, and in their haste to retreat left behind a vast quantity of supplies – oxen, camels, grain – which the starving Viennese fell upon joyfully. In hot pursuit of the fleeing army went troops of Ukrainian Cossacks, who caught up with them at Parkany, near Budapest, where in the ensuing battle the Turks were finally broken. The defeated Vizier struggled back to Istanbul to be greeted with the painful disgrace of being strangled in front of his family. Lurking amongst the provisions left behind at Vienna were some five hundred pounds of coffee, which no one recognized, coffee being unknown in the city at that time. The valiant Kolschitsky, having been rewarded with 100 ducats for his feats of derring-do, again stepped into the breach and offered to relieve the authorities of the burden. The money he applied to purchase of a property, and he soon opened the Blue Bottle coffee house, happily combining the spoils of war and the skills he had learnt in Istanbul. It was a great success, and the rest, as they say, is history.

Unfortunately the same cannot be said of the story itself. An eyewitness account by an Englishman in the service of the Austrian army detailed the great victory and the booty left behind, and coffee is conspicuous by its absence from the list. Although the bravery of Staremburgh warrants specific mention, Kolschitsky does not feature in the account. While it is hardly to be expected that a lowly spy should receive any accolade in a report that concerns itself primarily with the chivalrous behaviour of the noblemen in victory, if indeed Kolschitsky's bravery had averted disaster, then the action, if not the perpetrator, would surely have warranted a mention.

Neither does the Franz Georg Kolschitsky who is the hero of Viennese coffee history feature in the mainstream works concerning the siege. He was probably a small player on a large field of intrigue and espionage, one of many spies operating on behalf of the besieged Viennese. Indeed, another spy, Johannes Diodato, is credited by some with opening the first coffee house. Kolschitsky's reward of 100 ducats is well documented, but so is the fact that he immediately started harassing the city council with demands for more money and permanent premises, recalling in his letters 'with measureless self-conceit and the boldest greed' the treatment of various classical heroes, including, coincidentally, the fantastic rewards heaped upon Pompilius by the Lacedaemonians, whose Spartan 'black broth' we met earlier in these pages. Perhaps worn down by the weight of classical allusions, the council eventually relented and gave him a property at 30 Haidgasse worth over 1000 gulden. It has not been possible to establish whether this in fact became Vienna's first coffee house; nonetheless,

Kolschitsky's keen sense of his own worth has etched itself on the history of Viennese coffee, so that he has become the hero he almost certainly never was. His statue can be found adorning the exterior of the Café Zwirina.

However flawed his character may have been, it is the case that the Viennese did take enthusiastically to coffee after the siege. They may have been helped in adjusting to the new taste by the invention of the croissant, or, as it was then known, the *pfizer*. Supposedly created by a Viennese baker who had discovered a Turkish mining operation whilst working at night in his bakery, the curved bread roll was based on the crescent moon that featured prominently on the Ottoman flag, as it still does on that of many Islamic countries. In these highly charged days, it is salutary to recall that, every morning, many in the Christian world celebrate the crushing of Islam in a kind of unconscious anti-Communion.

The Siege of Vienna saw the end of expansion of the Ottoman Empire as a European coalition fought to regain lost territory. The Sultans became increasingly mired in debt, and the slave girls poised with their fine porcelain coffee cups at the lips of the Sultan gave way to the vulgar diamond-encrusted self-service coffee cups of the late imperial era, which can still be seen in the treasury of the Top Kapi Palace in Istanbul. Under Kemal Atatürk (1881–1938), Turkey finally turned its back on its Ottoman history, became a secular society, and, mysteriously, took up tea drinking, as if four hundred years of glorious coffee culture had never been.

The curious role of coffee in the lifecycle of these early empires was thus complete: the Sufis and the Ottomans had developed coffee drinking as a result of observing tea drinking during one of the rare forays of officials of the Chinese Empire into the Arabian Sea. The coffee habit, initially ritualistic, had fuelled Ottoman expansion during the heyday of their Empire, only to be handed on like a relay baton to the Habsburg Empire and to other European nations, where coffee, stripped of its spiritual function, in turn catalysed the creation of aggressive mercantile cultures linked with European imperialism. As the Ottomans slowly collapsed, so they reverted to drinking what was perhaps the inspiration for their love affair with coffee. Turkey is now the third largest consumer – and fifth largest producer – of tea worldwide.

4

THE MOCHA TRADE

Traces of the history of the expansion of European maritime nations into the East, their adoption of coffee drinking at home, and their involvement in the trade itself can all be found on the tiny South Atlantic island of St Helena. To the visitor, who must approach by sea, the island looms out of the dawn, its high peaks swathed in funereal clouds, and the enormous, bare, red-black basalt cliffs glisten with the remorseless damp of aeons of isolation, creating a seemingly impregnable fortress. As the boat draws closer and skirts the cliffs around the island towards the miniature capital of Jamestown on the north coast, the impression is of an unfathomable gloom.

This is partly because St Helena is further from anywhere else than anywhere on the planet. If the island were the size of the earth, the nearest land would be four times the distance of the moon away. Ascension Island, some seven hundred miles away, is closest – 'another meer wart in the sea', as a Dr Fryer noted in 1679. Madame Bernard was to remark during Napoleon's exile: 'the devil sh-t this island as he flew from one world to the other'. St Helena wears its remoteness like a damp, suffocating cloak.

The fierce, naked cliffs of basalt defy the heavy, sluggish swell of the South Atlantic and the unending battering of the south-east trade winds. It is hard to believe from the sea that, in 1502, the 47-square-mile island was regarded by its discoverer, the Portuguese Admiral Juan da Nova, as a veritable Eden. It was densely forested all over with gumwood, oak, and ebony, with no large animal inhabitants except sea-lions, sea-birds, seals, and turtles; it had no predators, no snakes, no poisonous insects, but 120 endemic kinds of beetle. The only usable access to the interior lay through the narrow valley that now contains Jamestown, where the early visitors built a small chapel, collected fresh water, and gathered fruits. Da Nova left a number of goats, and thus the untouched Eden that had first exploded out of the ink-blue waters of the South Atlantic some sixty million years previously commenced the inexorable fall from grace that only contact with man's intrusive ways can bring.

The goats bred rapidly, and herds of hundreds, huge and fat, roamed the island eating young trees. Rats had escaped from the Portuguese ships and proliferated, along with great poisonous spiders from Africa, and there were packs of feral cats and dogs. The island continued to be the secret solace of Portuguese sailors, but as other European nations began to flex their maritime muscles it was inevitable that the secret of St Helena would out. An English adventurer, James Fenton, came across it by accident in 1582, and hatched a suitably piratical plot to oust the Portuguese and have himself proclaimed King, from which he had to be dissuaded by William Hawkins, his second-in-command. In 1583 three Japanese princes stopped there en route for Rome, on an embassy inspired by the indefatigable Jesuits. By chance, two other Japanese, captured off California from a Spanish ship, the *Santa Ana*, by Thomas Cavendish on his round-the-world voyage, would also have visited St Helena when the captain stopped there in 1588. He had been able to locate the island by taking prisoner the navigator from the *Santa Ana*. He stayed twelve days on the island, surveying it meticulously, observing the herds of goats nearly a mile long, the Persian partridges and Chinese pheasants, and stands of imported fig, lemon, and orange trees, as well as herbs and vegetables.

St Helena, despite its isolation, already bore the heavy stamp of man. Having finally been put on the map by Cavendish, it was inevitable that St Helena should become the unfortunate battleground of later European rivalries. A Dutch pilot in the service of the Portuguese, Jan Huygen van Linschoten, put in on the way back from India a year after Cavendish had left and heard stories of the Englishman's sojourn. He described the island as 'an earthly Paradise for the Portuguese ships', so well placed in the vast wastes of the South Atlantic as to appear to be evidence of God's beneficence. In those early days, there was virtually no piracy and no rival European navies to worry about, so the Portuguese ships sailed their own course from India to convene in St Helena before making the voyage home together. St Helena's very isolation made it a uniquely valuable piece of real estate, in a bizarre sense obeying the estate agent's mantra of 'Location, Location, Location'. There was literally nowhere else to go.

Cavendish's discovery that the island was the gathering place for the returning Portuguese East India fleet meant that it quickly became the haunt of English warships in search of easy – and lucrative – prey, to such an extent that, by 1592, the fleet return-ing from Goa had specific orders to avoid St Helena at all costs. Captain James Lancaster stopped on the island in 1591 on the first English commercial voyage to the Indies. He was to be the commander of the first East India Company fleet ten years later, using Portuguese maps of the Spice Islands which, ironically, had been stolen by van Linschoten from the Archbishop of Goa. These maps had excited so much interest in Holland and England that they gave the initial impetus necessary for the formation of merchant companies to exploit the knowledge they revealed. St Helena had already started to be the stage upon which many of the main characters of the coming European dominance of the East were to be first seen.

European sailors returning from the Cape of Good Hope, the Arabian Sea, and the East Indies beyond could run before the south-easterly trade winds that blow almost unceasingly from the Cape across the expanses of the South Atlantic. To avoid running into the same winds, outgoing ships mostly swung out towards the Brazilian coast, eventually making a much more southerly passage to the Cape. Frequently, the boats that had made the long journey to the trading ports of the East were in poor shape by the time they returned, and St Helena became a sanctuary for battered, weary sailors and their broken ships. The island's history at the beginning of the seventeenth century reflected the waxing and waning of European fortunes in the East. Portugal, after it had become united with Spain in 1580, became embroiled in a war of attrition against the Dutch, who in turn flexed their muscles upon achieving independence at the conclusion of that war and lost no time in filling the vacuum left by the decline in Portuguese trading activity in the East by sending large well-financed fleets to the Spice Islands. This thwarted similar ambitions harboured by the English, who set up the 'Governor and Company of Merchants of London trading into the East Indies' (to become known as the East India Company) in 1600 with precisely the same aim. The First Voyage (as each individually financed fleet was termed) of the Company came to St Helena after a particularly gruelling passage of the Cape, during which the Commander, James Lancaster, having lost the rudder of his flagship, the *Red Dragon*, ordered the accompanying *Hector* to sail on, writing poignantly in his log: 'I live . . . at the devotion of wind and seas.' Fortunately for Lancaster, the captain of the *Hector* refused to obey the order, and the two ships eventually limped into St Helena for repairs.

For most English people, the East India Company is principally associated with the tea trade with China, which indeed it initiated in the 1660s and which largely sustained it until 1833, when it ceased to be a trading company and effectively became the managing agency of India. However, from the earliest years of the Company, its factors (as the merchants were known) had identified coffee as a potentially interesting trading commodity, and by the 1620s were actively trading coffee from Yemen throughout the Arabian Sea at a time when coffee was virtually unknown back in England. As St Helena became a vital safe haven for the increasing number of Company voyages that put in there, so it also became part of the intricate web of connections created by the coffee trade. The involvement of the Company in the trade pre-dated the period of rapid expansion of European coffee consumption, but coincided with the first reports of the beverage. The traveller Leonhard Rauwolf from Augsburg went to Aleppo in 1573 where he observed the use of 'a very good drink, by them called *chaube*'. Another early reference to 'this drink called *caova*' was by Prospero Alpini, a physician from Padua who travelled to Egypt in 1580 and published a book on the plants of the country in 1592. Padua's university was at the centre of European medical learning at the time, and knowledge of the new drink thus disseminated rapidly. Preceding this was the report made by the Venetian Gianfrancesco Morosini to the Senate in 1585. He had been living in Constantinople and said that the Turks 'drink a black water as hot as they can suffer it, which is the infusion of a bean called *cavee*, which is said to possess the virtue of stimulating mankind'. Coffee was well established in the Ottoman Empire by the time these observations were made, and was also being widely consumed in Persia and Moghul India. Where did all the coffee to fill the cups of Islam come from?

It is common for the coffee industry to assert that, whilst Ethiopia was the cradle of coffee, Yemen, having imported plants from Ethiopia, was the first country actively to cultivate and trade in the new beverage. In fact, until the mid sixteenth century, the demand for coffee was met by Ethiopia entirely. Evidence of coffee exports from Zeila, near Djibouti on the western Red Sea coast, can be found in reports of the jurist Ibn Hadjar al-Haytami of Mecca in the late fifteenth century as well as in an account of a boat captured by the Portuguese in 1542 on the way to Shihr in Arabia.

According to some sources, exported coffee was harvested from the wild bushes in Kaffa province in the western highlands. However, recent genetic research into the spread of coffee plant species has suggested that the source of the Yemeni coffee strain was not the type found in Kaffa province, but that found in the east near Harar. As it is clear that the Harar type evolved from the Kaffa type, this would imply that there had been a migration of the plant to the Arab province of Harar *before* the plant went on to be cultivated in Yemen. This strongly suggests that the original domesticated (cultivated) coffee plant came from Harar, and that this would also have been the source of the Ethiopian coffee traded in parallel to that of Yemeni origin through the port of Mocha. This places Harar securely at the epicentre of the genesis of the world coffee trade: its cultivated varietal was the source of coffee traded in the earliest days. The strain of coffee plant produced there today is still the original type, Harar longberry, which is close in flavour to its Yemeni progeny and, although 'unwashed' (generally considered to be a less satisfactory method than wet processing), is one of the world's most prized coffees.

There is no clue to suggest how the coffee plant came to be cultivated in Harar, although there is some anecdotal evidence that the slave routes from the Oromo region (the Harar Arabs were incorrigible slavers) were lined with coffee plants discarded by the coffee-chewing Oromo captives. This would not account for the domestication of the plant, however, which required the application of specific skills. As there was a sudden surge in demand for coffee in the first half of the sixteenth century, it would have made the cultivation of coffee commercially worthwhile, and Harar was in any case a great deal more convenient for Arab traders than distant Kaffa. The presence of a domesticated coffee plant in the Arab-controlled Harar region would have made the transplanting of that variety to Yemen virtually inevitable as Mocha consolidated its position as the chief coffee port.

Although the coffee trade remained relatively insignificant, and the records concerning its usage remarkably thin in the era up to 1550, it would appear that the groundwork, in the form of tacit social acceptance, along with religious and imperial approval, had been done on the basis of Ethiopian coffee alone, and that the cultivation of the plant had first commenced in the Harar region. The pretensions of Yemeni coffee to hold the monopoly on the early coffee trade are hollow indeed.

However, the switch of the principal source of coffee production from Ethiopia to Yemen can be dated with some confidence. In 1544 the Imam banned the cultivation of *qat* in the Jabal Sabir region of Yemen and introduced coffee plants 'from which the population will derive great benefit'. The same date is ascribed to the introduction of coffee in a later Arabian chronicle. The Ottomans took the neighbouring city of Ta'izz in the following year, and it is under their auspices that the cultivation of coffee became a significant feature of the economy. Indeed it was in many ways a classic colonialist venture: cultivated in a conquered country, coffee was principally consumed in the main cities of the conqueror. The only element missing from the later European model was the use of slaves, for it appears that the rapid expansion of coffee drinking throughout the Ottoman Empire had created a golden opportunity for Yemeni farmers. The mountains overlooking the Tihama – the coastal plain which had previously been relatively uncultivated – proved to be perfectly suited to coffee growing. Farmers from the Tihama and inland plateau moved there: an immense project of terrace building and irrigation works was implemented, financed by the burgeoning coffee trade throughout the Ottoman Empire.

Situated at the south-west corner of the Arabian peninsula, Yemen defies any mistaken preconceptions of unrelenting heat and equally unrelenting sand dunes. It is as if the peninsula had been stood upon, like a sheet of ice, in the north-east, raising the south-west Yemeni portion into ranges of mountains sliced through with precipitate gorges strewn with rocks and vegetation and watered by seasonal streams. The Tihama, bordering the Red Sea, is intensely hot and humid, but only thirty kilometres inland the mountains soar straight out of the plain to heights of well over three thousand metres. Whereas the Tihama remains relatively dry almost throughout the year, the mountains catch the monsoon clouds, and short, intense bursts of rain are frequent, resulting in *sayl* – flash floods in the dry river beds. From this dramatic landscape the coffee farmers fashioned a yet more dramatic way of life; to catch the sporadic rainfall, the precipitate hillsides are covered from peak to trough with terraces held in place by stone walls. It may take a wall five metres high, snaking around the craggy contours, to create a cultivatable terrace two metres wide. Looking up from below, it sometimes seems as if the whole mountain is one gigantic man-made dry stone wall stretching into the clouds. In order to harness the rainfall in an elaborate system of irrigation channels and tanks, Yemeni villages are deliberately built away from the terraces – the only such place available being on top of the mountains. Since the vernacular architecture favours houses in the form of five- or six-storey square-built stone mini-skyscrapers, the total effect is unique and astounding. Villages of perhaps ten of such houses are perched in the most improbable clusters on the top of jagged mountainsides, whilst below them row after row of terracing planted with windbreaks of wolf's wood and screw pine fall into the infinity of colossal ravines, home to wild roses and prickly pear, baboons, rock hyrax, leopards, and weaver birds.

There are no records concerning the terrace building project. However, the mass migration to the coffee mountains is still recalled in many oral family histories in the country. It was in its time as significant as the California gold rush. By the end of the sixteenth century, Arabia Felix was universally seen to be the origin of coffee production, totally eclipsing Ethiopia in a matter of half a century. When Europeans first heard of coffee, and when their merchants gathered intelligence regarding the trading potential of the mysterious new drink, it was to Yemen they looked. Yemen had usurped the Ethiopian claim to be the unique source, and farmers brought coffee to the busy entrepôt of Bait-al-Faqih at the foot of the mountains, from whence it was transported in camel trains down the Tihama to the port whose name soon became synonymous with the coffee trade: Mocha.

The name Mocha is so enmeshed with that of coffee itself that it appears on everything from Ethiopian coffee to a variety of brewing machines, to coffee blends, or coffee made in myriad ways, including, in the case of one coffee bar, 'espresso, steamed milk, chocolate, richly blended, topped with fresh cream', which would seem about as far removed from the austere majesty of the Yemeni original as it is possible to be. The reason for this ubiquity is simple: for a hundred and fifty years Mocha was celebrated as the sole port supplying the world's coffee, at a time when coffee drinking was booming in the Islamic world and Europe. Today, it is hard to believe that the town was very prosperous, with six thousand houses and a stone-built Governor's mansion 'with very fayre and large stayres'. It is now a godforsaken, fly-blown spot, strewn with the inevitable mounds of plastic bags and mineral-water bottles that are the unfortunate detritus of Yemen's *qat* chewing habit. The sand dunes have reclaimed much of the town, and the most permanent buildings are made from redundant shipping containers. Even in the mid nineteenth century it was described as 'a dead-alive mouldering town'. However, one can still find some signs of its former glories: the ruinous brick walls that have not been buried by the sand show signs of having been richly decorated with ornate plasterwork – these would have been the villas in which the wealthy coffee merchants lived. Likewise the mosque dedicated to Shadomer Shadhili, patron saint of the town, rises like a pearly mirage in the distance through the hot, dusty air, and the curving stairs of the ruins of what is said to have been the lighthouse, marooned half a mile from the sea, can still be visited, as long as the smell of human dung can be endured. This is one feature of Mocha that has not changed since the first descriptions by Europeans, who found it handsome and whitewashed along the waterfront, but 'unbearably filthy within'. The other is the unrelenting heat and humidity. The Tihama is as airless and humid a place as can be imagined, and early European merchants who ventured there in their doublets and fustian must have been horribly uncomfortable. The squalor and the heat contributed to the town's reputation for being an unhealthy place, 'a hell of heat and humid air, of infected drinking water and without a breath of wind'. The villa owners built verandas on the top of their houses, shaded by reed screens and designed to admit the slightest of breezes.

Mocha, according to one early account, 'standeth hard by the waterside in a plaine sandye field'. The local soil was barren because of salt contamination, and the only thing that grew there was date palms, from which toddy was made. It was hardly an ideal place for a port, but it was the best that was on offer on the Tihama coast. Aden, one of the world's great natural harbours around the corner on the Arabian Sea, was too far away from the coffee-producing mountains to be of use. Although fourteen fathoms deep, Mocha's anchorage was 'open and dangerous with very shoali water a mile off the town'. These shallows were eventually to be the death of the port as they accreted silt and became increasingly treacherous: today the water is only four fathoms deep as far as four miles off the town. This natural tendency to silt up was not helped by American trading ships in the early nineteenth century dumping their ballast in the anchorage before taking coffee on board.

By the time the first European traders arrived in the first decade of the seventeenth century the prosperity of Mocha was assured, with the coffee supplied by new plantations developed on the towering Yemeni mountains hard by. However, the increasing dominance of the Ottomans on both sides of the Red Sea meant that the strain of coffee that had been successfully introduced to Yemen continued to have a rival in the form of the Ethiopian Harar coffee. That coffee was under Arab control, and it was shipped to Mocha before being sold to other merchants. Hence the so-called monopoly held by the port of Mocha was a monopoly on the trade, not on the origin of the coffee. At times, the quality of coffee being shipped to Mocha from Ethiopia exceeded that of the local Yemeni coffee, and it achieved a better price. The East India Company's chief factor at Mocha, Francis Dickinson, wrote as late as 1733: 'There has been about Three hundred Bales of Abbysine coffee imported this Season, but as that is now cleaner than the Coffee generally brought to this Market, it sells for a higher price, and was all brought up for the Busseroh Market.' It has long been a puzzle to those interested in the coffee trade as to how the name 'Mocha' has been misappropriated by Ethiopia – in line with the assumption that the world's first cultivated coffee came from Yemen, it was believed that the Mocha sobriquet should properly be applied only to coffee from that country and that Ethiopia was guilty of barefaced theft. Since we have now demonstrated that, historically, Ethiopian coffee was sold alongside Yemeni coffee through the entrepôt of Mocha, that mystery has been solved.

It was widely reported that, in order to maintain their 'monopoly' on coffee production, the Yemenis boiled or part-roasted their green coffee beans to prevent them germinating. A Company report dating from 1640 describes the beans as having been 'cooked'. In this way the Yemenis supposedly foiled the early plans of the European traders to propagate coffee in their nascent colonies. The story is widely repeated today, although there is no evidence of the practice other than in second-hand accounts. In any case, the existence of the 'Abbysine' coffee origin shows that the supposed monopoly on production was chimerical, and thus did not need protecting. In addition, the logistical problems of actually boiling coffee to sterilize the seed would have been formidable, and the resultant effect on the quality of the coffee and its keeping qualities potentially disastrous. What is certain is that the authorities did what they could to control the export of coffee seedlings and seeds, and fines were imposed if traders were caught attempting to smuggle them out. It is probable that the spurious story of sterilizing the beans was circulated to discourage smuggling. It also happens to be the case that green coffee beans become increasingly difficult to germinate after a long lapse in time such as a sea voyage, and so it could well have appeared on the face of it that the rumours concerning boiling were true.

As reports of the new beverage started to circulate through Europe, so merchants, alert to every opportunity, started to take notice. The East India Company's early involvement in the coffee trade was, against expectations, nothing to do with importing it to England but with participating in the traffic of the commodity between the already developed markets in Persia and the parts of India under Islamic rule. This came about because the Company had failed to fulfil the designs of its original Charter, which were to fill the void in the spice trade from the East Indies left by the decline in Portuguese power. The Dutch, better financed and equipped, had quickly established themselves there to the exclusion of the Company. To make the best of its presence east of the

Cape of Good Hope, the Company bought such spices as it could pick up at secondary entrepôts, and also traded within the Indian Ocean itself. For this reason, early contact was made with the virtually unknown Moghul India, and the Company started to trade textiles from Surat (a western Indian port to the north of Bombay) to Java and Sumatra in exchange for the elusive pepper, nutmeg, and cloves. Coffee thus presented an ideal opportunity to develop another trading string to its bow within the Indian Ocean.

Through their links with the Levant Company, chartered in 1579, the Governor and Merchants of the East India Company had received intelligence about the potential significance of coffee, although it was at that time virtually unknown in Europe. The Levant Company and the East India Company had many prominent merchants in common and had shared offices at an early stage. They were aware that coffee could be obtained only from the port of Mocha. The *Ascension*, a boat of the Fourth Voyage, called at Mocha with John Jourdain aboard. His journal is the first detailed account of the Yemen and the potential of the coffee trade.

Jourdain was born in 1572 in Lyme Regis, Dorset, at the time a significant port. His father became mayor of the town a few years before his death in 1588, and evidently was a man of some prosperity as he left a considerable inheritance to his family. John became a trader in his own right, taking seventy sloops as far south as Portugal and the Azores. For reasons that are not entirely clear he signed on as Chief Factor for the Fourth Voyage of the East India Company, which had raised a subscription of £33,000 from 550 adventurers, some of whom had directly subscribed no less than £550 each, selling smaller parcels to 'underadventurers'. The flagship of the Voyage, under its General (the name for the Commander at that time) Alexander Sharpeigh, was the *Ascension*, a boat that was already a veteran of the First and Second Voyages and which had been sold to the Fourth for £485 17s. 6d. Another brand-new boat, the *Union*, cost a further £1250. Until the arrival of the concept of 'Joint Stock', whereby the profits or losses of previous Voyages were absorbed by the Company as a whole, each Voyage was an autonomous, self-financed entity that turned a profit or otherwise for its subscribers in its own right. Under strict instructions from the Court of Directors, the Fourth Voyage was ordered to sail to St Augustine's bay in Madagascar, there to build a pinnace (the parts of which had been shipped disassembled) and from thence make their way to Socotra, an island off the horn of Africa, to buy aloes. From Socotra, they were to explore the trading possibilities of Arabia Felix, particularly the ports of Aden and Mocha, although they were to avoid missing the monsoon that would take them to India. Detailed instructions regarding possible variations on their movements all the way to Bantam and the Spice Islands were issued.

The Voyage set sail in March 1608, eventually reaching Aden – 'this famous and stronge place' – on 7 April 1609. The port was, like Mocha, in the hands of the Turks but was in decline, as Mocha was more accessible to the trading caravans and ships making their way from Suez, and to Indian merchant ships both ports were much the same. Sir Edward Michelbourne, an independent adventurer who was later to be a thorn in the side of the Company in the East, had described Mocha as 'governed with merchauntes onlie and a place of spetiall trade'.

The Governor of Aden was a Greek renegade called Rajab, who obviously regarded unaccompanied European ships as fair game and set about luring the foreigners into his trap. Sharpeigh was welcomed royally, 'entertained with tabour and pipe and other heathen musicke', and given a house and assurances regarding commerce and duties. Rajab did his best to encourage the English merchants to bring their ship into port and their goods on shore.

Disputes arose over duties, and Jourdain was sent to seek the judgement of the Pasha at Sana'a, the capital. This was the first journey by an Englishman into the unknown country of Arabia Felix. He set out on 28 May 1609 on a journey that took him across a plain where he came upon a 'cohoo howse' and later, on 5 June, the mountain Nasmarde (properly Nakil Sumara) where he recorded his appraisals of the cultivation of coffee and observed that it was 'where all the cohoo grows . . . the seeds of this cohoo is a greate marchandize, for it is carried to Grand Cairo and all other places of Turkey, and to the Indias'. The audience with the Pasha was inconclusive, but Jourdain managed to obtain permission to trade from Mocha, to which his party then travelled. There he found Sharpeigh and his officers exposing themselves to the risk of capture on the shore, much to his disapproval, for 'the Turks themselves saye: if thou wilt have anie thinge of an Englishman, give him good words and thou shalt bee sure to wynne him'. Although Jourdain continued on to the East, his reports went back to the Directors in England, and the Company diverted the three ships of the next Voyage in expectation of good business between Mocha and Surat.

At first all went well. The fleet, under the command of Sir Henry Middleton, included the brand-new *Trades' Increase* and *Peppercorn*, and arrived at Mocha in October 1609. They appeared to be made welcome by the local Turkish official, but then suddenly the situation turned hostile. Their house was besieged, eight crew members were killed, and Middleton was held prisoner. Refusing to order his fleet to surrender, he was transported clapped in irons to Sana'a. He established from the Pasha that the Mocha merchants were concerned about the English buying up all the Indian goods and strangling their trade; Middleton promised that they would not do so, whereupon he was taken back to Mocha, still a captive. When he finally escaped in a water butt, he made off with his fleet for Surat but later returned to

Mocha to wreak his revenge by confiscating the goods of fifteen Gujerati trading ships waiting to enter port. While this might have satisfied Middleton, it ruined the Company's reputation in Surat and undermined negotiations already underway in Mocha with a new official there. Far from finding a way to participate in local trade, the Company had managed to alienate all those who might have helped it. It took the embassy of Sir Thomas Roe to Agra in 1615 to re-establish good relations. As he smoothed ruffled feathers, he observed the consumption of coffee at the Moghul Court, and he could be the subject of an illustration showing a European drinking coffee there.

Thanks to Roe's good offices, the Company's reputation at the Moghul Court was restored and trading concessions granted at Surat. While Roe may have considered that this was the result of his aristocratic 'qualitie' and courtly demeanour, it may have been that the Emperor was more impressed by the Company's victory in a naval battle against the Portuguese at Swalley Hole, off Surat, in 1613. The pilgrim route to Mecca from India required protection, and Jehangir was careful not to alienate the nation that appeared best able to provide it. As a result of the concession, the Company was soon in the coffee trade in earnest. After a firman granting permission had been received from the Sultan in Istanbul, a factory was established at Mocha in 1618 under Joseph Salbanke, and William Finch, previously Hawkins's loyal number two, fetched up as agent there in 1619 and was soon busy sending consignments of coffee to colleagues in Surat in preference to those in Persia, as it 'was worth more in Surat than your advice valued it there'. William Burt wrote to the Company from Isfahan in 1630 that 'if ships go to Mocha with a well-chosen cargo they will do well, especially if invested in cowa seeds, which find vent both in Surat and Persia unto your large advantage'.

The words and spellings that the English used for coffee varied significantly during the early years of their coffee trading:

Jourdain's 'cohoo' and Revett's 'coffe' were followed by references in the Company's factory records to 'cowha' (1619), 'cowhe' and 'couha' (1621), and 'coffa' (1628). In the first reference to coffee-related merchandise, on 8 May 1640, the Court of Committees in London recorded that 'Mr Methwold, being in court, alleges that Arlington, when employed with Mr Wild to Goa . . . certain coho dishes were committed to his care'. There were no more than twenty Company factors in Persia, based principally at Bandar Abbas on the coast, and coffee was but one of the many items they traded. However, the market for coffee amongst the courts of the Muslim rulers of Persia, as well as the Moghuls and their subject sultanates in the Deccan, generated sufficient demand to fuel a small, but profitable trade.

Although coffee had been familiar to a small number of well-educated Englishmen since the travellers' tales of the likes of Sir Anthony Sherley, Sir George Sandys, and William Biddulph were published in the first decade of the seventeenth century, it would seem that the merchants of the City of London were well ahead of the chattering classes in their direct knowledge of the beverage. The first coffee to be actually consumed in England may have been that reported by John Evelyn, when he describes in his diary having seen the Greek Nathaniel Conopios, the future Metropolitan of Smyrna, drinking coffee at Oxford in 1637: 'It was observed that while he continued in Balliol College he made the drink for his own use called Coffey, and usually drank it every morning.' The physician William Harvey (1568–1657) was likewise reported by the diarist John Aubrey to have been a coffee drinker before the beverage became generally known. He had possibly learnt the habit from his close family connections with the Levant Company, or, more likely, whilst training at Padua in Italy, where coffee had been described and tried in the last years of the sixteenth century. Upon his return to England in 1602 it seems that Harvey brought the new beverage back with him. Aubrey describes Harvey as 'filled with energy of a high-output kind', and writes of how 'his thoughts working would many time keepe him from sleepinge'. These are recognizable symptoms of a caffeinated man. Harvey, it is sometimes claimed, was led to his great discovery of the circulation of the blood by his observations of his own reaction to the caffeine rush, and he left in his will his remaining fifty-eight pounds of coffee beans for his colleagues at the London Society of Physicians to consume once a month in his memory. Harvey represents the intellectual bridge between the consumption of coffee and the Age of Enlightenment.

Although there is no record of the Company's ships bringing coffee back to London with them, it is hard to imagine that the Directors would have encouraged trade in such a novel commodity without being curious about it, or that the factors themselves would not have brought some back for personal consumption.

The Company's internal trade within the Arabian Sea was of relatively little interest compared to the mysterious allure of the mighty Moghul Empire. Shakespeare displays some acquaintance with the customs of India in his works, but makes no reference to Arabia or coffee. To this day, the Company's involvement in the early coffee trade has remained almost unknown, but its survival after the difficulties encountered with the Dutch in the East Indies depended on its ability to participate in the internal trade of the Indian Ocean. Coffee was evidently one of the commodities that enabled the Company to stay in business, and to maintain commercial and political links with Moghul India. It was from this fragile foundation that the formidable Company Raj in India arose, which was later to become Britain's eastern empire.

The Dutch themselves came hard on the heels of the English Company's merchants to Mocha. Pieter Van dan Broek brought the first coffee back to Holland in 1616, and the first commercial shipment was sold in Amsterdam in 1640 by a German merchant. Such coffee as was consumed in northern Europe came via Holland up until 1660. The first English coffee houses were supplied by beans from this source until the East India Company started to sell it at auction in London. The Committee of the General Stock first ordered ten tons of 'coho seede' from Surat in 1657, and two years later doubled the quantity in a second order. The General Court of Sales of 1 August 1660 records the sale of 'cotton yarn, coho seed, Lahore indigo, benzoin' and the coffee fetched 71s. 11d. per hundredweight. It marked the beginning of a revolution in the political, economic, and cultural life of the country.

5

COFFEE AND SOCIETIES

'And then homeward to the Coffee-house to hear news.'

Diary of Samuel Pepys, 4 November 1664

The first European merchants on the shores of the Red Sea had not arrived there by chance, nor merely for profit, although that figured significantly. Both the English and the Dutch had emerged from long struggles to throw off Catholicism, and the new spirit of merchant venturing in the East was also an assertion of their Protestant nationhood. Spain and Portugal had had their heyday in the sixteenth century; the former remained pre-eminent in South and Central America but its expansion had essentially run out of steam, and the latter had loosed the iron grip it had been able to maintain over trade in the Indian Ocean by superior firepower. France was preoccupied with maintaining its European power, and the Holy Roman Empire was both too land-bound and too absorbed with the Counter-Reformation to participate meaningfully in the scramble for overseas possessions. All were unable to rival the new merchant fleets unleashed from the North Sea.

For the English, in particular, the expansion of their maritime trading activities was an outward projection of the new-found self-belief that had formed during the Elizabethan era. John Dee, the Queen's astrologer, mathematician, cartographer and magus, is often credited with the conception of the British Empire – he reportedly outlined the idea in the mud on the banks of the Thames at the Isle of Dogs for a suitably impressed Christopher Marlowe. He was also the first to posit the creation of a 'petty Navy Royall' for the protection of trade. The establishment in the late sixteenth century of the chartered trading companies of the City of London – the Muscovy, the Levant, the Virginia, and the East India Companies – required a psychic paradigm shift for England, which had up until recently considered itself to be a second-tier European power, under the thumb of the Catholic monarchs of Spain and France. The Reformation under Henry VIII spurred the reorientation of Christian spiritual life, but it was the vision of a Protestant Empire of Albion governed by a Virgin Queen that provided the crucial dynamic. In time, Britannia would rule the waves, but it required a great deal of practical magic to get her there. Mysteriously, coffee was to be part of that process.

As Dee realized, it is in part necessary to dream an empire into being, and such dreams were the stock-in-trade of the Hermeticist. Hermeticism, which, as we have seen, had been preserved in Islamic culture during the European Dark Ages, was the hugely influential esoteric philosophy that became one of the intellectual fuels of the Renaissance, and was also the undercurrent of the Enlightenment. It found expression in diverse forms, one of which was the early seventeenth-century Rosicrucian movement. A key tenet of the Rosicrucians was the existence of an 'Invisible College', an ethereal academy of seekers after truth. There is more than an echo of the 'Invisible College' in the informal, yet highly instructive environment of the London coffee houses. They were often called 'Penny Universities' because the price of entry was a penny, but the knowledge that could be gleaned there was invaluable.

The seventeenth century saw the emergence of Coffee House Man. Close observation of the workings of nature, and the ensuing discoveries of the apparently immutable laws that governed her actions, signalled the birth of science and reasoning. Detached, objective reason could grapple equally with social, political, and scientific issues. The results could be shared, debated, and refined in the society of like-minded men in the coffee house. The Enlightenment in England was born and nurtured there.

The central role that the coffee house played in the City's commercial life is illustrated as late as 1805 in a finely calibrated memorandum: when news of the victory at Trafalgar and Lord Nelson's death arrived at the Admiralty, the First Secretary, William Marsden, 'sat up the remainder of the night . . . in order to make the necessary communications at an early hour to the King, the Prince of Wales, and other members of the Cabinet, and to the Lord Mayor, who communicates the intelligence to the shipping interest at Lloyd's Coffee-house'. In contrast to their role in Ottoman life, the coffee houses of England could make no claim to be the first secular public meeting places for taverns had been around for hundreds of years; the difference was that they were sober establishments, where men of reputation and high social standing could meet others from all walks of life. This rich social milieu in turn encouraged the formation of societies, associations of men with similar interests, whether literary, commercial, scientific, or political. Some of the informal business associations coalesced into formidable City of London institutions. The 'shipping interest at Lloyds Coffee-house' became Lloyds, the powerful insurance underwriter. The Stock Exchange emerged from Jonathan's Coffee House in Exchange Alley. The East India Company made the Jerusalem Coffee House in Cowper's Court its unofficial headquarters, to the extent that it became known as the 'Jerusalem and East India Coffee House'. Between the arrival of coffee in England in the 1650s and its gradual eclipse by tea, the country became the dominant global economic force, and by the late nineteenth century had created an empire. While the role of the commercial institutions in underpinning the emerging empire is well documented, the more subtle roles played by societies formed in the coffee house in fields such as politics and science were also significant.

It is almost impossible to distinguish the cultural effects of the coffee house from the physical effects of the coffee served in it. The environment of the 'Penny University' undoubtedly encouraged a degree of association between men who might otherwise never have met, but would they have formed societies without the intellectually stimulating nature of the beverage? It has been argued that, until the arrival of coffee, the population of northern Europe had existed in a constant state of mild intoxication, since the quality of water was such that many people drank the weak beers of the time morning, noon, and night. By switching to coffee, they were not only reducing the muddle-headedness resulting from alcohol consumption, but also ingesting a powerful new drug. Indeed, it could be said that the introduction of coffee to England led to a second 'brain explosion' like that which had rocked our Ethiopian ancestors.

As might be expected, the arrival of coffee was accompanied by intense interest from medical science. It was subjected to a debate that drew much from the Islamic tradition, which itself had evolved from Galen and Hippocrates. In its early days in England, coffee was regarded as a medicinal substance with powerful effects requiring careful administration, and doctors had a vested interest in trying to preserve coffee's status as a medicine, rather than a recreational drug. One way of doing this was by devising novel ways of delivering it into the body. Thus can be found curiosities such as the celebrated 'provang', a three-foot length of flexible whalebone with a silk pad at the tip which was inserted into the stomach, sword-swallower fashion, via the throat. An 'electuary' was taken beforehand, made from butter, honey, sallet oil, and coffee grounds. The combination of the provang and the electuary was designed as an emetic, for which purpose it was surely well suited.

Coffee attracted its share of opprobrium, exceeded only by the fantastic claims made for its virtues as a universal panacea: 'Do but this Rare ARABIAN cordial use, and thou mays't all the Doctors Slops refuse.' It was claimed that it could cure drunkenness (still a common myth today), the plague, melancholy, 'smallpox, measles, headache, dropsy, gout, scurvy, stomach pains, corruptions of the blood, indispositions of the brain . . . some drink it with milk, but it is an error, and as such may bring in the danger of leprosy'. (The warning against the use of milk is of Islamic origin, and accounts for its absence in Arabian coffee drinking today.) Coffee's detractors thought it induced melancholy and paralysis, as well as the trembling of the limbs which today rejoices in the clinical name 'restless leg syndrome'. These controversies swirled around coffee even as coffee houses became a familiar feature of metropolitan life.

The first coffee houses opened in Oxford, where the beverage had made its English début. In 1651 one Jacob, a Lebanese Jew, took a room in the Angel Inn on the High, where coffee 'was by some who delighted in noveltie, drank'. Cirques Jobson, another Jew, opened the second a year later. Encouraged by a group of young students, an apothecary and royalist, Arthur Tillyard, opened the third in 1655, to sell 'coffey publickly in his house against All Soules College'. With Cromwell's Commonwealth in power, and Oxford a hotbed of royalism, it seems that these coffee houses expressed something of the spirit of the city at that time, dedicated to pleasure and the restoration of the monarchy. This sybaritic conservatism, albeit flying in the face of the status quo, is at odds with the usual association of coffee with zealous revolution.

The entrance fee for Tillyard's was a penny, and the coffee cost twopence. The customers were mainly students who formed clubs, read poems, and distributed pamphlets – the eighteenth-century

Utilitarian Jeremy Bentham was said to have found his famous axiom 'The greatest happiness of the greatest number' in an old Oxford coffee-house pamphlet. A significant early contribution to the understanding of coffee also emerged from Oxford. In 1659, Edward Pococke, Laudian Professor of Arabic at the University, translated and published anonymously part of a text by Da'ud b. Umar al-Antaki a-Basir titled 'The Nature of the Drink Kauhi, or Coffe, and the Berry of which it is made, Described by an Arabian Physician'. Pococke had lived in Aleppo and Istanbul for ten years until 1640, where he had come to appreciate coffee and had brought the habit back to Oxford with him. This pioneering coffee drinker perhaps published the translation as a result of the rising popularity of coffee houses in the town. These preceded the institution of the Common Room in colleges and became such a popular distraction that in 1679 the city's mayor banned them from opening on Sundays.

However, the real significance of Tillyard's lies in the fact that it was the coffee house in which was founded the Royal Society, which was to become the most illustrious scientific institution of the age. The Society was arguably the most visible manifestation of the 'Invisible College', for it is curious that, once again, as had been the case with the Sufis, coffee drinking was adopted by men with alchemical leanings. One of the leading figures behind the Society was the enigmatic Elias Ashmole, whose collection formed the basis of the eponymous museum in the city. Ashmole was a believer in hermetic philosophy and a collector of alchemical texts and had discovered and transcribed the coded works of John Dee. Ashmole, who lived in South Lambeth, was a friend of Newton, Boyle, and Hooke and most of the other leading scientific men of learning of the day such as Dr John Wilkins, Bishop of Chester. Ashmole was a keen follower of the German Hermeticist Jakob Boehme, later to be a significant influence on Goethe, who in turn prompted the discovery of caffeine.

During the 1640s, a group gathered regularly at Gresham College in London that included Ashmole, Robert Boyle, John Wilkins, John Wallis, John Evelyn, Robert Hooke, Christopher Wren, Sir Robert Moray, and William Petty. During the period of instability engendered by Cromwell, a splinter group formed at Oxford, meeting at Tillyard's. It was here that the idea of formalizing the group into what became the Royal Society took shape. It gained the patronage of Charles II in 1662. The Society came to be dominated by Isaac Newton, who assumed the chairmanship in 1672. Although the Society's membership and its work were formally Cartesian, its existence was rooted in the Rosicrucian tradition of the 'Invisible College'. While alchemy, an essential component of Hermeticism, is widely ridiculed in modern scientific circles, it then existed as a world view that encompassed the unfolding empiricism. Newton himself, that colossus of cause-and-effect, was a practising alchemist all his working life, even at the time he was devising calculus and defining gravity. He regarded his esoteric studies as the more important, and sought the key to integrating his scientific discoveries into the esoteric whole. Ironically, the mechanistic Newtonian description of the universe, which effectively provided the rational structure for scientific developments up until the development of quantum mechanics, is increasingly undermined by new discoveries that lead back towards aspects of alchemical thinking. The seemingly fanciful notion of 'action at a distance', dear to the heart of seventeenth-century alchemists and metaphysical poets alike, has found its theoretical validation in the concept of 'entanglement' in quantum physics and, more recently, practical exposition in experiments with sub-atomic 'spin'.

The first coffee house in London was opened in 1652 by Pasqua Rosée, an Armenian, in St Michael's Alley in the City. Coffee houses grew in popularity very rapidly, and, as they had done in the Ottoman Empire, attracted controversy. As the medical debate raged, so the pamphleteers joined in. One such was the forthright (but anonymous) 'Women's Petition against Coffee', a broadside published in England in 1674, which complained that, as a result of spending all their time in the coffee house, 'Never did Men wear *greater Breeches*, or carry *less* in them of any *Mettle* whatsoever . . . They come from it with nothing *moist* but their snotty Noses, nothing *stiffe* but their joints, nor *standing* but their ears.' The women's objections were possibly just, as they observed that men had recourse to the coffee houses in order 'to *Soberize* themselves with Coffee', having become 'Drunk as a Drum' in the taverns. 'The Men's Answer to the Women's Petition against Coffee' claimed, in equally graphic terms, that coffee 'makes the erection more Vigorous, the Ejaculation more full, adds a spiritualescence to the Sperme'.

The political hue of coffee house culture attracted opposition from the establishment, and Charles II sent spies to report on what was being said at these gatherings. He also sought a judicial opinion, which was that they 'might be thought as common nuisances'. On 23 December 1675 Charles went so far as to issue ' A Proclamation for the suppression of coffee houses' that talked of the 'very evil and dangerous effects' they had. From 10 January the following year, he ordered, all licences to sell 'any coffee, Chocolet, Sherbett or Tea' would be withdrawn. There was public uproar as a result, and the proclamation was revoked on 8 January. Estimates vary on the number of coffee houses in London around that time: the most accurate assessment, based on the new London Directories of 1739, is that there were 551 at that date, with 144 in the City. Half of the buildings in the area around St Michael's Alley where Pasqua Rosée had first set up were coffee houses.

As well as commercial and scientific ideas, some key political concepts likewise emerged in the coffee house. The idea of the secret ballot, the one-man-one-vote concept that lies at the heart of democracy, was brought to the attention of the East India Company in 1619 when the then Governor found his position under threat. Although the use of the ballot box was rejected at that meeting (as well as the box itself, which found its way into the possession of the Saddlers' Company) on the grounds that 'the Lords and others present, houlding it a noveltye not formerly used nor known in their elections, [thought it] but a meanes to disturb the whole buysines', the idea re-emerged in 'The Coffee Club of the Rota', which was attended by Samuel Pepys, John Aubrey, John Milton, Andrew Marvell, and William Petty. This republican club met at the Turk's Head in Westminster, and when a member wished to sound out the meeting's view of the subject under discussion, he could call for 'the wooden oracle' to be consulted. The Club of the Rota was a typical coffee house institution, bringing together the thinkers of the day in relatively informal free association to discuss issues of the constitution and politics in a way that was both provocative and productive. Not all coffee houses were so serious: the Chelsea Coffee House on Cheyne Walk, kept by James Salter, was home to a collection of curiosities displayed in seventeen glass-fronted cases. The exhibits included 'A piece of Queen Catherine's Skin', 'Skeletons of Mice', 'A very curious young Mermaid fish', and 'Instruments for scratching the Chinese Ladies backs'. Salter, known waggishly as 'Don Saltero', would practise his former profession of barber on the premises, as well as extracting teeth and bleeding customers if requested.

There was considerable overlap between the patrons of coffee houses and the societies that emerged from them. The names of Ashmole, Wren, Evelyn, and other leading men of their time recur frequently in different coffee house contexts. The 'Invisible College' was embodied by its membership rather than by bricks and mortar, and so remained almost undetectable. These members of an imperceptibly affiliated group of like-minded people could be collectively termed 'Coffee House Man'. They were both the founders and the products of that coffee house culture that distinguishes so much of seventeenth- and eighteenth-century English urban life. Springing from the same source, Freemasonry was founded in the same era. The ubiquitous Elias Ashmole was the first to be inducted into a Masonic lodge, as he records in his diary, in Warrington in 1646. If the location is mysterious, then so is the year: by general assent confirmed sightings of Freemasons and their lodges in England are very rare during the seventeenth century. Ashmole had evidently travelled to Warrington especially for his induction, and left the next day for London – a considerable inconvenience that indicated the importance he placed on his membership. As a founder of a Rosicrucian lodge in London, which is seen by some as the precursor of English Freemasonry, he may have thought the trip particularly necessary. The members of Freemasonry overlapped that of the Royal Society (Ashmole, Moray, and probably Wren); again, the meeting place was a public building, although more often the tavern than the coffee house. This was probably because taverns were – and frequently still are – provided with private function rooms, and the nature of Masonic rituals required that they were conducted away from the curious onlooker. Coffee houses generally had only one room, and the business that was conducted there was open to all. Inspired by the Rosicrucians, Freemasonry was another branch of the 'Invisible College' that was to grow enormously.

Any mention of Freemasonry in Britain inevitably calls to mind the police, for the two are widely believed to march hand in hand. The idea of a police force was the creation of an archetypal Coffee House Man, Henry Fielding. He was a novelist and magistrate in the 1740s at Bow Street in Covent Garden, the heart of London's literary scene. He recognized that the damage – in the form of social disorder, envy, and crime – that the increase in wealth from trade had brought to England could be curtailed only by a reformed legal structure for law enforcement. He was not only the first to identify the problem, but also the first to propose a solution, with the foundation of the 'Bow Street Runners'.

Covent Garden had been conceived by its owner, Francis Russell, the Fourth Earl of Bedford, as a speculative property development – new, private houses for the wealthy, exhausted by the turmoil and rank odours of the City. It was designed by the Palladian architect Inigo Jones, brimful of his Italian experiences, who came up with the idea of the Piazza, a Latin city square of a kind that London had never seen before. From the residents' point of view this had the unfortunate effect of creating a public space where hawkers could sell their goods, and in their wake came all manner of undesirables. By 1670 the Earl had bowed to the inevitable and applied for a Charter from Charles II to formalize the status of the market, which by the end of the century became the biggest vegetable and flower market in London. The wealthy fled west, first to Soho and, when that was overrun, to Mayfair. Coffee houses proliferated in the now rather down-at-heel area, and what had once been the homes of the gentry became those of the prominent artists and writers of the time. Will's Coffee House at the corner of Bow Street and Russell Street was the favourite haunt of the literati; the poet Dryden was reserved a chair by the fire in winter, and one in the window in summer: 'The poet, who loved his ease, speaking of these as his winter and summer quarters respectively. From this coign of vantage he expressed his view on men and books, surrounded by an admiring crowd who said ay to all his remarks.' Other coffee houses included the Bedford and the Tavistock in the Piazza itself, the Turk's Head (which had a Turkish Bath attached), the Burton, the Garrick's Head, Hoyland's, Hummum's, Slaughter's, the Rainbow, and Richardson's. Their frequenters included

Steele, Pope, Hogarth, and Sheridan, as well as Fielding himself, whose favourite was the Bedford.

Fielding's experience as a magistrate brought him into regular contact with the ubiquitous, ill-defined mob that peopled the streets of London and arbitrated events like a volatile combination of a theatre audience, a jury, and sentimental lynch mob. At one moment they might side with the whore in a fight with her bawd, enabling her to escape; the next they might intimidate a witness to perjure himself to save a highwayman. The disorderly London mob, from whom 'The Thief-Catcher is in danger of worse treatment . . . than a Thief', was the prime object of Fielding's attention.

Fielding had formed a group of 'thief-takers' in 1749 and issued a report concerning the formation of a 'Watch and Ward' police force to Parliament that same year. This recommended the appointment of Commissioners in each Parish from the legal profession whose job it would be to supervise a constable. These, in turn, would manage as many as forty 'watchmen', who would be armed and carry a 'large sonorous bell' with which they could attract the attention of their fellow watchmen scattered around the parish in watch houses built by the Commissioners. Corruption within the system, which Fielding correctly identified as one of its potential flaws, would be dealt with by dismissal, fines, and imprisonment. New criminal legislation was followed by the transformation of the 'thief-takers' into the so-called Bow Street Runners in 1754, a group of ten scarlet-uniformed 'Robin Redbreasts' forming the first mobile unit of its kind, serving writs, patrolling the streets, and pursuing and apprehending suspected wrongdoers. They achieved a high level of success, although it was not until Sir Robert Peel formed the Metropolitan Police in 1829 that their success was emulated. Fielding's ill-health meant that he had to leave the day-to-day management of the Runners to his blind half-brother John, whom he had instructed in the law. John Fielding was later knighted, and his magistracy in Covent

Garden, combined with the 'Robin Redbreasts', integrated law enforcement and the administration of justice for the first time.

It would be wrong to attribute the genesis of the police force directly to the coffee house – as one can more plausibly in the case of Lloyds and the Stock Exchange – but in the figure of Henry Fielding we have a late-flowering example of Coffee House Man: energetic, self-motivated, political, practical, reformist, well-connected, cultured, and philanthropic. The police force was a creation of this conjunction of characteristics.

The rapid developments in science, commerce, politics, and the arts emerging from the revolutionary social structure afforded by the coffee house allowed societies of men with common interests to form and flourish elsewhere too. In France, Spain, and America these achievments led to the development of actual revolutionary movements, whereas in England they spurred the formation of societies, frequently questioning of authority and challenging to the status quo, but nearly always contributing to the robust debate that characterized the development of British political, social, philosophical, and commercial activity. The catalytic influence on the formation of societies within society was the key contribution of coffee house culture to Britain. That these societies consolidated into institutions that were no longer based in coffee houses reflects their evolutionary success and the adaptability of the coffee house culture, which could inspire the creation of august commercial institutions such as the Stock Exchange and Lloyds, a magazine such as the *Spectator*, the first use of the ballot box, the Royal Society, Freemasonry, and the police force.

This London-centric account of coffee house culture is the inevitable result of the fact that so many well-known institutions sprang from it. But the provinces and Scotland also witnessed a coffee house boom, and with it the rise in women coffee house keepers – for example Mrs Ashton in Birmingham, Sarah Tysack in Newcastle, and Widow Smith, who took over the Turk's Head in the Strand. Keeping a coffee house perhaps offered a respectable way of earning a living for women of modest means. Certainly there is no hint of disapproval in the letter written by an Edinburgh gentleman to an agent in Holland: 'Sir, my nices has a Coffee house which ther servants keepes and stands in neid of some Coffie berrie'. Coffee houses had become common in Edinburgh by the early 1700s and may in some measure have acted as the spur for the Scottish Enlightenment, from which emerged the influential figures of David Hume, the philosopher, Adam Smith, the economist, and many other prominent men in the arts and sciences. It was Hume who provided the succinct definition of the Enlightenment as 'a sudden and sensible change in the opinions of men . . . by the progress of learning and liberty'. The coffee house provided an environment in which both qualities flourished side by side.

6

THE FALL OF MOCHA

The spread of coffee cultivation from Ethiopia and Yemen to other parts of the world was largely the result of the expansion of European trade and colonization and led to the decline in importance of the port of Mocha. Prior to that era, there are unsubstantiated reports that Arab traders established coffee plantations in Ceylon (as it was then) in the late fifteenth century using Abyssinian plants. Likewise, the Indians claim that, around 1600, a Muslim pilgrim named Babu Budan returning from Mecca smuggled seeds 'strapped to his belly' which he planted outside his hermit's cave in the Chandragiri Hills, from which origins sprang India's coffee industry, currently the seventh largest in the world. However, there is no documentary evidence for this, and the earliest reliable report dates the presence of coffee in India to 1695. Just as Shadomer Shadhili, the patron saint of Mocha, is credited with the introduction of coffee to Yemen, so Babu Budan is still revered in India for his initiative, and his mountain cave attracts many pilgrims. While it would have made some commercial sense for Arab traders to have taken plants to other locations suitable for coffee cultivation, it is possible that they were hindered in their attempts to do so both by the desire of the Mocha authorities to limit the spread of the plant and by the fact that the market was overwhelmingly within the Ottoman Empire.

It does appear that, as early as 1616, the Dutch obtained a coffee plant from Mocha – said by some to have been of Abyssinian origin – to take back to Holland. Seeds from this plant were sent to Ceylon in 1658. The Dutch had gradually replaced the Portuguese in Ceylon from 1630 onwards, but the Directors of the VOC (The 'Vereenigde Ooste Indische Compagnie' – the Dutch equivalent of the English Company) did not manage to attract the diligent farmers they hoped for to the new colony. The coffee initiative failed, but more success attended their efforts in Java, where coffee plantations were first successfully established in 1699 with cuttings from Dutch possessions at Malabar in India. These in turn may have originated in Yemen or Abyssinia.

Once the Javanese coffee industry was established it very quickly rivalled, and then eclipsed, the Mocha trade – or at least it did for Europeans: in 1700 it is estimated that Yemen was producing 20,000 tons of coffee a year, the vast majority of which was sold into the Muslim world. The Dutch initiative was a classic case of early European colonialism. They introduced an expensive commodity to a suitable territory under their control, cultivated it intensively, and had the plantations worked by locals at the lowest possible rate – in the Dutch case, for nothing, through a quota system imposed on the islanders. It proved to be a hugely lucrative initiative: by 1731 the VOC had given up buying coffee from Mocha altogether and had restarted plantations in Ceylon. These were later to be devastated under the British in 1880 by an outbreak of leaf rust, and the island took up tea cultivation instead, with outstanding success. In the 1790s ships from the USA could be found buying coffee from Batavia and Padang, giving rise to the nickname 'Java', as coffee is often known in that country. The growth continued unabated into the nineteenth century, and by 1822 the Dutch East Indies, which included Java, Sumatra, and Celebes (Sulawesi), produced 100,000 tons of the world's total consumption of 225,000 tons. Thereafter there was a steep drop in production caused by competition from international rivals such as Brazil, whose slave coffee economy was even more cost effective than the Dutch quota system. By 1902, the East Indies were producing 50,000 tons of a total world consumption of a million tons.

Nonetheless, it can be seen how the introduction of a new commodity into a plantation economy could swiftly change the complexion of international trade. One victim of this shift was Mocha itself, which went into a slow decline during the eighteenth century – it was even bombarded by the French in 1737 for reneging on treaty obligations – as its European market dwindled and its European colonial rivals expanded their production. It should be remembered, however, that even in the early eighteenth century, when the European trade at Mocha was at its height, they bought only an eighth of the coffee that was sold through the port – the rest supplied the needs of the coffee houses of the Ottoman Empire, Persia, and Muslim India. Mocha's prosperity was largely the result of trade within the Islamic world. European colonial coffees not only supplied European needs but encroached on Mocha's traditional customer base.

In 1715 French traders of the Compagnie des Indes took a leaf out of the Dutch botanical book, shipping plants from Yemen to the island of Réunion, which stands in curious counterpoint to St Helena. It is a little more southerly, and as far from the east coast of Africa as St Helena is from the west. It is much less isolated, however: Madagascar, the world's fourth largest island, stands between it and Africa, and Mauritius, another of the Mascarene Islands, is but a hundred miles away. Réunion is also noticeably larger than St Helena (300 square kilometres), and considerably taller at over 3,000 metres. It was colonized by the French in 1646, only thirteen years before the East India Company claimed their lonely rock: unlike the polite, formal acquisition of St Helena by the English, the French claim was represented by a boatload of convicts dumped on the beach. However, the Ile de Bourbon (as it was then called, until it was renamed Réunion in 1792 after the Revolution had disposed of the Bourbon monarchy) was to assume a major role in French geopolitical strategy when it came to the struggle for hegemony between the Compagnie des Indes and the East India Company in South India. The relative proximity of the naval base on the island proved to be a thorn in the English side in the 1740s as fortunes ebbed and flowed between Madras, home of the English Company's Fort St George, and Pondicherry, the Compagnie's main base. Like St Helena, Réunion has remained in colonial hands, although its racially mixed population benefits from the considerably more generous treatment that France metes out to its possessions, having full departmental status, a regular influx of Parisian sunbathers, and subsidized travel. The island's claim to a place in this narrative, however, rests on an earlier discovery.

Whilst coffee history usually crowns Ethiopia as the sole source of wild coffee, it seems that Réunion, and its neighbour Madagascar, harboured pretenders to the throne. The Malagasy wild coffee strain was discovered in the eighteenth century but was never commercialized, whereas that of Réunion, 'Bourbon pointu', enjoyed a very brief moment in the spotlight. These two relatively unknown strains are original, wild varieties, along with one from East Africa: owing to the biological stresses encountered in its spread across Africa and elsewhere, the DNA of later coffees becomes considerably more complex than that of these initial varieties. The native coffee strain, also called 'marron' coffee, was found on Réunion in 1711 near St Paul, at a height of more than 600 metres. It was similar to the type now known as Mauritania and was believed at the time to be as good as Arabian Mocha ('Bourbon rond'), although others found it bitter tasting. The Mocha varietal was introduced to the island in 1715 by Captain Dufresne d'Arsal, a sailor from St Malo. He had managed somehow to acquire sixty live trees. Forty died on the voyage and a further eighteen died shortly after landing. He gave one of the two remaining trees to a M. Martin of Saint-Denis and the other to the parish priest from Saint-Suzanne. By 1719 the trees had produced a small harvest and a hundred beans could be bought for a piastre. It was pointed out that the bushes resembled the native coffee bushes, and the government decreed that all the inhabitants should cultivate this latter varietal. They were obliged to supply the government one pound each per year. Unfortunately the bitter taste of marron coffee found no favour in France, and it also had the disadvantage of being difficult to propagate and could be harvested only every two years. The Governor of the Mascarenes, Desforges-Boucher, thus decided to establish a nursery of 7800 genuine Mocha plants derived from the two originals, and by 1727 the island was producing 100,000 pounds of coffee.

In the coffee trade, the name 'Bourbon' has come to be associated with a variety of coffee plant originating in Yemen which spread into South America from the island. Another Yemeni type, 'Typica', was spread by the Dutch to Asia and found its way to Latin America. Indeed whilst Réunion was developing Mocha plants, Louis XV already had some flourishing in his greenhouse at Versailles. He was particularly passionate about them, tending to them personally, and harvesting, processing, roasting, and brewing them himself. He had Madame du Barry portrayed as a Sultana, coffee cup in hand. Louis's coffee plants had been propagated from the gift of a single mature plant to his predecessor, Louis XIV, from the Mayor of Amsterdam, and were in turn probably a descendant of coffee bushes taken from Yemen to Holland in 1616. It was a surprisingly short-sighted present for the usually commercially minded Dutch: these royal obsessions were to become the supposed progenitors of most of the coffee industry of the West Indies and Brazil.

Réunion's role in coffee's global odyssey has been much overrated, and, as with the name 'Mocha' in coffee marketing, the significance of the 'Bourbon' botanical nomenclature should not be taken too seriously. Both 'Bourbon' and 'Typica' were varietals of Yemeni origin, and even the 'Bourbon' plants found in Brazil may have missed the island entirely in their migration. The plants found on St Helena are 'Bourbon' and these, as we know, were directly imported from Yemen. Probably the most direct contribution of the island to the spread of coffee – and a very significant one in quality terms – was made in the recent past, when missionaries introduced coffee from Réunion to Kenya in the early 1900s.

To ensure the success of the new Mocha plants, each farmer on Réunion was bound to grow two hundred coffee trees for every slave he had, and uprooting a coffee tree was punishable by death. So prolific had coffee become by 1738 that the brilliant Governor La Bourdonnais (who was also to cause havoc with the English in India with his *ad hoc* navy) decided that Réunion was producing too much coffee, and so in 1743 new planting was prohibited. The subsequent defeat of the Compagnie in India by the British, followed by its remorseless decline, deprived the island of a certain market for its coffee, and it was unable to compete with the coffee produced in the French West Indies, which were also much closer to their European market. Thus, although for the rest of the century Réunion had a reasonably lucrative and steady coffee industry based on the imported Mocha Arabica varietal, it failed to grow beyond the production levels of the 1730s. When a cyclone devastated the island's plantations in 1805, coffee growing was largely abandoned. Then, in 1810, a new, more resistant variety, 'Leroy', was introduced, apparently from the Atlantic coast of Africa. It is strange that this variety of Arabica came from there, for the Atlantic coast is best known as the home of the inferior Robusta variety, and at this stage in history there were still few departures from the 'Bourbon' Arabica type, which was itself mistakenly assumed to have spread from Réunion. Such confusions are typical of the botanical history of the coffee plant – it is only through genetic research that we have spared the plant a long journey from western Ethiopia to Yemen and back to eastern Ethiopia, a mythical route previously attributed the status of fact.

Given the early involvement of the English in the coffee trade in the Arabian Sea, it might seem surprising that the East India Company was relatively slow off the mark when it came to establishing its own colonial plantations. But the Company's only Indian territorial possessions at the time were the small pockets of land surrounding the three Presidencies (and ports) of Calcutta, Bombay, and Madras, and its business was trade, not settlement and cultivation. St Helena was, in effect, its only secure colony with the appropriate growing conditions for coffee and, unlike the Dutch Java and the French Ile de Bourbon, its size dictated that there was no possibility of large-scale cultivation of coffee. At best coffee would always be a marginal economic endeavour. Nonetheless, the Directors' belated decision to procure plants was relayed to Francis Dickinson, the grandly titled 'Commissary for Affairs of the English Nation at Mocha'.

Having first been to Mocha in 1722, Dickinson was posted there once more in 1728, the Company's factory having been closed for two years as the result of 'the unexpected revolution that happened last year in Arabia'. He instructed his assistant at Bayt-al-Faqih, John Hanys: 'He may chose whatever is conducive to the interests of the Company but he should be careful to observe that coffee was good, dry, clean and well-garbled.' Dickinson evidently left for Bombay with Hanys in the summer of 1732, and their return to Mocha on the *Caroline* on 1 April 1733 was recorded in the diary that Dickinson kept from that day until the following August. It provides an insight into the dull but dangerous life of an East India Company factor shortly after the very peak of Mocha's prosperity. It also allows us to identify the moment when the Company finally managed to obtain coffee plants from Yemen to create its own coffee plantation on St Helena.

When he returned to Mocha, Dickinson took note of the competition: a Dutch ship from Batavia, the *Pondicherry*, a French ship from that Indian port, a local coastal grab from Surat, and the *Nogdy Sanay*, an Indian ship flying Portuguese colours. He paid his compliments to the Deputy Governor and then inspected the Company's factory, where he found 'six hundred and sixty bales of Beetlefuckee coffee being part of a thousand and thirty eight bales purchased there before our arrival by our Banians [Indian merchants]'. The humorous name 'Beetlefuckee' was frequently used by Englishmen in reference to the town of Bayt al-Faqih, which lay at the foot of the mountains about ninety miles north of Mocha. The mention of 'Beetlefuckee coffee' is interesting because it suggests that what was generally known as Mocha coffee could be from various local sources – Dickinson later describes Mocha coffee as coming from a number of villages that lay some days' journey to the south, towards Aden. Indeed 'the reason why little coffee comes to Mocha is that it is previously sold at Bayt al-Faqih where the Turks buy three-quarters of the country's coffee produce', he reported. From his account it would appear that the true coffee entrepôt, the mart that lay at the hub of the coffee trade, was not Mocha at all, but the flyblown town of Bayt al-Faqih in the hot, humid, dry Tihama desert. The town was described by the Danish explorer Carsten Niebuhr in 1766: 'There were only a few stone-built houses; the majority of the population lived in straw huts in random confusion in the narrow dusty street, where the coffee traders passed by . . . traders from Hijaz, Persia, Egypt, Syria, Constantinople, Habash, Tunis, Fez and Morocco . . . even buyers from India and sometimes Europe meet here.' In our own times Bayt al-Faqih remains an unlikely setting for the genesis of the world's largest commodity industry after oil, lacking any buildings of size, let alone merit, with the winding avenues of the market covered in green plastic tarpaulins to provide shade from the relentless sun.

Hanys was sent off to this remarkably unremarkable town and again instructed to ensure that his purchases were 'good, dry, clean and well-garbled' – the latter expression seeming to mean of an even colour and appearance. Shortly after his arrival, Hanys advised Dickinson that there might be a good opportunity to buy cheaply during the coming 'Hodge' (Haj) feast, when there would be no competition from the Muslim merchants, and indeed he and 'the French Second' would have the field to themselves. Although they occasionally colluded, by and large the French merchants were seen as unwelcome competitors, and any fresh intelligence concerning the whereabouts of French ships bound for Mocha was covertly circulated. 'We must inform you that a very large French Ship from Europe is come in with us, and it's not improbable that the Arrival of these two Ships may somewhat enhance the Price of Coffee . . .', the Supercargo on the *Prince William* wrote to Dickinson on 27 April.

This news may have led to hurried purchases up at Bayt al-Faqih, and as a result to the delivery of some underweight bales to Mocha, for Dickinson advised Hanys 'to complain to the Governor and endeavour either to get the Muccadum [headman] of the Camels punished or threaten'd, so as to prevent the Camel drivers pilfering the Bales on the Road'. More seriously, there was a confrontation with the Governor, recently returned from Sa'ana with orders to extract customs duty for the Imam. There were also disturbing rumours of a war between the Imam and his powerful brother that could lead to an attack on Mocha.

None of these concerns prevented Dickinson from acting reasonably promptly on the orders of the Directors. On 14 May 1733 he asked Hanys to procure some coffee trees for 'the Company's station on St Helena'. A few days later the Governor attempted to extort 5000 Spanish dollars in customs arrears, but his representative received short shrift from Dickinson: 'We represented to him the unreasonableness of his Demand, which if he did not relinquish, he might be assur'd our Hon'ble masters would know, in whose power it was to utterly destroy this place.' The warning, no idle threat, seems to have worked, as there are no further entries in the diary on this subject. Dickinson then summarized a letter he had received from Hanys on 26 May: 'He had got the Camel fellow imprisoned whose Bales came short, and as to the Coffee Trees we ordered him to procure, he believes it impracticable, the Government having formerly fined one of our Banians Five hundred Spanish Dollars for attempting to get some, but if we desire it, he will get some Coffee Seed which the planters made use of for raising young trees which he believes will answer to the same purpose.' Plainly the Yemenis would not let actual coffee plants leave Mocha – perhaps they had learnt from the experience with the French some years earlier – but, mysteriously, they seem to have been altogether more sanguine about the export of 'seed' – the berries of the coffee bush, which kept the bean safe and fertile within. Apparently there was no necessity for secrecy, because there appears to have been no danger attached to taking seeds. Exactly why the authorities should have sought to ban the export of plants and not of the seeds is unknown. Dickinson wrote back to Hanys explaining that 'if a little of the mould that is most natural to the Coffee Plant can be got without inconveniency from the Places where the best Soil grows, it would be acceptable'. Shortly afterwards Hanys was reported ill, and a Dutch doctor had to be dispatched from Mocha to attend him. Dickinson noted that 'the Dutch have bought no Coffee this Season . . . having such vast quantities of their own so much cheaper from Java and Ceylon, and we are told that they make but a small Difference in Europe between that and Arabia coffee'. The fall of Mocha was gathering pace.

After another altercation with the Governor, who refused to allow Dickinson and Hanys to embark without the payment of a substantial advance on next year's customs duties, the *Prince of Wales* sailed for Bombay on 11 August. Evidently they had left behind the elusive coffee seeds, as the Supercargo of the *Houghton,* a 460-tonne ship then at anchor off Mocha, wrote in a letter to the Directors dated 22 August 1733: 'We have used all possible means to procure some coffee plants but to no purpose, it being so dangerous a consequence that no one would undertake to bringing any down.' He then had some better news: 'but we have got some seed which we are told will do as well'. The seeds were finally aboard a ship bound for St Helena.

However, St Helena was not in the best of states to receive these precious coffee seeds. Since the beginning of the seventeenth century, European rivalries had spilled over on the island: mariners, principally English, Dutch, Portuguese, and Spanish, frequently took pot shots at each other as they came and went from the anchorage. The island had lost its initial peace and tranquillity; by 1610 the Portuguese found their Catholic chapel vandalized by the Protestant Dutch, a large carved stone crucifix broken up, and plantations ravaged. The Dutch claimed that the Portuguese had – in breach of a tradition that was supposed to transcend national rivalries – purloined letters left behind by Dutch mariners for their compatriots, and the Portuguese responded by tearing up the plantations of lemon and orange trees. It was reported that 'Some years ago, the Hollanders ruined all that was good, only to spite the Spaniards, who afterwards did the same, that the English etc. might have no benefit of it.' Whilst the Europeans squabbled, the rest of the island, with the exception of the goats, hogs and other animals gone feral, remained pretty much as it had always been, the high hills covered in dense forests of ebony and redwood, and the seas still teemed with fish.

There were inevitably some serious skirmishes – a cannon from a Portuguese ship sunk by the Dutch in 1608 was recently dredged up from the Jamestown Roads – but it was not until 1633 that anyone thought to take legal possession of the island. By then the Portuguese had lost nearly all interest in what had become a dangerous spot for them, and it was the Dutch who took formal possession, or rather they purported to do so, for they never sought to enforce prior claim when the English eventually took the island in 1659. The evidence of the Dutch claim was found in the State Archives in the 1930s, on a document which still bore the perforations where it had been nailed to a tree in Chapel Valley in the manner prescribed for making territorial claims under international law of the times. Had the Dutch enforced possession by due process, the history of St Helena might have been very different, for it was under English rule that a remarkable procession of great soldiers, scientists, scholars, poets and politicians put in at Jamestown, with the result that, in the words of the South African writer Lawrence Green: 'It holds more of the strong meat of history than any other town in Britain's colonial possession.'

Perhaps the reason the Dutch left St Helena alone was that they had been hatching a plot to settle the immediate hinterland of Table Bay at what is now Cape Town. Like St Helena, this had been a common haunt of European sailors for years, with the advantage that it was a suitable port for ships both on outward and return voyages. In 1652 a Dutchman laid out the ground plan for the fort and a vegetable garden, and permanent settlers arrived in 1657. This seems to have spurred the Directors of the English Company into viewing St Helena in a different light, for it was the Dutch settlement of the Cape, along with concerns about the Spanish war and frequent incidents of piracy all the way from the Cape Verde Islands to the Channel, that finally made them take the plunge. The Court Minutes of 15 December

1658 noted 'the great conveniencing and concernment that it might prove, both to the Company and to this nation, for to fortify the island of St Helena . . .'.

So it was that, on 5 May 1659 Captain John Dutton, with a band of settlers from England, and charged with setting up a garrison and permanent fortifications, formally took possession of the island on behalf of the East India Company. As Governor, Dutton was able to judge all but the most serious crimes by the laws 'usually exercised in other English plantations, according to the laws of England'. This perhaps unremarkable appropriation had an extraordinary genesis: Dutton had originally been bound for the tiny nutmeg-producing Spice Island of Pulo Run with twenty-seven colonists with suitably pioneering backgrounds – bricklayers, carpenters, smiths, gardeners, and their wives. Pulo Run had been a bone of contention between the English and the Dutch companies since the early years of their rivalry, but a lull in the hostilities between them had determined the Directors to settle the island, and Dutton was appointed Captain of the proposed expedition. When it suddenly appeared that war might break out again, at the last moment they redirected the hapless settlers to St Helena. A decision taken at East India House in Leadenhall Street had the effect of diverting a putative community of colonizers from Pulo Run, where they would have been wafted by the nutmeg-scented breezes of the Spice Islands, to St Helena, a mere 10,000 miles to the west, where they were battered by the south-east trades instead.

It was expected by the Directors of the East India Company that the nascent colony would be self-sufficient in food in little more than a year (their optimism was fantastically misplaced, for 350 years later the island is still, as it always has been, dependent on subsidies to avoid starvation). Gradually the infrastructure of the plantation (an early term for a colony) was installed: plants, seeds, fortresses, slaves, settlers, and government. The Castle, originally named James Fort, became the seat of government, a moated stronghold overlooking the roads at the head of Chapel Valley. Behind it sprang up the fledgling Jamestown. Once they had realized the reckless optimism of their forecast, the Company provided the colony with necessities such as shoes, beer, and fishing tackle, and every ship returning from Surat in India was ordered to bring back a ton of rice for the islanders. In 1661 Dutton was told that he could proceed, as originally had been planned, to colonize Pulo Run. Whether it is a reflection on the charms of St Helena or those of Dutton is hard to say, but only two of the original colonists chose to stay on the island despite generous offers of land, the rest electing to chance their arms with Dutton in the Spice Islands. There the perfidious Dutch refused to abide by the treaty agreed in Europe and the settlers found themselves once again at sea; where they finally ended up is not recorded.

St Helena had thus lost as many settlers as she had attracted, and the new Governor, Stringer, had a difficult time securing the island. Thirty refugees from the Great Fire of London arrived to find a population of only fifty white men and ten white women, and the Company's subsequent efforts to attract more Londoners failed. The conditions imposed on settlers were quite onerous: in exchange for land, they had to undertake sentry duties and to man the fortifications whenever a ship was sighted. The island was in effect a huge fortress in the deserts of the South Atlantic, and like a lonely garrison anywhere, the occupants complained about the inadequacy of the provisions, the boredom induced by their duties, and the harshness of the governing regime. The settlers failed to make the island a self-sufficient, self-determining community and sank into a simmering, occasionally mutinous apathy. The internal wranglings on the island caused them to ignore the sudden danger the Dutch now presented.

Having initially congratulated themselves for their foresight in opting for Table Bay as a colony instead of St Helena, the Dutch had found that the anchorage was not as safe as it might have been, and vessels returning from the East were frequently blown by the trade winds and carried by the current beyond the safety of Cape Town, with the next possible stop being St Helena. The Directors of the Dutch East India Company ordered that a search be made of the South Atlantic for another St Helena, and a hypothetical 'S. Helena Nueva' conveniently made its appearance on some contemporary maps. However, the only real candidates were Tristan da Cunha and Ascension, the one being too hostile a climate and the other too barren. In the meantime, Dutch vessels landing at the real St Helena covertly introduced dogs and bitches, which they hoped would kill the wild goats and further impoverish the island. Eventually the Directors, in their pragmatic Dutch way, realized that the best St Helena was the original one and in December 1672 they sent a small fleet from Table Bay to capture it, England and Holland then being at war. Although the Governor had some intelligence concerning the likely Dutch attack, the island's fortifications and garrison were ill prepared. After an unsuccessful attempt on Jamestown, the ships were led to a safe landing by the signals of a treacherous islander, and 500 Dutch soldiers came ashore, swiftly overcoming all opposition. The Governor and the garrison in Jamestown, realizing that the game was up, escaped to some English ships then at anchor and fled to Brazil, spiking the guns and destroying all powder and provisions. Through a combination of foresight and good luck, a small English squadron sent to escort the East India fleet home learnt of the capture of the island, promptly bombarded the Castle, and secured the Dutch surrender.

The English East India Company had realized through its temporary loss what an important strategic asset St Helena was and urgently arranged for more soldiers, settlers, arms, and provisions to be sent out there, and although discontent continued to rumble through the basalt like a simmering volcano, at least the island's future was reasonably secure. In 1676 the astronomer Edmund Halley, a precocious 20-year-old Cambridge drop-out, was sponsored by the East India Company to go to the island to undertake the first comprehensive mapping of the stars of the southern hemisphere and to witness the transit of Mercury. He quickly discovered that St Helena's weather was wet and cloud cover very frequent. While his astronomical ambitions were thus often thwarted, he made good use of his time observing the effects of the southern trade winds and developing his pioneering theories concerning large-scale, high-altitude meteorology that would eventually be published in his world map of 1686. Whereas he spent his two years on the island looking skywards at the air currents, recent observations from space reveal that the formidable presence of St Helena creates a perturbation in the flow of the south-east trades that can be detected as far as two hundred miles north of the island. Halley's work on the southern star map was to earn him a place in the Royal Society, and he was able to witness at least some of the transit of Mercury across the face of the sun before clouds got in the way.

Slavery was an established practice on the island, in line with all other colonial possessions. With the settlers themselves occasionally mutineering against the island's government, usually fuelled by arrack from home-made stills, it was inevitable the slaves would follow their lead and, in 1694, some rebelled. White mutineers might be hanged; the eleven slaves were too valuable to be slaughtered wholesale, so three were executed – disembowelled and publicly quartered *pour encourager les autres* – while the rest were merely flogged, branded, and returned to their owners. In later years seven tried to escape in a stolen boat: the authorities, being well aware of the island's isolation, did not even make a token effort to recapture them, but simply recorded their certain deaths. Attempted escape from the island became a favoured, if forlorn, pursuit, mainly of slaves but sometimes soldiers as well.

Otherwise life on St Helena continued placidly enough. There was a gold rush, which turned out to be a fool's gold rush, and a similarly futile copper stampede. Strong governors were sent out to repair the damage wrought by weak ones – the notably energetic Governor Roberts created more fertile land by irrigation, discovered a source of lime on the island, and created a factory making bricks and tiles, saving the Company a great deal in shipping costs. Such an industrious intelligence was anathema to the traditions of St Helena and had to be offset somehow; the local tanners took to boiling the bark of the native redwood trees that grew in the Great Forest in the east of the island to extract an acid which they then used in the process. They did not strip the bark in a way that would allow the trees to recover, and as a result the trees simply died and became the strange skeletal home of roosting rats, who took to the trees to avoid the plague of cats, which in turn decimated the island's birdlife. Woodland disappeared at an alarming rate. The island's endemic ebony had been cleared by the Company to make pastures that were rarely viable; goats ravaged the rest, but when the Governor sought permission to shoot them he was told by London that: 'The goats are not to be destroyed, being more valuable than the ebony.'

Within two hundred years of its discovery the island's environment was starting to collapse as a result of the profligate predations of man and beast. The delicate micro-climates changed, leading to unheard of droughts and floods, and without the forest to hold it, much of the immensely fertile topsoil, which had accumulated over millions of years, was simply washed away. On one occasion, 'water descended with mighty floods and torrents, carrying away the soil in an incredible manner, with both grass, trees, yams and stone walls before it'. So much fine earth was washed away that the sea for miles around the island was discoloured by the mud. When the population was not hastening the destruction of the land it depended on, the inhabitants took to destroying themselves with arrack, supposedly to counter the ill-effects of a diet of yams. In 1717 the ever-patrician Company wrote to the island Council with concern: 'People will be apt to say that at this island the old proverb is true about settlements, that where the English first settle they build a Punch House, the Dutch a fort, and the Portuguese a Church.' The census of 1723 revealed that St Helena had by now a population of 1128: 50 white men and 79 women, 251 children, 610 slaves, and 18 freemen. There were 120 officers and other ranks, and 124 cannon in eight locations around the island. The government was corrupt and frequently unjust: the Company's accountant beat his slave boy to death but the matter was hushed up by the incumbent Governor, Smith.

His successor was Governor Byfield, and it was during his enlightened rule that the idea of coffee cultivation was first mooted. He wrote to the Court of Directors in London: 'We believe that coffee would grow well here . . . we remember that there was once a coffee tree which grew very well in the worst part of the country.' This mystery coffee tree had never been previously recorded, and its mention may have been simply part of Byfield's general strategy to get the support of the Company to encourage the island's agriculture; his possible white lie certainly had the desired effect, for the Directors responded to his report by ordering the procurement of seeds from Mocha.

Governor Byfield's was an unusually beneficent term, with an almost unheard of level of goodwill amongst men. The Sessions record in 1727: 'There being a very good harmony and agreement amongst the inhabitants and no person having entered any action against his neighbour, Sessions adjourned.' The Governor, through fencing off forests and strictly enforcing regulations banning the grazing of animals in the Company's young plantations, restored at least some of the island's sadly depleted forests. A survey he commissioned revealed that the erosion of topsoil continued at an alarming rate after each heavy rainfall. His glad hand with the inhabitants was revealed by his ability to cause them to have the idea, which they had previously resisted, of culling the island's goats. As soon as this was implemented, young indigenous trees sprouted spontaneously. These and other actions saved the Company some £25,000 over four years, which they recognized by awarding a substantial cash bonus to Byfield of £400. Such a Golden Age could not last long: in March 1731 a group of wealthy islanders made unfounded reports of corruption and injustice concerning him to the Court of Directors. Although exonerated, Byfield was so disgusted by their ingratitude that he resigned. Thus it was his successor, Isaac Pyke (who had already served as Governor, and was heartily detested), who witnessed the arrival of the first coffee plants on the island.

The *Houghton*, out of Mocha, arrived at St Helena on 10 February 1733. The Council Proceedings noted: 'The Super Cargoes told us that they could not get us any Coffee plants but brought us a good quantity of the berries for seed which wee will plant as fast as the season will permit us.' Remarkably, after all the trouble that had been taken to procure the seeds, coffee disappears off the record until shortly before Napoleon's exile to the island. Despite Byfield's suggestion, there seems to have been no concerted effort to cultivate coffee as a cash crop. This may have been because coffee can quite happily, if erratically, grow in the wild, which nicely coincided with the St Helenan farmer's natural temperament. In contrast to the success of the Dutch and the French in Java and Réunion, the East India Company's introduction of coffee to St Helena was a damp squib. It was not until 1814 that coffee plants were spotted at Bamboo Grove in Sandy Bay on the south side of the island by the distinguished botanist William Roxburgh, formerly superintendent of the Company's Botanical Gardens in Calcutta: 'some of the finest coffee trees I ever saw . . . in every stage from the blossom to the ripe berry'.

While coffee may have kept a low profile, the eighty years between its arrival and the arrival of Napoleon were crammed with incident of a typically St Helenan kind. The island's life seems to have been an eclectic concatenation of English village life, with its petty crimes, petulant priests, and innate, rural conservatism, and patrician, colonial despotism coloured by an international cast of marauding mariners, slaves, pirates, and soldiers, most of whom seemed less than eager to stay. Repeated escape attempts were mounted during coffee's wilderness years: ten slaves with the long boat in 1744, nine slaves in the Company's boat in 1745 (although they foolishly left the rudder, sails, and oars on the shore), four slaves in 1747, then another five slaves, and a further fifteen in the long boat, all in the same year. There is no evidence that this haemorrhage of slaves and boats ever led to a successful escape. For experienced mariners, St Helena's isolation represented an enormous obstacle; for ill-equipped, inexperienced, undernourished slaves there was virtually no chance. It is a measure of their desperation that they continued in the attempt: life on an island where four white men who beat a slave woman to death were fined £6 10s. each could have had something to do with it. Or perhaps the fact that when a white woman stabbed her black slave woman with a carving knife, she was acquitted of murder since the only witness to the crime was a black slave, whose evidence against a white was inadmissible in law. Even freed slaves were judged by different standards: one free slave woman had an illegitimate child by a soldier and, being found guilty, was re-enslaved, along with her child.

7

SLAVERY AND THE COFFEE COLONIES

Do you remember the days of slav'ry?
And how they beat us
And how they worked us so hard.
And how they used us.
Till they refuse us.
Do you remember the days of slav'ry?

'BURNING SPEAR' (WINSTON RODNEY),
'Slavery Days' (1975)

Slavery may not be the oldest profession – after all, the whole point is that its services are provided free of charge – but it is nearly as old as mankind. Although in our times it has come to be associated with the horrendous treatment meted out to black Africans, in ancient times it was charmingly indiscriminate: slaves were plucked, regardless of race, colour, or creed, from the fringes of power to be redeployed at its centre. Slavery has always had a pronounced imperial character, and has been traditionally one of the principal spoils of war. The Children of Israel were thus enslaved in Egypt, and it is estimated that the early Roman Empire had a slave population of some two million – one-third of its total. They included Russians, Slavs, Goths,

Gauls, Celts, Britons, Nubians, and Ethiopians. The Romans, and the Greeks, along with the Byzantine Christians later on, all felt moved at some stage at least to discuss and rationalize the enslavement of their fellow humans, usually falling back for justification on the Will of God. Nonetheless, manumission (the emancipation of slaves) was frequent, and the laws of these respective empires were in fact surprisingly concerned with the treatment of slaves. Islam took on the attitude of its regional predecessors without skipping a beat, and it was the spread of that religion across North Africa and down into West Africa that opened up what was to become the single biggest source of slaves during the heyday of the Atlantic slave trade. Arab merchants traded freely in East African slaves: black eunuchs were a particular favourite of the Chinese imperial Court. The Arab occupation of the Iberian peninsula not only involved the enslaving of some of the Christian population – it is estimated that there were 30,000 Christian slaves in Granada in 1311 – but also a share of the trafficking of as many as twenty thousand slaves a year northwards across the Sahara from the Muslim kingdoms of West Africa. These in turn became wealthy on the trade, with supplies made up by raids on weaker neighbours.

The countries of northern Europe had more or less abandoned the practice of slavery in the eleventh century, opting for the more sophisticated mechanism of serfdom. This had the advantage, in colder climes, of making the serf fend for himself in the long winter months, thus reducing the labour overhead. It was the onset of colonialism that reintroduced the use of slavery and its attendant evils to the north: the slave trade followed the flag. The process started when the Portuguese, through the voyages of discovery instigated by Henry the Navigator, were able to creep gradually down the unknown west coast of Africa until Bartolomeu Dias finally rounded the Cape of Good Hope and opened the way for Vasco da Gama's voyage to India in 1498, enabling the creation of the Portuguese trading empire in the

East Indies. In the meantime, the slave traders followed in their progress: the Spanish enslaved the beardless *guanches,* the indigenes of the Canary Islands, whilst the Portuguese established factories on the Slave Coast (between Dahomey and Togoland), which effectively circumvented the traditional Arab trans-Saharan slave routes. The first cargo of black slaves to be directly imported by sea to Portugal was sold at Lagos on the Algarve in 1444. The island of Madeira became the prototypical colonial slave economy: sugar plantations worked by slaves were established there in the late fifteenth century, and may well have given food for thought to Christopher Columbus, who had lived on the island and married the daughter of a local governor. As well as working as a sugar buyer for a Genoese company, Columbus had direct knowledge of the slave trade from his visits to the Guinea coast. A fine explorer but a poor colonizer, he was nonetheless at the crest of the black slave wave that was to crash onto the shores of the New World, bringing first sugar, then coffee in its wake.

Shortly after Columbus discovered Hispaniola – now divided between the Dominican Republic and Haiti – he enslaved a party of Taino Indians and sent them back to a friend in Seville. This was followed by another cargo of some four hundred slaves in the following year, 1495. Thus the notorious Atlantic slave trade, which was to lead to the forcible transportation of millions across from Africa to the western hemisphere, began with slaves being sent in the opposite direction, to Spain. The experiment was not a success – half of the second consignment of slaves died, and they were regarded as 'not people suited to hard work, they suffer from the cold, and they do not have a long life'. In any case, even in the Caribbean, through a combination of smallpox, cholera, and conquest, the native Indians were to be virtually wiped out within a generation. It was into this rapidly growing void that the slaves of Africa – robust, disease resistant, and productive – were to be sent.

In 1510 King Ferdinand authorized the first shipment of black slaves – 'the best and strongest available' – to work the mines in Hispaniola. The floodgates were thus opened, and black slaves were to play an increasingly important part in the forging of the Spanish Empire in the Americas. They accompanied Velázquez on his invasion of Cuba, Pedrarias to Panama, Cortés in his conquest of Mexico, and Pizarro into Peru. The slaves frequently played an active part in these invasions – Pizarro even raised one of them to be a commander, and another to be a captain. The black slaves and their white masters thus formed an unholy alliance in New Spain against the dispossessed indigenes, creating a social and political hierarchy that left the Indians below the blacks of slave origins at the bottom of a very stratified heap. When coffee production was introduced into these Spanish-held territories during the late eighteenth century, the same hierarchical structure came into play, and it can still be observed in the struggles over land and exploitation by the remaining pockets of indigenous people in the highlands of Central and South America, from Chiapas in Mexico to Peru.

With the exception of Australia and New Zealand, the East Indies never became colonies in the 'white settler' style. They were controlled by a small number of Europeans exerting power over much larger native populations through superior force of arms, wealth, and organization. Throughout the whole western hemisphere the story was radically different, and its reverberations can be felt to this day. There, embattled Indians were partially or entirely exterminated by European settlers, either militarily or by disease. Plantation economies were established based on black slave labour imported from Africa. The white masters ruled the roost. The pattern was initiated by the Spanish, followed by the Portuguese in Brazil in the late sixteenth century, and later by the British and French in the West Indies, and perfected in the American colonies.

The Portuguese in the East Indies and the Spanish in the West Indies began to feel the effects of competition from their northern European rivals in the late sixteenth century. Initially semi-piratical in nature, as exemplified by the activities of Drake in the Caribbean and Pacific, it quickly grew to become a serious, structured threat to their previous monopolies. The great Spanish treasure fleets that made off with the booty of America and the Philippines were increasingly vulnerable to attack in the West, whilst Portuguese naval power was swiftly eclipsed by that of the English and Dutch in the East. The French and the British established colonies on the seaboard of the North American continent, and gradually picked up colonial possessions in the Caribbean that were to become important centres of coffee production – the English captured Jamaica from the Spanish in 1655, and the French seized the west of Hispaniola in 1605 from the Spanish, renaming it Saint-Domingue in 1697. Martinique, a Windward Island, was colonized by the French in 1635. Many of the Leeward Islands and pockets of the coast of the isthmus were disputed between the two powers over the coming years. The Dutch were dominant in the East Indies, and perhaps too stretched to make an impression in the West, where they colonized only Guyana.

Initially, and for much of the eighteenth century, the economies of the Caribbean colonial possessions of France, Britain, and Spain were dominated by the cultivation of and trade in sugar, an enormously valuable commodity that depended entirely upon slave labour for its production. When coffee arrived in the early eighteenth century, it became quickly established, not only because of the fertile soil of the islands but also because the plantation economy, and the slave infrastructure, was already in place. Coffee flourished in the more mountainous areas of the larger islands, thus making it possible to extend the existing system into previously uncultivated areas, further enriching the landowners. The cultivation of coffee was not in competition with that of sugar, but complementary to it. By the 1770s a plantation might yield £25 per acre, representing a profit of between 400 and 500 per cent.

In addition, the British had already established that there were profits to be made in the slave trade itself: the Royal Adventurers into Africa, chartered in 1660, boasted the Duke of York amongst its shareholders, and its own currency, the guinea, was made from gold from that coast. The Company was soon offering 300 slaves to the first Governor of Jamaica, and the slave population of that island quickly rose to 10,000 in 1673, and by 1700 it had imported a further 25,000 from the Royal Adventurers' successor, the Royal Africa Company (Governor: James, Duke of York). The French were relatively dilatory as a slaving nation, with the total slave population of Martinique, Guadaloupe, and Saint-Domingue being at that time 44,000, the majority of whom were in Martinique. It is estimated that some 400,000 slaves had been imported from Africa to Brazil by 1700, principally to work the sugar plantations. There was to be a sudden upsurge in the slave numbers in Brazil as a result of the discovery of gold in Minas Gerais in 1698. As was the case in their eastern possessions, in particular Goa, the Portuguese had a surprisingly relaxed attitude to miscegenation, and planters frequently married or took as their mistresses former slave women. The relatively tolerant racial *mélange* that is Brazil today is partly the result of this. By 1640 the Spanish Empire had imported 150,000 slaves into Peru, 25,000 into Central America, 12,000 into Venezuela, and 80,000 into New Spain, of which 25,000 were in Colombia: the second half of the seventeenth century was to see demand in the region of 40,000 slaves per annum for the Spanish territories. All of these countries had yet to discover coffee production, but it is clear that without the massive previous influx of slaves its widespread cultivation could not have been contemplated. The continuing importance of the western hemisphere in the world of coffee today is derived from the former colonial plantation economies of the region, based on slavery.

Despite these enormous numbers, it was the eighteenth century that was to see the fullest development of the slave trade and the first seeds of its eventual abolition, initially by the English and then the French. By the end of that century, Saint-Domingue would be in the hands of the rebel slaves led by Toussaint Louverture, its white planters having fled to Cuba to start that country's coffee industry, and Martinique would be in the hands of the British. Independence movements against Spanish colonial government were starting to coalesce in New Spain and Venezuela. Slavery, and the plantation economies built on it, was also by then an integral part of the dynamic of empire in the western hemisphere.

The introduction of coffee to the Caribbean is generally credited by the coffee industry to Gabriel de Clieu. A picturesque story concerning his voyage to Martinique in 1723, during which he used the last of his water ration to feed the coffee plant he had purloined from the King's greenhouse in the Jardin des Plantes, would usually be recounted at this point. The reader will be spared the details, as they are almost certainly untrue. Equally improbable is the claim that the plants were the forbears of the coffee industry of the entire hemisphere. The pragmatic Dutch had already taken seedlings to Surinam by 1718, and the French themselves were growing coffee on Hispaniola by 1715. Although there is reason to believe that de Clieu did actually take some coffee plants from Paris to Martinique, his heroism is somewhat diminished by the knowledge that he could have got them from a neighbouring island. The prime source for the story is de Clieu himself, who, as an impoverished former colonial governor, had a vested interest in any vestigial celebrity he could muster.

Whatever its actual provenance, coffee spread through the hemisphere very quickly: the British introduced it to Jamaica in 1730; the Spanish brought it to Cuba in 1748, to Guatemala in 1750, to Peru in 1764, Costa Rica in 1779, Venezuela in 1784, and to Mexico in 1790; the Portuguese had introduced it to

Brazil in 1752. The one common feature of all these countries was that they had large existing slave populations that enabled coffee growing to be established with startling rapidity: Venezuela, for example, was the third largest producer of coffee worldwide by 1800.

To service the needs of colonial plantation economies, the Atlantic slave trade boomed during the eighteenth century. The folksy tale of de Clieu's introduction of coffee to Martinique conveniently ignores the fact that the island had at least 100,000 slaves by the time he arrived with his precious seedlings. Saint-Domingue (now Haiti), that prodigious source of most of France's sugar, chocolate, and coffee, received a slave boat from Africa every week, provided by the slave shippers of Nantes. Richard Lake, one of the pre-eminent coffee planters on Jamaica, was also a respected slave dealer, whilst Sir Alexander Grant had 11,000 acres on the island from which he exported sugar to England on his own ships, which then went to Sierra Leone for slaves to bring back to the island. The British, owing to their domination of the sea, had an estimated half of the total slave trade to the Americas by the time of the Abolition. It was principally financed by the wealthy traders of Bristol, London, and Liverpool, but the other inhabitants of those towns could join in the speculation, buying shares in a particular slaving ship. The local haberdasher, grocer, or tailor in Liverpool, with his $\frac{1}{32}$ interest in the voyage of a 'Guinea Cargo', was as concerned to turn a profit as the wealthiest merchant. Slaving crossed religious barriers: English Anglicans, American Quakers, French Catholics and Huguenots, Dutch Calvinists and Portuguese Jews all managed to square their conscience with their respective religions and profit from the trade. John Newton, a slave captain who was to become Vicar of St Mary's, Woolnoth, wrote the hymn 'How Sweet the Name of Jesus Sounds' whilst the groaning captives lay mired in their own filth on the decks below. Slaving was no obstacle to respectability – indeed, it was so profitable that it was often the means of obtaining it.

The general European view was that the slave trade was a way of 'redeeming an unhappy people from inconceivable misery'. That the misery of life in Africa was frequently the result of the wars and privations brought about by the trade itself was not often considered until the end of the eighteenth century, when the Abolitionist movement brought detailed reports concerning the realities of the trade to public attention. Even then, those against Abolition, such as James Boswell, could argue that 'To abolish this trade would be to shut the gates of mercy on mankind.' However, his mentor, Dr Johnson, had firmly and consistently opposed slavery and had once, to Boswell's horror, proposed a toast at Oxford: 'Here's to the next insurrection of the negroes in the West Indies.'

The Atlantic slave trade also benefited other trades and manufactures, as the slaves had to be paid for and the rulers in West Africa had specific needs. Arms and gunpowder were top of the list, as they were also the means by which new slave supplies could be acquired, and the gunmakers of Birmingham were happy to oblige, shipping 150,000 rifles in 1765. 'Guinea' cloth, a heavy indigo-dyed cotton from South India, was popular on that coast. It was brought to England by the East India Company – the Charter of which did not allow it to take part in the Atlantic trade – and then re-exported to Africa. New England produced copious quantities of rum, 130 gallons of which could be exchanged for a slave. Swedish iron became a unit of currency. Fine linens from Germany, Japanese silks, and even English woollens – the Gulf of Guinea experiences some surprisingly cool winds – all found their way to Africa. Thus even those not directly involved in the slave trade might find that they profited handsomely from its existence.

The conditions on slave ships were, of course, appalling: even the crews suffered an average death rate of some 20 per cent on a round trip. Once they had reached their destination, the slaves were cleaned up and fed, then auctioned off to start their future life, which consisted almost entirely of work, from sun-up until ten at night, encouraged by the lash. Any spare time would have to be spent tending the vegetable garden from which they had to supplement their pitiful rations. Marriage in general was not encouraged: most slave owners believed that it was cheaper to buy a new slave than to rear one, although after the abolition of the trade in the USA in 1808 the breeding of new slaves became a more cost-effective option than an illegal purchase. It mattered little whether the plantation was given over to sugar, coffee, tobacco, or chocolate, as the work was equally, unremittingly hard, and the punishments terrible: 'Have they not hung men with heads downwards, drowned them in sacks, crucified them on planks, buried them alive, crushed them in mortars? Have they not forced them to eat shit?' reported one slave from the French colonies.

Echoing the trade in the commodities they produced, slaves were shipped, sold, stocked, and smuggled through an elaborate web of financiers, shippers, and middlemen. Kingston in Jamaica became the main entrepôt for the illegal sale of slaves into the Spanish Empire, and Havana, Cuba, became the hemisphere's largest slave market after Abolition. Profits could be as high as £40 per slave, but in general they were more like 50 per cent at the beginning of the century, declining to 10 per cent by 1800.

The American War of Independence was to change the dynamics of empire in the western hemisphere, leading to the occlusion of the European interests, principally those of the Spanish, and the rise of American hegemony. Ironically, the symbolic trigger for Independence was a squabble over tea. When Americans forswore that beverage, they made up the loss with one of the principal products of the slave colonial system in the hemisphere – coffee.

In 1772, the Lords of the Treasury of Her Majesty's Government were threatening to sue the East India Company for the non-payment of tax on tea. The Company's monopoly on the tea trade from China, combined with the apparently insatiable appetite of the British for the beverage, had led them to overestimate the amount they needed to ship: the problem was that cheap, smuggled tea, which had evaded precisely those taxes the Company was now being forced to pay, provided a more than acceptable alternative for many in England. The Company was, not for the first time, facing ruin. The precipitate actions of the Company and the Crown to solve the problem of excess tea led, quite literally, to the loss of the North American colonies, which pointedly turned their back on tea and wholeheartedly embraced coffee. The Boston Tea Party, deceptively trivial as the *casus belli* might seem, in fact marked a turning point in the affairs of mankind. As a consequence of it, the British Empire, the Empire of Tea, would strut the stage for the next century as the imperial superpower, though the seeds of its eclipse had already been sown, whilst the USA, the future Empire of Coffee, could build on its new-found freedom to carve out a nation with vast natural resources on the North American continent, inconvenienced only temporarily by the native Indians. The pioneers, gold rushers, wagon trainers, traders, trappers, bordello madams, and Custers of the Great West were destined to sit round their campfires drinking coffee, not tea.

The background to the Boston Tea Party is complex. The Company's imports from the East were frequently re-exported to the North American colonies, which had, naturally, developed a taste for oriental luxuries at the same time as the Mother Country. The Charter of the Company did not allow it to conduct the re-export trade itself, but there was no shortage of merchants willing to undertake it, and textiles and tea became the most important British exports to America, along with ironware. As tea had supplanted coffee in the affections of the British, there were signs that it would do the same in the American colonies. They were, however, behind the times, and the tea trend that had swept Britain had not yet been picked up at the expense of coffee. The two beverages carried on a respectable co-existence, frequently served, and given equal importance, in the same establishments. In the 1920s the respected American historian of coffee William H. Ukers dredged the historical sludge for the slightest evidence that coffee drinking in America pre-dated that of tea. This was part of an almost pathological tradition of seeing coffee as a peculiarly American beverage, a patriotic one even. He resorted to suggesting that a perfectly ordinary pestle and mortar that can be shown to have come over on the *Mayflower* was 'later used to make "coffee powder"'. Ukers's uncritical pursuit of the equation Tea=British=Bad, Coffee=American=Good serves to illustrate how deep it used to run in the American psyche. As he himself concedes, the first mention of coffee in the New World occurs in 1668, by which time the Dutch burghers of New Amsterdam had had ample time to infect the nascent colonies with that pernicious brew, tea.

In fact tea had been very popular on the north-eastern seaboard of America since the 1650s. It was a well-established favourite in New Amsterdam even before it became widely known in England, and after the city became New York in 1674 – exchanged with the Dutch for the same island of Pulo Run that had been the original destination of St Helena's first settlers – tea gardens modelled on those of London such as Vauxhall and Ranelagh flourished on Manhattan. Coffee came not far behind, and coffee houses became as popular in the cities as they had done in Europe. These two well-liked beverages, with cocoa coming a respectable third, continued to thrive in parallel, and by the 1760s America was importing over a million pounds of tea a year. Most of it, however, was smuggled, to avoid the punitive and much resented duties imposed by the Crown, even on tea re-exported from England. After 1767, to counter the smugglers, merchants could 'draw back' the full amount of duty paid, and the result was the near-total eradication of smuggling. However, taxation issues between the British Government and the American colonies were a political hot potato, and when a new tea tax was imposed, the revenues from which were to go to paying the salaries of British officials, protests broke out. New Englanders were exhorted to give up tea in favour of a root from Labrador with 'a very physical taste':

> Throw aside your Bohea and your Green Hyson Tea
> And all things with a newfangled duty.
> Procure a good store of the choice Labradore,
> For there'll soon be enough here to suit ye.

There was no sudden surge in demand for 'Labradore', but legitimate tea sales plummeted to only 100,000 pounds in 1770, and smuggling thrived again. At that time, not only was the East India Company in debt, with the Treasury threatening legal action, but it had also built up substantial stocks (21 million pounds) of tea in London. The Company came up with an elegant, if entirely colonial, solution: they persuaded the government to draft the Tea Act of 1773 to allow them to send tea to America and to sell it there at a price that included the duties the Company, but not the colonists, could draw back. As a result of political horse-trading, the Bill was passed on the nod. 'No Bill of such momentous consequences ever received so little attention on its passage through Parliament', an American historian has observed. With the Company dumping their vast surplus on the Americans at low prices, legitimate traders as well as smugglers were threatened.

As revolutionaries were soon to do in Paris, disaffected colonists met in the coffee houses, mainly those of Boston, and in particular the Green Dragon in Union Street. Its upstairs room was home to the St Andrew's Lodge. Freemasonry was to play an important role in the American Revolution, and in particular the lodges affiliated, not to the Grand Lodge of England in London, but to the Grand Lodge of Scotland. Scottish Freemasonry blossomed in the North American soil, and it is an odd coincidence that the rituals which previously had served as a framework for Jacobin dissent against the Hanoverians became an important factor in the American Revolution. Freemasonry could be found on both sides of the coming war between the colonists and the Crown, and although there is no clear evidence of collusion amongst masons from opposing camps, the fact that the British made some extraordinary military errors has aroused suspicions. Sir William Howe's failure to pursue Washington after expelling him from New York, and Sir Henry Clinton's wilful failure to link up with Burgoyne's army marching south from Montreal in 1777, are the two most conspicuous examples.

As in England, taverns commonly provided rooms for Masonic meetings, and the Green Dragon was no exception. The St Andrew's Lodge that met there was a Provincial Grand Lodge, which meant it was entitled to warrant the creation of new lodges, and its Grand Master, Joseph Warren, was the designated Grand Master for North America. The Lodge bought the Green Dragon in 1774, and American historians have long regarded it as the 'Headquarters of the American Revolution', and one of its offshoots, 'The Sons of Liberty', is generally considered to have been the organization behind the Boston Tea Party.

While the idea that the downfall of the Empire of Tea was plotted in a coffee house is beguiling, the Green Dragon was, as was common in New England at the time, also a general tavern. Coffee was only one of the many drinks on offer, including wines, ales, chocolate, and tea – ironically, coffee itself was subject to heavy colonial taxation, but it never attracted the opprobrium heaped on tea. However, the Freemasons who swore oaths and fomented revolution were a sober, solemn body of men, amongst them a number of luminaries of American Independence, and it is more likely that they restricted themselves to cups of coffee rather than indulging in anything stronger. It is very unlikely that they would have drunk tea, with its already unacceptable associations. The Green Dragon hosted not only the St Andrew's Lodge but also mysterious subgroups such as the 'Committee of Correspondence', which co-ordinated revolutionary actions throughout the North-East and included Paul Revere (who rode to New York and Philadelphia with news of the Tea Party) as well as Joseph Warren; the 'North End Caucus'; the 'Sons of Liberty', which included Samuel Adams (a renowned hot-headed agitator who had incited the 'Boston Massacre' of 1770) and also Paul Revere; and the 'Loyal Nine', the particularly militant core of the Sons of Liberty. Although not all members were Freemasons, Masonry provided the structure for the coming Revolution, both literally in the form of the lodge meetings at the Green Dragon, and metaphorically, for the exchange of ideas and creation of loyalties. In England in the seventeenth century coffee had become the fuel of the Enlightenment; in North America, where it arrived some twenty years later, it became indelibly associated with the struggle for independence.

Boston, the most prosperous trading city in New England, was the centre for both commerce and dissent. The city was known for its coffee houses from the beginning of the eighteenth century, although tea and coffee remained parallel cultural forces until the Revolution made its final determination. As well as the Green Dragon, Boston had the Crown Coffee House, the King's Head, the London, and the British. The names themselves suggest the strength of loyalty to the British that persisted before the Revolution, and even during it: the War of Independence was also very much a civil war, with loyalists and patriots ranged against each other, assisted by the British and native mercenaries of the loyalist side, and latterly the French on that of the patriots. The clientele of the British coffee house, which had been a meeting place for redcoats and loyalists, was ideologically opposed to that of the Green Dragon, and with the defeat of the English changed its name, in a U-turn of admirable directness, to the American.

By the time the Tea Act was passed and the tea put on board ship in England, Boston was rife with sedition. John Adams urged that 'Tea must be universally renounced', adding in a letter to his wife that 'I must be weaned, and the sooner the better.' The Continental Congress agreed, resolving against tea consumption. In October Warren and Revere decided to publish a Resolution of the North End Caucus: 'To oppose the vending of any tea sent by the East India Company . . . with our lives and fortunes.' In November the Sons of Liberty nailed a notice to the Liberty Tree stating that the consignees of the tea were to resign their commissions as tea agents for the East India Company. 'Ignore this at your peril.' It was ignored, principally because amongst the consignees were Governor Hutchinson and his family who stood to make a great deal of money.

Into this maelstrom sailed the ships bearing the Company's tea from England. The Company had had trouble finding exporters willing to involve themselves in the doubtful enterprise, and eventually the tea had to be shipped on the Company's account, but not in the Company's ships – in order to remain within the spirit of the Charter. The ships with the first consignment – the *Dartmouth, Eleanor, Beaver*, and *William* – berthed at Griffin's Wharf, Boston during December 1773. The Committee of Correspondence distributed handbills: 'The detestable Tea shipped for this port by the East India Company is now arrived in this harbour. The Hour of Destruction on manly Opposition to the Machinations of Tyranny stares you in the face.' The North End Caucus formed a guard on the wharf, ostensibly to protect the ships but in fact to prevent the consignees from unloading the tea. Members of the various subversive groups who met at the Green Dragon were now all fully engaged. A song exhorted:

> Rally, Mohawks – bring out your axes!
> And tell King George we'll pay no taxes on his foreign tea!
> His threats are vain – and vain to think
> To force our girls and wives to drink His vile Bohea!
> Then rally boys, and hasten on
> To meet our Chiefs at the Green Dragon.
> Our Warren's there, and bold Revere,
> With hands to do and words to cheer
> For Liberty and Laws! Our country's 'Braves' and firm
>   defenders
> Shall ne'er be left by true North-Enders,
> Fighting Freedom's cause!
> Then rally boys and hasten on to meet our Chiefs at the
>   Green Dragon.

Although legend and contemporary pictures disguise them as Indians, with feather head-dresses and moccasins, the 'Mohawks' concealed their identities only with blankets and lampblack. On 16 December they boarded the ships unopposed, watched by two thousand people on Griffin's Wharf. The sixty 'Mohawks' brought out their axes and emptied 90,000 pounds of tea into the briny waters of Boston Harbour, ignored and even in some cases assisted by the crews of the ships. Bohea (a black tea) chests at that time weighed nearly 400 lb, and the manoeuvring and emptying of them would have taken the efforts of a number of people. By the following morning the tea had gathered like seaweed at the water's edge.

Tea had become the symbol of British oppression, its destruction a symbol of the Colonists' Revolution, and the adoption of coffee now became a patriotic imperative. This was the prevailing myth: in fact, contrary to expectations, the East India Company was back in business selling tea to America in the early 1800s. For the British, the loss of the North American colonies was in some measure compensated for by the creation of their Empire in the East. General Cornwallis, who had been defeated at Yorktown in 1781, a critical battle in the struggle for independence, went on to distinguish himself as Governor-General in India, particularly during the Third Mysore War, and increased the Company's territorial domination in the south of India, where coffee plantations were later established. However, had it not been for the success of the American Revolution, the western colonies might have been added to the eastern for another century at least, and the British Empire would have been truly globally dominant. Critically, the emergence of the USA as a global power and the imposition of its global hegemony would have been significantly delayed. The Empire of Tea might have maintained its polite stranglehold on the world to this day.

In April 1789 George Washington, the most successful patriot commander, came to New York as President-elect, and he was officially received by the Governor of New York State and the mayor outside the Merchants' Coffee House. New York coffee houses in the eighteenth century followed the European mould as centres of business and politics but failed to emulate their literary cast. This was entirely due to the absence of writers of any repute in the colonies at that time. Coffee houses frequently doubled as court house and council chambers, however, and during the Revolution were a vital nexus for the spreading of news. The Exchange Coffee House was opened in the 1730s and became an unofficial auction house and commodity exchange. It moved several times and was soon eclipsed by the Merchants' at the corner of the present Wall and Water Streets. The Merchants' was, amongst other things, the scene of slave auctions, as an advertisement in a 1750 newspaper shows: 'Just imported a parcel of likely Negroes to be sold at Publick Vendue, To-morrow at Ten o'Clock, at the Merchants' Coffee House'. During the War of Independence the Merchants' was effectively the seat of the revolutionary government, witnessing many of the seminal events of that time. When the British occupied the city, it became the loyalist centre of trading and news. After the peace, this role continued and the Merchants' became, as Lloyds had become in London, the main centre of all news concerning shipping. A register of distinguished visitors to the city was also kept there and their local addresses, emulating the practice of publishing the names of illustrious visitors to European spa towns in local newspapers. The Merchants' also hosted the meetings of Masonic lodges and innumerable worthy societies; the meeting at which the Bank of New York was founded (the city's first); and likewise the first meeting at which stocks were publicly traded by brokers. The Merchants' contained within its walls a distillation of the commercial activities of all the separate City of London coffee houses such as Lloyds, Jonathans, and the Jerusalem. It was burned to the ground in 1804 and never rebuilt. Its place as the centre of stock trading had in any case been taken over by the Tontine Coffee House opposite, which had, appropriately, been financed by the sale of £200 shares to 157 individual investors. The Tontine was converted into offices in 1834, having outgrown its usefulness as an exchange. The subsequent gradual disappearance of New York's other coffee houses reflected the increasing institutionalization of financial and business organizations and the creation of purpose-built premises for their activities.

The coffee houses of the City of London that had burgeoned during the late seventeenth century had attracted a specific commercial clientele and had coalesced into more formal institutions – whether commercial societies, social clubs, or restaurants – by the mid eighteenth century. New York's coffee houses underwent a similar process nearly a century later, reflecting that city's later development as a pre-eminent commercial centre. There had always been taverns, in both London and New York, but that environment was neither suited to the collective pursuit of money nor to the elevation of worthy causes. Coffee houses provided a decent and sober meeting place for the serious men who built commercial empires, and the coffee they provided fuelled the strictly practical, dispassionate thought processes that helped them to achieve their aims.

The Boston Tea Party was a reaction to oppressive Crown taxes as represented by the dumping of surplus Company tea on the North American market. It was, *per se*, neither a reaction to tea nor the expression of a preference for coffee; nonetheless, it transformed the drinking habits of the fledgling nation. The whole range of physiological, psychological, and psychodynamic effects of coffee drinking were thus, by an almost arbitrary act of the British Government, suddenly thrust centre stage in the process of the flowering of the American people and their national identity. Just as the Ottoman Empire had seized upon coffee and made it part of the web that bound it together commercially, culturally and spiritually, so coffee for the Americans was hard-wired into its own empire-building. The remorseless logic of the westward expansion was to be fed by coffee from the new plantations of the Caribbean and South and Central America.

The Revolutions in America and France, fomented in the coffee houses, had far-reaching consequences for the slave trade. The Americans, when fighting to be released from the colonial yoke, were quick to think of themselves as slaves of Britain, but slow to appreciate that their own negro slaves had any cause for complaint. A Quaker noted that Washington had asked God to deliver Americans from oppression, whilst at the same time 'sighs and groans' could be heard from the far more oppressed slaves. Although the import of slaves was officially proscribed by the

Continental Congress of 1774, the decision was never enforced. With a slave population at the time of 650,000, the newly independent United States was nearly as dependent on slavery as the West Indies as a whole, where there were 800,000 of them. The Constitution of 1787 mentioned the issue, but only to determine that any discussion of Abolition should be put off for twenty years. When the debate was reopened in 1808, Abolition of the trade in slaves swiftly followed. By that time, however, the slave population itself had risen significantly: during this period it is estimated that the USA probably imported more slaves than had been brought to North America since it was first colonized. It is a sobering reflection on the ideals and character of the American Revolution that with one hand it could bind whilst with the other it sought to cut loose. There was in fact an increasing intellectual and political opposition to the slave trade: and there was every reason for the Revolution to embrace the principles of the Declaration of the Rights of Man all-inclusively. The main reason why this failed to happen was political: the southern states would not have joined the Union if slavery had been federally abolished, and it was felt 'better to let the southern states import slaves than to part with those states'. Thus while individual states could, and some did, abolish both slavery and the slave trade, there was no federal ruling. In addition, slave merchants in the northern states had a vested interest in the trade. The legacy of this fateful pragmatism was reaped in the Civil War, and the overweening power of the southern conservative political establishment in our own times contains a disturbing suggestion that the issue still remains unresolved.

The debate concerning slavery had a profound effect on the pre-Revolutionary thinkers who gathered at the Café Procope in Paris, including Montesquieu, Rousseau, and Diderot. The ethics of the slave trade were discussed whilst its very fruits were consumed, a dark liquid produced by dark skins in the depths of dark despair. Diderot wrote that the trade 'is a business which violates religion, morality, natural law, and all human rights', whilst Rousseau railed against the supposed right to enslave as 'absurd and meaningless'. By the time the Revolution broke out in France in 1789, slavery had risen up the agenda of the States-General. Thomas Clarkson, the engine behind the British Abolition movement, came to Paris to test the water there, bringing with him a diagram of the *Brookes*, a Liverpool slaver, which showed in mechanistic detail the layout of the slaves on the decks. This celebrated image moved Mirabeau of the National Assembly to have a wooden replica built with tiny, black-painted figures to represent the slaves. It shocked all who saw it, but apparently not enough to cause any alteration in the status quo: it was argued that France's prosperity depended upon the colonies and the slaves that served them. In 1791, however, the National Assembly became the first ruling body in Europe to condemn the trade, even though it made only small alterations to the law. The quality of debate at least exceeded that of the British Parliament, where Tommy Grosvenor, the Member for Chester, argued that the slave trade was 'not an amiable trade, neither was the trade of a butcher an amiable trade, and yet a mutton chop was, nonetheless, a good thing'.

Events in France had been followed with great interest in Saint-Domingue, which had a population of 450,000 blacks compared to only 40,000 whites and 50,000 mulattos. The island was a byword for cruelty to slaves even in this cruellest of systems, for the whites lived in terror of a slave uprising and subjugated them ruthlessly. The colony was forced by the French Government to sell all their produce to France at fixed prices, so that the wealthy white planters were in a similar position to that of the former colonists in America, and they likewise chafed at the home Government's bit. The mulattos, often wealthy slave owners themselves, were resented by the poorer whites, and the slaves occupied their customary place at the bottom of this volatile heap. In the remote hills could be found the marrons, the escaped slaves who practised voodoo and to whom rebellious slaves naturally gravitated. The island at that time was believed to be the richest of any European colony anywhere, and also produced half the world's output of coffee. Dr Johnson's toast became reality in 1791 when the slaves rose, put as many whites as they could lay hands on to the sword, and destroyed the sugar and coffee plantations. Months of savage fighting followed, with the various factions brutally defending their interests. When war broke out between France and Britain, the unfortunate island became the field upon which all the political dramas of the late eighteenth century would be played out in a tempestuous, tropical form. Revolution, invasion, independence, colonization, emancipation, regicide, race, disease, and war all featured in what was to be the only successful slave revolution in history. Toussaint Louverture, the slaves' leader, led his people blinking into the light of the next century. Coffee production had dropped by half, and most of the white coffee planters had fled to Cuba, where they could resume the cultivation of coffee with slaves without fear of insurrection. All Louverture had to deal with was the small matter of Napoleon.

8

THE CONTINENTAL SYSTEM AND NAPOLEON'S ALTERNATIVE TO COFFEE

Coffee, (which makes the Politician wise,
And see thro' all things with his half-shut Eyes) . . .

ALEXANDER POPE, *The Rape of the Lock*,
canto iii (1714)

Born into the minor nobility of Corsica in 1769, Napoleon Bonaparte hovered like an eagle – his imperial emblem – over the early years of the nineteenth century. To his supporters, he was close to divine. He rose to power during the later years of the French Revolution, initially because of his military genius; but he quickly showed himself to be a visionary administrator and statesman, with a far-reaching sense that the potential created by the Revolution could be harnessed to the glory of France. After his occupation of Egypt between 1798 and 1799, in rapid succession he became Consul, then First Consul, then was crowned Emperor in 1804, by which time his rule had spread over most of the European continent, underpinned by his monumental Code Civil. His ambitions were all for France, and he considered himself the 'People's Emperor'. He was reviled as a tyrannical ogre by his arch-enemy, the British, and the white heat of their hatred forged two of that country's greatest military heroes,

Nelson and Wellington, who were over time to bring about his eventual downfall. His restless energy was both his strength and his weakness: Napoleon's notorious winter retreat from Moscow in 1812 was an epic *folie de grandeur* prompted by his lifelong fault of impatience. Defeat led him to be exiled briefly to Elba, from which Mediterranean island he returned to meet his Waterloo in 1815. Expecting to be exiled to a country house in England as befitted his station in defeat, his final exile on St Helena was the bitterest of pills, the damp confines of Longwood House, a converted barn, providing no possible consolation to the man who was, in Lord Rosebery's memorable phrase, 'wrecked by the extravagance of his own genius'.

Napoleon's was an empire that spread slowly from his European core, and tropical plantation colonies inspired little interest in him. His dream was far grander: after his invasion of Egypt he professed to having wished to carry on to India: 'I saw myself founding a new religion, marching into Asia riding an elephant, a turban on my head, and in my hands a new Koran I would have written to suit my needs'.

It was after peace had been signed with Britain in 1801 that Napoleon, who had by that time become First Consul, decided that the situation in Saint-Domingue would have to be addressed. The colony was too important to the French economy to be allowed to assume independence. Toussaint Louverture was nominally Governor-General on behalf of France, having fended off an invasion by the British and double-dealt with the Spanish, who had ceded their half of the island, Santo Domingo, as part of a treaty in 1795. Napoleon's plan, to be implemented by his brother-in-law General Charles Laclerc, was to send an invading army to restore French rule, initially by undertaking to allow the former slaves representation in a new government, and then treacherously arresting all the troublemakers and re-enslaving all the blacks, thus returning the island to the status quo *ante*

Louis XVI, but with Napoleon in charge. The fact that he had revived the slave trade in France in 1802 must, however, have sent clear warning signals regarding his likely intentions to Louverture.

The invading force took most of the coastal towns in early 1802, although the wealthiest of them, including Cap François, the 'Paris of the Americas', were burnt to the ground by the retreating forces of Louverture. Soon Laclerc had secured the surrender of most of the rebel leaders on promise of good treatment; then, as had been ordered by Napoleon, he had them shipped back to France, where Louverture himself died miserably in prison. However, when Laclerc sought to disarm the remaining blacks, news of Louverture's death spurred another final rebellion, which the French forces, fatally weakened by yellow fever, were unable to counter. When war once more broke out with Britain in 1803, it was clear that the French would have to leave, and a truce was organized to cover the retreat. Napoleon took the news badly: 'Damn coffee!', he said with feeling, 'Damn colonies!' The independent republic of Haiti was declared on 1 January 1804.

The Emperor's disaffection with Saint-Domingue was reflected in his attitude to all his Caribbean colonies, and certainly led in part to his offer to sell Louisiana to an astonished Jefferson for a total of $15 million. In Napoleon's mind, the strategic and economic function of the North American colony was intimately tied in with that of Saint-Domingue, and the fall of the island made Louisiana redundant. The problems of the resumed European war also loomed large in his mind. The Louisiana Purchase – complete with the coffee houses of New Orleans – brought the problem of the slave trade to the forefront of legislators' minds. The newly acquired state was the scene of rapid expansion of cotton production, a crop which, it was generally agreed, poor white paid labour was too enfeebled by the climate to work. While they had doubled the size of the Union, the price was higher than might at first appear: they had also shifted the balance against the early abolition of slavery. Thus the success of the Haitian slave rebellion ironically contributed to the development of the USA as a world power, itself long dependent on slavery.

The failure of the French campaign in Egypt had quelled Napoleon's fantasy of developing an eastern empire to match his western one. He claimed to have spent much time in Egypt learning about Islam: 'I always had seven coffee-pots on the boil, while I was discussing with the Turks, for I had to stay awake all night, talking over religious matters with them.' The defeat by Nelson at the Battle of the Nile destroyed much of his navy, and, after having disposed of his prime American colonial interests, Napoleon was forced to turn his attention to Europe. His domination of continental Europe was now matched by the equivalent domination of the seas by the English navy, especially after the Battle of Trafalgar in 1805. Colonial products, including coffee, upon which the continent had become dependent, were suddenly unavailable, and so Napoleon, ever the innovator, set up the 'Continental System' in 1806, whereby European manufacturers and farmers under the domination of France were encouraged to achieve self-sufficiency in all products. The cultivation of sugar beet to feed the craving for sweetness was one successful and lasting result of this initiative. The use of chicory as a coffee substitute was a less successful equivalent, though it still lingers in France to the perplexity of its neighbours – in all other respects France is a gourmet nation *par excellence,* but the continued use by the French of chicory mixed in their coffee when economy no longer demands it is puzzling.

The concept of the Continental System seems at first sight perverse: it was a blockade of the British Isles, which had control of the seas, by continental Europe, which had few remaining ships. However, by denying access to British ships to all the ports of the continent, including those of Russia, Napoleon achieved by default what a dominant navy might have given him. The British, marooned off the continental coast, were no longer able to trade with their nearest and most important neighbours. Thus to bring the Continental System to the heights of strategic perfection it was necessary that Europe should become fully self-sufficient, no longer reliant on imported goods, neither the manufactures of Britain nor the familiar commodities of the colonies. In the meantime, without its most important trading partners, it was hoped that British maritime trade and industrial manufactures would wither on the vine. The Continental System was pure economic warfare, and depended on the skill and inventiveness of French science and industry to respond to the challenge, which was considerable: England was way ahead of the rest of the world in terms of manufactures and industry. Necessity, albeit self-induced, is the mother of invention, and an industrial revolution swept France. Napoleon told one industrialist: 'We are both of us making war on England, but your method of warfare is even better than mine.' Manchester cottons, Bradford woollens, Staffordshire pottery, Sheffield steel, and countless other British products previously taken for granted now had to be made in France. American cotton? Grown in France. Cuban cane sugar? Sugar beet grown in France. Saint-Domingue coffee? The climate would not allow its cultivation in France, and so whereas the want of other necessities brought forth acceptable substitutes, the lack of coffee could prompt only a very pale imitation: chicory.

This pale-blue flowering, indigenous European plant had no distinguishing features other than a long, brownish root like that of the cornflower it resembles. Not needing to fend off tropical pests, chicory contains no caffeine, nor indeed anything resembling the wonderful complexity of flavours and aromas of coffee. It was, however, the nearest thing to coffee that the wit of man could devise. The roast and ground chicory root had been first developed as a coffee substitute in Germany, at the time when Frederick the Great's campaign against coffee was in full flight. Frederick had witnessed an explosion in coffee consumption in Germany during his long reign and believed it to be the ruination of the working classes – its effects on those who could afford to buy it were another matter. In the libretto of J. S. Bach's 'Coffee Cantata' (1732) a young bourgeois German woman threatens her father:

> No lover shall woo me
> Unless I have his pledge
> Written in the marriage settlement,
> That he will allow me
> To drink coffee when I please.

Frederick was furthermore convinced, on medical advice, that coffee could cause men to become effeminate and women sterile. In his particularly Prussian way, in 1777 he issued an edict advocating the consumption of beer: 'It is disgusting to notice the increase in the quantity of coffee used by my subjects, and the amount of money that goes out of the country in consequence . . . My people must drink beer. His Majesty was brought up on beer, and so were his ancestors, and his officers.' He proceeded to impose heavy taxes on coffee, and to make its roasting subject to rigorous licensing regulations. Those amongst the working classes who failed to take up beer drinking were forced to look for substitutes for their favoured beverage. It was as a result of this exhaustive search, which saw experiments with wheat, barley, figs, and corn, that chicory came top of a very substandard class.

Before coffee's introduction the German population had been accustomed to swilling considerable quantities of weak beer throughout the day. This was a common northern European trait, and it has been argued that the sudden get-up-and-go that the people of these northern nations exhibited in the seventeenth century was the result of the exchange of a state of permanent inebriation for permanent caffeination. Although the flavour of coffee found favour in Germany, its effects did not: if it was drunk in the profligate manner in which the Germans were used to drinking beer, it caused all the symptoms of caffeine abuse. So when a Major von Heine launched a new roasted chicory powder, it was a success both because of Frederick's strictures and because of the natural health concerns of the people themselves.

Although he did not invent the use of chicory as a coffee substitute, Napoleon embraced it warmly as the Continental System's answer to the coffee problem. He effectively decreed that chicory should be welcomed as a perfectly acceptable coffee substitute, although he evidently found it difficult to convince his pleasure-loving friend Junot, who he discovered had managed to import forbidden luxuries: 'The ladies of your household should drink Swiss tea; it is just as good as Indian, and chicory is just as healthy as Arabian coffee.' Whereas today it takes an army of marketeers to persuade us of the merits of a particular consumer choice, Napoleon was able to change the taste of the populace in a suitably grand manner: marketing by imperial fiat.

Despite the collapse of the Continental System after the retreat from Moscow in 1812, and the final collapse of the First Empire after the defeat at Waterloo three years later, the French partially retained the chicory habit, perhaps as a result of some sort of perverse nostalgia. For the economic logic of the Continental System had long since been undermined, first by the smuggling of English goods, then by a relaxation of the rules to allow the French to sell desperately needed grain to England in exchange for gold. Then, instead of the total prohibition of English imports, heavy duties were imposed. In 1813 coffee that was priced at 40 shillings a hundredweight in London fetched 500 shillings in Hamburg. In the end it was the English who, realizing that the French war effort was being substantially financed by trade, decided to block-ade the Continent. Conventional thinking triumphed in the end, despite the best efforts of Napoleon's unconventional genius. Napoleon had thought that the Dutch, Germans, and Swiss would be willing to make some personal sacrifices for the freedom that his imperial rule brought them: in the end, as he remarked, 'When I think that, for a cup of coffee with more or less sugar in it, they checked the hand that would set free the world!'

9

NAPOLEON AND ST HELENA

St Helena, a little island . . .

NAPOLEON BONAPARTE,
note in his atlas as a young lieutenant at Auxonne

Napoleon arrived on St Helena on 16 October 1815 after the defeat that summer by the British and Prussians at Waterloo. The likelihood of his escaping was as remote as the island itself. The fortifications were truly formidable: gun emplacements bristled from every strategic point overlooking the ocean, and the lessons of the Dutch invasion had been learnt, so that inland passes were covered from the heights. One first-time visitor reported: 'Batteries now appear in every direction; guns, gates, embrasures, and soldiers continually meet the eye.' St Helena was in effect an impregnable ship of the line permanently at anchor in the South Atlantic.

Although the coffee plants that had been planted from the Yemeni seeds nearly a hundred years previously had disappeared from sight until Roxburgh's report in 1814, there is an apocryphal report that during his exile Napoleon said: 'The only good thing about St Helena is the coffee.' The idea that the ex-Emperor, architect of the Continental System and noted coffee drinker, might have endorsed the qualities of the neglected crop is compelling, and rewards further scrutiny. As befits the most written-about man in history, there is much that can be learnt about Napoleon's sensual habits, and a gift of coffee, ironically, was to be the *casus belli* between him and the man he came to detest as his gaoler, the Governor, Hudson Lowe.

Coffee was not the only crop that had been brought to the island. Captain Bligh, late of the infamous *Bounty*, called by in 1792 with some Tahitian visitors on his way back from the South Seas, leaving ten breadfruit plants from the supplies that he was taking to Jamaica, as well as seeds of mountain rice and sago. The Council wrote to him before he left, describing 'the inexpressible degree of wonder and delight to contemplate a floating garden transported in luxuriance from one extremity of the world to the other'. Bligh's visit took place at the start in earnest of the era of worldwide economic botany, promoted chiefly by Sir Joseph Banks, an adviser to the East India Company. St Helena's own botanical garden was but one of many such, spread strategically around the burgeoning British Empire. The aim was scientific to the extent that research into plants and their ability to adapt to strange environments was partly scientific; but the underlying *raison d'être* was to encourage the growth of potentially valuable crops in British territories, reducing the nation's dependence on fickle foreigners for its essentials, and making sure that the profit remained in British hands. Coffee, as we have seen, was amongst the earliest plants to be treated thus, and everything from cinchona (the plant from which quinine is derived) to tea was to be evaluated for its potential commercial benefits. The process of globalizing the regional produce of a particular area was an essential tool of the Company's, and later the Empire's, economic dominance. It removed monopolistic strangleholds, enabled new plantation technologies to be profitably deployed, and, most importantly, kept the produce under British control. As John Stuart Mill, one of the Company's chief apologists as it faced abolition in the 1850s, remarked in another context: 'Our West Indian colonies [are] the place where England finds it convenient to carry out the production of sugar, coffee and a few other tropical commodities'.

A few years prior to Captain Bligh's visit, the island had suffered one of its periodic mutinies, this time the result of restrictions placed on the rights of soldiers to visit punch houses. Ninety-nine soldiers were captured, and nine executed. This was nothing out of the ordinary; from the time of St Helena's annexation by the East India Company mutinies had been a regular feature of island life. It is interesting that when St Helena was mooted as the location of Napoleon's exile, concerns over its history of mutiny and insurrection were never raised. Far from an attempted rescue from the sea, perhaps the real danger lay in the possibility that the Emperor would exert his considerable powers to rally the disaffected on land. Given that the number of soldiers would increase tenfold, and the island's isolation and privations diminish not a jot, it is odd that the thought of mutiny did not occur. It would have been a fitting end to an extraordinary career for the Emperor, too, to have taken over his accursed island prison at the head of a renegade army, and then defied the British to recapture it. They could have reinstituted the Continental System in miniature. The effect if Napoleon had ruled the island would have been spectacularly beneficial, if the experience of Elba was anything to go by. In the ten brief months of his exile on that island – which was four times the size and had four times the number of inhabitants of St Helena – he was a busy, improving Emperor: paving the streets, organizing rubbish collecting, and installing street lighting in Portoferraio, the main town; designing a flag, building a theatre and mounting performances by his beautiful sister Pauline; improving the agriculture, bottling and selling the mineral water, and planting chestnut trees on the mountains to combat soil erosion. St Helena – denuded of trees and topsoil, with a catalogue of failed agricultural initiatives, overrun by goats, cats, and rats, run by a corrupt, petty and parochial Government – would have benefited immeasurably had the extravagance of Napoleon's genius been turned upon it. As it was, all that remorseless energy had nowhere to turn but inwards, to poison its possessor.

By Napoleon's standards, the Governors of St Helena in the first years of the nineteenth century were layabouts. By St Helena's standards they were positive dynamos. But although Governors Beatson and Wilks were committed agricultural improvers, no mention is made of the coffee plants introduced to St Helena at some personal risk. The former wrote prolifically on the subject of goats, which, despite the best efforts of his predecessors, still held back the progress of forestry and horticulture on the island: his appointment of the Senior Chaplain, Mr Samuel Jones, as 'Inspector of Strayed Sheep and Goats' perhaps reflected the importance he placed on all forms of pastoral care. Goats, gum-trees, martinets, and mutinies – all parochial concerns evaporated when the *Icarus* arrived on 11 October with breathtaking news that Napoleon Bonaparte, the most feared man in the world until his recent defeat, was to arrive in a few days on the *Northumberland* to commence his exile on St Helena.

The latest census had revealed that St Helena had a population of 700 whites, 975 soldiers, 1400 slaves, and 450 'free people of colour' – some 3500 inhabitants all told. For six years their lives would be turned upside down by the presence of the ex-Emperor in his isolated eyrie at Longwood House, the converted barn destined to be the scene of the claustrophobic *grand opéra bouffe* that was the Exile. A curfew was imposed between nine at night and daylight, unless a written approval was given by the Field Officer for the day. The population was nearly doubled by the eventual presence of 2280 additional soldiers and 500 officers, which brought on shortages of food and accommodation.

Everything – beef, mutton, pork, turkey, potatoes, geese, fowl and duck – went up in price. Eggs that had been three shillings a dozen became a shilling apiece. Shipping was tightly regulated: other than Company ships, none could come into the Jamestown Roads unless inspected and found to be in severe distress. Two brigs constantly patrolled the island, and at the sight of any boat within sixty miles an alarm was sounded and 500 guns swiftly manned. Fishing boats had to be licensed, and then could fish only close to shore and during the day, causing a shortage of fish where before there had been abundance and limiting its consumption to the rich. Evidently not everything was in short supply: 279 newborn illegitimate children were baptized on the island during the Exile.

The knowledge that he was doomed to be imprisoned on this forbidding rock must have struck Napoleon with dread: as he approached for the first and only time in 1815, he examined the island through his telescope from the deck of the *Northumberland* and remarked with admirable understatement: 'It's not an attractive place. I should have done better to remain in Egypt.' No dwelling had yet been settled upon for him. Before he landed, Admiral Cockburn and Governor Wilks made a tour of various properties on the island to assess their suitability. Cockburn agreed with the Governor that Longwood seemed the best candidate, but it required considerable work. The decision was made in haste: the climate at Longwood is perhaps the worst on the island, its exposed position at an altitude of 1760 feet making it prey to unending wind and remorseless damp. The building itself, the former barn, was ill equipped to fend off the weather; the chimneys smoked, the floorboards in many rooms were laid directly on the earth, the roof was tarred canvas, which heated up unbearably in the intermittent sun, and the walls were of insubstantial wood. Its only virtue, if such it be, was that there was plenty of room on Deadwood Plain for the garrison of the 2000 soldiers considered necessary to guard the exiled Emperor.

Napoleon came ashore at night to avoid the crowds who were waiting to catch a glimpse him, but they lit torches so that he could not pass unseen. He spent the night at the house of Mr Porteous, the Company's Superintendent of Lands, who lived in the grandest house in Jamestown, then rode next day with Cockburn to inspect Longwood. His opinion of the house, if indeed it was sought, is not recorded. He did not wish to spend another night in hot and stuffy Jamestown being gawped at, and on his return over Two Gun Saddle he spotted a house called The Briars, an airy property occupied by the family of William Balcombe, who worked partly for the East India Company and also as a general purveyor on his own account. There was a small but pleasant pavilion in the garden with one room large enough for the old campaigner to install himself in, setting up the camp bed in which he invariably preferred to sleep.

By a twist of fate typical of the historical landscape of St Helena, Napoleon's nemesis, the Duke of Wellington, had like-wise stayed in the same pavilion some ten years earlier whilst returning from India, having made his name there as Sir Arthur Wellesley during his campaign against the Mahrattas, particu-larly in the decisive battle of Assaye, which he reckoned to be the toughest of his career – tougher even than Waterloo, the defeated commander of which battle now occupied his same quarters on St Helena. Wellington was not impervious to the irony when he heard about it and wrote to Admiral Malcolm, Cockburn's successor, with typical bluster: 'You may tell "Bony" that I find his apartments at the Elysée Bourbon very convenient, and that I hope he likes mine . . . It is a droll sequel enough to the affairs of Europe that we should change places of residence.'

His stay at The Briars was the only passably happy time Napoleon spent on St Helena, mainly due to the presence of the five Balcombe children, and particularly Betsy, a lively teenager who enjoyed an easy familiarity with Napoleon that awe-struck adults could not manage. When he attempted to teach her billiards, she amused herself 'trying to hit his Imperial fingers with the ball'. Betsy's intimacy with the Emperor was to have a deep effect on the life of her family: her father became a general purveyor to Napoleon and his suite – it is likely that he supplied the coffee drunk at Longwood – and they were all sent home in disgrace when he was implicated in an attempt to smuggle letters from the island.

Although an admirer of female beauty, Napoleon himself was not greatly interested in sensual pleasures. He was reckoned an indifferent lover, and food and drink did not excite him: he had upset Admiral Cockburn on the *Northumberland* because he always left the table early, 'not wishing to sit at a table for two or three hours like the English, guzzling down wine to make myself drunk'. He seems to have found the drinking habits of the English very interesting. He quizzed a group of officers who came to pay their respects to him at Longwood: 'Do you drink?', in French, then in his poor English, 'Dreenk? Dreenk?'. Betsy Balcombe wrote that 'He had formed an exaggerated idea of the quantity of wine drunk by English gentlemen, and used to ask me after we had had a party, how many bottles of wine my father drank, and then laughing, and counting on his fingers, generally made the number five.' On one of his rare excursions from Longwood late in his exile he paid a surprise visit to Mount Pleasant, the house of Sir William Doveton, and closely questioned his daughter, Mrs Greentree, as to how frequently her husband became drunk, and was evidently quite put out when she told him that it was some years since she had seen him like that. (Sir William was the distinguished St Helenan who, on his only visit to London, having met a lady of his acquaintance in the street, suggested that they defer their conversation 'until the procession had passed'.) Napoleon himself liked to drink a little Gevrey Chambertin with water. One of his complaints about his treatment on St Helena was that the red wine the English made available, although of excellent quality and plentiful, was always Bordeaux.

Napoleon had been a fast eater all his life: as First Consul he advised a visitor 'If you want to eat well, you eat with the Second Consul, if you want to eat badly, with the Third Consul, but if you want to eat quickly, you eat with me.' He always left the table abruptly, 'as if he had received an electric shock'. Sir George Bingham, when a guest at Longwood, remarked: 'It was a most superb dinner which lasted only forty minutes, at the end of which we retired into the drawing room to play cards . . . the dinner was stupid enough; the people who lived with him scarcely spoke out of a whisper; and he was so much engaged in eating that he hardly said a word to anyone. He had so filled the room with wax candles that it was as hot as an oven.' Sir George was polite enough not to refer to the scores of rats that scuttled around the diners' feet, and which Napoleon regarded with indifference – even when one jumped out of his hat as he was about to put it on – believing them less of a blight on his life than the sentries stationed around Longwood.

It was noted by his amanuensis, Las Cases, who accompanied Napoleon to St Helena before being banished for attempting to smuggle messages out, that the Emperor had an exceptional sense of smell. On board the *Northumberland* the smell of the ship's paint was enough to make him sick, and he sent his aides to the newly redecorated Longwood before moving in to ensure that there was no residual paint smell, falling into a rage when it was reported that there was. It was not just paint that troubled him: he had once hired a pretty Madrileno maidservant who had taken his fancy but peremptorily dismissed her when he had discovered that he could not bear her smell. One biographer remarked: 'It has been explained that allergies were the cause of his acute sense of smell. For Napoleon the ideal woman was one that gave off no smell at all.' He claimed that he could always tell when he was getting close to Corsica even with his eyes shut, and complained of the damp, mildewy smell of Longwood. He was a fastidious bather, spending long hours in the bath there, and being daily rubbed down with eau-de-Cologne. When supplies on St Helena ran out, his valet Marchand made up a formula from the herbal material available: this recipe was later recreated by the couturier and perfumer Jean-Charles Kerleo at Jean Patou in Paris, and the perfume can still be savoured on request, but not bought. Longwood today is pervaded by a palpable compound of mildew and melancholy, the aroma of the Exile, despite the fact that the house has been totally rebuilt and only the stone steps leading to the front porch are original.

Despite his general indifference to food, Napoleon was a regular coffee drinker whilst on St Helena, taking it daily with breakfast at six and after lunch at ten. Dinner at eight always finished with coffee served from a silver pot in his much prized cups, commissioned by him from the Sèvres porcelain factory in 1806. These were small, blue, and decorated with gold hieroglyphs and hand-painted pictures taken from *Scenes of Egypt* by Vivant Denon. The cups had been noted by Bingham: 'The dessert service was Sèvres china, with gold knives, forks and spoons. The coffee cups were the most beautiful I have ever seen: on each cup was an Egyptian scene, and on the saucer the portrait of a bey or other distinguished person. In France they cost, one cup and saucer, twenty-five guineas.' Napoleon, ever generous, gave one to Lady Malcolm, whose husband had replaced Admiral Cockburn. On a visit to the house of one of his aides, Maréchal Bertrand, near St Matthew's vicarage, Betsy Balcombe, accompanied by Napoleon, drank 'delectable coffee' prepared by La Pages, but gives no hint as to its origins. Cold pie, potted meat, cold turkey, curried meat, dates, almonds, oranges, a very fine salad, and coffee had been served at the impromptu picnic lunch he had taken to Sir William

Doveton's house. Mrs Greentree had tasted the coffee, which had been brought from the house, and which she found 'acid and disagreeable'. Mount Pleasant is in the Sandy Bay area of the island, and within five hundred yards of Bamboo Hedge, which is where the original coffee from Yemen was planted in the 1730s. It is tempting to suppose that Sir William would have told Napoleon about this old coffee plantation, which is in sight of his house, and that he might even have prepared the coffee from Bamboo Hedge for the Emperor – though as there was no expertise or equipment for the processing of coffee cherry on the island it is very likely to have been poorly prepared. This could have created the 'acid and disagreeable' flavours Mrs Greentree complained about. The fact that she did complain, and in the presence of the Emperor, is interesting. She would surely not have had the bad manners to have done so had the Emperor brought the coffee with him, and, unless it was the focus of particular interest, would not have insulted her father's hospitality either. What actually happened during the picnic on the lawn at Mount Pleasant will never be known. The incident took place in October 1820, after Napoleon had conceived a sudden interest in gardening and had planted coffee trees as the centrepiece of his new plan. They died in the winds that constantly lashed Longwood.

Napoleon had evidently drunk coffee since early adulthood: when he was courting his first wife, Josephine, in 1795, she used to serve him coffee that had been grown on her family's estates in Martinique. Her family, the Taschers, had had plantations there since the seventeenth century, initially growing sugar but taking up coffee cultivation when it was introduced to the island by Gabriel de Clieu. They had 150 slaves, evidently well treated, but the plantations produced no income for Josephine as the island was, when she met Napoleon, in the hands of the British. Perhaps it was Josephine's influence that had led to his reinstituting the French slave trade in 1802. He had certainly been under pressure from the slaving interests at Nantes, Bordeaux, and Marseilles and had seen from the example of the rebellion on Saint-Domingue how economically damaging the loss of a colony could be.

In the case of St Helena, however, it was maintaining the colony that now came at a heavy cost. Although St Helena was still in the possession of the East India Company, during Napoleon's exile its government was taken over by the Crown, which also paid for the vastly increased expenditure necessary to keep the island in a constant state of high alert. The estimable Governor Wilks was pensioned off and replaced temporarily in turn by Admirals Cockburn and Malcolm, until the Crown's chosen successor, Sir Hudson Lowe, arrived in April 1816. A taciturn, unimaginative man, the Exile was a formidable challenge to which he could only fail to rise: Montholon, one of Napoleon's so-called Four Evangelists (the others were Bertrand, Gourgaud, and Las Cases) who accompanied him into exile, wrote: 'An angel from heaven would not have pleased us as Governor of St Helena.' Whatever his other merits, Lowe was no angel, and as his relationship with Napoleon quickly soured, he became obsessed with the safekeeping of his charge inside what was jokingly called 'Hudson Fort'. He would wake in the middle of the night and feverishly scribble down new ideas to increase the security there. He had a bitter, bored, and ruthless opponent: Napoleon himself said in December 1818: 'Whatever they say, I can make or unmake the reputation of the Governor . . . all I choose to say of him, of his bad behaviour, of his ideas of poisoning me, will be believed.'

Their first meeting appears to have been friendly enough, however. Lowe had been commander of the Corsican Rangers, knew Egypt, and had fought in some battles opposite the Emperor, who noted: 'We probably fired guns at each other. With me that always makes for a happy relationship.' Napoleon was always keen to measure what he called a man's 'draught', and in Lowe's case the initial result seemed favourable enough: 'This new Governor says very little, but he seems polite,' he is reported to have said, although in another account he remarked: 'I have seen Prussians, Tartars, Cossacks, Kalmucks and many others, but never before in my life have I seen so ill-favoured and forbidding a countenance.'

Curiously, despite the frequent mentions of Napoleon's coffee-drinking on St Helena, there are no references to coffee amongst the detailed accounts of deliveries of food and wine to Longwood – with the exception of an incident when Hudson Lowe made a gift of coffee to the Emperor, which played a part in their falling out at their second meeting in April 1816. By then a considerable agenda had built up. It is not certain where the coffee came from, and although it is tempting to assume it was from the plants that had lately been seen at Sandy Bay, Montholon asserts that Lowe had received it from Réunion, the small French island in the Indian Ocean. On the face of it, that would seem unlikely, as East Indiamen rarely called there, and French ships would not have been welcome on St Helena. However, Réunion coffee was at that time being sold in significant quantities at the Cape, and there was a flourishing private trade between the island and Cape Town. It is thus perfectly possible that on this occasion coffee from Réunion did find its way to St Helena and on, via Lowe, to Longwood.

Whatever its origin, the coffee became a bone of contention as Napoleon's resentments against Lowe surfaced after his request to be able to roam unaccompanied on the island was refused. Napoleon told Las Cases after the meeting: 'What an ignoble, sinister face the Governor has . . . being left alone in the company of a man like that would be enough to put one off one's cup of coffee.' Another account has Napoleon melodramatically ordering a servant to throw the coffee out of the window after Lowe had left, convinced that it had been poisoned. Montholon reports that Lowe sent the coffee to Longwood and that the household suspected that it was poisoned, until Napoleon had it sent to the kitchen saying, 'Good coffee is a precious thing in this horrible place.' This may be the origin of the apocryphal remark often attributed to Napoleon, 'the only good thing about St Helena is the coffee'.

Whatever really happened at that fateful meeting, it is a fact that their relationship deteriorated beyond recovery, and until Napoleon's death in 1821 Lowe saw his captive only once more. It was a brief and antagonistic meeting at which the Emperor sought to provoke Lowe with insults, which he met with sullen composure. In a parody of the Latin temperament frustrated by northern implacability, Napoleon said afterwards that he wished Lowe had slammed the door when leaving.

Because Napoleon met Lowe in private, the accounts are second-hand, and even if Napoleon's comments were objectively reported, that by no means ensured their objectivity. Napoleon brazenly cheated at cards and chess, and was no less brazen when it came to manipulating opinion to his advantage. This was not idle mischief-mongering: he hoped to inflame public opinion in England concerning his treatment through the leaked reports which, remarkably, made their way to his supporters in London. The Balcombe family were banished from the island on suspicion of conveying just such secret messages. The *Remonstrance* supposedly written to Lowe by Montholon, but in fact dictated by Napoleon, was published in London in 1817 and defended by Lord Holland in the House of Lords. The Colonial Secretary, Lord Bathurst, dismissed his concerns and was criticized in the subsequent *Observations* by Napoleon, published in 1818, in which he claims that St Helena was chosen to bring about 'a death sufficiently slow to be apparently natural'.

St Helena's very isolation in the sea lane from India ensured that there were continuous comings and goings of East Indiamen, and, despite the security, intrigue was rife. Thus whilst it might be presumed that within the tiny enclave of Longwood everyone would know each other's business and that it would be easy to obtain a factual account of what happened there, in fact the reports differ widely and are frequently self-serving. Napoleon's entourage, with the honourable exception of Maréchal Bertrand, seem to have written with an eye to publication, rather than history. In any case they were infected with the pervasive melancholy of their extraordinary situation: the writers of the history of the Exile were like dying planets revolving around a star slowly collapsing in on itself.

The Exile continued, steeped in ennui. Napoleon briefly took up gardening, built a Chinese Tea House, and planted coffee bushes as the centrepiece of what became known as Marchand's Garden, outside the Emperor's bedroom. The coffee bushes wilted in the winds, and died along with Napoleon's enthusiasm and, soon after, the man himself. The cause of death is still much disputed, although stomach cancer remains the official explanation. It was recently revealed by one of her descendants that, whilst visiting the island, Mme Montholon became Napoleon's mistress and that her child, Joséphine, born on the island in 1819, was his. According to this account, when she left the island her husband administered tiny doses of arsenic to the Emperor, not in order to kill him in a jealous rage, but rather to trigger the symptoms of an illness that would require his return to Europe, thus also taking Montholon back to his errant wife: the arsenic reacted badly with other medication that Napoleon was taking and carried him off by degrees. While arsenic has indeed been found in samples of Napoleon's hair from St Helena, it also exists for unexplained reasons in samples from as early as 1805, as well as in the hair of his three sisters, which rather undermines any suspicion that Napoleon was poisoned on the island.

A few days before the end, Maréchal Bertrand recorded that Napoleon kept begging for coffee and that his new 'doctor', Antommarchi (he was in fact a dissecting room assistant), allowed him a few spoonfuls. Then, as the Emperor declined further, Bertrand writes:

> That morning, he had asked twenty times if he could be allowed some coffee. 'No, Sire'. 'Might the doctors allow me just a spoonful?' 'No, Sire, not at the moment, your stomach is too irritated, you would vomit a little earlier, perhaps.' He had already vomited perhaps nine times during the day. What a great change had overtaken him! Tears came to my eyes, seeing this formidable man, who had commanded with such authority, in a manner so absolute, beg for a spoonful of coffee, seek permission, obedient as a child, asking again and again for permission and not obtaining it, without ever losing his temper. At other times during his illness, he would have thrown his doctors out, flouted their advice and done as he wanted. Now he was as docile as a child. So, here is the great Napoleon: pitiful, humble.

Napoleon died at 5:49 in the evening on 5 May 1821 in his camp bed, which had been moved to the drawing-room at Longwood. The body was inspected by Lowe – his first sight of Napoleon for nearly five years – who asked for confirmation from one of the entourage that it was indeed who it purported to be. The autopsy was performed by Antommarchi, who at last was in his element. Five English doctors were on hand to confirm the result, which was that death had been caused by stomach cancer. One dissenter noted that the liver appeared enlarged, but Lowe excised this opinion from the final report, thus bringing into being nearly two hundred years of conspiracy theories, further fuelled by the omission of Antommarchi's signature, which he had refused to attach because the report referred to General Bonaparte, not the Emperor. Petulance and pettiness from all sides pursued Napoleon to the end, and beyond.

After the autopsy, the race was on to secure portions of Napoleon's person for posterity – even his pickled penis is proudly displayed at a museum in France. A death mask was required, and the plaster of Paris with which to make it was scarce. Dr Burton bought up all the plaster figurines of Greek goddesses, poets, composers, and other heroes that he could find in Jamestown, pounded them up, and with the resultant powder made the death mask. There is something rather satisfactory about the thought that the mould for the sole surviving image of Napoleon in death was composed of an *ad hoc* hotchpotch of gods and geniuses. The face portion of the mould was filched by Mme Bertrand, leaving Burton with a far from satisfactory back of the skull. The corpse was dressed in Napoleon's favoured dark green uniform of a colonel of the Chasseur of the Guards, and laid in state for first the dignitaries and later the general inhabitants of the island to pay their respects. For nearly everyone it was their first glimpse of the man who had spent almost six years in exile amongst them, who had dominated unseen their daily lives. The island was thrown into a turmoil of post-exile uncertainty: property prices plummeted, and a horse that would have fetched £70 when the Emperor was alive was worth only £10 now that he was dead. The island suddenly lost its unsought *raison d'être*.

The Emperor's will had directed that 'I desire that my ashes should rest on the banks of the Seine, amid the French people whom I have so loved.' However, the British considered his body to be a threat to national security: Lord Rosebery remarked that 'The arrival of a dead Napoleon in Europe would be second only in embarrassment to the arrival of the living.' So he was condemned to a further exile *post mortem*. A burial site was selected

The grim basalt cliffs of St Helena, the world's most isolated island, which is also the unlikely source of one of the world's most expensive coffees. Napoleon was exiled here in 1815.

The dramatic landscape of the Yemeni highlands where coffee was first produced on elaborate terracing in the sixteenth century. Villages are perched on the heights to leave as much cultivatable land as possible.

A crumbling merchant's villa in the formerly celebrated port of Mocha which controlled much of the world's coffee trade for two hundred years.

Painting by a Moghul artist showing Europeans, believed to be Englishmen, drinking coffee at the court in Agra.

The nearest to be found to an eighteenth century coffee house in London today, Berry Bros & Rudd in St James Street originally sold coffee, not wine.

The Green Dragon at Boston, sometimes called the headquarters of the American Revolution. The coffee house/tavern was much frequented by the early Revolutionaries, and the Boston Tea Party was plotted here.

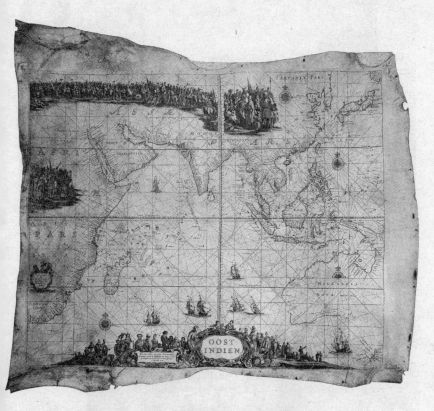

The British and Dutch Empires in the East by Pieter Goos. Such maps were intended to give general information; the actual navigators would have relied more on written directions called 'rutters'.

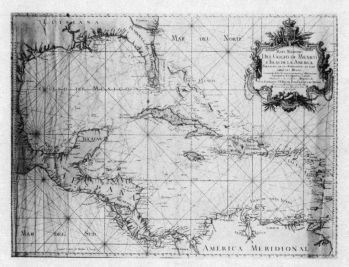

The Spanish Empire in the West. A map of the Gulf of Mexico by Thomas Lopez and Juan de la Cruz, *c.* 1755.

A box made from the iron ball attached to the ankle chains of a slave. After his emancipation, the slave remodelled it as a gift to William Wilberforce, who led the movement for abolition of the Slave Trade. The hands are those of his great-great-great-great grandson.

Napoleon's Sèvres coffee service, with pictures of Egypt by Vivant Denon. It was much commented upon by English visitors to Longwood, his house on St Helena.

The dining room at Longwood. Almost windowless, insufferably hot and plagued with rats – which the Emperor studiously ignored.

The effects of various psychoactive drugs on the web-weaving abilities of the common house spider. a) Marijuana b) Benzedrine c) Caffeine d) Chloral Hydrate. Caffeine causes the most serious impairment.

for him situated in a pretty valley close to Hutts Gate, by a spring from which he had always insisted that his personal drinking water at Longwood be drawn: coincidentally, it was called the Sane Valley. The funeral took place with all due pomp and ceremony, the route lined with every member of the 3000-man garrison. The hills resounded to the boom of cannon from ship and shore, and a band played solemn martial music. After the burial, the young willow trees surrounding the grave were stripped of leaves and twigs by souvenir hunters. The great man worked his magic from beyond the grave, and his memory was starting to be exploited.

The tomb was constantly guarded by three soldiers; as the soldier in charge reported, 'I have a sentry promenading on each side of [the grave] to catch him if he gets up.' The soldier was later to make a visit to Longwood and admired the Denon coffee service, 'the most beautiful, I suppose, that was ever made'. The significance of the crockery at Longwood should not be underestimated: the English porcelain company Wedgwood have to this day obtained considerable mileage from their 'Napoleon Ivy' porcelain set, which is one of their best selling lines. The bottom of each item is marked conspicuously with 'Napoleon Ivy. As used at St Helena 1815'. The company's own records tell a different story, however. At the request of the Prince Regent they did send to Longwood, via a government agent, their classic pale blue breakfast service and a dinner service in white and gold with each plate hand painted with an 'elegantly executed landscape of British scenery'. The latter would have been particularly galling to Napoleon as he had nursed hopes that he would be exiled to a suitably grand house in the English countryside. The tea and coffee sets that Wedgwood sent were 'embossed Vineleaf' china, a completely different design from the 'Napoleon Ivy'. There is no evidence that any of the services was ever used.

The genuine article, the Denon coffee set, now resides in the Louvre, acquired in 1950 from Princess Napoleon. Displayed in a silk-lined case, it is quite as remarkable as the contemporary descriptions suggest, although the *faux* hieroglyphs in gold against a deep lapis blue – curved ladders entwined with rope, feathers, and arrows – have a slightly comical air. The painted scenes are impeccably detailed but, surprisingly, feature more river views, mosques, and tricolour-flying forts than ancient temples. The portraits of Egyptian notables on the saucers are identified in detail: one fine gentleman is 'Muley-Palamé, frère ainé du Roi de Maroc'. A few of the cups are cracked or chipped, lending the patina of usage to the ensemble: with half-closed eyes, it is easy to imagine the guttering candles and stifling heat of the salon at Longwood, and the clatter of cup in saucer as coffee is served. Did the Emperor drink from all of these cups – or did he, like a child, have a favourite that evoked special memories – perhaps the 'Vue de Thebes' from across the river, the palm trees caught in mid sway? He could have immersed himself in the detail of the exquisite picture, a momentary escape from the Exile. He said when he first saw St Helena that he would have done better to have remained in Egypt: the Denon coffee set brought Egypt to him.

In the manner characteristic of St Helena, which wears its history with a sublime indifference, Longwood, having outlived its usefulness as a post-imperial residence, reverted to farm buildings. Just nine years after his death, it was reported that Napoleon's bedroom suite had become a home to cart horses, and that the place between the windows of the drawing-room where the Emperor had breathed his last was taken by a threshing machine. Strips of wallpaper had been torn off as relics of the Exile, and the plaster was covered with graffiti, mainly in French, commemorating the late occupant of the desolate rooms.

Napoleon's remaining entourage left the island a few weeks after the funeral on a passing cattle ship, followed by Sir Hudson

Lowe, who, though reviled by the French contingent, was fondly remembered on the island as the man who abolished slavery there. After a furore over the whipping of a young slave girl, he had quietly pointed out to the island's Council in 1818 that St Helena was the last territory in the East India Company's possession where slavery was tolerated and secured the necessary vote in favour of abolition in ten minutes flat. Not that his abolition was as dramatic as all that; in line with prevailing practice, the condition of existing slaves was to remain unchanged, but their children would be born free, although compelled to attend church and Sunday school. On leaving the island in July 1821 Lowe was presented with an address from the islanders that noted his achievement : 'A prominent measure of your Excellency's was a proposal which might have been expected to have been unpopular in a colony where slavery had long been recognized: yet, Sir, it met with the instantaneous and unanimous approbation of the inhabitants; a result which offers no slight proof of our entire confidence in your concern for our welfare.'

The new Governor, once again a Company appointee now that the Exile was ended, was a Brigadier-General Walker who, in line with his more enlightened predecessors, attempted to institute agricultural reforms, educational programmes, and other worthy works. In turn his successor, Governor Dallas, built the 900-step staircase up Ladder Hill from Jamestown that is still the single most discussed tourist attraction on the island. Mynah birds were introduced from India in 1829, eventually becoming a serious threat to fruit growers on the island.

Amidst all these parochial concerns, great events were brewing that would impact on St Helena more than anything in its history, including the Exile. The mighty East India Company was faced with enormous parliamentary opposition to the monopoly trading rights in China that gave it control of the tea trade and eventually succumbed. No longer would it enjoy sole access to

Canton; in fact, it ceased to be a trading company at all and instead became a managing agent in the Indian subcontinent on behalf of the Crown. Shares could still be bought and sold in the Company, and it was a mine of invaluable patronage; but in essence it had ceased to be what it had always been intended it should be, a commercial enterprise based on trade, becoming instead what it had always disavowed, a territorial power. As part of the deal, in 1834 the island of St Helena passed from Company to Crown control. Whereas the Indian subcontinent was to be governed by a Company no longer interested in trade – what Macaulay called 'the strangest of all governments . . . designed for the strangest of all empires' – St Helena was to be brought under conventional Crown colonial control. This was a seismic event in the island's life, and one which still resounds today. The £90,000 annual subsidy the island received from the Company largely evaporated; salaries were slashed; generous Company pensions were crudely culled; and soldiers and civil servants were dismissed. This ruthless cost cutting had a devastating knock-on effect throughout the island's economy, and the inhabitants were reduced from relative prosperity to penury at the stroke of a pen. The Company, in a manner reminiscent of modern corporate practice, denied any responsibility for its former servants and directed all complaints to the Crown, where they fell on deaf ears. The Crown, meantime, regarded the position of the Governor of St Helena as an opportunity to reward superannuated servicemen with a comfortable berth, and Plantation House was from then on treated to a succession of crusty colonels and apathetic admirals who were not expected to evince much interest in the island's affairs.

The poverty was apparent to Charles Darwin, who stopped by in the *Beagle* in 1836. With characteristic zeal, he conducted an in-depth survey of the island's flora and fauna in the six days he remained there. Strangely, he failed to spot the unique wire bird, the island's only endemic bird. However, he did note that many of the newly emancipated slaves had borne the brunt of the new government's parsimony, which had left them unemployed and extremely poor. Ironically, while its own freed slaves were suffering severe hardships, the island itself was becoming an operations centre for anti-slave trade activities. A Vice-Admiralty Court was established and Royal Navy men-of-war plied the West African coast apprehending slaving vessels and bringing them to St Helena, where the owners would be tried, the vessels broken up, and the slaves fed and clothed at the 'Liberated African Depot' in Rupert's Valley. Once recovered – and the condition that they arrived in was frequently so appalling that many did not survive – the slaves were shipped out to the West Indies or to British Guiana, where there were employment opportunities for them. Some ten thousand slaves passed through the depot before the naval squadron left in 1864. This anti-slavery activity had one devastating consequence for the island: a Brazilian slave boat was brought to the island in 1840, duly broken up, and the timbers stored in a lumberyard in Jamestown. They were infested with white ants, a particularly persistent termite that proceeded over the next fifty years to devour the island. They started first with books, especially the theological works in the Public Library (on account of the fact, said the cynics, that they were the least read), but eventually the beams in all the houses of Jamestown were infested, and the town collapsed as if struck by an earthquake. Even the Castle fell to their predations and had to be entirely rebuilt. The ants spread gradually into the countryside, devastating both buildings and live trees.

10

SLAVERY, BRAZIL, AND COFFEE

Brazil had long been one of the principal outlets for the traffic of slaves to the Americas. Indeed, as it was a Portuguese colony, the Brazilian requirements of the Atlantic trade were mainly met by Portuguese slavers operating out of Angola and, later, from round the Cape at Mozambique. As Angola lay to the south of their favoured slave ports, it was rarely frequented by English, French, Dutch, or American slave ships, and thus the Portuguese trade was relatively self-contained, and even had its own patron saint, St Joseph. The notorious slave-holding sheds, the 'barracoons' of Luanda, were operated by Portuguese who had taken up permanent residence on that coast. From the outset the number of slaves involved was enormous. The colony of Brazil had been established by the Portuguese as a result of the Treaty of Tordesillas in 1494, which followed hot on the heels of Columbus's discovery of the New World. This sweeping treaty was a sublime example of the vaunting ambition of the early Catholic colonial mindset, and was to have far-reaching consequences. The issue was simple: how to divide up the planet between the rival interests of the Spanish and the Portuguese. The determination made by Pope Alexander VI was signed at Tordesillas, an otherwise unremarkable town in northern Spain. A line of longitude was drawn 100 leagues west of the Azores; Portugal was allocated everything to the east of it, Spain everything to the west. Thus when da Gama hoved to off Calicut on the coast of India in 1498, it was because the Portuguese had been permitted by the treaty further to pursue their exploration of the Indian Ocean in pursuit of 'Christians and spices'. The conquests of the Aztecs by Cortés in 1521 and the Incas by Pizarro in 1532 were likewise the result of Spain paying scrupulous attention to their treaty obligations. Inevitably, the wording of the treaty had not been drafted with a fully rounded vision of the world, so that by 1543 Spain had sailed west through the Magellan Straits and claimed the Philippines, a few hundred miles north of the Spice Islands that the Portuguese had gained after sailing east.

Brazil was discovered by Pedro Cabral in 1500, six years after the treaty. It fell within the Portuguese hemisphere of influence, and the indigenous Indians there suffered the dubious pleasure of Portuguese colonial custom as a result: of the seven million originally to be found as few as two hundred thousand survive, driven ever deeper into what remains of the Amazon jungle. Although the Portuguese were slow to colonize the interior, the coast of Brazil soon saw the introduction of sugar and slavery, and by 1820 there were an estimated two million slaves in the country, whose average life expectancy once having arrived was a mere seven years. The entire population of Brazil was at that date around four million. With Portugal maintaining a tight colonial grip on the traffic, and taxing every slave sold in Brazil, the home country had also become increasingly dependent on the revenues that the slave trade brought. As the merchants from Bahia wrote to the King in defence of the trade: 'Any objections to the slave trade are attacks on the population, the commerce and the income of Your Majesty.'

In 1822, Dom Pedro, the son of the King of Portugal who had fled to Brazil in 1807 from Napoleon's invading army, declared the country independent of his homeland and himself its Emperor. Ironically, this revolution was itself inspired by the influence of Napoleon, and the success of revolutionary France which had led to many of the colonial regimes in South America seeking their freedom from the European yoke. The exiled French Emperor had often mused on the possibility of leading a Latin American Revolution. He had long considered that colonialism was doomed to failure, and had written to the Legislature in 1809: 'The Emperor will never oppose the Independence of the continental nations of America . . . Whether the people of Mexico and of Peru should wish to remain united with the motherland, or whether they should wish to elevate themselves to the height of a noble independence, France will never oppose their desires – provided that these people do not form any relation with England.'

In 1831 Pedro abdicated in favour of his young son, who was proclaimed Pedro II in 1840, the same year that the captured Brazilian slave boat introduced white ants to St Helena. That island's position in the South Atlantic made it uniquely well placed for the interception of slave boats from the Angolan coast bound for Brazil.

Although Brazil had nominally banned the slave trade in 1831, in fact it continued unabated, and the activities of the slave port of Rio de Janeiro gained further impetus from the introduction of coffee growing in the nearby Paraiba Valley in the southeast of the country. Brazilians are fond of recounting a romantic tale concerning the introduction of coffee to their country – so romantic, indeed, that it eschews any pretence of fact. According to this account, French Guiana and Dutch Guiana, neighbours on the South American coast east of Venezuela, each grew some coffee but jealously prohibited the export of seed to their neighbour, or indeed to anywhere else. During a border dispute between the two colonies, a Brazilian diplomat, Francisco de Mello Palheta, was asked to arbitrate: the wife of the French Governor fell for him and, after a passionate affair, she gave him a bouquet as a parting gift that contained a number of ripe coffee cherries from which sprang the entire, fabulous, world-beating Brazilian coffee industry. It is remarkable how coffee mythology repeats the same themes, in this and the stories of Gabriel de Clieu and Babu Budan, of insuperable obstacles being overcome by wily outsiders leading to the triumph of coffee in a particular country. The addition of sex to the tale is a typically Brazilian contribution, but overall it is no more credible in this case than in the others. More prosaically, coffee was in fact introduced to Brazil in 1774 by a Franciscan friar, José Mariano da Conceição Veloso, who received the seeds from a Dutch friend, a Mr Hoppman. He planted them in the garden of St Anthony's monastery.

Romance aside, the harsh reality was that the world's greatest coffee economy was founded on the continuation of slavery long after it had been banned in Europe. Brazil only definitively banned slavery only in 1888. The impact on the coffee economy was enormous. As one Member of Parliament was to say in 1880: 'Brazil is coffee, and coffee is the negro.' However, at the beginning of the nineteenth century Brazil's economy had been based on sugar, so much so that it was said that 'sugar talked Portuguese'. It was Napoleon's discovery of the uses of sugar beet during the era of the Continental System that had successfully freed the world from the domination of tropically grown sugar cane. The less successful substitution of chicory for coffee failed to effect such a liberation for caffeine consumers, and it was the growing demand for coffee that suggested to Brazilian plantation owners that the move should be made from sugar to coffee. Whereas sugar had been grown principally in the north-east around Bahia, coffee flourished in the more moderate climate of the south. The over-exploitation of the land in the cane plantations had exhausted the soil, and so planters and their slaves relocated like a swarm of locusts to the area with the fabled *terra roxa* north of Rio. This purplish virgin earth had grown rich with millennia of forest humus: naturally, the first step was to clear the trees. Thus began a version on an industrial scale of traditional 'slash and burn' farming – forest clearance and the *roca* (burning) – followed by massive coffee planting, with the nutrients in the earth gradually depleted and dramatic soil erosion. Once the capacity of the land to recover was exhausted, it was abandoned and the process started once again. With small-scale slash-and-burn activity the surrounding natural environment quickly re-encroaches on the cleared land, which can then recuperate. By contrast, as operated by nineteenth-century Brazilian coffee farmers, the economies of scale went hand in hand with the inevitability of widespread environmental devastation.

Coffee harvesting requires considerable manpower. Deploying slave labour on a continental landmass, it was possible for Brazilians to farm coffee on a scale hitherto unimaginable. Vast *fazendas* covering tens of square miles stretched out over the hills, the endless rows of coffee bushes giving the impression that the entire landscape had been passed over by a gigantic rake. The plantations were unrelieved by shade trees as the local climate did not necessitate the protection that coffee bushes usually required.

The sheer size of these plantations, combined with the slave labour prohibited elsewhere, made Brazilian coffee unbeatably competitive internationally. In addition, the rapid introduction under Pedro II of the essential infrastructure of a modern economy – roads, railways, ports – made the distribution and export of the country's vast coffee production cheap and efficient. Technology also helped ensure the adequate provision of slaves – the first steam slave ship crossed the Atlantic in 1848 to Angola. Brazil was seen as a safe investment by the burgeoning international banking community: the railways, for example, were financed by Barings Bank of London. The wealth generated by coffee was substantial. Slave-owning plantation owners were often fabulously rich, and inclined to inflict horrific suffering on their slaves: unremitting labour, near starvation, cruel punishments, murder and unrecorded deaths, rape, torture, sexual orgies . . . Children, too, worked on the plantations. The Brazilians had previously subscribed to the theory that it was cheaper to import new slaves than to allow the raising of 'home grown' ones. With the realization that 'children of a very young age can go and pick coffee' the view shifted, and increasingly slaves were able to marry and raise children. Child labour remains a problem issue in the coffee industry to this day.

When slavery was finally abolished in 1888, the ban was politically acceptable to the plantation owners only when it became apparent that the slaves could be replaced by cheap immigrant European labour, particularly from Southern Italy. The fall in the value of the real eased the transition from slave to paid labour. Powered by vast plantations, the Brazilian coffee industry has until today remained hugely competitive, and although it is not immune to the vagaries of the markets – at one stage even its trains were fuelled by surplus coffee beans – its terrain has meant that new innovations such as mechanical harvesting have kept costs down. At its height, in the decade before the First World War, coffee represented 90 per cent of Brazil's gross domestic product, with most of it being exported to the USA and, to a lesser extent, Germany. It produced ten times as much coffee as its then nearest competitor, Venezuela, and at its height had as much as 90 per cent of the world market. Upon the foundations of slave labour Brazil developed its unassailable position in the coffee world, and its delay in freeing the slaves – it was the last country in the western hemisphere to do so – maximized the period in which the production of coffee could be increased at a low cost. The legacy is a coffee industry where the economies of scale can still be deployed to full advantage.

11

THE GREAT EXHIBITION

In 1840 the English finally agreed that it was safe for Napoleon to go home. The exhumation on St Helena was a solemn affair: it began at midnight on the exact anniversary of Napoleon's arrival on the island twenty-five years earlier, by torchlight in torrential rain. The stone slabs, cement, and other obstacles were removed by soldiers, and eventually the glint of mahogany was visible. It was by then full daylight. When the coffin was opened, Napoleon's body was perfectly preserved, and the onlookers were moved to observe that he appeared more, rather than less, lifelike than when they had last seen him. In death, he had grown stubble and long fingernails.

The body was taken to Paris, where it now lies in six coffins in a monumental sarcophagus of Finnish red porphyry in the crypt of the Church of the Dome, surrounded by weeping generals and sculpted plaques celebrating his victories. A Messianic cult had grown up around the dead Emperor. Writers and artists frequently commemorated him in a way that was frankly idolatrous. The writer Honoré de Balzac, whose other distinction was the consumption of sixty cups of coffee a day, wrote *Le Médecin de campagne* in which Napoleon was compared on equal terms to Jesus. The return of the Emperor was not simply a major event in the national psyche of France, but also in that of countries such as Poland, which chose to elevate him as the sacred liberator of their homeland from the Russian yoke.

In a muted, but nonetheless powerful form, the cult of Napoleon still exists. Every year an official service is held to commemorate the anniversary of Napoleon's death in the church of St Louis in Les Invalides: a reminder of how revered the Emperor still is even in the Third Republic. At the front the seats are reserved, rather poignantly, for 'Famille'. Against the outside wall of the church a little memorial garden has been built incorporating the two great gravestones, railed around and planted with willows to 'evoke' the tomb as it first was when he was buried on St Helena.

As a result of the Napoleonic connection, the island had achieved a measure of celebrity and its cottage coffee industry enjoyed a brief renaissance. The owner of the estate at Bamboo Hedge, G. W. Alexander, sent a sample to a coffee broker in London, William Burnie & Co., who pronounced it 'of a very superior quality and flavour' and suggested that it might fetch as much as £7 per hundredweight. Encouraged by the potential of 'a very valuable and secure source of income', Alexander increased the area under cultivation, and by 1845 was able to achieve the highest price of any coffee on the London market by a penny per pound. In 1851 a Mr Magnus entered his St Helena coffee into competition at the Great Exhibition in the specially constructed Crystal Palace in Hyde Park. It was exhibited amidst exotic displays gathered from all around the world, including the Koh-i-noor diamond recently taken as war reparations from the Sikhs and presented to Queen Victoria. Other curious exhibits included an expanding pianoforte for use on yachts and artificial teeth carved from hippopotamus ivory.

The Great Exhibition of the Works of Industry of All Nations was one of High Victorian Utilitarianism's crowning achievements, and its catalogue and accompanying Report of the Juries provide a compendium of the labyrinthine workings of the imperial mind. Although the Exhibition was the brainchild of Prince

Albert, the overall jury Chairman was Viscount Canning, who presided over a council consisting of the chairmen of the numerous juries judging the myriad categories. The chairmen could award the Council Medal to an exhibitor, the highest accolade. Individual juries could award Prize Medals or Honourable Mentions. Coffee came under the class 'Substances used in the Preparation of Drinks', which had six jury members. The Chairman of that class was Edward de Lode. His reports on behalf of the jury reveal that they were required to make an assessment of curiosities such as 'Dr Gardner's Prepared Coffee Leaves', 'worthy of note, as affording a really palatable drink when infused as tea is . . . but as the leaves can only be collected in as good state, at the expense of the bush, it is doubtful whether the coffee produced by the berries be not after all the cheapest, as it is certainly the best.'

The jury were disappointed by the deficiency of coffee specimens from the most important producing countries, but acknowledged that there were 'some of excellent description from British Colonies, which have never before been known to produce this article'. A sample of Borneo coffee from Sarawak was submitted and was awarded a Prize Medal 'for its great superiority in colour and weight. It is the first sample from that country ever seen by the Jury.' 'Norfolk Island sends an excellent sample of coffee, apparently of the Berbera variety; it is of good colour, well-adapted for roasting, and is a most desirable novelty . . .' As indeed it would be today, if it still exists. Berbera is an ancient port on the African coast of the Red Sea. The report also mentions that 'The native, wild, or indigenous coffee of Ceylon is also exhibited, which, like the wild plant of Bengal is of no value' – which aside is enough to give coffee historians sleepless nights.

'Portugal sends a very valuable series of coffees from various of her colonies: of ordinary description from ST THOMAS; tolerably good from the CAPE DE VERDE ISLANDS; bad from

TIMOR; and excellent from Madeira.' Other than Timor, these coffees are virtually unknown today.

The home team comes in for some severe criticism. 'The samples of Aden coffee contributed by the HONOURABLE EAST INDIA COMPANY are not superior . . . the specimens are dirty, and not sufficiently garbelled [picked]. Aden, alias Mocha coffee, is along with the other coffees of the Red Sea, sent first to Bombay, by Arab ships, where it is "garbelled", previously to it being exported to England. The bean is always broad and small, and the climate of India is supposed to improve its flavour.' This bears out reports that from the earliest days of the trade the usual route for coffee shipped by the Company was from Mocha to Bombay, thence to England. The practice of 'monsooning' Indian coffee to simulate the effect of the long sea voyage may have arisen as a result of the improvement of flavour noted here.

Amidst this glamorous competition appears 'ST HELENA – There is an excellent sample of coffee from this island, from a private Garden of Mr S. Magnus of which Honourable Mention is made.' As Honourable Mentions are made of a good quarter of the exhibits, this is not a spectacular coup for the island, but a solid endorsement nonetheless. The coffee fared better than its other entry: 'St Helena contributes Snuff-boxes made from the willow-tree under which the remains of the great Napoleon rested until their removal to France . . .'

As well as giving the British an opportunity to demonstrate how advanced they were in matters of agriculture, commerce, engineering, and manufactures, the Great Exhibition marked a significant shift in the psyche of the nation, then in possession of the greatest empire the world had ever seen. New, heavily mech-anized ways of producing goods and distributing them had been invented, and the Empire provided a vast market for these goods as well as a cheap source of raw materials. Britain had become the world's pre-eminent economic power. That wealth was conceived of as a sign of God's beneficence, a divine pat on the head for a job well done. God had been transplanted almost unnoticed from the Church to the Temple of Mammon. He still presided over Creation, but mankind had dutifully taken on many of the more practical tasks. The simple plough-the-fields-and-scatter days were giving way to the Modern Age of hissing steam engines and roaring foundries. Entire structures such as bridges could be fabricated in iron and shipped in pieces to their unseen, faraway destinations. Consumer products poured off production lines in unheard-of volumes. In the commercial hierarchy, coffee was still an old-fashioned tropical commodity harvested by hand that could be judged (as it was at the Exhibition) in the raw, with little standing between the bean and the natural processes that had produced it. The Exhibition was a harbinger of what lay in wait for coffee when the industrial and marketing might of the twentieth century was brought to bear on it.

With the Honourable Mention to encourage it, St Helena went through one of its periodic spurts of activity as landowners decided to plant coffee, although as the island's newspaper reported, 'the reason why coffee is not cultivated on a much larger scale by landowners is . . . a want of means'. Nonetheless it seems that some enterprising coffee farmer found a market for his produce in the salons of Paris, cashing in on the Napoleonic connection after Longwood became a French property. In France, St Helena coffee was considered 'to be equal if not superior to the best Mocha' and commanded a price of 1s. 6d. a pound (slightly more than the Burnie valuation). This represented a small premium on the prevailing market price of coffee at that time, sufficient, it was hoped, to encourage immigration to the island of planters with some capital. However, in 1871 the administration was found to be heavily in debt, and the island on the verge of bankruptcy. Expenditure was cut by pensioning off many government workers with a flat

£1500, and they promptly used the money to emigrate. The loss of capital and labour was near catastrophic, and many settlers likewise left for home or the Cape of Good Hope. The development of coffee plantations was thereby stopped in its tracks, and by 1883 the horticulturalist Dr Daniel Moriss, later to be knighted as Director of Kew Gardens, saw 'very fine patches of coffee', although 'somewhat neglected', growing at a number of locations on the island, including Plantation House. He thought the island was capable of producing 'a fair quantity of very fine coffee'. The observation was accurate, but on St Helena the problem had always been acting on potential. Eventually there was one plant, flax, introduced in 1874, that became the island's staple crop. For the first time the government developed a lasting enthusiasm for an agricultural project, and the income of sorts that it generated. Nearly all thoughts of coffee were set aside in the scramble for flax planting. The coffee trees were neglected, seldom picked, and no one on the island drank such coffee as they produced.

In 1876 Arthur Rimbaud, ex-poet and soon-to-be coffee trader, put in at Jamestown on board a Scottish ship, the *Wandering Chief*. He had come from Java, having enlisted with the Dutch army as a mercenary to fight in their colonial war against Achin, a war which had been predicted by the writer Multatuli in *Max Havelaar, or the Coffee Auctions of the Dutch Trading Company*. Rimbaud had no sooner landed than he deserted, obtaining a passage home on the Scottish ship by pretending to be a sailor. The *Wandering Chief* had been dismasted at the Cape in a storm and, like many before it, had limped to St Helena for repairs. As the penniless Rimbaud did not have the £1 landing fee required, he covertly swam to the shore and made his way up to Longwood, where he is said to have signed the Visitors' Book, although it has since disappeared. There is no record that he knew anything about the island's coffee, but within a few years he might have appreciated its history at least: the Harar coffees in which he was to trade were the linear forbears of the Yemeni stock from which St Helena's coffee was derived. Thus the 22-year-old Rimbaud paid an illicit visit to the former home-in-exile of his country's most successful imperial ruler while on the run from another country's colonial war, which had been predicted in a campaigning work concerning a fictional coffee trader – a career he was shortly to adopt in reality. And, unknown to him, the breezes that buffeted him at Longwood secretly carried the scent of coffee blossom drawn from the same genetic stock he would come to know so well. The strangeness of this concatenation of events would not have eluded France's finest symbolist poet, who had explored and popularized synaesthesia – a rare neurological condition causing the sufferer to hear colours, taste shapes, and other sensory blendings – as an aesthetic form. His part in the weaving of coffee's fine web through history, botany, and empire around the world might have pleased him.

12

HARAR AND RIMBAUD: THE CRADLE AND THE CRUCIBLE

empereur, vieille démangeaison, tu es nègre . . .
('emperor, old itch, you are a negro . . .')

RIMBAUD, *Une Saison en enfer* (A Season in Hell)

The only certain things in this world are coincidences.

LEONARDO SCIASCIA

Rimbaud must surely be a suitable anti-hero for a dark history of coffee. He crops up in three of the obscure outposts that feature in the story – St Helena, Batavia, and Harar, the cradle of coffee itself. And, improbably, he became a coffee trader, making him history's one and only celebrity coffee merchant. Above all, his dark, restless, visionary nature could have been born in the same crucible that brought forth the mysterious alchemy of coffee. Napoleon, all high deeds and daring, has been our hero thus far, with coffee running like a trapped nerve through his Empire and Exile. Rimbaud, inspired and deranged, is his polar opposite, but voluntarily chose the same exile's fate.

By giving up the giddy success of his literary career at the age of twenty, Rimbaud achieved the kind of immortality usually granted to the prematurely deceased. The great puzzles have always been why did he do it, and is there any glimmering in his subsequent career of the incandescent genius that characterized his youth? It has been suggested that his renunciation was an act of supreme arrogance, in that he believed himself to have already accomplished everything that he was capable of. The bulk of his writings after 1875 consists of letters to his family, often on the subject of money, and business correspondence, which are fascinating only because they have no literary merit whatsoever: it is as if he had deliberately excised that aspect of his sensibility.

Rimbaud has been the single most influential figure on late twentieth-century rock lyrics, and his practice of the 'derangement of the senses' found obvious, if rather crass, parallels in the drug culture associated with the music business. Bob Dylan's post-Newport sixties lyrics owe much to the poet, and Jim Morrison virtually recreated himself in his image, both as a lyricist and in terms of his Dionysian excess. Patti Smith also acknowledges a debt. Rimbaud has been more written about than any other French nineteenth-century writer, and the loyalty of his fans is legendary: some have so desired to emulate their hero that they have sought to have a leg amputated in Marseilles, a fate that he suffered shortly before his death.

Rimbaud was born in a provincial town in northern France in 1854. His father was a soldier who abandoned his family, whilst his mother was of stern, bourgeois Catholic stock. The young Arthur excelled at school, where he was considered an exemplary pupil, although one astute master noted that his angelic looks and penetrating light-blue eyes could not conceal a character that could all too easily run to the bad. Which, indeed, it proceeded to do, spectacularly, even within the terms of his less conventional contemporaries, who considered his violent affair at the age of seventeen with the older fellow-poet Paul Verlaine utterly scandalous. This was accompanied by rude, boorish, lecherous and drunken behaviour on an operatic scale, which made his society intolerable to most. However to some, such as Verlaine, he was a magnificent poet and a volcanic creative force. Rimbaud believed that the poet could fulfil his function as a seer only by the derangement of the senses, and absinthe was generally the preferred agent. This in turn led to his interest in synaesthesia: his celebrated poem 'Vowel' assigns a colour to each vowel in the text, and he played compositions on the piano in which he ascribed a colour to each note of a chromatic scale. These experiments, along with his urgent, vivid, non-rhyming prose-poetry, came to influence a whole generation of French painters and writers alike.

Rimbaud was first published at the age of fifteen, but *A Season in Hell*, the work for which he is best known, was written at the age of eighteen in the aftermath of his estrangement from Verlaine, who, having tried and failed to strangle his wife, had abandoned her to live with Rimbaud in London. They fell out over a herring, Verlaine went back to the continent to attempt a reconciliation with his wife, Rimbaud followed and Verlaine shot him in the hand, leading to his imprisonment and Rimbaud's desolate *A Season in Hell*. For a young man whose life to date, although not without incident, had been steadfastly European, the poem displays a vivid fascination with the desert, the tropics and negritude, written in the hallucinatory Orientalist style of a spiritually bankrupt proto-Kurtz. It is an extraordinary, visionary masterpiece.

He then travelled around Europe a great deal, often penniless, often on foot. Between 1873 and 1875 he wrote poems and reflections on his travels that were later published at the instigation of Verlaine under the title *Illuminations*. After these he wrote no more. To have retired so finally from creative life at the age of twenty must be something of a record. The rest of Rimbaud's life has been the object of fascination for his admirers and biographers alike, but from a literary standpoint it is like trying to identify an aeroplane by the trail it has left when it has long disappeared over the horizon. As we have seen, he spent a month in Batavia before his desertion in 1876, and subsequently visited Longwood. He went to Cyprus, Hamburg, and, bafflingly, Scarborough. He helped his family repair their house in Roche: he wanted to become a practical man, to turn his back on what he had so forcefully expressed in *A Season in Hell*.

> *J'ai horreur de tous les métiers. Maîtres ou ouvriers,*
> *tous paysans, ignobles.*
> (I have a horror of all metiers. Bosses and workers,
> all peasants, abject.)

In 1880 he moved to Aden from Cyprus and was taken on by a Lyons-based coffee trading company, Mazeran, Viannay, Bardey et Compagnie. His role was humble, sorting and packing coffee bales, and so was his salary, but he impressed M. Bardey enough to be appointed to the new office that he had just opened in Harar. Rimbaud, prone to exaggerate his importance, wrote home to his family that he would make 2 per cent commission on all trade that he managed there – in the event his contract gave him 1 per cent. After a twenty-day journey from the coast, he arrived in Harar in November 1880.

The high country around the city of Harar was home to the strain of coffee that had found its way to the new coffee cultures of the Red Sea, from Mocha to Mecca and thence to Cairo. Harar is the only walled city in Ethiopia. It is likely that it was founded in the seventh century by immigrants from the Hadramaut. By the tenth century the ancient ports of Zeila and Berbera were export-ing many slaves to Arabia, with Harar the chief inland entrepôt. The city had become the capital of the Muslim state of Adal, which co-existed uneasily with the Christian Ethiopians and the Oromo tribe to the west. It was considered the fourth city of Islam after Mecca, Medina, and Jerusalem.

The city's walls contained the one-storey buildings that housed everything from the slave marts to the palace. Outside, the hyenas gathered nightly for the day's rubbish to be fed to them. As an Arab enclave between the tribes whose people were enslaved and the hostile deserts leading to the Red Sea port of Zeila whence they were exported, Harar was perfectly placed as a slaving entrepôt. It has been suggested that the very existence of coffee plants in Harar was a result of the slave trade: the Oromo, in whose tribal lands in the Western Highlands coffee first grew wild, were particular favourites of the Arab slavers. These were the same Oromo who traditionally used coffee in their blood-brotherhood ceremonies, and whom the eighteenth-century explorer James Bruce observed eating 'the berries of the Coffee tree *roasted* and *pulverised*, which they mix with grease', rolled into a ball and kept for use on long journeys. One ball, he said, 'will support them for a whole day'. The slave trails from the west to Harar are supposedly dotted with coffee plants that have grown up as a result of the detritus of that energy food. This fails to take into account the fact that the beans were roasted and ground before being mixed with the butter, which would have destroyed their ability to germinate. It may have been that the Oromo had simply carried coffee cherries with them to eat, spitting out the beans as they were led by the slavers to Harar, and from these fertile seeds coffee trees found their way to the region.

Harar remained a remarkably closed city, unknown to Europeans until the visit of the explorer Richard Burton in 1855, who commented on the coffee plants growing in the area and on the continuing slave trade. He had an audience with the Emir, who 'did not disdain to be indoctrinated with the principles of free trade in coffee and cotton'. After ten days he returned to Berbera on the coast, his journey 'a mere adventure of uncommon hardships'. It was the difficulty of this journey from Harar to the Red Sea ports that may have first inspired the planting of coffee in Yemen: the trail across the deserts crosses some of the most hostile areas of Africa. The Danakil tribe in particular were feared for their habit of wearing the dried testicles of those they had killed strung on a necklace.

Things had not changed much when Rimbaud arrived twenty-five years later. He soon slipped into the boredom that bedevilled him, dreaming of going to Panama to assist with the canal project and complaining that the weather was 'grumpy and humid' and that the work he did was 'absurd and mind-numbing'; he concluded that 'existence in general is absurd'. His notes and letters concerning the details of the trade in coffee bear more than a passing resemblance to those of Francis Dickinson at Mocha 150 years previously. He went back to Aden in December 1881, writing that he would probably never return to Harar. He spent his time dealing almost exclusively in 'moka', which term, in continuation of the tradition, referred equally to coffee from Yemen or Ethiopia. He found the work, 'slaving away like a donkey', so boring that he feared he might become a complete idiot. So boring, in fact, that he soon signed a new contract to go back to Harar, where he mounted further expeditions: his report on a trip to the Ogaden was published by the Society of Geography in Paris in 1884. On one trip to the Galla tribe, he was served green coffee beans cooked in butter, and on another had to take coffee with the Sultan of Zeila, Mohammed Abou-Becker, whose permission he required in order to travel in the area. The Sultan was also a brigand with a particular interest in raiding European caravans, which naturally failed to endear him to the coffee merchant. He summoned coffee by clapping his hands for a servant, 'who [came] running from the next straw hut to bring *el boun,* the coffee'. Although he does not describe the brewing method, it is likely at that time to have been the steeped, roasted bean. Rimbaud's travels, following on those of Burton and Bruce in the same regions, exposed him to the various, possibly ancient uses of coffee. He was in this sense an explorer of coffee's mysterious origins as well as a dealer in its daily delights.

Rimbaud also started taking photographs with equipment sent out from France, and tried the local *qat*, which he found unremarkable. But again he became bored: 'Alas! What is the use of these comings and goings, and this tiredness and these adventures among strange races, and these languages of which the memory is filled, and these troubles without name . . . But who knows how long can last my days in these mountains? And I could disappear in the middle of these tribes, without the news ever coming out of it.' In the meantime, the Egyptians, who had been occupying Ethiopia since 1875, withdrew and the country fell increasingly into chaos. European imperial interests were creating tensions that could be felt even in remote Harar. He returned once more to Aden, where he bought coffee for the company, spending an average of 200,000 francs a month. It is rumoured that he had installed an Abyssinian mistress in his house. As usual he started planning to travel to other countries with a brighter future: India, Tonkin, and Panama (again) all make an appearance in the same letter home. Soon, Rimbaud decided that he would probably do better as an arms dealer, supplying guns to Menelik, King of Shoa, who was fighting the Abyssinian Emperor, Johannes. The French backed Menelik, mainly because the British were backing – and arming – the incumbent. Rimbaud teamed up with two other French partners, one of whom promptly died of cancer and the other of a stroke. Menelik gave him a poor price for the arms, and Rimbaud spent most of the proceeds paying off the creditors of his deceased partners. This is not uncharacteristic; he was known as an honest, hard-working, scrupulous trader, and was generous to the poor while living a relatively austere existence himself. His two years in the arms business were unprofitable for Rimbaud, but the triumph of Menelik ensured Ethiopia's independence during the European scramble for Africa, and brought honours to Rimbaud's Swiss engineer friend from Aden, Alfred Ilg, who became Menelik's Prime Minister. Rimbaud returned to Harar, and in 1890 started to receive letters from literary circles in Paris addressed 'Dear Poet!' His reputation was growing, but this was of no interest to Rimbaud. He was the 'négociant français' in Harar, dealing in coffee, gums, ivory, musk, textiles, saucepans, helmets and occasionally arms. His connection with Ilg, and hence with the court of the new Emperor Menelik II, seems to have been good for business. However, he did not retain a high degree of respect for the coffee he sold – in a series of letters to Ilg he variously refers to 'this scum known as coffee', 'this damned coffee', and 'this filth mixed with the scrapings of the floors of Harari houses'. Nonetheless his letters and accounts show that he remained active in the trade.

Since the publication of *Illuminations* (1886) his writing had been confined to his letters, many of which were to his mother and sister Isabelle. They are much concerned with money, as he was remitting some of his income to the household in France, with the climate of 'ce satané pays', and with complaints of daily life and health: 'As for Harar, there is no consul, no police station, no road. One gets there by camel, and one lives exclusively amongst the negroes. But one is free, and the climate is good.'

However his health deteriorated greatly, and the flaring up of a congenital cancer of the knee led to his painful departure from Harar, hauled by stretcher on the twelve-day journey across the desert to Zeila on the Red Sea coast. He saw a doctor in Aden who advised his immediate return to France, where, in the faintest of echoes of the fate he forecast for himself in *A Season in Hell*, he was nursed by his sister Isabelle through his final illness, including the amputation of his leg, in Marseilles.

I will come back with limbs of iron, with dark skin, and angry eyes: in this mask, they will think I belong to a strong race. I will have gold: I will be brutal and indolent. Women nurse these ferocious invalids come back from the tropics. I will become involved in politics. Saved.

Saved, he was not, at least physically. He died in 1891 at the age of 37 – the same as that of his great follower, Jim Morrison. In Harar, the hyenas still prowl without the city walls, but the coffee trade as a whole has lost most of the romance it may once have had. No longer is it steeped in obscure origins, strange discoveries, and shady deals in sunny places: in the twentieth century coffee entered the modern world, packed, packaged, branded, and marketed in line with almost all other consumer goods. It kept step with the spirit of the century, marching with soldiers into war, following peacekeepers into occupation, tempting consumers from supermarket shelves, enticing them into franchised bars. It needled the ambitions of the new middle classes, fuelled baby boomers' business plans, and fell into the clutches of a handful of transnationals who bent it to their will. Those who actually produced coffee were somehow left behind, as, by the end of the twentieth century, coffee had been commoditized and corporatized as only the West knew how.

13

MODERN TIMES

The main obstacle preventing coffee becoming a fully signed-up member of the consumer society was packaging. As long as coffee had to be distributed in green form, to be roasted in small batches for a local market, it could never become the plaything of big business. However, the technical issues surrounding roasting and packaging of coffee were surprisingly difficult to solve.

There are a number of machines for industrial coffee roasting, usually depending on the scale of the operation. The most common amongst specialized roasters – who do not necessarily want to turn out vast amounts of a homogenized blend but need to roast smaller quantities of a large variety of coffees – is the drum roaster. This resembles a large-scale tumbler drier, usually heated by gas from below, with a cooling tray in front into which the hot beans pour after the hinged front of the roaster is opened. The unroasted green coffee is first blown through metal tubes into a hopper above the roaster, passing en route through a de-stoner which removes extraneous material by suction. When the required temperature – about 220 degrees centigrade – is reached, the coffee is dropped from the hopper into the roasting drum, which rotates both to ensure an even distribution of the heat on to the metal drum and to make sure the surface of the beans never stays in contact with the hot metal for longer than a few moments. The coffee takes about ten minutes to roast. The colour of the beans is usually assessed by the man in charge of the roaster, who decides by eye against a sample when the coffee is sufficiently roasted to achieve the desired colour. This decision is both critical and difficult: it is impossible to cease the roasting process immediately, as the heat of the coffee beans persists after they spill into the cooling tray. This tray is a large circular dish of perforated metal through which cool air from the factory is drawn down by powerful pumps. Metal paddles circulate the beans, ensuring that they all cool at the same rate. The craft of the man in charge of the roaster is revealed only when the beans are finally cooled to room temperature: if he has calculated correctly, they should now be the colour that was originally intended. The judgement is anticipatory, and highly skilled. In eighteenth-century Paris, there were reckoned to be only two men capable of properly roasting coffee, and although the technology has evolved, the basic principle of a rotating drum over a source of heat remains essentially the same.

During roasting, a series of complex chemical reactions take place that develop the characteristic coffee aroma and flavour. Most visible of the results is the change in size – roughly double – caused by the action of interior water on the cell structure of the bean – and the change in colour from light green to brown, the result of the caramelization of sugars from broken-down carbohydrates. The most important change takes place when the interior of the bean becomes hot; by a process known as pyrolosis, the carbohydrates and fats form new molecules, generally known as oils. These contain all the flavour and aroma we associate with coffee. They are not present in the green bean but are created in the act of roasting. Over eight hundred different chemical ingredients have been identified inside the coffee bean, glorying in such names as furfurylthiol, furfuraldehyde, oxazole, and ethyl-furaneol. Another, trimthylamin, exists in minute quantities: it is also found in putrefying fish. Like perfume, coffee uses the most *outré* of ingredients to work its wonders.

Most coffee oils are immensely complex and have foiled the best efforts of scientists to simulate them adequately, which explains why artificial coffee flavouring is without exception of a poor standard. Although these oils constitute less than 3 per cent of the end product by weight, without their presence coffee would neither smell nor taste of anything. In effect, 97 per cent of the coffee one buys by weight is tasteless, baked vegetable matter and caffeine, which is unaffected by the roasting process and constitutes between 3 and 6 per cent of the final weight of the coffee. Considering that a roasted coffee bean is about a sixth of the weight of the cherry that gave birth to it and nurtured it, it can be seen that the whole purpose of the bean's cycle from coffee bush to cooling tray is to extract the 2 per cent of its original weight that has any flavour value.

In the oils that appear during the coffee's ten-minute ordeal by fire lies the miracle that is the transubstantiation of coffee. From the moment it spills, still smoking, from the roaster, the fight is joined to retain those precious oils. Ironically, the biggest obstacle to doing so is the coffee itself, as it produces large volumes of carbon dioxide gas – 12 litres per kilo, or about six times its own size per average household pack – in the twenty-four hours after roasting. Thus a complicated technical packaging solution is required. Unlike the other key bits of coffee machinery, the roaster and grinder, which are really of interest only to the trade, coffee packaging and its associated technology confront the consumer directly on the shelf, and the various solutions that have been adopted offer an insight into the curious behaviour of coffee after roasting.

Coffee is a substance that is so commonly ill-treated in its storage that it is difficult to remember how delicate it really is, and how much flavour and aroma are lost if it is not handled properly. Its appearance – dry brown beans or grounds – belies coffee's acute sensitivity, which is why it can frequently be found stuck for weeks in storage jars on obscure kitchen shelves. This is particularly true in predominantly instant coffee cultures, such as the UK, which tend to treat the two utterly different substances in exactly the same way, mainly because instant coffee manufacturers have gone out of their way to make their product look as much like the real roast and ground coffee as possible. However, whereas instant coffee can quite happily survive in its jar for weeks or months after opening, real coffee requires much more careful handling. The reason coffee's flavours become exhausted is because the volatile oils are extremely vulnerable to oxidation, which in turn causes a rancidity experienced by the palate as a stale, sickly sweetness.

In an ideal world, coffee should be roasted, ground, and prepared at the same time – this is part of the general practice of the traditional coffee ceremony throughout Ethiopia and Yemen, and amongst the nomadic Bedouins of the Middle East. As well as the distinctly enhanced sensory experience of seeing the green coffee beans being roasted before one's eyes, it lengthens the time for the serving of coffee to take place, which reflects a higher level of courtesy to a guest than other, short-cut methods. It has a practical dimension, too: green coffee can be stored for long periods of time, whereas it immediately starts to lose its flavours when roasted. Technically, if our traditional Bedouin were to decide to store the remains of the roasted coffee in a tightly sealed tin, the pressure of the gas would blow the lid off within a day. Even if that problem were surmounted, the roasted coffee beans would immediately start becoming subject to staling by the oxygen shut up inside the container, because, given that only a very small proportion of the roasted bean actually smells or tastes of anything at all, it likewise requires only a very small amount of oxygen to cause staling. Thus a sealed container effectively improves matters only a little. Roasted beans themselves, however, are a reasonable first line of defence against oxidation: their closed cell structure ensures that there is not too great an exposure to the air, and they can survive without undue impairment for a few days. For longer storage, the beans need to be kept out of the light, which speeds up oxidation, and in a cool place, such as a fridge or preferably a freezer, which slows it down considerably, giving a reasonable storage time of a month. Grinding coffee opens up the cell structure of the bean and greatly increases the surface area of the coffee open to attack by oxidation: some staling is evident after twenty-four hours. As we can see, our traditional Bedouin tent starts to require a generator and a range of white consumer goods merely to store coffee properly, which would put something of a damper on the envied freedoms of the Bedouin fold-the-tents-and-silently-depart lifestyle.

The problems of gas production and staling make much more of an impact in a developed consumer marketplace, where roasted coffee has to make a succession of long journeys over a considerable period of time before it is finally brewed and drunk. Roasters have applied the ingenuity of modern packaging technology to the apparently mutually exclusive aims of letting the explosive gas out of the container whilst at the same time preventing destructive oxygen from getting in. Engineers will immediately shout 'Valve!', and that is indeed the most elegant solution; but it took a century before a valve system could be effected reliably and economically.

A method has been developed whereby the coffee is put into large bins that are then flushed through with an inert gas such as nitrogen or sometimes carbon dioxide. A valve allows the excess pressure to be released. This method is used as the precursor for the classic vacuum retail pack and for the gas-flushed sachet more often used in the catering trade. In order further to preserve ground coffee against air, industrial grinders sometimes also have the facility to flush their mechanism continuously with nitrogen. Using such systems at the end of the gassing-off period, the coffee has thus far been relatively untouched by air. It can then be packed.

The vacuum, either in the form of a tin or a foil pack, is both the oldest and most ubiquitous form of industrial coffee packaging. Pioneered by Hills Brothers of San Francisco in 1900, it gradually became the packaging system of choice in North America and beyond. It creates the comforting illusion in the consumer's mind that, since the coffee comes in a vacuum, it must be perfectly preserved. This is simply not the case. Although it has been protected from oxygen initially, it is not economically viable to keep the coffee in a totally inert environment whilst it is being packed. This would require all ambient air being excluded from the feeder systems for the coffee and the packaging materials, as well as from the machine itself. The whole point of vacuum packing, however, is to suck out any vestige of air from the pack, and thus to eliminate coffee's greatest enemy. The problem is that it is impossible to create a perfect vacuum in a manufacturing environment, and there will always remain a little 'residual oxygen' inside the pack. As in the case of the Bedouin and the sealed container, the presence of even this small amount of oxygen is sufficient to cause noticeable staling, particularly over the long periods of time that are the norm in the distribution chain for coffee. The finite amount of residual oxygen inside the pack means that the damage is not as severe as it would be in a non-hermetically sealed pack; nonetheless, the end product is far from perfect.

But a worse problem awaits vacuum-packed coffee. Having more or less effectively sucked everything out of the can or foil pack, the process has also evacuated any gas from the very cell structure of the coffee itself. When opened, the rush of air into the vacuum pack that reassures the consumer that their coffee has been properly cared for penetrates every nook and cranny of every cell of every coffee ground, and immediately starts the oxidation process the manufacturers have been at such pains to avoid. Once a vacuum pack is opened, the coffee is much more prone to rapid staling than coffee packed by other methods.

Valve technology is the best means of preserving coffee's flavour and aroma. The principle is to harness the power of the gassing-off of the coffee *after* it has been packed to flush out the residual oxygen left after the pack has been flushed with gas. A soft foil pack of coffee with a valve on it is packed by a gas-flushing system immediately after roasting and grinding. The coffee starts its gassing-off, the volume of gas thus produced effectively flushing out through the valve all the remaining oxygen from the inside of the pack. After a few days, the coffee inside is in an inert, virtually oxygen-free environment, and staling is prevented. The shelf life of coffees produced using the valve method can be very long, with marginal deterioration compared to a completely fresh coffee after as long as a year. Moreover, there is no sudden rush of air into the soft pack when it is opened.

Valves on coffee packs assume a variety of shapes and forms, from the white plastic nipple of the Goglio system to almost invisible transparent tabs. The simplest and most elegant valve is that produced by Bosch, of Stuttgart in Germany, the brainchild of one Dr Dumke. First introduced in the 1980s, it has become the valve of choice for coffee *cognoscenti*, both roasters and consumers alike. Being a proprietary system, it works only on Bosch's own packaging machines, which means that a considerable investment is required to run the system, and in addition the valves cost a few pence each. It also requires strict production line disciplines to ensure that all aspects of the machinery are in alignment and functioning properly; but if they are, the benefits to the consumer purely in the freshness of the coffee are outstanding. Confronted by a strange selection of coffees in a strange land, one could do far worse than to select the one with the little transparent patch on the front: it is unlikely that a manufacturer would have invested in the system without putting decent coffee in the pack, and in any case it is likely to be the freshest there, which compensates for much else.

Historically, vacuum packing was the system that effectively delivered coffee from the tyranny of the here-and-now. An exclusively industrial process, it allowed the development of advertised coffee brands, lengthy distribution chains, and centralized buying and production. It brought coffee into the modern age. The other way in which coffee was corporatized was through the invention of instant coffee. The creation of a soluble beverage that appears to be an acceptable and much more convenient alternative to the coffee from which it is derived has been one of the great success stories of the twentieth century. There are few comparable examples of an ersatz version of a beverage that enjoy such a dominant position in the market.

A patent for a coffee compound was filed as early as 1771 in England, and Scotland produced Camp Coffee essence in the late 1800s, of which the bottle, a fine example of the Empire school of design, sports a pukka sahib in a kilt being served coffee by his dark-skinned be-turbanned orderly outside a tent that flies a flag with the cryptic message 'Ready Aye Ready' on it. Camp Coffee has perhaps inevitably become something of a postmodern camp classic, finding particular favour in America. A Japanese inventor, having first created a soluble tea, invented an instant coffee in the United States in 1901 which was used on the Ziegler Arctic expedition. This was followed by the appropriately named Faust Instant Coffee in 1906. A Belgian named George Washington living in Guatemala started his eponymous company with a secret recipe that was covertly replicated by the family physician. Dr Frederico Lehnhoff Wyld, a Guatemalan German, set up an instant coffee factory in France that was bankrupted by the outbreak of the First World War. That war was the first in which coffee became an essential component of the soldier's diet. As conditions for brewing coffee in the trenches were far from ideal, there was a sudden surge in the army's demand for instant coffees, which had started to appear in America, peaking at 16,800 kilos a day by the end of the war. Water could be boiled quickly for instant coffee, or indeed it could be made with cold water for the caffeine kick alone. As such, it was the American soldiers' friend, part of their emergency rations, and as comforting and familiar as a cigarette. While instant coffee flourished in the Great War, it could not survive the peace, and after the Armistice the fledgling industry went into a steep decline. The Second World War brought it back into popular favour.

Again, convenience was the key. With American domestic consumption of coffee at an all-time high in 1941, it was no surprise that when the country went to war after Pearl Harbor in December of that year, coffee went too. The average annual consumption of a GI during the war was 14 kilos, nearly double the already peak national level. The combination of intense wartime factory production and the fighting itself made caffeine a vital chemical ingredient of the war effort. If there is any truth in the idea that capitalism depends upon caffeine because it lengthens the productive day to a theoretical twenty-four hours, then the war provided further proof. While the coffee that was consumed domestically in America was roast and ground, the instant manufacturers found that literally everything that they could produce was requisitioned by the army.

Having already established itself as an acceptable drink, it was easier in the post-war years for instant coffee to grab market share from the roast and ground manufacturers. This happened not only in the USA, but globally. It was as if World War and the concomitant World Peace had opened the door to instant coffee in countries that previously had little acquaintance with it. Even the European heartland of traditional coffee drinking found itself assailed by the new beverage, and in America itself instant coffee had a third of the market by the late 1950s. By that time, however, the quality of American regular coffee had declined so much that the distinction between real and instant had been significantly eroded. This global explosion came about as a result of a combination of factors: the ubiquitous presence of US troops, the fact that the increased use of cheap Robusta coffee in instant coffee drove down the price in austere times, and the new convenience culture. There was also a fashion factor: in MacArthur's Japan, for instance, coffee drinking reflected a vogue for all things American, and the *kissaten* (coffee house) that had been catching on slowly since the 1920s suddenly sprang up everywhere.

Instant coffee is now ubiquitous. In their respective international hotels, it is hard to find proper Yemeni coffee in Yemen or Indian coffee in India, but always possible to find a Nescafé. In a globalized culture, the brand means more than the brew. Continuing in this fine tradition, it is reassuring to find that it has recently been suggested that the residue of instant coffee manufacturing could be of use in the poultry industry.

The main similarity between instant coffee and real coffee is the use of the word coffee to describe them both. Beyond that, any resemblance is largely coincidental. That does not mean that instant coffee has no place in society, but it should be recognized for what it truly is: a convenient, sometimes pleasant, caffeinated coffee-style hot beverage. The instant coffee manufacturers' principal aim, however, is to blur as far as possible the consumer's perception of the difference between the two, for as soon as a simple taste test is conducted between an instant coffee (albeit the best on the market) and a nondescript real coffee the game is up. There are two thrusts to the manufacturers' attempts to confabulate the ersatz with the real thing. One is through technological development, and the other is through marketing.

The technology for making instant coffee has been the subject of tremendous investment by the major coffee companies, and Germany and England have the dubious honour of being at the cutting edge. In essence, instant coffee manufacture consists of creating a brew of coffee on a vast scale and then concentrating it by one of a variety of methods, including evaporation and low-pressure extraction. The resulting concentrate can then be turned into powder, granules, or freeze-dried granules. The secrets of those technologies are closely guarded by the individual manufacturers. Massive research and development programmes, as well as substantial capital investment backed by enormous advertising budgets, have meant that instant coffee has become a very big boy's game indeed. In the UK it is dominated by the archetypal transnational, Nestlé. That company has achieved almost legendary status with its coffees, having maintained quasi-monopolistic market share and a premium price position through quality of product and extremely effective advertising. The company also enjoys profit margins of some 27 per cent on its instant coffee products, something that has been called 'commercial heaven' – other food product sectors typically operate at between 5 and 15 per cent margins. The UK sector of Nestlé's global instant coffee operations is reckoned to be the most profitable single business sector for the entire company.

The reality for the instant coffee manufacturer is that, however hard he tries, he is unable to make his product as good as the real thing, and so he has to resort to massaging the consumer's perceptions in his favour. It is no coincidence that the better quality instant coffees closely resemble the appearance of ground coffee; this heightens the expectations that a real coffee flavour will be delivered, and underscores the unconscious convenience food mentality that says 'Well, they look the same, so maybe they're just about the same really.' Likewise there is a cunning technology known by the attractive term 'plating on', which consists of injecting the top of the jar of instant coffee with a reasonable simulation of the aroma of ground coffee, so that when the seal is broken, the first impression is of a fresh, coffee smell. That it neither lingers nor represents the aroma of the coffee when brewed, is immaterial. What most betrays the inferiority of instant coffee is the fact that it does not stale significantly, even after the jar has been opened. Those delicate volatile oils that are such a vital part of real coffee's flavour and aroma have been roundly abused in the manufacturing process, so there is no need to make much of a fuss about preserving them afterwards. While it does not have an indefinite shelf life, there are generally few on-pack storage suggestions. Instant coffee does not go stale because there is little of real interest left to go stale.

Instant coffee has a number of additional hidden vices. It contains a higher proportion of caffeine per cup than roast and ground coffee, higher even than a pure Robusta. It also tends to smooth out the worst features of Robusta coffees, making an irresistible temptation for manufacturers to include it in their blends. The combination leads to the further caffeination of the nation.

Some instant coffee manufacturers try to make their cheaper products resemble those of their more expensive rivals. Thus we find agglomerated powder masquerading as freeze-dried granules. Spray drying, the original instant coffee technology, imparts a strong 'Ovaltine' flavour to the end product, upon which modern freeze-dried products, launched in 1965, are certainly an improvement. But the real problem with instant coffee is that it breaks the fundamental rules for good coffee making – freshly roasted, freshly ground, freshly brewed – and nothing can be done about that. Its success is entirely due to its convenience, but it has wheedled its way into the hearts and minds of the consumers, and such is its ubiquity that many people genuinely seem to prefer it to the real thing. The issue of the deliberate confusion between what is real and what is not is becoming increasingly heated as the instant manufacturers adapt to the new market conditions arising from the espresso boom. Some machine manufacturers have produced instant coffee brewers for caterers which to the unsuspecting look like genuine espresso machines. Other instant coffee/powdered milk/chocolate mixtures disingenuously call themselves 'cappuccino'. All this causes uproar amongst honest, upright, espresso-loving citizens who see their beloved beverage being perverted for profit. The practice is, however, merely an extension of the misguided decision that allowed manufacturers to call their instant beverage coffee in the first place.

The distinction between real and instant coffee is also blurred in the marketing. The underlying approach is to treat instant coffee and real coffee as if they were both equally satisfactory subspecies of the genus coffee. Frequently, instant coffee manufacturers also sell roast and ground coffee, so it is in their interests to promote the 'House of Coffee' idea, under which flag sail numerous variations, all supposedly distinguished by the high level of care and expertise lavished on them by the manufacturer or retailer in question. Thus the freeze-dried Costa Rica Arabica is given equal pride of place to the real coffee equivalent, and the consumer is left with the impression that the difference is not fundamentally one of flavour, but of lifestyle. The net effect has been that instant coffee has dragged itself up the social ladder on the bootstraps of the real thing. In the UK, where the market is dominated by instant coffee, which represents 80 per cent of all coffee sales, this has had repercussions throughout the coffee trade, which has nurtured this giant cuckoo in its midst while at the same time trying to promote the virtues of good coffee. This means that the trade tends to obscure rather than reveal the differences between the two products. The UK is almost unique globally in that it has so heartily embraced instant coffee. This is partly the result of the nation's pre-eminent affection for tea, partly due to its historical indifference to food culture; but most of all it is because, in the late 1950s, it was sold on the notion that there was no discernible difference between real and instant coffee by Nestlé and Maxwell House at a time when the country was emerging from wartime rationing and was sniffing the air to see what new and wonderful things could be bought with its increased disposable income. Instant coffee caught the *Zeitgeist* of the emerging middle classes (the staunch 'I'm-Alright-Jack' working classes regarded coffee as effete), and its undoubted convenience struck a chord with housewives seduced by anything promoting itself as labour saving. Instant became aspirational, a sign of discernment the tea packers could not emulate. By the time coffee consciousness was raised in the 1990s, instant coffee was so entrenched in the national psyche that the opportunity for real coffee to trade off instant's patent inadequacies had passed.

Instant coffee brands also used commercial television, established in 1956, as their chosen advertising medium: while tea took more than the three-minute advert break to brew, instant coffee could be made without missing the programme. Those who chose to remain by the television could watch instant coffee advertisements preparing them for the next break. The curious symbiosis between television and instant-coffee culture was established. In part, this testifies to the success of the advertising campaigns themselves, particularly those of Nestlé, which are treated with some veneration by marketing students. Their advertisements over many years have been phenomenally successful in terms of recall and increased propensity to purchase.

By and large, the focus of health concerns regarding coffee is naturally its most active ingredient, caffeine. NASA scientists came up with one of the more interesting demonstrations of the effects of caffeine on living beings, in this case the hapless *Araneus didematus*, or common house spider. A particularly fiendish experiment was devised to administer doses of various psychoactive substances to spiders and analyse the resultant webs compared with those of their sober cousins. The chosen substances were caffeine, Benzedrine, marijuana, and chloral hydrate – the latter a sedative and hypnotic when used on humans. The result was bad news for caffeine consumers: the spider stoned on marijuana created a near-perfect web, save only for forgetting to finish it off; the speed-crazed one did little patches quite well with great gaps in between as if it kept getting distracted; the chloral hydrate head offered up a zonked-out *reductio ad absurdum* minimalist web; but the caffeine-crazed spider produced something that in no respect resembled the hub-and-spoke pattern of the conventional web. The conclusion was that spiders' web-building capabilities were far more grievously impaired by caffeine than by the other psychoactive substances.

We humans are not spiders, and too much can be read into the results of the experiment. Whether or not we choose to interpret the frantic, misplaced energy of the caffeine-inspired spider as a neat simulacrum of the chaotic output of the student downing endless cups of instant coffee, it remains the case that caffeine, mankind's drug of choice, used by 50 per cent of us on a daily basis, was intended by nature as a powerful insecticide and anti-bacteriological agent. Its effects are indeed so powerful that ultimately caffeine kills the coffee bush itself.

It is typically louche of mankind to have become addicted to, of all things, an insecticide. Not content with tea and coffee, we have discovered that about sixty evergreen tropical and semi-tropical plants have evolved the cunning strategy of generating the bitter alkaloid caffeine in their leaves, beans, and stalks to give sundry beetles, borers, ants and others stomach ache and prompting nervous collapse. As well as tea and coffee, these plants include cacao, cassina, kola nuts, guarana nuts, and maté. Coffee in its own right can boast some nine hundred insect enemies, including leaf miners, stem borers, scale insects, berry moth, berry borers, and mealy bugs. Evidently it needs to create all the caffeine possible, as infestation by any one of these can cause an average 10 per cent crop loss.

The effect of caffeine in tea was first described in China in around 500 BC, and Chinese medicine ascribed a range of benefits to it, including the stimulation of digestion, the burning of fat, cleaning of infected skin, and washing of the eyes. Caffeine delivered in the form of coffee entered the pharmacopoeia much later, as we have seen. The first 'head to head' experiment to assess the difference between the two beverages was performed in the late eighteenth century. It was infinitely easier to conduct interesting scientific experiments in the days before human rights were invented, especially if you happened to be a King. Gustavus III of Sweden was greatly interested in the controversy surrounding the drinking of tea and coffee and he was able to exert his *droit de seigneur* to set up an experiment on live human beings. The King commuted the death sentences on a pair of identical twins who had been found guilty of murder on condition that they would both suffer life imprisonment, with one drinking three bowls of tea a day, the other, three bowls of coffee, accompanied by an otherwise similar diet. The tea drinker died first, at the tender age of 82, proving beyond reasonable doubt that coffee was healthier, which may explain why Swedish per capita coffee consumption today is among the highest in the world.

The inspiration for the discovery of caffeine came from Johann Wolfgang von Goethe, the poet, philosopher, and scientist, who in 1819 asked a young Swiss chemist named Gustav von Runge to demonstrate his discovery of the effect of belladonna in dilating the pupil of a cat's eye. Satisfied with Runge's abilities, Goethe then showed him some coffee beans and challenged him to analyse their chemical structure, leading to Runge's discovery of caffeine (or trimethyloxpurin, known to chemists as

$C_8H_{10}N_4O_2$) some months later. When he left Goethe's house Runge almost forgot to take his cat with him, until Goethe reminded him not to leave behind his 'familiar' – a reference to the tradition that witches and alchemists always kept a cat in their company.

The reference was not without relevance to Goethe's own early life, when he had pursued the study of alchemy. From his youth he had also been a keen coffee drinker and a regular visitor to Florian's in Venice and Café Greco in Rome during his time in Italy. Evidently he perceived some deleterious effect from his habit, because he deliberately cut back on his consumption of coffee and alcohol from his thirtieth birthday in 1779. This coincided with a subtle change in his attitude towards alchemy that developed into an interest in the scientific study of what he called 'encheiresis', the mysterious connections that bind nature together. This required an analytical approach more in keeping with the spirit of the times, and although Goethe was to excel primarily as a writer in later years, his scientific studies of botany, geology, and colour theory were very influential. Optics and colour theory had also been interests of that other towering figure of science and alchemy, Isaac Newton, about a hundred years earlier. It is perhaps a manifestation of the very encheiresis that he endeavoured to describe that the historical threads of alchemy, coffee, and Faust met in the protean figure of Goethe, and that he inspired the discovery of caffeine, the chemical filament that weaves the web of coffee's dark history.

Runge's discovery of caffeine was swiftly followed by the isolation of 'thein' in tea by Oudry, and the subsequent discovery that they were, in fact, both the same by Jobat. The isolation and naming of the active ingredient did wonders to contain the controversy that had previously surrounded tea and coffee drinking, and coincided with an enormous global rise in the consumption of both during the nineteenth century. Caffeine use or abuse has never since been seriously challenged, with the result that it is fully integrated into the lives of 80 per cent of mankind, whether in the form of coffee, tea, or myriad soft drinks. However, in order to expand, the caffeine industry has to find new consumers, and has started to target the young. The consumption by teenagers of soft drinks with added caffeine has overtaken that of milk-based beverages in the USA, whilst children under five years drink 16 per cent less milk than in the late 1970s and 23 per cent more soft drinks. There is concern that Europe is heading the same way. On top of this there has been a shift in marketing strategy. Whereas previously soft drinks manufacturers justified the addition of caffeine on grounds of taste, the new generation of 'energy' drinks use the language of drug culture to describe their effects, such as 'buzz', 'lift', and 'high'. This ominous move, as far as the caffeine industry's detractors are concerned, habituates young consumers to the idea that the use of chemicals to alter mood or performance is acceptable, or even, as the Red Bull studies of driver fatigue would seem to suggest, a positive duty.

There have been occasional flurries of opposition to caffeine consumption, mainly from those having an alternative product to promote. The 'Postum' toasted cereal coffee invented by Charles Post was introduced in 1895 in the USA, inspired by disapproval of tea and coffee by the evangelical nutritionist John Harvey Kellogg. Post carefully nurtured consumer fears concerning caffeine by innovative advertising campaigns that are considered masters of the genre: his headline proclaiming that 'It is safe to say that one person in three among coffee users has some incipient or advanced form of disease' is a fine example of this Late Snake-Oil Salesman style. Post was able to build a multi-million-dollar business from his 'Postum Food Coffee', although he was eventually forced to remove the word 'coffee' from his packs.

Meanwhile in 1906, one Ludwig Roselius of Hamburg filed a patent for a coffee decaffeination process he called Kaffee

Hag, and many others followed suit in the USA and France. The coffee industry was sufficiently impressed with the commercial potential for decaffeinated coffee products to have continued to research and develop at great expense a variety of techniques for removing the caffeine from green (unroasted) coffee beans. In most coffees caffeine accounts for between 1–2.5 per cent of the total dry weight of the bean, with high-grown quality Arabicas containing almost half the caffeine of coarse low-grown Robustas. Instant coffee has almost double that of ground in the cup, but espresso has less as a result of the rapid extraction and lower weight of coffee used. The prize for the least caffeine-bearing coffee bean goes to a little-known wild Malagasy varietal, which unfortunately tastes unpalatably bitter. Botanists have been working overtime to effect the marriage of this naturally occurring decaffeinated coffee with a decent tasting Arabica. The union has thus far proved unsuccessful.

The decaffeination of coffee involves soaking the green beans with a solvent. Over time, and in the light of a number of health scares (the decaffeinated consumer having a heightened health consciousness compared to his caffeinated counterpart), the solvent used has changed. Hag's process initially used benzol, then methyl chloride was introduced, which was subsequently banned by the Food and Drug Administration in the USA when it was shown to be carcinogenic if taken in huge doses by rats. Ethyl acetate, which occurs naturally in small quantities in coffee itself, then became solvent of the month, which led to a rash of manufacturer's claims to produce 'naturally' decaffeinated coffees even when the solvent was brewed synthetically in huge chemical plants. Then in 1979 a Swiss company, Coffex, introduced a 'water process' that has achieved huge success, in part because the term 'Swiss Water Process Decaffeinated Coffee' has irresistible echoes of lush alpine meadows and pristine edelweiss. A newer method, which produces a better quality product, the

'Supercritical Carbon Dioxide' method, has been unable to take the commercial high ground it might otherwise have been expected to do as it conspicuously lacks the Heidi factor.

In all cases the use of the solvent has a damaging effect on the flavour, but again this varies from process to process. As caffeine itself is a bitter alkaloid, of which there is sufficient quantity even in Arabicas of the highest pedigree to be discernible, decaffeinated coffees tend to have an underlying sweetness about them. This can be further exaggerated by the effects of staling, to which, after the indignities suffered in the processing, decaffeinated coffee is particularly prone.

Because many leading brands of both roast and ground, and instant coffees have managed to introduce decaffeinated coffee into their marketing mix, serious criticism of the effects of caffeine has been muted. Consumers who might purchase the decaffeinated product are appealed to in the gentlest terms, hinting at possible sleeping problems or unspecified 'preferences'. Of course, a more aggressive campaign citing urinary incontinence and a tendency to see UFOs roaring out of the night sky might not reflect favourably on the rest of the brand's stable. As a result, some fine source material for potential Postmodern Snake-Oil Salesman-style advertising has thus been neglected, and the world sadly will never see campaigns on the lines of 'I thought all men had restless leg syndrome, until I bought my husband Dexter's Decaff . . .'.

14

COFFEE, SCIENCE, AND HISTORY

It would be tempting to assume that coffee cultivation had somehow emerged from the shadow of colonialism and empire into the sunshine of a more enlightened era. However, it is becoming increasingly clear that, although the players have changed, the orchestra is producing the same tune. Local labour on subsistence wages produces coffee at the lowest possible cost for markets in the developed world. The main difference is that instead of living by the old maxim that 'Trade follows the Flag', powerful corporations have realized that it is easier to dispense with the burdensome responsibilities of actual colonization, and use modern transnational institutions such as the WTO, the World Bank, and the IMF to impose their will from the boardrooms of Manhattan, Paris, and Berlin. For the impoverished farmer whose national politics bend to the needs of these transnational institutions and the corporations they serve, the notion of democracy is a spurious validation of the yoke under which they are forced to work. Packaging technology, as we have seen, paved the way for the corporatization of coffee. The science associated with coffee not only created the theoretical base from which such developments could spring, allowing the transnational coffee companies increasingly to control the market, but has now started to influence government policy and academia. Coffee science, it would appear, is quietly falling victim to the interests of coffee corporations.

On the fourth floor of a quiet house in the elegant 8th arrondissement of Paris lies the secret heart of coffee science. The secretariat of ASIC (Association Scientifique Internationale du Café) administers the organization that co-ordinates the dissemination of the latest scientific research dedicated to the world's most valuable agricultural commodity. It is an independent freelance business that acts for various organizations, including the European Tea Federation. Its function for ASIC is to act as a clearing house for correspondence and, most importantly, to organize the biannual conferences that are the showpieces for the presentation of the voluminous coffee research that issues from the laboratories of the world. Coffee is the most scientifically scrutinized foodstuff in the world.

Those who are concerned by the extent to which academia has been overtaken by commercial interests would find ASIC an interesting case study. It was founded in 1966 by René Coste as a research branch of a French government department. It was Coste who had famously masterminded the creation of 'Arabusta', a hybrid combining the flavour virtues of the Arabica plant with the hardiness of Robusta. The only drawback was that the plant was sterile, which in itself was sufficient to make it of no commercial value, although it remains a botanical curiosity. Over time ASIC evolved from an organization run on a shoestring out of an existing government department to one that admitted industry representatives, then industry finance. Today ASIC has ceased to be a French government body at all, although Coste remains its Honorary President. ASIC proudly maintains that it is 'the only completely independent organization in the world whose scientific vocation is specifically devoted to the coffee tree, the coffee bean and the coffee drink'. However, claims that the organization is perpetually short of money are undermined by the reluctant admission that it is chiefly financed by the coffee industry. A glance at the 2002 board confirms that the industry is extremely well represented: Gerry Baldwin of Peet's in California, President; Ernesto Illy, First Vice President; A. Illy, Vice President; R. Liardon of Nestlé Product Technology Centre, Scientific Secretary; M. Blanc of Nestec Ltd, Secretary and Treasurer; executives of Kraft (owned by Philip Morris), Doewe-Egberts (owned by Sara Lee Inc.), and Integrated Coffee (the pioneers of GM coffee in Hawaii) are also on the roster. The claim of 'complete independence' is inevitably compromised by the nature of the membership, funding and management of the organization.

ASIC's conferences are held alternately in coffee-producing and consuming countries. In Kyoto in 1995 the opening speech was made by the head of the Ueshima Coffee Company, Japan's largest roaster, who summarized the contents of the presentations, finishing up with the remark 'there are only five technical papers on physiology. This is because coffee is already recognized as a healthy beverage.' So, as they say, that's all right then. The Kyoto conference was a typical ASIC effort, with 12 keynote speeches and 138 presentations, of which 43 were by Japanese scientists. Delegates could immerse themselves in topics as varied as 'Studies on the management of rust resistant Cafimor varieties in Papua New Guinea', 'The effect of coffee aroma on the brain function: results from the studies of regional cerebral blood flow through positron emission tomography and event related potential (E.R.P.)', and 'In-mouth coffee aroma: breath-by-breath analysis of nose-space while drinking coffee'. They could learn that 'coffee aroma can be used to improve the unpleasant feeling in some psychiatric illness without any side effect because it acts on the areas associated with emotion' owing to 'the unique effect of coffee aroma on brain function'. The breadth is staggering and the depth daunting: to have a well-informed overview of the field would require an extraordinary degree of multi-disciplinary scientific expertise.

Many of the research papers come from academic bodies, the French being particularly strong in the field with ORSTOM in Montpellier, a government institution dedicated to tropical plant botany – the genetic research that enabled us to track the coffee plant as it moved east across Ethiopia to Harar and thence to Yemen was conducted by a team headed by an ORSTOM scientist. Equally, a significant amount of research comes from the coffee industry itself, which is only to be expected. The problem is that it is difficult to know if there is an invisible censor at work.

Although the precise nature of the relationship is difficult to pinpoint, ASIC is part of a network of acronym-rich coffee research organizations across Europe which are reluctant to declare their interest in the coffee health debate. In the leafy purlieus of Chipping Norton in Oxfordshire lurks CoSIC (the pan-European Coffee Science Information Centre), which purports to present a balanced analysis of the issues arising from coffee science. CoSIC was established in the UK in 1990 by ISIC, the Institute for Scientific Information on Coffee, which is 'based' in Switzerland, although it appears to be a virtual organization, sharing its secretariat with ASIC in Paris. According to Maurice Blanc – who works for Nestlé and is also a Secretary and Treasurer of the ASIC board and organizes their conferences – ISIC came into being in 1990 in response to industry concerns about possible problems with research then being conducted by IARC – the International Association for Research on Cancer, particularly in relation to caffeine and bladder cancer. ISIC was founded by a coalition of Nestlé, Lavazza, Kraft, Paulig, Tchibo, and Doewe Egberts – a roll-call of European coffee industry heavy-hitters. ISIC then decided it needed an information wing, and so funded the foundation of CoSIC, and a scientific wing, for which reason it took over and funded a pre-existing team of academics called PEC, the Physiological Effect of Coffee Group.

According to its publicity material, 'The aim of CoSIC is to provide accurate, balanced and consistent information to all audiences across Europe who have an interest in coffee, caffeine and health. The primary objective is to bring balance to the coffee and health debate.'

This conceals the fact that CoSIC is entirely funded, via ISIC, by the coffee industry, which may explain why the three examples of recent research carried on its web site are good news for coffee drinkers: STUDY SHOWS CAFFEINE DOES NOT INCREASE DEHYDRATION (21 June 2002); HOMOCYSTEINE NOT THE CAUSE OF HEART DISEASE (1 March 2000); COFFEE DRINKERS HAVE LOWER RISK OF GALLSTONE DISEASE (9 June 1999). CoSIC's scientific advisor is Dr Euan Paul, a long-standing industry figure. CoSIC may wonder whether it is able to maintain its claim to work with independent scientists now that Dr Paul has also taken on the mantle of Executive Director of the newly formed British Coffee Association, whose members are the principal UK coffee companies, including Kraft UK and Nestlé UK. Amongst the BCA's roles is to 'act as industry spokesperson on issues affecting the coffee industry' and to 'represent the coffee industry's views on relevant legislative and technical issues'. When Oxfam recommended that the grave international coffee crisis could be solved by producers being paid a dollar a pound, the BCA dismissed the proposal as being 'too short term'. Dr Paul evidently believed that the crisis can be more simply solved 'if every consumer drank one more cup worldwide'. However, with his CoSIC hat on he maintains that moderate caffeine intake, which he fails to define, is harmless. (The recommended safe dose of caffeine according to some is 300mg; ergo, just under four Red Bulls @ 80mg per can, three demitasse espressos @ 90mg each, or five cups of tea @ 60mg each.) Dr Paul thus appears to be saying that the problems of Third World coffee producers can be solved, but at the risk of possibly pushing First World coffee consumers over the threshold into what might be defined as excessive caffeine consumption. Such are the difficulties encountered by a scientist on the playing fields of commerce.

It is increasingly difficult for a reasonably sceptical non-scientist to take seriously the quality of science that is being put forward in these reports. A few years ago the tea industry gleefully jumped on research indicating that green tea had been shown to possess anti-oxidant qualities. Lo and behold! in 2001 new research apparently demonstrated that coffee had suddenly been imbued with anti-oxidant properties *four times stronger than tea*! It may well be the case – only a scientist would dare gainsay it – but to the layperson it smacks of opportunism. As with all food-related health issues there is a crying need for genuinely objective information. One of the problems caused by the increasing preponderance of science-at-the-service-of-industry is that such information is hard to find, and it is usually the industry-funded science that shouts loudest and longest. This is not to say that the science produced by the coffee industry is *per se* biased or inaccurate; however, when the presentation of scientific information starts to assume the characteristics of a co-ordinated marketing campaign, credibility inevitably suffers.

In the meantime, and in the public domain, the issue of the effect of caffeine on health is not so easily dismissed. In 1997 a group of eminent American scientists and physicians affiliated to the Center for Science in the Public Interest in Washington wrote to the Head of the Food and Drug Administration (FDA) presenting a clear case for the labelling of the caffeine content of all food and beverages and urging them to undertake an authoritative study of the effect of caffeine on health. In 2000 the Australia and New Zealand Food Authority commissioned a report into the dietary effects of caffeine and were particularly concerned by the arrival on their shores of so-called 'energy' drinks which were heavily caffeinated, such as Red Bull. The working group for the report included Professor Jack James, who dissented from the group's conclusion. Professor James, now Head of the Psychology Department at the National University of Ireland in Galway, is a respected academic working to bring scientific balance to the activities of what he calls 'the caffeine industry', having published two books and numerous papers on the subject. Certainly he is sufficiently respected for it to be a surprise to find that his efforts have been completely ignored by the likes of ASIC and CoSIC. He suggests that the caffeine industry has successfully seduced individual scientists to concentrate on issues favourable to the industry, and that it is becoming increasingly difficult for the scientist, let alone the public, to ascertain what is or is not objective research. He points to two myths about caffeine that have been sustained by what he believes to have been a co-ordinated effort to cross-reference back to, and ignore subsequent refutations of, faulty research. One concerns the myth that caffeine enhances performance, the other that habitual caffeine use builds up a tolerance to the raised blood pressure associated with the drug. His belief that the myths are kept alive by the industry is sharply at odds with that of Dr Euan Paul of the BCA, who claims: 'Over the last 10 to 15 years the old myths and fallacies have very much been laid to rest. There has been a lot of scientific work showing that there is no risk in the consumption of coffee as long as, like everything else, it is done in moderation.'

Professor James believes that, as academic departments in universities come under increasing pressure to find industry funding, so the results that they produce are increasingly open to question. He points to the fact that Vanderbilt University Medical Center at Nashville in the USA recently received a $6 million grant from the coffee industry to set up a department, the 'Vanderbilt Institute for Coffee Studies', established for 'the study of the health benefits of coffee'. 'An International Advisory Board comprising leaders from the world of coffee has been established to promote the I.C.S. Academic independence is ensured by the fact that all I.C.S. scientists are members of Vanderbilt University's faculty, all publications appear in peer-reviewed scientific journals without censorship by funding groups, and I.C.S. research programs are regularly reviewed by leaders in relevant scientific fields,' trumpets the University. As the aim of the ICS, and the basis on which it received its funding, is to discover the health benefits of coffee, it is unlikely that the issue of its academic independence will ever arise, as it is constitutionally precompromised.

Professor James also maintains that the caffeine industry has adopted the strategy of discovering or only emphasizing the purported benefits from caffeine consumption. As research bends to the corporate buck, so does government. He resents the fact that more and more of his time is spent drawing people's attention to 'the potential for corruption of scientific enterprise' rather than on his own research. The European Commission, which partly sponsors his current studies, does not escape his criticism, but he has written in *Addiction*, an academic journal, about the threat to research integrity of one particular research body, the International Life Sciences Institute. In 1958, caffeine was listed under 'generally recognized as safe' by the Food and Drug Administration in the USA, but in the late 1970s there was considerable pressure on the FDA to remove it from the list from lobby groups, including the Center for Science in the Public Interest. The International Life Sciences Institute was founded with funding from the soft drinks industry to counter this threat. By 1980 the FDA was warning pregnant women against excessive caffeine consumption: the ILSI countered with the publication of a work on the effects of caffeine, but when it came to dealing with the potentially negative effects seemed selectively to employ research to support the case of the caffeine industry that caffeine was essentially benign.

The commercial stakes in the scientific game are very high: largely as a result of the increasing concerns about caffeine, coffee consumption in the US declined by 39 per cent between 1962 and 1982. The fall was reversed by 1990, a success that has been widely attributed by the caffeine industry to its own campaign to counter scientific concerns. The ILSI has become a worldwide body purporting to sponsor research to 'make a difference' to happiness and health. While it has recruited many notable scientists to its subsidiary Research Foundation, the control of the organization and of its purse strings is firmly in the hands of its corporate membership, which reads like a litany of the usual suspects in the global food and drink industry – Coca-Cola, Mars, Nestlé, Procter & Gamble, and Unilever, amongst others. It also includes members from the chemical and pharmaceutical industries such as Du Pont and Bayer. ILSI's association with the World Health Organization has provoked concern within that body that there may be echoes of the tobacco industry's attempts to counter the efforts of the WHO to look into the harmful effects of tobacco. Indeed the ILSI was identified by a WHO working group as an organization that – according to Professor James – funded 'seemingly unbiased scientific groups [i.e. third parties] to influence political and scientific debate concerning tobacco and health'. The fact that ILSI is also participating in a European Union programme, 'Food Safety in Europe: Risk Assessment of Chemicals in Food', causes concern, particularly as it still trumpets its 'independence'. The key issue, whether it be for food in general or caffeine in particular, is one of scientific objectivity, and the difficulty that scientists have in countering threats to their objectivity when they are lone voices.

The process is illustrated by the report 'Falling Asleep at the Wheel', produced by the Sleep Research Department at

Loughborough University. As BBC Scotland reported, 'The study found that one can of an energy drink could counteract "moderate levels of sleepiness" and two cans will almost eliminate the problem entirely . . . Research centre director, Professor Jim Horne, said: "Drivers should plan their journeys and get off the road if they feel at all tired. Once stopped in a safe place they should drink a can of energy drink and, if possible, take a short nap for more than 15 minutes."' The BBC noted that Red Bull had been the energy drink used in the experiments, but not that the research had been fully funded by that company. Listening to the report, it would be perfectly possible to reach the conclusion that the answer to the problem of driver fatigue was simply to buy two cans of Red Bull (current global sales, 1 billion cans a year). Key elements of the results then cropped up in pamphlets launched by the Road Operators Safety Council in conjunction with Loughborough, a body whose membership includes 40,000 bus and truck drivers in the UK. Red Bull would seem to have derived considerable commercial benefit from the scientific credibility of reports that they themselves commissioned.

The use of science by the coffee industry to shield products from possible criticism on health grounds is an expensive pastime, but ultimately the cost is borne by coffee farmers in the form of low coffee prices. To some, the only way to cope with the crisis is to find a First World roaster with the means to help them 'add value' to their coffee. The burgeoning interest in 'specialty' coffees is now a worldwide phenomenon. Initially it was a roaster-led initiative, uncovering a latent desire in consumers for more interesting, better quality coffee – understandably, given the prevailing standards in the USA in the 1970s. Now, with the catastrophic price crisis, qualification as a specialty coffee is probably the only hope of survival for the coffee producer.

Coffee, at its higher reaches, has become a fashion business. The market requires innovation and novelty, and the roasters and producers fall over themselves to supply them, and try to turn their previously unsung coffees into something of extraordinary pedigree. Because there is not enough to go around, new plantations spring up, backed by investment from seemingly unrelated sectors such as travel and leisure groups. A hundred hectares are being planted on Fiji, which was last reported to have exported the grand sum of 1140 kilos to New Zealand in 1980. Nepal, which had no coffee industry at all, has now sprouted 'Mount Everest Supreme'. The Galapagos Islands, Panama, the Cape Verde Islands, the Azores . . . Coffees are pitched to a specialty roaster's marketing department like scripts to Hollywood producers: 'It's Hawaiian Kona Kai meets Yemeni Mocha, but more accessible . . . and we think we can get the Moghul Emperor on board.' The Holy Grail is exclusivity; the roaster wants to have the sole rights to the property so that no rival can snatch it from under his nose. The coffee becomes his alone to promote and cannot be gainsaid.

While existing producers seek to enhance their credentials, and new producers choose suitably exotic locations for their plantations, the coffee buyers trawl the world for some undiscovered coffee masterpiece. As with sunken vessels, historical research is an invaluable tool of the trade; this book itself will have made alert buyers aware of a few previously unknown potential treasures.

The specialty coffee phenomenon is the corollary of the control of the supply chain by Western corporations. The workaday coffees of the world are produced and sold at rock-bottom prices, but the needs of the wealthy, discriminating consumer must also be met. Thus whilst the rest of the world's coffee consumption converges on the cheap coffees of Brazil and Vietnam, a small but significant market has developed for designer coffee. Its existence is a reflection of how much the actual quality of the coffee is only one component in the marketing mix: the ability to 'add value' by drawing on other aspects of the coffees in question is a skill which, by and large, only the companies in consuming countries possess. Some, though very few, producing countries, such as Jamaica, have managed to retain control of their 'brand' (in their case, Blue Mountain), and some regions, such as Antigua in Guatemala, are striving to reinforce it. However, these are only minor and isolated successes compared with the brand equity created by coffee companies such as Starbucks and Nestlé, and the huge profits that are reaped by creating a premium positioning for their products.

To be able to join the pantheon of specialty coffees, the fundamentals of a new coffee's taste must be sound, and preferably distinctive. It should certainly have no harsh flavours, no 'off' notes. Thus whilst the slightly metallic acidity of some Central American coffees is a desirable characteristic whilst it is held in check by a full body, if that body is thin, as is the case with some Mexican coffee, then the acidity ceases to be in balance, and becomes less desirable. The coffee does not necessarily have to taste like another – although the language used to describe coffee has evolved, like other languages, from shared experience, and even a new sensation is described using the building blocks of previous ones.

It is easy to see how influential the sense of place is in the way in which coffee is marketed in developed countries. The very names of the varieties on the shelf – Kenya, Costa Rica, Java et al. – are designed to stimulate interest, much like a travel brochure, and are often accompanied by a suitable image to evoke the country in question. The power of taste experience refreshed by imagination is not to be underestimated. One of the trials of a coffee taster's life is to meet people newly returned from holiday clutching a pack of Togolese Robusta, Peruvian Arabica, Jamaican Blue Mountain or some such. They thrust it into your expert hands fully expecting confirmation of their opinion that it is 'marvellous'. Perhaps it was marvellous in Togo, with the fufu sellers' cries echoing across the market, or in the Andes with the breeze carrying a half-promise of snow, or in Jamaica with the parrots swooping amongst the jacarandas. But on the cold workbench of a seasoned taster it will usually be either low quality or very stale, or most probably both. The travellers have stirred their memory of the country into the cup, the ultimate sweetener. The taster, on the other hand, knows how that sleight of mind works and how it helps marketing departments to beef up their copy. This sense of location is most imaginatively manifested by the preference of Japanese consumers for Tanzanian coffees over Kenyan. It may be in part due to the difference in the levels of acidity; it is certainly also due to the chance resemblance of Mount Kilimanjaro to their sacred Mount Fuji. Images of Kilimanjaro adorn many manufacturers' packs of Tanzanian coffee in Japan.

The sense of place becomes more refined higher up coffee's social scale; regional identifiers come into play, such as Antigua and Kona Kai; and, at the top, estate names. The more specific the sense of place attached to a coffee, the more it requires 'explaining', in the form of the inclusion of history in the proposition. In a world of proliferating consumer choice, history has the merit of bestowing lineage and breeding on a product, and just as every American heiress in the 1920s wanted to marry an English Duke, so the discerning consumer would like to think of himself (or herself) as a connoisseur. The origins of the historical marketing approach lie in the historical facts that surrounded certain coffees, and the undoubted cachet that accrued from them. Thus to learn, as was commonly believed twenty years ago, that the Queen had Wallenford Estate Blue Mountain Coffee flown to her via the diplomatic bag had considerable allure. It was impossible to buy bona fide Wallenford Estate coffee at that time, and it had been unavailable for years, but this supposed 'history' contributed powerfully to Jamaica Blue Mountain's long-standing pre-eminence amongst coffees.

What such ambient history lacks, of course, is the history of the coffee beans themselves. Ideally the coffee plants would have traceable origins, and preferably more than a limp and unsubstantiated claim like that of the Federación Nacional de Cafeteros in Colombia, which insists that coffee plants 'were introduced during the sixteenth century by Jesuit missionaries'. As we have seen, this was an era when Europeans had yet to discover coffee at all. The Caribbean likewise is littered with coffee plants apparently derived from those introduced to Martinique by Gabriel de Clieu, undermining whatever value this already highly suspect pedigree possesses.

It is a pity that Napoleon did not drink St Helena coffee on the historical record. Along with Churchill, Napoleon is the most collectable of historical figures, and it would have been a great coup to have been able to report a moment when he actually drank the coffee, and, even better, commented on it. We have seen that it is quite probable that he did so, and that evidence in its own right provides an interesting background to the coffee. We have found him drinking coffee regularly, we know where the water with which he brewed it came from on the island, and that he briefly grew coffee trees in his garden: we just haven't managed to catch him *in flagrante* with St Helena coffee.

15

THE BATTLE OF THE HEMISPHERES: THE OLD EMPIRE OF TEA VERSUS THE NEW EMPIRE OF COFFEE

We can divide the world of coffee conveniently into two hemispheres: the Americas and the rest. There are pressing geopolitical reasons why the plantation industries in the colonies of the old British Empire, focused on tea, differ from those of the American Empire, focused on coffee. The former British colonies are now major consumers of the beverage they grow: the latter operate through corporate colonialism, which obviates the need for territorial occupation and any concomitant responsibilities, however poorly discharged. By effectively tying coffee farmers to a small number of transnational buyers and creating, through institutions such as the World Bank, trading conditions that demolish any internal, national controls on the trade, the corporations have profited hugely while the farmers' share of the revenue pie has diminished from 40 per cent in 1991 to 13 per cent at the present time. Historically, tea also differed from coffee in that there was very substantial existing production and consumption of the beverage in pre-colonial China, Japan, and other Asian countries, whereas the discovery and rise of coffee coincided almost exactly with the expansion of European colonial power. The increased demand for tea in Europe could for a long time be met by the expansion of Chinese production, and it was not until the 1830s that the East India Company made serious efforts to introduce tea planting to India and other colonial territories. One result is that, of the top ten tea producing countries of today, four are former British colonies, and of the top ten consuming countries five are producers themselves, a further three are other ex-British colonies, and number five is Britain herself. These figures reveal an interesting legacy of the British Empire: it initiated the production of tea in some of its colonies and consumption was enthusiastically taken up by the people of its adoptive countries.

TEA

Top Ten Producers '000 tonnes		Top Ten Consumers '000 tonnes	
1. India	806	1. India	655
2. China	676	2. China	478
3. Sri Lanka	284	3. Turkey	166
4. Kenya	249	4. Russia	153
5. Turkey	171	5. United Kingdom	137
6. Indonesia	165	6. Japan	137
7. Japan	89	7. Pakistan	108
8. Iran	60	8. United States	93
9. Argentina	50	9. Iran	91
10. Bangladesh	47	10. Egypt	73

(Source: *Economist World in Figures* 2002)

It is also interesting to find the presence of significant tea drinking in countries of the former Ottoman Empire – Egypt and Turkey – which would seem to suggest that tea is the favoured drink of waning empires. Once Islam had gone into a general decline, Muslim countries, such as Iran, adopted what some see as the more introspective, less excitable tea to accompany the contemplation of their former glories.

THE WESTERN HEMISPHERE

The French invasion under Napoleon of the Iberian peninsula in 1808 led to the collapse of the Spanish and Portuguese monarchies. The most far-reaching effect of this was on their former colonies in the western hemisphere, in South and Central America. Coffee production in many of those countries was to become a very significant force in the economic and political life of those fledgling nations. Coffee, from being an exotic plant of the mysterious East, became a vital product of the post-colonial West.

As we have seen, the monopoly on coffee cultivation held by Yemen and Ethiopia was broken relatively quickly, and the colonial powers, initially the Dutch, English, and French, but later also the Portuguese and Spanish, introduced coffee under a plantation system into whatever appropriate colony was to hand. For the French and the English the conditions most favourable to the introduction of coffee planting could be found in the West Indies, where colonization and imported slaves had already combined with brutal efficiency. The Dutch, in their colonies in Java and Sumatra, had to find rather more subtle means to get the local population to do their dirty work, a more difficult task but one they set their minds to with a vengeance. When America achieved independence and turned its back on tea, it therefore had within its backyard the means to satisfy the increased demand for coffee. The islands of the West Indies initially supplied their needs, but then, as consumption expanded both in America and Europe, the newly independent countries of Central and South America took up coffee production. They had nearly all abolished slavery, as being inconsistent with their own revolutionary ideals. However, they exchanged the overt colonial masters of Spain and Portugal for the more discreet domination of the British Empire. A phrase that to modern ears sounds like jingoistic hyperbole, 'Britannia Rules the Waves', was a profound global truth after the defeat of Napoleon. The sea was the means whereby international trade was conducted and military force exerted; domination of the sea lanes by the Royal Navy gave unparalleled control of the conduct of international affairs to Britain. After successful independence movements of the 1820s had freed many Central and South American countries from Spain, George Canning, the British Foreign Secretary, could remark with assurance in 1824 that 'Spanish America is free and, if we do not mismanage our affairs sadly, she is English.' The assumption that freedom and Englishness amounted to the same thing was a fundamental quality of the British imperial mindset.

Britain had by then done a curious and unprecedented thing: she used her immense naval power for the imposition of the greatest act of imperial philanthropy the world had yet seen. The official abolition of the slave trade in 1808 was enforced, initially hesitantly but later with greater and greater resolve, by ships of the British West Africa Squadron. Countries such as Denmark and Argentina, which had a minor interest in the trade but a great interest in British goodwill, swiftly joined the campaign. Others, more dependent on the slave economy, fell into line much more slowly. Whilst the implementation of the abolition of slavery was riven with contradictions, there is no doubt that it was British perseverance, allied to British power, that finally removed the scourge of legitimate slavery from most of the world. Indeed it was only because she was a global imperial power that Britain was able to impose her will in this way. Rival contemporary European powers often sought a hidden motive for Britain's apparent philanthropy, and saw it as a 'grab for power'. Why else should the foremost slave trading nation at the end of the eighteenth century seek its abolition early in the nineteenth? The answer was God, or at least that

God who had apparently endorsed slavery as a manifestation of his divine will, had suddenly had second thoughts and had determined that it was vile and despicable. Ably represented by the Abolitionist movement and their champion in Parliament, William Wilberforce, God got his new message across to all social levels of the nation. The seed of doubt, once sown in the fertile soil of the collective conscience, grew with startling rapidity: it was the speed with which Britain reversed her position on slavery that, more than anything, aroused the suspicions of her rivals.

With the inexorable rise of American power, Britain gradually lost its influence over the western hemisphere. The brief occupation of Cuba in 1898 signalled the first tentative step of American imperialism, and that country's influence over its backyard increased exponentially during the twentieth century.

Of the top ten coffee producing countries today, four are in Central and South America and Indonesia still figures in fifth place – in part a legacy of the Dutch era, although the country now produces a great deal of Robusta coffee. The top ten consuming countries, with the exception of Brazil at number two and Ethiopia at nine, are America first, and then other Western European countries plus Japan at four. In other words, and in contrast to tea, the flow between coffee production and consumption is primarily from developing countries to Western countries, and there is far less of an internal market for the major producers than there is with tea. Coffee thus continues to be a much more overt product of the historical colonial system. India and China have a significant national interest in the well-being of their tea industries. With the partial exception of Brazil, which consumes 40 per cent of what it produces, the same principle does not apply readily to coffee.

COFFEE

Top Ten Producers '000 tonnes		Top Ten Consumers '000 tonnes	
1. Brazil	1941	1. Unites States	1121
2. Vietnam	676	2. Brazil	765
3. Colombia	560	3. Germany	567
4. Mexico	387	4. Japan	404
5. Indonesia	361	5. France	319
6. Cote d'Ivoire	328	6. Italy	307
7. India	324	7. Spain	188
8. Guatemala	312	8. United Kingdom	138
9. Ethiopia	210	9. Ethiopia	98
10. Uganda	186	10. Netherlands	95

(Source: *Economist World in Figures* 2002)

The European powers used to maintain a significant commercial loyalty to their former colonies when it came to their coffee-buying habits. The French, having made the mistake of colonizing the Robusta producing countries of West Africa, formed an affection for its particular taste that stood in stark contrast to their discernment respecting other foodstuffs. The Dutch still relish the heavy body and low acidity of Indonesian coffees. The British, having colonized Kenya, discovered to their surprise that they had the makings of one of the best coffees in the world, and aristocratic Europeans flocked there to establish plantations – most famously Karen Blixen ('Isak Dinesen'), who discovered to her chagrin that the land she had bought was above the height limit for coffee growing, leaving her plenty of time on her hands to fly around the country with tousle-haired Old Etonians. Since the 1970s, with the onward march of globalization, such historical trading patterns have been increasingly blurred. The French have discovered the virtues of good coffee, ending their years of gustatory exile, and are increasingly replacing Robustas with high-quality Arabicas. The British have discovered espresso and cappuccino, and thereby reduced links with their old East African partner – Kenyan coffees perform poorly in espresso machines. Only the USA has remained consistently loyal to its backyard: of coffee drunk there, a higher proportion (75 per cent) comes from the western hemisphere than would be expected on a pro rata basis.

THE AMERICAS

The western hemisphere produces two-thirds of the world's coffee and consumes a third of it. As the biggest single consuming nation (some 25 per cent of worldwide production) the USA has, with impeccable economic foresight, regarded the countries of Central, and to a lesser extent South, America, as Uncle Sam's backyard. Although overt colonialism is making a comeback, the USA, until relatively recently, has adopted a covert approach to the achievement of its economic hegemony in Central and South America. Much of this was driven by two considerations: countering the threat of 'Communism' (or indeed anything with the faintest taint of socialism), and maintaining regimes 'sympathetic' to America and American business in place, which have in nearly every case been oligarchical or military. As the latter created the conditions in which the former flourished, there was always a fundamental structural weakness in the strategy, causing problems that could be countered only by ever more repressive regimes. Thus in support of this flawed approach these countries have witnessed, and continue to witness, an unending series of acts of state terrorism perpetrated by the US in the form of interference in the electoral process through violence and intimidation, assassination, funding of guerrilla armies and death squads, illicit gun and drug running, and, when considered necessary, direct military intervention.

Until recently the coffee industry played a very significant role, being the means by which the élite got and maintained their wealth, and conversely was the principal cause of the grievances of the poor and dispossessed peasantry. This historic imbalance lurks in the foundations of the political and social structures of the region, even as they transform themselves into 'modern' economies. With the collapse of the Soviet Union, the perceived 'Communist' threat has substantially diminished while the US economic stranglehold on the region has likewise increased through the North American Free Trade Agreement (1994) and its possible replacement, the Free Trade Area of the Americas (2005), will encompass the entire hemisphere except Cuba.

The net effect for coffee producers has been that the USA no longer feels any political need to address their problems through the International Coffee Agreement, which collapsed in 1989 when it withdrew its support. The threat of economic sanctions (usually applied through the World Bank and the IMF) is sufficient to cow most of the population. The remaining 'hardliners' (Communists, trade unionists, and other dissenters) can be dealt with through military action, usually via the provision of equipment and technical support to the preferred regime. Under these circumstances it is very difficult for a left-leaning regime to get elected, or, once elected, to stay in power. With control of the media remaining in the hands of the oligarchy, and with the global financial markets reacting favourably or unfavourably to candidates according to their sympathies, elections have become increasingly a meaningless sham, designed principally to maintain the fiction for the American public that their country stands for freedom and democracy.

The islands of the Caribbean were the pre-eminent global producers of coffee whilst under the direct rule of European colonial powers, principally France in Saint-Domingue but also Britain in Jamaica and Spain in Cuba. The Napoleonic Wars devastated demand from Continental Europe, and many of the islands converted to sugar cultivation. When normal trade was resumed, the competition from the newly established mainland coffee industries of Brazil, Venezuela, Guatemala, and Costa Rica was too strong for the residual island plantations. The abolition of slavery dealt the final blow, and whilst the Caribbean remains a small producer of coffee, the real action is in the continental Americas.

Coffee books traditionally take the reader for a comforting stroll through the flavour variations of coffee, country by country. We will take that walk through Central and South America also, pausing now and then to admire the local history and politics as well. In some countries we judge to be of particular interest, we will halt, and look in some detail.

CENTRAL AMERICA

The doleful consequences of US hegemony and that nation's support of any anti-Communist activity, however venal and anti-democratic, with the concomitant litany of human rights abuses, death squads, and impoverished citizenry, can be read like a roll-call in a southward sweep through Central and South America. With the exception of Mexico, which has had a more diversified economy since it became the great source of cheap manufactures for North America, the states of Central America are – or were until the recent collapse in prices – all heavily dependent on coffee for their export income. Coffee sustains their economies, but also sustains the entrenched land-owning oligarchies that control the industry, and hence the political and military machines that preserve the status quo. Historically, since the establishment of coffee growing in the late nineteenth century, many of these coffee countries had been effectively near-slave states. The wealthy coffee plantation owners (frequently foreigners, and in the case of Guatemala of German origin) would, in cahoots with the government, coerce migrant labour down from the neighbouring highlands, the menfolk often selling their wives' labour in exchange for an advance, with the women then perhaps being subjected to rape or abuse. Frequently the land that the coffee was grown on – by definition, fertile and at high altitude – was appropriated from indigenes who then became the first guerrillas to fight against the same government policies that had allowed their communal lands to be stolen. The refrains of 'Land Reform' and 'Liberal' politics in Central America were frequently the high-minded packaging in which the government endorsed the theft. The creation of wealthy land-owning coffee farmers to whom the nominal government was deeply beholden created a cycle of suppression of political debate and the press, the use of the police and bureaucracy as an instrument of fear, and the replacement of any government that failed to behave in an accommodating fashion towards the coffee oligarchy. Under these circumstances, the only expression of opposition was out-and-out rebellion: in El Salvador in the 1880s the displaced Indians rebelled, to be faced with well-armed militias; in Nicaragua the Indians laid siege to Matagalpa, and more than a thousand were killed by the army.

In modern times left-wing insurgency in all these countries has been countered ruthlessly by the army or police, themselves often trained at the notorious School of the Americas at Fort Benning in Georgia, which used to be under almost permanent siege by protesters against human rights abuses. In the 1960s, the School was known in Latin America as the *escuela de golpes* or 'coup school', owing to the high number of ex-alumni who became involved in overthrowing Central or South American governments. When some of the Spanish-language training manuals used at the School until 1991 were released by the Pentagon in

1996 after pressure from activists, a *New York Times* editorial commented: 'Americans can now read for themselves some of the noxious lessons that the United States Army taught to thousands of Latin American military and police officers at the School of the Americas during the 1980s'. A training manual recently released by the Pentagon recommended interrogation techniques like torture, execution, blackmail and arresting relatives of those being questioned.' Other lessons to be learned included assassination, mind-control, and electoral fraud. The School has recently vowed to change its ways, but the fact remains that the political and economic structure in most of these countries is inherited from this strong-arm approach allied to coffee interests.

Mexico

Coffee represents 1 per cent of Mexico's export earnings, and employs 4 million people directly and indirectly on 120,000 farms, 100,000 of which are less than 5 hectares. Two hundred thousand indigenous Indians farm less than 2 hectares of coffee. Mexican coffee has a pronounced acidity but has a tendency to a lack of body. Mexican politics has a tendency to dictatorship and corruption and, more recently, an accommodating attitude to every economic policy that the USA suggests. Whilst the government bends over backwards to provide tax breaks to sweatshop manufacturing industries, it virtually ignores the plight of its coffee farmers, whose coffee is fetching such a low price that they cannot afford to pick it. Coffee fields may be torn down to make way for corn so that the families can at least eat. The environmental damage this causes will be serious, for coffee plantations are often a halfway house between forest and field.

Much Mexican coffee is grown in the Chiapas region in the south of the country bordering Guatemala. Chiapas is the most rebellious of the Mexican provinces and is home to the Zapatista revolutionary movement, which is being ruthlessly suppressed by the government, supported by a fleet of US 'advisors'. Severe disruption in the early 1990s by the Zapatistas was ascribed to low coffee prices: the area was subsequently militarized under the guidance of graduates of the School of the Americas, who now routinely terrorize the indigenous population. The main reason for this appears to be that the Zapatistas' desire for autonomy conflicts with the aims of President Vicente Fox's 'Plan Pueblo Panama', which envisages the use of the province for the large-scale production of a range of export crops. This, along with the current coffee price collapse, seems to have prompted widespread migration from the area, contributing further to the chaos in the cities and desperate attempts to enter the US illegally: in Arizona in 2001, fourteen former coffee pickers from Chiapas were found dead, suffocated in the back of the truck that had smuggled them in.

Guatemala

Guatemalan coffee is traditionally amongst the best in Central America: Guatemalan politics have traditionally been amongst the worst. Coffee directly or indirectly supports the lives of a third of the population of 6 million, and the country is the eighth biggest producer in the world. The largest fifty or so haciendas are owned mostly by families of German origin, but there are some 60,000 very small family holdings. Even in today's market, coffee represents nearly 10 per cent of the country's export income.

Nowhere better typifies the very worst of Central American politics than Guatemala. The alliance of Central American states that declared independence from Spain in 1821 lasted only until 1838, when it fractured into its component parts. The Mayan indigenes of Guatemala found themselves forced off their lands, and to avoid effective slavery fled to the high mountains. Coffee started actively to be grown in 1853, but it was found that the best land for its cultivation, the Pacific side of the country in the rich volcanic soil around Antigua, was occupied by lately exiled Mayans. The standard-issue liberal land reform statutes were enacted, which legalized the dispossession of the Indians, and coffee became a major industry, relying heavily on the forced labour of those same Indians. They in turn developed an understandable tendency to try to escape from the plantations, and the result was the development of a disproportionately large army to stop them doing so. A wave of German immigration in the late nineteenth century consolidated the larger farms: they, and the economy of the country as a whole, were still dependent on the exploitation of the labour of local Indians, and the army to enforce it.

Thus a tight knit, largely German coffee oligarchy supported by a ruthless army became the *de facto* government of the country. This became rather alarming when the Second World War broke out, particularly as many in the German community were openly sympathetic to the Nazis. Those Germans who opposed Hitler were placed on a secret Gestapo hit list, to be disposed of on victory. The end of the Second World War saw the first attempts at social reform in Guatemala, particularly under the nationalist Jacobo Arbenz Guzman, who nationalized land that was lying fallow, some belonging to an American business, the United Fruit Company. That could not be tolerated: he had to go, and he did, in a CIA-engineered coup of 1954. The ill-substantiated threat of 'Communist infiltration' provided the necessary justification, and the CIA's new man in charge ensured that the ownership of all lands was returned to the status quo *ante* existing before the date of the reforms. Arbenz was no Communist: he had merely wanted to change Guatemala from a 'dependent nation with a semi-colonial economy into an economically independent country'. Independent also of US hegemony, which proved to be his downfall.

Having lovingly crafted a repressive, one-party regime, the

US spent the next thirty-six years trying to keep it, and its later manifestations, in place. The coffee élite had no complaints: they were still able to rely on the cheap labour that the military helped keep cheap by employing the tried and tested techniques of the School of the Americas on 'subversives', including the rape and torture of an American nun, Diane Ortiz, who was later to claim that one of the perpetrators was actually an American. The former Defence Minister, Hector Gramajo Morales, later memorably explained his social policy: 'We instituted civil affairs [in 1982] which provides development for 70% of the population, while we kill 30%. Before, the strategy was to kill 100%.' Whatever the percentage, it is estimated that some 200,000 people were killed in Guatemala up until 1996.

Bill Clinton stated in 1999 that US support for oppressive regimes in Guatemala had been 'wrong', which must have brought great comfort to those who had suffered from its effects for thirty-six years since Arbenz's death. The highly fragile truce in the civil war currently holds, but largely in name only: there are still death squads who pick off 'subversives', and the military is still substantially armed and trained by the USA. The larger coffee plantations are still owned by the élite, protected by high walls and armed guards, and the workers are still housed in barracks where they may or may not receive the statutory minimum wage of $2.48 a day, and the basic education and health care that the law provides for.

El Salvador

Ten per cent of the 6.5 million population of El Salvador are dependent directly or indirectly on coffee, which represents 15 per cent of GNP and over 5 per cent of export earnings, down from 96 per cent in 1936 and 50 per cent in 1990. (Fifty-seven per cent of export earnings now come from the garment industry.) The high-grown coffee of nondescript quality was mostly exported to Germany until the recent price crisis – some of the wealthy coffee plantation owners are of German origin. Forty thousand jobs have recently been lost and 70 per cent of the small farms are effectively abandoned, meaning that no cleaning, pruning, or fertilizing is taking place.

In July 2002 a Federal Court in West Palm Beach, Florida ordered two retired generals from El Salvador to pay $54.6 million dollars in damages to three Salvadorean citizens tortured by security forces twenty years previously. The generals, one a former minister of defence and the other the head of the National Guard, had been honoured by the USA and were living a respectable retirement in Florida. They had previously been acquitted of complicity in the murder of three American nuns, their defence lawyer claiming that their courageous defence of democracy could be likened to that of Thomas Jefferson and John Adams. This echoes President Reagan's infamous characterization of the Contras in Nicaragua as freedom fighters in the mould of the Founding Fathers. Abuses of history are as much part of the armoury of American statecraft as abuses of democracy. On this occasion the mountain of evidence from credible witnesses connecting the defendants directly to the torture of the plaintiffs was irrefutable, and stories emerged of how government troops hunted down suspected guerrilla sympathizers, leaving bodies littering the streets and killing entire villages. El Salvador was, and is, heavily dependent on coffee. The American support of the oligarchy was thus mainly support of the coffee élite. In the case of El Mozote, where up to a thousand elderly men, women, and children were brutally murdered, ten of the twelve soldiers eventually accused of the massacre had trained at the School of the Americas.

The lives of Salvadorean governments have been 'nasty, brutish, and short', usually involving the military – also, since the Second World War, often trained at the School of the Americas.

Rios Montt, a particularly unsavoury President during the 1980s, ensured that not only were supposedly left-wing agitators disposed of under his regime, but also indigenous Mayan Indians, many of whom inhabited the highlands most suitable for the cultivation of coffee. Over 100,000 of these indigenes are supposed to have been killed during his time. This was, however, only a continuation of an honourable Salvadorean tradition dating back to the nineteenth century, when liberal land reforms led to the appropriation of the lands of the indigenes for coffee farming and the concentration of that land in the hands of fourteen families. Indians revolted throughout the 1880s, but were violently suppressed by well-equipped militias.

Honduras

The coffee industry of Honduras today represents some 10 per cent of export income, down by over a third from five years ago. Six hundred thousand of the population of 3 million are dependent on it. There are about 45,000 farms, some organized into co-operatives. Honduran coffee, particularly that grown at the highest altitudes, can be very decent, if rarely exceptional. In general it is a good, clean-cupping, reasonably priced 'filler' coffee for use in blends. Honduran politics have been dire since the end of the Second World War, its large production of bananas making it the political model for the 'Banana Republic'.

Military dictatorships, assassinations, torture, CIA-advised counter-insurgency operations – the whole gamut of the USA's patronage can be seen at work in Honduras, especially during the 1980s when the country housed the celebrated Reagan-era Contras, a rag-tag partly mercenary army of US-funded 'freedom fighters' set up to oust the Sandinistas in Nicaragua, who were in some danger of running the country with a semblance of social justice. Oxfam, as we have seen, commented at the time that the Sandinistas were 'exceptional in the strength of that government's commitment . . . to improving the condition of the people and encouraging their active participation in the development process'. Naturally they too had to go, and the Contras were put together to do the job from Honduras. The only problem was how to get them funded without arousing the suspicions of Congress. The three-year investigation undertaken by the Kerry Committee of the Senate found out how it was done: 'There was substantial evidence of drug smuggling through the war zones on the part of individual Contras, Contra suppliers, Contra pilots, mercenaries who worked with the Contras, and Contra supporters through-out the region . . . In each case, one or another agency of the US Government had information regarding the involvement either while it was occurring, or immediately thereafter . . . Senior US policy makers were not immune to the idea that drug money was a perfect solution to the Contras' funding problems.'

The US Government had covertly adopted Colonel Oliver North's idea of funding the actions of the Contras by drug running. It is this concept that appears to have matured into a fully fledged part of US government subculture, and which is increasingly being played out against the volatile backdrop of Colombia.

Nicaragua

Coffee represents nearly 15 per cent of the export earnings of Nicaragua on about 17,000 farms. It is estimated that some 300,000 people formerly dependent on coffee for their livelihood have been made unemployed by the current coffee crisis. The coffee is light- to medium-cup, with a fairly metallic acidity, more fragrant in the best qualities. Not amongst the best coffees of Central America, but quite drinkable as a 'single origin' coffee. The country's politics, however, are one of the most depressing examples of the baleful influence of the USA's avuncular role in Central America.

The notorious Anastasio Somoza García came to power in the 1930s. As well as ruling with an iron rod, he and his family owned forty-three of the largest coffee plantations in the country. Any sign of dissent was ruthlessly suppressed until finally the Sandinistas (named after the nationalist leader Augusto César Sandino) came to power in 1978 by deposing the old tyrant and setting up reform programmes with progressive social ideas such as building schools and hospitals. Initially, President Jimmy Carter did what he could to lessen the threat of 'another Cuba' through conventional diplomatic and economic channels. The election of Ronald Reagan in 1980 led to the formation of the Contras, who burnt down the schools and hospitals. Horrific scenes of rape and pillage took place, all paid for by the US Government who also took the opportunity to engage in some illegal harbour mining in the area.

After a decade of constant struggle, the 1990 election saw the defeat of the Sandinistas by a population exhausted not by their rule but by the trouble that their rule brought in its wake. Some elements of the Sandinistas' social reform programmes, in particular the land reforms, have remained in place, and Nicaragua is still a country where co-operative movements flourish, particularly in the coffee industry. One such, PROODECOOP, was started in 1993 to help its members with finance and with production and marketing advice. It has 45 co-operatives on its books supporting 2500 families, each of which farms about ten acres. PROODECOOP is also involved in the construction of schools and clinics and provides legal advice for members. It has also initiated an innovative project in conjunction with Global Exchange in San Francisco (which promotes Fair Trade coffee) whereby interested parties are invited to pay their way to Nicaragua for the coffee harvest, staying a minimum of two weeks and having their expenses there paid. This suggests that the problems experienced by Nicaragua in the 1980s still resonate with Western consumers, and that the country remains something of a byword for social justice.

Whilst this is encouraging – and many such Fair Trade initiatives can be found throughout Central and South America – it is evident that these self-created pockets of a more just society have been forced into a marginalized existence within the kind of globalized macro-economic environment as represented by NAFTA and its progeny.

The Nicaraguan government is believed to be corrupt and inefficient: it has also signed up to an agreement with the IMF to maintain a minimum balance of international reserves, which means that a fund set up from coffee farmers' contributions in better times to support coffee farmers in lean ones, such as currently exist, is effectively frozen. Another initiative to suspend all foreclosures on coffee farmers for 300 days was unanimously passed by the Nicaraguan National Assembly in 2001 but vetoed by the President under pressure from the IMF and the Inter-American Bank, which latter threatened to suspend a $50 million loan. Thus farmers who may have acquired a modest 10-acre smallholding as a result of the Sandinistas' land reforms may see that holding repossessed as a result of the pressures of the international financial institutions that wield effective power over the governments of states that have borrowed from them.

Costa Rica

Three hundred thousand of the 2.5 million inhabitants of Costa Rica are dependent on coffee for their livelihood, many on smallholdings that are linked in co-operatives that are in turn members of a Federation that processes and exports their coffees. With its reputation for very high quality – good Costa Rican coffee, particularly from the Pacific side of the country, has all the best attributes of Central American coffees – the country has been able to benefit significantly from the boom in the specialty coffee trade in the USA.

The survival of Costa Rica as the 'Switzerland of Central America', a democratic, stable, and relatively prosperous state amidst the chaos and poverty of its neighbours, is something of a mystery. It may be coincidental, but it is also the country that dispossessed fewest indigenous people in the colonial and post-colonial era. This was not necessarily the result of a benign social policy, but more because there were few Indians there to begin with. Nonetheless, the land was not overly stained by the blood of displaced indigenes, and has rewarded its current occupiers with the finest coffees and a largely untroubled political landscape.

Panama

Panama completes the southwards tour of the Central American isthmus. Its two million inhabitants grow a small amount of coffee, but it has increasingly become a popular origin for new speciality coffee for the US. As the country is always associated with the canal, it is surprising to find that the landscape of much of Panama is very mountainous.

The country was carved away from Colombia in 1903, and its all-important canal remained under US control until 1999. As a warning to the future guardians of the canal, and to send clear signals to its neighbours, the USA invaded Panama in 1989, ostensibly to get its President, General Manuel Noriega, who was accused of drug smuggling – to which the US had turned a blind eye to while he was a useful ally. Thousands of innocent Panamanians were killed or wounded, and Noriega sought refuge at the Vatican Embassy from where he was eventually prised by the unbearably loud rock music that the Americans blasted at him.

SOUTH AMERICA

The coffee-producing countries of South America include Colombia, Venezuela, Bolivia, Ecuador, Peru, and, of course, Brazil.

Even Paraguay and Argentina have modest coffee industries, leaving the coffee continent only Uruguay and Chile short of a full country set. However, South America is also a continent where many other vital commodities – oil, copper, coal, tin, sugar, soya beans, iron ore, and gold to mention but a few – can be found in significant quantities, as well as manufacturing and other industries. Thus on the whole, the dependence of the countries of the region on coffee is markedly smaller than in Central America, and the effects of the coffee trade on the economy and politics of a given country is less marked. Brazil, as we have seen, was dominated by coffee interests in the nineteenth century, but although it is still the number one producer worldwide, today its economy is much more mixed.

However, one country, Colombia, which is currently vying with Vietnam for number two status, is in a highly volatile state at the time of writing, and deserves to be looked at in some detail for what it can tell us about coffee in the world today.

Colombia

Colombia exported $866 million of coffee in 2002, down from $1.7 billion five years earlier. This represents one-sixth of the value of petroleum and related exports, and about the same as that of coal. It has some 300,000 coffee farms, of which 40 per cent are less than a hectare in size. Half a million people – of a total population of 40 million – live off the coffee industry, directly or indirectly. Good Colombian coffee should have a medium body, a clean cup, and a fine acidity. Unlike Kenya coffees, in which the acidity is allied to a pronounced fruitiness, the Colombian acidity is allied to a nutty flavour. The additional refinement of a Supremo overlays these characteristics with an element of sweetness.

Until recently, the Federación Nacional de Cafeteros (FNC), the non-governmental organization that controls the coffee industry in Colombia, was a model of good order and the envy of exporting countries the world over. Undermined by war, terrorism, and disastrously low coffee prices it was in danger of imploding, its funds exhausted, and the consequences for the peasant coffee farmers of Colombia, already in desperate straits, would have been terminal. Drastic layoffs and restructuring have enabled it to secure a reprieve from the government, predicated on a return to a more favourable coffee market by 2005. It would take a brave gambler to bet the farm on that.

Colombia used to be, until the appearance of Vietnam on the world stage, the second largest grower of coffee after Brazil, producing about a million tonnes in an average year. The general quality is significantly higher than that of its big rival, partly a result of higher altitude – the three cordilleras on which it is grown run up the spine of the country and are part of the Andes range – but also because the coffees are all washed, whereas those of Brazil are natural, or unwashed. Most of the coffee is marketed through the FNC, which buys the parchment coffee from smallholders, mills and grades it, and handles its distribution and what happens in sales. Unlike what happens in many countries, where the peasant smallholders are frequently the first to suffer from the vagaries of the international marketplace, or forced to wait many months for a return on their crop, the FNC has a long-standing and largely patrician relationship with the growers. For example, until recently, in times of very low coffee prices, the FNC would effectively subsidize the price it paid to the smallholders from funds built up in more prosperous times.

Enormous quantities of Colombian coffees are exported to the USA and find their way into the ubiquitous, infinitely refillable American breakfast mug, where the coffee is usually so weak as to be unrecognizable, and whatever qualities it may possess are destroyed by the 'cream'. The European market is more demanding, and as a result a more carefully processed grade known as 'European Preparation' is produced for that market. For a coffee blender, the overriding feature of Colombian coffee is its consistency. It sets a high standard and sticks to it tenaciously. This consistency is a result partly of the well-run industry, but may also be a consequence of the fact that, uniquely amongst producing countries, Colombia's coffee trees have no season and are harvested all the year round. Colombian coffee is thus an ideal component of a blend, being of good quality, readily available, and very reliable.

This reassuring portrait of Colombian coffee production presupposes that all is well in the Colombian body politic, that its economy is reasonably stable, and that the FNC can continue to smooth out the peaks and troughs without outside interference. However, all that is under threat: the civil war is escalating as the US seeks to defend its oil interests, World Bank strictures have led to a doubling of unemployment in the last ten years, and there has been a 30 per cent drop in real terms in the national average income. Agriculture, formerly the mainstay of the nation's economy, has gone into steep decline, with 2 million acres of arable land lying vacant whilst imports of food have soared. And the FNC – that remarkably enduring experiment in a centralized, planned, co-operative organization – can hardly hold back the tidal waves of free trade and globalization. Coffee farmers in the 'Zona Cafetera' are abandoning previously flourishing coffee farms, or taking to coca and poppy planting to supplement their income. In the south, where such plants are more widespread, US planes spray them from the air with Monsanto's Roundup or Roundup-Ultra (its more virulent form), killing all and any crops, polluting the rivers, and causing widespread health problems, as well as laying waste over a million acres in the last five years. When a demonstration of the sprayer's accuracy was mounted to impress visiting US Senator Paul Wellstone, a Democrat opposed to American military aid for Colombia, he and his aides were accidentally drenched in the herbicide. Before it could be determined what long-term harm may have befallen him as a result, Wellstone was killed in a plane crash in the run up to the 2002 Senate elections. The death of the most vociferous Democratic critic of the then potential war in Iraq, just as sabres were rattling ever louder, was seen by some as an eerie coincidence, suggesting that the Executive had made a closer study of the history of Byzantium than might at first appear.

Monsanto were one of the suppliers of chemicals for the Vietnam War including the notorious Agent Orange. Whilst Monsanto acknowledge, in the 130 countries worldwide where they are marketed, that Roundup and Roundup Ultra should be used with caution to avoid damage to humans, animals, and other flora, it has long been suspected there has not been adequate research into the possible effects on humans of enhanced Roundup Ultra Cosmo Flux 411 F, which apparently has been deployed by the US Government without the knowledge of the Colombian Government. The US 'War on Drugs' has frightening implications for the Colombian ecosystem, and if coca and poppy planting continue to move into the areas where coffee is grown, the health effects of the spraying could be felt globally. Within the USA, Monsanto's reassurances regarding the safety of their operations have been shown to be lamentably wanting: they were recently found guilty by a court in Alabama of conduct 'so outrageous in character and extreme in degree as to go beyond all possible bounds of decency so as to be regarded as atrocious and utterly intolerable in civilised society'. The case concerned the long-term poisoning and systematic cover-up of the toxic pollution of the poor community of Anniston. The company was heavily fined as a result, but it is clear that, for this corporation at least, the wages of sin substantially exceed the costs of virtue.

Appallingly, worse is yet to come. The US administration is contemplating the use of mycoherbicides, genetically engineered pathogenic fungi, conjured up by the US Department of

Agriculture's experiment station in Beltsville, Maryland. These are being produced with US funds by Ag/Bio Company, at a private lab in Bozeman, Montana, and at a former Soviet bioweapons factory in Tashkent, Uzbekistan. Fusarium oxysporum is designed for use against marijuana and coca plants and Pleospora papaveracea is engineered to destroy opium poppies. Neither the human health implications of their use nor the likely effect on other plant species has been determined. The Colombian rainforest is one of the most biodiverse remaining on the planet, and the inevitable spill-over of aerial-sprayed mycoherbicides could trigger an ecological and human catastrophe that would make Vietnam seem like small change. The destruction of the forest plant life would be very convenient for mining, logging, and oil interests, however. The Convention on the Prohibition of Military or Any Other Hostile Use of Environmental Modification Techniques (ENMOD) was adopted by the UN in 1976, with the US as a signatory, as a result of the worldwide condemnation of the use of Agent Orange during the Vietnam War. Peru and Ecuador oppose the US plan, citing not only ENMOD but also the non-proliferation section of the Biological Warfare Convention, which proscribes the transfer between nations of such weapons. It is a telling comment on Colombia's subservient colonial status that it is likely to be forced into accepting a provision within the 'Plan Colombia', shortly to be agreed by Congress, whereby massive US aid and weaponry will be given to the Colombian Government to wage war against the FARC guerillas ('Frerzas Armadas Revolucionares de Colombia') only if the former agrees to the use of mycoherbicides. The rural people, ecology, and coffee industry of Colombia are thus threatened with devastation by their own government. The likely effect on the coffee crop remains to be seen, but there is no reason to assume that the coffee fields will be immune to the drifting herbicide sprays, or that this toxic soup may not enter the food chain via the endless cup.

Coffee came to Colombia as a result of Spanish colonization. The foundation of the cities of Santa Marta and Cartagena on the coast from the 1520s was followed by inland cities, including Bogotá, from where the new state was administered, absorbing the indigenous Indian tribes without much resistance. Cartagena grew to be a major mercantile and naval port of the Spanish Empire and was famously plundered by Sir Francis Drake. In time-honoured fashion, disease and hard labour laid waste to the local Indians, and miscegenation obliterated their culture: they were joined in their oppressed state by African slaves, who worked the mines and fields. The FNC claims that coffee was introduced by Jesuit missionaries in the sixteenth century: this remains both unsubstantiated and unlikely. Not only would this imply that the Jesuits knew about coffee when it was but a twinkle in the eye of other European traders, but that they had anticipated its value as an export crop. In general, the Spanish were slow to develop the coffee-growing potential of their Empire, and it is more likely that it was introduced in the late eighteenth century.

During the eighteenth century the Viceroyalty of New Granada was formed, incorporating modern-day Colombia, Venezuela, Panama, and Ecuador. Spaniards born in South America started to occupy key positions in the administration and army, and, whilst loyalty to Spain remained absolute, the seeds of independence were sown. Napoleon's invasion of Spain triggered an identity crisis amongst that Empire's subjects, facilitating the rise, during the early nineteenth century, of Simón Bolívar, 'The Liberator', who secured independence but at the cost of the secession of Venezuela and Ecuador. The country then had a million and a half inhabitants. Liberal reforms during the latter half of the century tended – as they did throughout Latin America – to consolidate the position of the wealthy through land reforms. Indians found themselves dispossessed of the little land that they had. The Conservatives sought to reintroduce the ties with the Catholic Church that the Liberals had broken, and bloody civil war was frequent. By the beginning of the twentieth century, Colombia was producing some 3 per cent of the world's coffee; twenty years later, it was 10 per cent, accounting for 70 per cent of the country's export income. It principally went to the US. Panama seceded in 1903 after the machinations of Philippe Jean Bunau-Varilla and Theodore Roosevelt over the Panama Canal, which the Colombian Government did not wish to be built. The Panamanians received annual payment from America in exchange for yielding sovereignty in the Canal Zone. Colombia greatly resented this intrusion by its powerful neighbour. The FNC was founded by 'cafeteros', coffee farmers, in 1927, and remains a non-governmental organization, and still exhibits unfashionable signs of democratic tendencies. Under President Lopez in the 1930s, laws were passed giving legal title to squatters of unused agricultural land, a radical reform that had a significant impact on the coffee industry, giving thousands of growers their own land. The return of the Conservatives after the Second World War saw a time of political turbulence and the rise of 'La Violencia' in which 200,000 people died in the period up to 1964. A military coup in 1953 resulted in a populist President, General Gustavo Rojas Pinilla, whose regime collapsed when world coffee prices fell dramatically in 1957. The Liberals and Conservatives then formed a National Front, in effect a power-sharing agreement amongst the élite, alternating the presidency between them. It ensured that at least no one else got a look in.

The 'Alliance for Progress', a US initiative for economic development in the region started in 1961, had the predictable side effect of increasing Colombia's dependence on the USA. Orlando Fals Borda, a former dean of the faculty of sociology at the National University of Colombia, describes the initiative thus: 'What we actually did was to mortgage the country in order to save a ruling class that was headed for disaster. It was already tottering when this stimulation came along to enable it to gasp out a few more breaths, the same kind of artificial breathing as that of a dying man who is fed oxygen, and equally expensive. The sad part is that this ruling class will not have to pay the mortgage it incurred. It will be paid, perhaps with the blood, certainly with the sweat of our children and the working classes, the innocent people who always in the last analysis pay for the broken plates.'

Inflation, unemployment, and corruption gave rise to popular mistrust of the National Front, and revolutionary Marxist movements emerged from the universities in the 1960s, including FARC. The latter remains the foremost revolutionary force in Colombia today. The rise of the Medellín and Cali cartels in the 1970s brought a new complication to the political scene: drugs. Colombia was initially the main supplier of cannabis to the voracious US drug market, and then subsequently cocaine. The return to some semblance of democratic choice with the demise of the National Front and the re-emergence of the Liberals and Conservatives was increasingly marred by the tendency of the drug cartels to kill unco-operative judges and politicians. The Marxist insurgents were pitted against the government-approved vigilante groups formed by landowners, and they all received funding from the drugs trade. Into this maelstrom strode the USA, providing massive aid to the Colombian military and assisting in every way short of actual participation to combat leftist insurgency. The victims were frequently simply political opponents – trade unionists, human rights activists, and left-leaning politicians – rather than guerrillas stalking the jungles. America justifies this under the banner of the 'War on Drugs', which conveniently ignores the involvement of all parties – government, paramilitaries, insurgents, and the CIA – in that same trade. The recently elected Colombian President has promised to double the police and triple the military in an all-out effort finally to deal with the guerrilla problem, with promises of US support that includes satellite tracking technology to keep tabs on rebel forces, whilst the coffee industry teeters on the verge of collapse and pushes those who have been critically affected into the arms of those same guerrillas. America's money is spent on copious military aid, divisive and destructive, but the idea of using that money to support a minimum coffee price, which would go some way to addressing the root cause of the problems, remains heretical. The humble Colombian cafetero trying to turn a dime on a coffee smallholding hardly registers on the global economic radar screen, but it's his country, his land, and his compatriots that suffer.

The FNC is by no means a perfect institution: in a dysfunctional democracy, in which coffee was by far the largest earner of foreign exchange, it could never be. The oligarchy was deeply involved in coffee, and the FNC to some became the means of reinforcing the patron/peon status quo. What it managed to ensure from its foundation in 1927 was a consistently high quality of coffee: this is no longer the case. The FNC has been forced by the crisis in world coffee prices to lay off over half its employees, cut back its representative offices worldwide, and reconsider its role. The fund for growers, accumulated in good times to cover the bad, is exhausted, and it is only by running a deficit that the organization can help growers with a paltry subsidy. They in turn cannot manage to produce and process coffee to the same high standard that had become a *sine qua non* in the coffee trade. The quality coffee that blenders and roasters could rely on has been compromised, perhaps fatally.

It is easy to forget, when reviewing the problems of Central and South America in relation to their northern neighbour, that a large proportion of the population of those countries descend from the Spanish colonists who killed (deliberately, by war, or accidentally, by disease), brutalized, or economically marginalized the indigenes they found there, and then introduced negro slaves to work the land for them. The prints of the bloody hands of empire builders of European stock can be found over much of the world today, and whilst the fortunes of individual nation states may have waxed and waned, the European gene-pool still has a pretty firm grip on the totality of the world's wealth.

As the western hemisphere produces two-thirds of the world's coffee and is dominated by the USA, which buys three-quarters of its needs from its neighbours, it is possible to fall into the trap of blaming that country for the problems besetting the coffee industry. This is also the result of the understandable instinct to blame the top dog when one isn't the top dog oneself, or, as is more frequently the case with European powers, one has ceased to be top dog some time ago. After all, the historical record shows at various times that Portugal, Spain, France, England, Germany, Holland, Russia, and even Belgium held substantial colonial interests, in some cases empires. The coffees of the world were mainly produced there for the delectation and delight of their various home markets, and, as we have seen, there is little to suggest, in the eighteenth century and much of the nineteenth at least, that the Dutch in Indonesia, the Portuguese in Brazil, or the British in Jamaica were running anything other than colonial regimes that would today be totally unacceptable. The reality is that the overt nation-state colonialism of the earlier eras has now morphed into a new transnational corporate colonialism in which all the Western nations have a stake, and in which the dominant force is the USA.

In the twentieth century, issues of social justice seemed to play a meaningful part in the political agenda of nation states. With the demise of the Soviet Union there are, at a national level, few remaining exemplars, however flawed, of societies in which social justice is a governing principle. The removal of the perceived 'threat' of such societies in Central America led directly to the dropping by the US of its support for the International Coffee Agreement and the ensuing free trade free-for-all that has brought coffee farming to its knees worldwide. Coffee consumers in Western countries may have 'benefited' from lower prices, although often at the cost of lower quality: national and international coffee companies, in the meantime, have benefited from substantially increased profitability. This is the fundamental aim of transnational corporate colonialism.

16

FAIR TRADE

Poverty, violence, exploitation, environmental devastation, political oppression, and corruption; these are not notably consumer-friendly topics, and in the coffee trade they are generally brushed under the carpet. To an increasing number of coffee drinkers in the West, however, the absence of one, some, or all of these negative factors has become a significant positive. Thus we have the rise of 'cause-related' coffees, and the proliferation of labels that go with them – 'Fair Trade', 'Shade Grown', 'Bird Friendly', and organic coffees. While the fundamental motives for making such purchases differ widely, the effect on the palate is similar: the bitterness of coffee's negative associations is mitigated, if not entirely removed.

The unhappy situation of the coffee farmers in Uncle Sam's backyard is reflected by the fact that 90 per cent of Fair Trade coffee eventually sold to consumers comes from Central and South America, with 30 per cent from Mexico and 20 per cent from Guatemala. Seventy-five per cent of the coffees produced by Fair Trade certified farmers comes from the region. However, at 2000 tonnes a year, the USA is only the fourth largest consumer of the available Fair Trade coffee (albeit rapidly growing), after Denmark, the Netherlands, and the UK. It would seem that while Central and South America have experienced some of the worst excesses of the coffee market, their giant northern neighbour has until recently done little about it. Perhaps the hemisphere simply needs the Fair Trade movement more than elsewhere.

The movement, which has assumed an increasingly high profile in recent years, originated in the coffee trade, and more precisely from an extraordinary book written in the middle of the nineteenth century by Eduard Dowes Dekker, a Dutchman using the pen-name 'Multatuli'. *Max Havelaar, or the Coffee Auctions of the Dutch Trading Company*, published in 1860, was deeply controversial, sending a 'shiver through the country' and prompting questions in Parliament. A multi-layered work that is considered a classic of Dutch literature, it is a polemical critique of Dutch colonial practices in Java, as well as a passionate condemnation of all such systems and their inherent injustice. For this reason the name *Max Havelaar* has become the call to action of the global Fair Trade movement. Multatuli had served as a colonial official in the Dutch East Indies: he writes with an insider's knowledge of the system that betrayed him. It is also startlingly relevant to the world of coffee today.

Max Havelaar is a highly entertaining literary work, as well as burning with what D. H. Lawrence called 'hate, a passionate honourable hate'. The 'Coffee Auctions of the Dutch Trading Company' referred to in the title is a book that has been commissioned from the fictional Mr Droogstoppel, a successful Amsterdam coffee broker given to insufferable hypocrisy. He receives some papers written by an old school friend who has fallen on hard times – thereby, according to Droogstoppel's lights, placing himself beyond the pale, and making the material he has on the Java trade fair game for Droogstoppel's borrowing. One of the stories recounted in the papers, that of Max Havelaar, the Dutch colonial official and fierce defender of native justice, is effectively stolen by Droogstoppel to meet his publishing deadline. The theme of misappropriation from the poor, and the pious, self-justifying logic that the rich apply to it, is thus established early on. It is then taken up in relation to Javanese peasants: Droogstoppel neatly encapsulates the importance of religion in reinforcing the colonial mindset. His firm has made a handsome profit: 'Doesn't it seem as if the Lord had said: "Here, here are thirty million to reward your belief"? Isn't it clearly the finger of God, who makes the wicked labour to preserve the just? Isn't it a hint to us to continue in the right path? A hint to get much produced over there and to stand firm in true faith here? Isn't that why we're told to "work and pray", meaning that *we* should pray and have our work done by that black scum which doesn't know its "Our Father"?'

The book then introduces the measured, indignant voice of the hero, Max Havelaar, whose incisive and devastating analysis of the structural flaws in the Dutch colonial system is a masterpiece of clarity and psychological perception, both of the body politic and the individuals who inhabit it. A central object of his attack is the 'Culture System', which imposed the cultivation of export crops on peasants, including substantial quantities of coffee. This frequently led to famine in Java, despite its rich soils. 'The Government compels him to grow on *his* land what pleases *it* . . . and *it* fixes the price it pays him . . . and since, after all, the entire business *must* yield a profit, this profit can be made in no other way than by paying the Javanese just enough to keep him from starving, which would decrease the producing power of the nation.' In terms of the drama, the main narrative thrust of Havelaar's story, however, concerns his attempts to persuade his superiors to suspend a native chief who has been abusing his privileges. Rather than the chief, it is Havelaar who in the end is forced to resign. The Havelaar story is in all its details Multatuli's own, and the book was also a conscious effort on his part, as the victim of a personal injustice, to be reinstated in the administration of the Dutch East Indies. Despite or because of the book's instant success, this never happened, and Multatuli, although briefly celebrated, led a poor and embittered life, finding even the reforms to the 'Culture System' that his book had engendered an object for withering contempt: 'Nevertheless, a show had to be put up of activity in a new direction, and the People, "shuddering" with indignation, had a succession of bones thrown to them, not really to appease their hunger for reform but to keep their jaws busy, even if it was only with blathering about what passed for economics and politics,' he wrote in his note to the 1875 edition. He could have learnt from the words of Lord Shelburne, Prime Minister in the days of the struggle against the slave trade: 'It requires no small labour to open the eyes of either the public or of individuals but when that is accomplished you are not got but a third of the way. The real difficulty remains in getting people to apply the principles which they have admitted and of which they are now so fully convinced. Then springs the mine composed of private interests and personal animosity.'

As Lawrence remarked, *Max Havelaar* is 'a book with a purpose . . . The Anglo-Saxon mind loves to hail such books. They are so obviously in the right. The Anglo-Saxon mind also loves to forget completely, in a very short time, any book with a purpose. It is a bore, with its insistency.' Multatuli's book, however, has not been forgotten, and the force of its passionate indignation can be felt as keenly today as when it was written, and is yet more relevant. As an object lesson on the immovability of economic and political institutions when faced with the oppression of those whom they are supposed to serve, the tale of Max Havelaar is essential reading for those concerned with global justice. If coffee is indeed the drink of revolution, then *Max Havelaar* is its manifesto.

The first flickers of the Fair Trade movement can be seen in the co-operative movement of late nineteenth-century Britain, but it was with the tentative trading initiatives of Oxfam in the UK in the 1960s that it started to become more clearly defined, aligning itself with expressions of support for the politically and economically marginalized. The coffee initiative in support of the

Sandinistas in Nicaragua in the 1980s, both in the USA and internationally, was one of the more conspicuous efforts, with President Reagan's embargo circumvented by committed coffee roasters – scions of the Gamble family ranged against the Folger's coffee produced by Procter & Gamble – and the then Greater London Council in London opting to buy only Nicaraguan coffee. Political alignment as a motive for coffee purchasing gave way to more complex producer support programmes and 'development trade', and a labelling initiative emerged in Holland in 1988 under the name 'Max Havelaar'. This gave meaningful definition to the concept of Fair Trade, with clear rules and qualifying criteria, and provided the consumer with a reasonable level of reassurance that they were not simply being taken for a ride by effective policing of the label.

At the core of the 'Fair Trade' concept is that the farmer achieves a certain price (currently $1.26) for his coffee regardless of whether the market is below that figure (as it is at the time of writing). There are numerous other factors that are taken into account: the absence of go-betweens, often and with justification called 'coyotes' in Central America, and educational, welfare, and health provision. Case studies of producers who have managed to become 'Fair Trade' registered provide a heartening counterpoint to the tales of doom and gloom that pervade the industry. Some of the qualifying criteria are controversial: large estates are unable to qualify, which in turn disenfranchises their workers who are as vulnerable to exploitation as any smallholder, if not more so. This policy was created to keep the initial focus of the 'Fair Trade' label on the 85 per cent of all coffee farmers internationally who have less than five hectares; over time it is anticipated that the qualifying criteria for the label will be extended to make them applicable to large estates. Likewise, another controversial area was the key strategic decision, taken early on, to allow roasters to package coffee with the 'Max Havelaar' mark alongside coffees that had been conventionally sourced. The juxtaposition on the super-market shelf of a Fair Trade coffee at a price premium and an ordinary coffee from the same roaster raises some strange conundrums – if this is Fair Trade, then the other must be Unfair Trade, in which case why produce it at all? However, the policy of supping with the devil enabled the 'Max Havelaar' mark to gain a vital foothold in mainstream retailers. It should be said that the dynamics of the international coffee trade at that time, just before the break-up of the International Coffee Agreement, ensured that the producers were shielded from the worst effects of the rollercoaster price ride that has traditionally been the coffee market. Indeed it is revealing that the political motivation for coffee purchasing, relating particularly to Nicaragua's Sandinista movement, changed into a more general Fair Trade motivation – leading to the invention of a 'Fair Trade' mark in 1994 – at the time that the ICA collapsed and the Sandinistas lost the 1990 election, in no small part owing to US interference. While the Sandinistas existed there was a genuine, identifiable, geopolitical alternative to US hegemony in Central and South America. With their disappearance, those with an interest in social justice have had to fight their corner from within the system. Instead of what might be called a 'Fair Trade' nation (Cuba being the last in the hemisphere) posing a functional alternative to neo-liberal capitalism, we now have a parallel 'Fair Trade' system running, with very little clout in the general scale of things, alongside 'Free Trade'. While 'Fair Trade' coffees might claim, with considerable justification, to be addressing localized problems, they cannot claim to be dealing with the issues of global inequity, political oppression, and environmental degradation, which are the background conditions of all coffee producers. As long as the entire industry is thus structurally flawed, the 'Fair Trade' movement remains an entirely laudable but ultimately inadequate attempt to staunch the bleeding from the most seriously wounded. And correcting the flaws of the coffee industry would itself require a complete re-evaluation of the prevailing global political and economic ideology: in other words, the creation of a 'Fair Trade' world.

This remains an unlikely global development under current conditions, although there is no doubt a powerful synergy between large-scale political movements, particularly anti-globalization, and the Fair Trade movement. Coffee is something of a pet subject for the anti-globalizers as it exemplifies, in stark terms, the neo-colonialist subtext of the neo-liberal agenda. In the UK in 2001 alone, sales of Fair Trade products rose by 40 per cent. Consumer-led boycotts of sweatshop labour, which have tended to expose the egregious inequity between high-priced fashion items and luxury goods and the squalor and degradation of those who make them, are complicated by other issues such as branding, 'MacJob' employment in the West, and all the emotive paraphernalia of modern consumerism. So far the Fair Trade movement has addressed only apparently simple agricultural products: coffee, tea, orange juice, bananas, cocoa, honey, mangoes. Plans are afoot to move into rice, dried fruit, nuts, spices, and cereals. But the apparent simplicity flatters to deceive: while a banana makes a fine background for a telling graphic (the tiny 1-pence portion at the tip of the fruit received by a worker from the sale of a 30-pence banana contrasting with the huge 15-pence central hunk gobbled up by the retailer), the same global corporate and governmental forces that have led to the explosion of Export Processing Zones (EPZ) can be found at play in the agriculture sector.

The EPZ 'sweatshop' model is notorious for 'swallow factories', which land in countries where the costs of production are lowest and labour regulations least enforced; then, at the first sign of the prosperity or desire for better working conditions caused in part by their presence, they make off to a cheaper, less regulated zone. The Mexican Maquilla zone on the US border has recently seen a wave of factory closures, with the lay-off of workers and concomitant social privations, although a few years ago this area was held up as a prime example of the success of the policy. If China comes to the fore as the next low-cost coffee producer and trounces Vietnam in the markets, where will that leave Vietnam's smallholder coffee industry, currently a 'success' story? The answer is clear: redundant coffee trees and redundant workers, to say nothing of the environmental effects. It would appear that this new EPZ-style coffee agronomy is being made possible by governments and institutions principally for the benefit of corporate profitability, and Western consumers end up with a limited range of low-price, low-quality coffee. The general verdict in the trade seems to be that the mass coffee market will be served more or less entirely by Vietnam and Brazil within a few years (the emergence of China as a force in the coffee market remains at the level of a rumour at the current time). Junk coffee – high in caffeine, low in quality – will be made available to the caffeinated masses at keenly competitive prices, whilst the traditional high-quality coffee producers will pack up their bags and head for the city. This is an industrial lay-off on an unprecedented scale: not thousands, not tens of thousands, not hundreds of thousands, not millions, but tens of millions of jobs are likely to evaporate.

Gandhi urged the Indian people to eschew the model of Western modernization because the world could not cope with a nation of 300 million people (as India then was) stripping the planet bare like a swarm of locusts. In the world of coffee, the day of the locust is upon us, and the tilling of the earth has become as precarious an occupation as the sewing of a sweatshirt. The entrance of China into the WTO, combined with the enormous lay-offs in its unprofitable state-run industries, has created a huge pool of cheap labour. Should China turn its attention to expanding its currently small coffee industry – an ironic departure for the country that gave the world tea – then other producers around the world must tremble. The 'race for the bottom', which is the inevitable result of trade liberalization, has already started in earnest.

How can Fair Trade co-exist with the globalized juggernaut that is the international coffee market today? The answer is that it can, but it is increasingly difficult for it to do so. It has yet to achieve the critical mass necessary for it to support a coffee supply chain that can survive independently of the world market. Thus while the registered growers of Fair Trade coffees could in principle supply 75,000 tonnes of coffee annually, the demand in 2001 was only 15,000 tonnes. For every bag of coffee for which the growers have received the Fair Trade tariff, four bags of that same coffee have been bought in the bargain basement free-for-all of the market, which is either of the low quality exemplified by Brazil and Vietnam, or has been produced at a cost greater than the price it has been sold for. This situation finds expression on the supermarket shelf where there is one Fair Trade coffee for every ten ordinary ones. Although the background is different from that described by Multatuli in *Max Havelaar,* effectively the break-up of the International Coffee Agreement, the influence of institutions like the World Bank and the IMF, and the power of global corporations in the coffee market have conspired to make the coffee we consume in the western world a product of what is far worse than the 'Culture System' described with outrage in that book. Instead of a single 'government' forcing peasants to grow coffee that is sold at a pre-fixed price and paying them just enough to avoid the starvation that would diminish productive capacity, governments, institutions, and corporations have forged a system that dispenses even with the responsibility felt by the then Dutch Government to try to avoid starvation in the native population. The campesinos of Colombia, the coffee pickers of India, and the highland tribesmen of New Guinea do not even have the luxury of a cruel colonial government to accept – or avoid – the burden of responsibility for their basic welfare.

The coffee trade as it is currently configured is creating, at this moment, vast social, economic, ecological, and political convulsions that are having a disastrous effect on the lives of tens of millions. At the same time, Western coffee companies are reporting record profits and the international coffee-bar market is expanding voraciously.

If Bert Beeckman, who started the 'Max Havelaar' labelling initiative in the late 1980s, had to decide today whether to allow a roaster to carry Fair Trade coffees alongside Unfair Trade coffees under the same brand, would his pragmatic strategy be the same? The problem is that the level of systemic inequity has increased so significantly that, whereas consorting with the enemy in those days was undesirable but not actually despicable, today it looks increasingly like actively condoning near slavery.

Consider the following (fictitious) scenario.

The owner of the Ahab Coffee House employs ten waiters and waitresses. They live in the damp basement under the shop with their families in squalid, cramped conditions. They have one gas ring between them to cook on, rudimentary sanitary facilities, and they sleep on flea-ridden mattresses on the floor. The children have no access to education, and health care is prohibitively expensive. The waiters and waitresses are paid just enough to prevent them from actually starving, and their wages are docked if they commit any kind of misdemeanour, real or imagined. They are not protected by any kind of employment legislation, have no contracts and no job security. The well-heeled clientele of the Ahab Coffee House notice the miserable and careworn condition of the serving staff and complain about it to Captain Ahab, the genial owner. He agrees that it is indeed an appalling state of affairs, but says there is nothing he can do about it, because if he puts up his prices to enable him to improve the workers' conditions, all his customers will go around the corner to his nearest rival and then the staff would all be kicked out onto the streets and be even more miserable than they already are. However, recognizing that there is a genuine concern amongst his customers, he agrees the following: he will undertake to employ one waitress who will be paid a salary that will enable her to rent an apartment of her own where she can live with her family, who will work on a long-term contract with reasonable hours, and with sick pay, holidays and retirement benefits. Thus Fair Trade, as she is called – her parents were unreconstructed hippies – comes to work at Ahab's, and the customers are relieved to note that she does not have the pallid complexion and snivelling demeanour of the others. In fact, Fair Trade is quite a hit, and Captain Ahab notes that her cheerfulness attracts a whole new crowd of customers who like to listen to her tales of how her children are doing in school, how she has at last bought a new television, and how her husband's lumbago is responding to treatment. And because of Fair Trade's sunny disposition and infectious *joie de vivre*, Ahab's Coffee House becomes quite the place to go, Captain Ahab buys a new yacht, and everyone is happy – except for the other staff, whose lot improves not one jot, indeed actually worsens as they have to work harder because the place has become so popular.

This analogy can be pushed and pulled in various directions according to taste. Why shouldn't Ahab call his staff the most content in town if it helps business? What do we think if he puts the odd coin in the collection box every week at church for the benefit of the world's underpaid workers? What if Fair Trade decides to share her salary and benefits amongst her colleagues? What would happen if Ahab decided to sack all the staff except Fair Trade and employ all her sisters and brothers on the same basis as her? Or if he unilaterally put all the existing staff on the same basis as her? These issues, which reflect real-world concerns in the coffee industry regarding branding, charitable contributions, co-operatives, and so on, are serious enough; but the real issue is what do we think of ourselves as we sit in the coffee house being served by half-starved staff whilst Fair Trade entertains the table by the door with her holiday snaps? Because that is what we are doing every time we visit a coffee shop that carries Fair Trade coffee alongside others, or when we buy from the supermarket a pack of Fair Trade coffee from a brand that sells other kinds. We connive at the underlying injustice.

The example of Ahab's Coffee House does not seek to disparage the sterling achievements of the Fair Trade movement, but it highlights how far there is still to go. The place of Fair Trade coffee in the general pantheon of trade-led initiatives, whether charitable, governmental, or international in complexion, has become increasingly important – particularly as the feeling grows inexorably that the developed world, far from addressing the issues of Third World poverty, is, through its imposition of the terms of the triumvirate of the WTO, the World Bank, and the IMF, merely creating an institutionalized, transnational corporate version of colonialism.

Many coffee manufacturers, particularly the small and medium-sized ones, are genuinely concerned about the terrible state of the global coffee market. While the major corporations that have profited tremendously from the global price slump tend to mouth platitudes and do nothing, it is left to these smaller businesses to carry the banner. However well intentioned they may be, they frequently set up independent initiatives, not wishing to be tied to the supply chain on offer through the Fair Trade movement, with much heartfelt talk about how their buyers build 'long-term relationships with growers', paying a fair price, educational and health standards, and so on. These self-regulated Fair Trade criteria may well be rigorously defined and policed – or not: the problem is that no independent organization monitors the process, and so the public can never really be sure. Furthermore, independent labelling initiatives can make seductive pitches to the more concerned consumer, unintentionally opening the door to the unscrupulous manufacturer who can all too easily jump on the bandwagon.

At the heart of nearly all the cause-related labelling initiatives lies the elusive concept of sustainability. Many of the initiatives overlap: IFOAM, the international organic regulatory body, has incorporated social justice issues into its organic criteria, insisting 'the rights of indigenous peoples shall be respected'. 'Bird-friendly' tends to run in parallel with organic. Fair Trade certification has some aspects relating to environmental practices. This all seems to point in the direction of a 'sustainable' superlabel that would somehow satisfy everybody's needs whilst at the same time reducing the proliferation of labels and the confusion that brings. Sustainability is, however, a word that can be found on the lips of the chairman of BP as well as hard-line ecowarriors, with entirely different meanings attached to it. To the former, the concern is for economic growth which does not cause the implosion of the societies from which it springs; for the latter, most of the global economic activity we already take for granted is depleting the earth's ability to regenerate.

Probably the two greatest issues of our time are the global economy and global ecology, and the finest minds bend to the task of reconciling them. This produces some strange inconsistencies: the Senior Policy Adviser at Oxfam UK praised the growth of Vietnamese smallholder agriculture as a means of eliminating rural poverty, but that same growth with respect to coffee from Vietnam threatens the livelihood of millions elsewhere. In a globalized world, in which the agricultural sweatshops switch to where the costs of production are lowest, one country's temporary success is usually bought at the price of another's impoverishment. But regardless of the economic arguments, nearly all human activity inflicts strains on the ecology: even ancestors of the Native Americans, today revered by many for their supposed oneness with nature, swept through the continent in a matter of centuries after crossing from Asia during the Ice Age in 12,000 BC, driving into extinction vast numbers of large native mammals such as elephants, cheetahs, camels, and ground sloths, in a frenzy of hunter-gathering.

The trade in coffee is an inheritance of the colonial system, produced by poor tropical countries and consumed by rich temperate ones. Ideas of Fair Trade, and of organic and bird-friendly coffees, are predicated on the assumption that the trade is immutable, and that the trick is to make it more just and eco-friendly. This of course ignores the entire supply and consumption chain. Even Fair Trade coffee is carried down to a tropical dock in a truck belching diesel fumes, shipped thousands of miles across the world's oceans, and hauled up and down a Western nation's motorways eventually to find its way onto the shelf of a supermarket built on an out-of-town greenfield site frequented by shoppers who arrive in gas-guzzling cars from the surrounding towns and villages. This, in itself, is hardly sustainable.

17

ESPRESSO: THE ESPERANTO OF COFFEE

Espresso is a wonderful system for making good coffee, but not a good system for making wonderful coffee. This apparent heresy demands an explanation, for most people in search of good coffee head for the nearest espresso bar.

Like Italian cars, football, fashion, food, and film starlets, espresso coffee has acquired an unmistakable aura of Italian glamour. It combines precision engineering, voluptuous lines, impeccable style, and consummate showmanship, allowing its exponents to build an entire café culture around the process of making a cup of coffee. Little wonder that in our damp northern climes we have been seduced by the concept, and have seen periodic attempts to transplant it to our culture. In the espresso bar boom in the England of the 1950s, espresso became a symbol of youthful rebellion: the bars were places where the black-clad young and the poetically disaffected met to blow smoke rings and plumb the depths of existential angst. Short lived, the craze that resulted in the opening of four hundred espresso bars in London alone, has been all but forgotten. In the 1980s, the domestic espresso machine became a fashion accessory, the first recourse of an advertising art director seeking to suggest yuppie cred. In its latest and most successful manifestation it has become inextricably linked with the general pillaging of other cultures for their most marketable elements, such as kilims, Cajun cooking, and the tango; espresso is the preferred coffee of the Global Village, the coffee Esperanto. However, the Italian original has been repackaged to make it more acceptable to the modern international big-brand consumer. This has given rise to a cultural miscegenation adapted to the exigencies of modern marketing. The principal exponent of this interbreeding has been Starbucks, who manage to persuade their customers that even the most ersatz of their pseudo-Italian fabulations are actually authentic, as though Marcello Mastroianni could regularly have been found supping *venti vanilla decaf frappaccino*.

Considering the pre-eminent position of the Italians in espresso culture, it is surprising to find that both the English and the French have valid claims to have invented the forerunner of the espresso machine. The French case rests on the machine invented in 1822 by Bernard Rabaut and refined by Edward Loysel that was a spectacular success at the Paris Exhibition of 1855. Some purists (usually British) are scornful of this machine, since it worked by merely creating a head of steam in a large boiler which forced water out through the coffee. (The English Ward Andrews patented coffee pot of 1841 was the first to suggest the use of a piston to force a measured amount of water through the coffee.) The credit for creating the progenitor of the Italian café espresso machine in 1902 is given to Luigi Bezzera. In 1945 Achille Gaggia devised the hand-pulled spring-piston system, which added considerably to the theatre of the brew. The modern machine is the result of gradual refinements of this, so that today the ideal machine will brew a single espresso coffee by pushing water at between 90 and 96 degrees centigrade under a pressure of 9 atmospheres (created by springs, hydraulics, or compressed air) through the coffee grounds in 20–30 seconds.

The speed with which an espresso coffee is dispensed, coupled with sound and steam effects reminiscent of the heyday of the Great Western Railway, probably led to the common misspelling in English, 'expresso'. Strangely, whilst the *Oxford English*

Dictionary (and many others) claims that *caffè espresso* means literally 'pressed-out coffee', some linguists suggest that the origin of the word is probably French, from *exprès* meaning 'immediately, for one purpose only'. It would appear that neither the machine, nor the word used to describe the method, is necessarily of Italian origin.

Whatever the etymology, there is no doubt that Italians have made espresso their own, maintaining that the espresso method extracts 'the heart of the coffee'. There is some justification for this passionate claim. In common with other aspects of coffee, the espresso phenomenon is the result of a highly sophisticated interaction of a number of factors. Contrary to the expectations raised by all that bubbling and hissing, a professional espresso machine, such as the type found in restaurants or cafés, brews the coffee at a temperature of around 92–4 degrees centigrade. Boiling water is damaging to the volatile flavour and aroma components in coffee, so the lower brewing temperature helps preserve these vital oils. In addition, the use of pressure to force the water through the coffee leads to a higher level of emulsification of the oils, which are not water soluble, than with other brewing methods.

As a result, the flavour and aroma of an espresso coffee is enhanced – quintessence of coffee, in effect. Italian experts would have us believe that suspended carbon dioxide in an espresso coffee inhibits the taste perception of bitterness, and that the *crema* (the froth on the top of the coffee) seals in the aroma. The higher viscosity produced by the oil content leads to a lower surface tension, which means that the flavours penetrate more deeply into the taste buds, and the 'polyphasic colloidal system' of the *crema* – a mixture of gas, oils, water, and fine grounds – leaves a satisfying aftertaste for up to twenty minutes after consumption. Owing to the speed of the brewing process, the amount of caffeine is also 30–40 per cent lower, per measure of coffee grounds, than that extracted by other methods. As if all these wonderful attributes were not enough, even the number of beans used per serving, fifty-five, is close to the number (sixty) that Beethoven used meticulously to count out for his ideal (non-espresso) brew. *Perfetto*: espresso is a wonderful system for making good coffee.

The *éminence grise* of the espresso world is Dr Ernesto Illy, chairman of the eponymous illycaffè created by his father in 1933. Possessing suitably impressive qualifications in chemistry and molecular biology, and armed with two sons in the business, one of whom is a professional photographer and boasts the title 'Image Manager', Ernesto Illy has done more to market the image of Italian espresso to the world than any other man, and in the process has made illycaffè an international success. This has been achieved on the solid foundation of unimpeachable product quality and sound science – the company boasts its own laboratories and is at the forefront of research in the field. The respected magazine *Scientific American* carried an article in June 2002 by Dr Illy entitled 'The Complexity of Coffee' in which the author managed to focus exclusively on espresso, with the alternatives only detailed in a separate section by different authors, presumably introduced in the interests of editorial balance. 'Connoisseurs agree', Dr Illy writes, with the kind of magisterial authority to which espresso evangelists have become prone, 'that the quintessential expression of coffee is espresso.' The subsequent chemical analyses, microscope photographs, pie charts, and graphs set out scientifically to prove the case. With the kudos attached to articles like this one, together with its scientific credentials, market credibility, and excellent quality, the company has transformed espresso into the lingua franca of the coffee consumer. And, without a doubt, a well-served illycaffè is unrivalled of its type. But a proselytizer can rarely resist going a step too far: Illy also wrote that 'Espresso is useful for our purposes as it is in effect a distillation of all the numerous techniques by which coffee can be made, including the Turkish method and various infusion and filter drip processes. To know espresso is to know coffee in all its forms.' Apparently, we can safely throw away all our filter machines, cafetières, and *ibriks* and install a Gaggia machine in the kitchen. The only problem is that if we then take out of the cupboard one of our favourite single-origin coffees, such as a Kenya AA, prized for its fruity acidity, and put it through a newly installed espresso machine, it comes out thin, overly acid, and lacking its unique fruitiness. It is not the quintessence of that particular coffee.

In fact the method fails to highlight the nuances and distinctive features of most of the pedigree coffees of the world. The key to good espresso is good blending, using a mixture of various coffees to create a balance of components that optimizes the characteristics of the brewing system. Neither illycaffè nor any of its rivals successfully market a single-origin espresso coffee: their reputation depends on the quality of their blends. In other words, espresso is not a good system for making wonderful coffee.

It is at this point that separating the myth and the reality becomes increasingly difficult. It has to be remembered that, as recently as the 1920s, Italy was one of Europe's poorest countries and was drinking half the amount of coffee that the UK, a dyed-in-the-wool tea-drinking nation, consumed. Waves of emigration to Brazil in the nineteenth century had established good relations with that producer of unwashed Arabicas, and by virtue of their brief colonial foray in the 1930s into Abyssinia, now Ethiopia, the Italians had access to the unwashed coffees of that country as well. Unwashed coffees – the cherry is sun dried before being removed – are considered an essential component of a good espresso blend, although the premium end of the non-espresso coffee market generally treats them as an inferior 'filler'. Likewise, one of the traditional benefits of the espresso brewing method has been that it smooths out the coarser flavours commonly found in cheap Robusta coffees – indeed, until recently, it was widely recommended that a certain amount of Robusta was an essential component of an espresso blend as it facilitated the creation of the *crema*, the thick froth that Illy tells us seals in the aroma and gives the lingering aftertaste. Illycaffè themselves have quietly introduced a pure Arabica espresso blend as their house blend, a development which neatly coincided with raised consumer consciousness regarding the difference between Arabica and Robusta coffees arising, not from espresso usage, but from the use of other brewing methods in which the coarseness of the Robusta was naturally highlighted. The company is understandably coy about admitting to having ever used Robusta coffees, and would prefer it to be believed that they have always used a pure Arabica blend, in keeping with their quality image.

The espresso brewing method was developed in Italy in the early twentieth century in part as a way of delivering, very successfully, a relatively high-quality brewed coffee from relatively low-quality raw material. With the arrival of increased consumer awareness people became interested in premium, single-origin coffees with distinctive tastes. Proselytizers quickly repositioned the espresso method as *the* best way of brewing coffee. However, while espresso conceals the faults of poor coffees, it fails to reveal the virtues of great ones.

One benefit that espresso has undoubtedly brought the world is the sure knowledge that when you order a cup it is freshly brewed on the spot. Nothing murders coffee more surely than keeping it on a hotplate or in a heated cylinder. Within half an hour it loses much of its flavour, and after an hour it is more or less undrinkable, having become thin and bitterly metallic. Such brewing systems are the bane of hotel restaurants and sporting events: the single-shot, freshly brewed nature of espresso makes it unsuited to the demands of rapid, mass service. Strangely, the country that glorifies espresso also invented the 'Slow Food' movement, which honours all things requiring patience in relation to food growth, preparation, and consumption.

When the 'Chief Global Strategist' of Starbucks, Howard Schultz, saw espresso bars for the first time on a visit to Italy, he realized that this was what the world had been waiting for: the business to be in was selling espresso-based drinks. Unfortunately, the company's self-serving myth machine attributes an earlier *coup de foudre* to Schultz, who apparently saw the original Starbucks coffee shop in Seattle's Pike Place market and fell in love with it. However, that particular Starbucks was a retailer of specialty coffee beans, not the desired espresso bar. Working on the Wildean principle that we always kill the things we love, Schultz bought the store and then inflicted a major makeover on it, turning it into the faux-Italian coffee shop of his dreams. Little evidence remains of the original Pike Place Market retail store in the current Starbucks get-up, but even as the company adds one store per day to its portfolio worldwide, it is helpful for it to have the homely 'mom and pop' passionate retailer image in its marketing back-pocket. It gives a small-is-beautiful gloss to the corporation. We have seen how the invention of vacuum packaging and instant coffee enabled coffee to be packed, branded, and distributed in line with other mass consumer products. Until recently, the specialty coffee retailer stood in contradiction to this modern corporate approach. A single shop, or a small chain, roasted their own coffee, frequently in the shop itself, and made their product knowledge and expertise their biggest single asset. Having annexed the qualities of blended coffee for the mass market, it was inevitable that the specialty retailer should be the next target of the corporate appetite. These retailers have now themselves been cloned, packaged, and marketed. Starbucks's principal conjuring trick has been to persuade us that, despite its global ambitions, it remains at heart a passionate specialty coffee retailer. The Pike Place Market store remains a central part of that myth, a message subliminally reinforced by the use of greens and browns in Starbucks's pamphlets, the casual-but-hip fit-up of its stores, and the jazz or world music playing in the background. In fact the effect is achieved by standard operating procedures laid out in standard training manuals, a standard look laid out in a Style Guide, standard greetings and standard ways of dealing with complaints: indeed the whole aim is to ensure that a Starbucks customer is never confronted by non-standard product, presentation or staff behaviour. Only then will they automatically head for the nearest Starbucks whether they are in Kansas or Kuala Lumpur. Familiarity breeds content, and far from celebrating a diverse world, as it appears to do in their coffees and their outward expression, Starbucks plays on the insecurities of the brand fashion-victims and conformists the world over.

The Seattle original in effect simply provided Schultz with a name to get into the espresso game and an ongoing folksy marketing tale; the Starbucks with ambitions to open 20,000 stores globally bears no relation whatsoever to its progenitor, despite its claim that it has 'achieved success one cup at a time, one store at a time'. It could be said that one store a day is indeed one store at a time, but it is hardly the behaviour of a company with modest ambitions. It should be noted that at Starbucks the pedigree single-origin coffees are brewed in a filter machine, which would suggest that, despite Schultz's love affair with espresso, he too thinks the unthinkable: espresso is a bad way to make great coffee.

One of the reasons for the success of coffee bars is that it is difficult and costly to make good espresso in the home. When the likes of Starbucks project the image of their coffee shops as a 'third place' environment, neither the home nor the office, but a prefabricated home-from-home peopled with clones of the cast members from 'Friends', they are exploiting the fact that the easiest place to get a real espresso is precisely not your home.

This fact also has a very significant effect on the prices that can be charged. If the customer can make the same at home, only much cheaper, he is much more likely to balk at the price. Trend-watchers have long anticipated the arrival of a new wave of tea bars capitalizing on the flagging momentum of coffee bar culture; the one outstanding problem they have identified is that tea is perceived as something that can be made better in the home than outside it, with the resultant effect on potential sales and the pricing structure.

The choice of espresso as the delivery vehicle for the core Starbucks experience was a shrewd one. The real benefit is that espresso makes an ideal base for the sweet, milky drinks widely loved in America. One can have a hybrid Italian-style coffee experience without actually having to taste the dark, bitter-sweet mystery of real coffee. It has been said that the coffee bar phenomenon is in reality about the delivery of sweet, milky drinks in a pleasant environment with a coffee theme.

The milkiness of the Starbucks range of coffees has also embroiled the company in one of the key public health debates in the USA, concerning the use of milk derived from rBST or recombinant bovine somatotropin. An ingenious product from Monsanto, it simulates the action of hormones that make a cow produce milk, and consequently increases lactation by 15 per cent. It was quickly cleared by the FDA in the USA, but ran into problems in Canada. There were increasing concerns that the product caused mastitis (udder inflammation) in cows that necessitated the use of antibiotics, with a concomitant danger to human health. More seriously, there was increasing evidence that the excess of natural insulin stimulated by rBST in the animal could cause colon and breast cancers in humans. A public row ensued that seriously called into question the integrity of the Canadian Health Ministry. A subsequent Senate review revealed manipulation by Monsanto, which in turn forced the FDA to review its clearance for rBST. It emerged that, in effect, the FDA had broken standard approval procedures in regard to rBST, and in the view of many it had ceased to be the guardian of public health but was instead 'an extension of the drug companies'. Many FDA staff involved in the rBST issue had previously worked for Monsanto, and the company was a major contributor to President Clinton's campaign funds.

Despite the uproar and mutual recriminations, the FDA still certifies rBST as safe to use, and labelling regulations in the US are such that it is very difficult even to say that the milk that you are selling is rBST-free – two retailers who attempted to do so were sued by Monsanto. The only way of ensuring that there is no rBST in milk is to buy organic. Starbucks has started to offer organic milk as an alternative on request, but the company refuses to engage in the scientific debate, preferring to see it as a simple matter of customer preference. Given that Starbucks is one of the largest outlets for milk products in the USA, its inclination to sit on the fence on a public health issue seems disingenuous, and has been ascribed to pressure from other transnationals such as Kraft and Pepsi, which the company denies. This is not a problem that will go away: with the European Union fighting a rearguard action against the legalization of rBST, despite enormous pressure from the USA, it could well soon affect Europe. It would be consistent with the past strategy of transnationals if the labelling regulations were forced through in the EU, which would mean that there would be no requirement to highlight that the milk contained rBST. A stance by Starbucks that reflected genuine health concerns rather than a generalized please-the-customer approach would significantly raise the profile of a scandal that has been mainly conducted behind the closed doors of governments, regulators, and corporate lobbyists. As a consequence, in the USA Starbucks has been heavily lobbied by environmentalists concerned with biotechnology products in the food chain. Its position as market leader and its high profile have made it a target of interest groups anxious to take the Starbucks scalp.

The local Chamber of Commerce of the City of Seattle must wonder from time to time why the seat of such icons of capitalist enterprise as Boeing, Microsoft, and Starbucks is also the spiritual home of grunge and anti-globalization. Starbucks was the target of rocks hurled by rioters in the anti-WTO demonstration in the city, and of all transnational brands it seems to attract the most opprobrium, despite or because of its attempts to present a caring face. In many ways Starbucks is the company that many people love to hate: its employment practices (anti union, pro part-time), its predatory property acquisition, and its heavy-handed defence of its feel-good trade mark have all exposed the iron corporate fist beneath the Peruvian yak-wool glove. Perhaps more than anything, it is the company whose lead product lays bare the ever-widening gap between the First and the Third World. Coffee is savoured by the senses and its effects physically absorbed, something that could never be said about a 747 or Windows. It is literally consumed, and with it, the contradictions of a conscience-stricken consumer society.

Coffee strips bare the difference between the image and the reality. The roasters and their marketing gurus would have us believe that the sun dapples through the banana fronds, chickens pick contentedly at the corn, children scratch their newly learned alphabet in the dirt, and the coffee farmer, tired after an honest day's labour in the field, eats a simple but wholesome meal surrounded by a loving family. They fall over themselves to portray the unique character of Costa Rica, Guatemala, Kenya, or Java coffees and the care and attention with which their buyers nurture and appreciate such differences, and so they are forced to draw attention to at least some aspect of each country's special quality. It is certainly a useful introduction to the geography of

Central and South America to visit a speciality coffee retailer, and a leaflet with a map of the world showing coffee-producing countries is the standby of virtually every coffee roaster, however basic their products. Coffee, by its very nature, projects a global vision, and consumers have willingly embraced its diversity. However, over the last ten or so years the post-colonial realities of the geography of coffee production have become increasingly harsh. As the world has woken up to coffee, it has also woken up to its geopolitics.

The case of Starbucks and East Timor highlights this. The company discovered that the country produced high-quality organic coffee and by 1999 was buying over a third of the crop. The romance of bringing a relatively unknown coffee onto the world stage seems undeniable, and the fact that it was also organic was a helpful bonus. However, the reason why East Timor coffee was organic was something that Starbucks was less keen to advertise. During over twenty years of a brutal and illegal Indonesian occupation, after an invasion that had been quietly pre-approved by President Ford and Henry Kissinger in a visit to that country in 1975, a monopoly over the sales of Timorese coffee had been granted to Denok, a company coincidentally controlled by the former head of Indonesia's armed forces. After the invasion, the company was also the biggest owner of coffee plantations, and farmers were forced to sell to Denok at rock-bottom prices. Denok did little to encourage or pay for fertilizers or other chemical treatments for the plants. This had the wholly unintentional result of making East Timorese coffee organic by default. When the monopoly was broken in 1995 as a result of rare US diplomatic pressure, farmers were free to sell on the international market and realized that their organic status, which they had had certified, yielded a premium price. Starbucks was quick to perceive the quality of the coffee. It was less quick to acknowledge the fact that East Timor was effectively under illegal colonial occupation by a brutal neighbour. That smooth, full-bodied, organic coffee concealed a very bitter taste indeed.

The transnational companies manufacturing trainers or shirts in their Third World sweatshops as far as possible conceal their products' origins and the conditions under which they are produced. While activists and journalists can, and frequently do, go behind the scenes to reveal the reality, the products themselves are distanced from their genesis. Coffee is entirely different in this respect, and this is the reason it has attracted such virulent criticism. No amount of image managing and recycled wheatstraw paper leaflets can create a distance between the corporation and the source of its products, and the more successful and high-profile Starbucks becomes, the more visible and disturbing the problem its success reveals. The very economics of the coffee bar in general work to highlight the gross inequities of the globalized market.

A pound of Arabica coffee currently fetches around 50 cents on the New York 'C' market. Let us assume, quite unjustifiably, that the farmer who grows this pound receives the full 50 cents. One pound of coffee makes roughly forty servings. Thus for every cup of coffee sold in Ahab's Coffee House, on the most generous of estimates, the grower receives just over a cent. And the average price of coffee in cafés around the world? Bangkok $1.44, Capetown $0.54, Istanbul $0.47, Hong Kong $1.45, London $1.94, Moscow $2.00, New York $2.00, Paris $2.00, Rome $3.10, Sydney $1.60, and Tokyo $3.57. Thus in London the café customer is paying over 150 times what the grower receives. If the grower were to receive ten times (1000 per cent) the amount he does currently, the price in the café would rise, on a pro rata basis, by only 5 per cent. The economics of a coffee shop are fairly complicated (and in some cities, such as London, scarcely profitable, despite the hype) and include rent, rates, staff, management, capital costs, the espresso machine, and so forth. Nonetheless, because the actual cost of the coffee in the cup is so low, there is ample scope for increasing that amount by a huge factor without burdening the consumer with more than they might leave as a tip, say seven pence. For this reason, hypothetically speaking, if there were to be a concerted attempt to redress the inequities of the coffee market, it should start in the coffee shop: the economics make sense – it benefits the growers most at the least cost to the consumer – and it is, after all, the place where all the best revolutions began.

It is also historically appropriate that the coffee bar should once again become the hotbed of what is in effect a political controversy, as it was the coffee house, not coffee itself, that was associated with revolt. To the major events of the French and American revolutions, in which coffee houses played a significant part, can be added the revolt against Austrian rule in Northern Italy, which was fomented in the coffee houses of Venice, Padua, and Verona, and the Madrid Revolution, which began in the Café Lorenzoni. Even the placid coffee houses of Vienna, which today resound to nothing louder than the clack of a billiard ball or the rustle of a newspaper, unknowingly played their part in a revolution. During the First World War a young Russian émigré frequented the Central Café for some years to play chess and talk each evening. In 1917, the Austrian Foreign Minister was disturbed in his office by an aide who told him excitedly that 'Revolution has broken out in Russia.' The Minister dismissed the news: 'Russia is not a land where revolution would break out. Besides who on earth would make a revolution in Russia? Perhaps Herr Trotsky from the Café Central?'

18

THE HEART OF DARKNESS

[Coffee is] 'slow poison'

VOLTAIRE

Vietnam
In the 1980s Vietnam was the 42nd ranked producer of coffee in the world, largely Robusta of a fair quality grown on what had been former French colonial plantations nationalized by the new government. The 67,000 bags it exported scarcely registered a blip on the radar of the world coffee trade.

In 2001 Vietnam produced some 15 million bags, making it the second largest producer of coffee worlwide. This massive increase has been blamed for the global collapse of coffee prices. The World Bank, which strenuously denies any miscalculation, is in turn widely criticized for financing the vast expansion of coffee growing. In the meantime there are unsubstantiated but persistent rumours concerning possible dioxin contamination of the coffee crop, a legacy of the widespread spraying of Agent Orange by the Americans during the Vietnam War. Vietnam is the country where coffee's dark history has come home to roost with a vengance.

The colonization of Vietnam started with the fall of Saigon to French forces in 1859. The attack was a manifestation of the aggressive capitalism of French imperial strategy under

285

Napoleon III. No self-respecting European nation could eschew the colonial action in Asia, and the French were no exception. Within a few years they had control of what they renamed Cochinchina, and by 1887 had amalgamated modern-day Vietnam, Laos, and Cambodia under the general heading of the Indochinese Union. The installation of the colonial fixtures and fittings (roads, railways, canals, ports, and French administration) was achieved in short order, and the French sat back to enjoy the wealth of natural resources and agricultural products that Indochina brought forth – minerals, coal, rice, and rubber. Coffee was not amongst them: although it was introduced in 1887, it would appear that the coffee grown there during the French era was for local consumption only. The region also provided a substantial market for French manufactures. There was little encouragement of economic growth, as French investors wanted quick returns, and profits were rarely reinvested.

Lands opened up by irrigation for rice cultivation were appropriated by the French or their Vietnamese sidekicks: although rice production quadrupled between 1880 and 1930, the average amount consumed by the peasants actually decreased. In an echo of the privations witnessed by Multatuli in *Max Havelaar,* landless peasants were forced to work for no salary to pay in kind for the taxes imposed by the French to finance the infrastructure projects from which they derived no benefit. There was little education, justice, or health care for the general population to compensate for the colonial yoke, and the Vietnamese were excluded from bettering themselves by participation in the new economy. In short, the traditional charges laid against European colonial powers find ample justification in the French treatment of Vietnam.

Under such circumstances it is not surprising that nationalist movements sprang up, and were suppressed, with some frequency. None of these endured until the foundation of the Indochinese

Communist Party in 1930 by Ho Chi Minh, who as a seaman had travelled extensively during his youth before settling in Paris and joining the French Communist Party there, subsequently returning to Vietnam. After several ruthlessly crushed false starts, the Party had made some headway when the Second World War broke out and the whole of Indochina became a French-administered Japanese territory. In an oriental echo of Vichy France, the French collaborated with the Japanese, allowing them to station troops in Indochina and use it as the launch pad for their extensions by force of the Greater East Asia Co-Prosperity Sphere. Only the Communist Party, led by Ho Chi Minh, assisted the allied war effort during the Second World War by undercover intelligence operations against the French and their Japanese overlords. In the power vacuum created by the Japanese defeat in 1945, Ho Chi Minh was able to seize de facto power of the north of the country, whilst the French held on to the south. In this division lay the origins of the Vietnam War.

The US President, Roosevelt, in wartime negotiations with Winston Churchill, had insisted that Britain should divest itself of its Empire. This was couched in the language of a moral imperative, but was also clearly aimed at creating new markets for American goods. There was also no particular threat of a Communist takeover in the colonies that he proposed Britain must vacate, although later Malaya was to prove the exception. The French were not expected to release their colonial grip on Indochina, however, because it was clear that, if they did so, Ho Chi Minh would take over, and because he was a Communist he was therefore not eligible for assistance in throwing off the colonial mantle. Far from it: he was the potential domino that could set in train the eponymous effect, and that was a sufficient *casus belli* as far as the US was concerned. France thus enjoyed America's support in the form of aid and equipment in what turned, after a period of uneasy co-existence, into the First

Indochina War. The result of this was a formal division of the country, leaving the Democratic Republic of Vietnam in the North. Ho Chi Minh was a fully Westernized, modernizing ruler of the fledgling state, who professed an admiration for America and incorporated elements of that country's constitution into his. The South fell prey to a totalitarian regime that relied heavily on the threat of the North to woo the favours of America. The pattern that played havoc in post-war Central America was present in Indochina, too, although coffee was not the driving economic force. Inevitably the ruthless suppression of dissent in South Vietnam fuelled the incipient support for the politics of the North, and aid and insurgents began to flow south, seeking reunification of the country. A military coup on 1 November 1963, authorized by President Kennedy, saw the assassination of President Ngo Dinh Diem and installed a succession of corrupt and incompetent generals in power, increasingly maintained there by American aid and military equipment. As long as this was used to counter the Communist threat, a blind eye was turned to the internal affairs. Seventeen thousand American 'military advisors' were stationed in the South by the end of 1963, propping up a regime that was under external pressure from insurgents and internal pressure from the popular National Liberation Front.

President Lyndon Johnson initiated the bombing of North Vietnam in 1965, in which year 75,000 American troops were stationed in the south. By early 1968 this number had reached half a million, sparking a wave of internal dissent in the USA that changed the strategic landscape for decades. Johnson, recognizing his inability to sustain this position, proposed peace talks, to be held in Paris in May. It was an election year, and it has become clear recently that these talks were sabotaged by the Republican candidate, Richard Nixon, who promised the South Vietnamese that they would get a better deal if he were elected. He was, and they didn't: the war dragged on for another three years, resulting in the loss of another 30,000 American lives and countless hundreds of thousands of Vietnamese. During the period up to their final ignominious withdrawal in 1973 the US hit Vietnam with more bombs than were dropped during the entire Second World War, the equivalent of a 500-lb bomb for every man, woman, and child. Each of the 2 million Vietnamese who died was killed at a cost of $50,000, making it a very expensive pointless war to boot.

The defeat in the Vietnam War haunts the American psyche in the way that no other of the interventions that have served to create the American Empire does. However, it has been argued that the defeat was in fact no such thing, and that the prime strategic aim of ensuring that Vietnam would not be able to demonstrate the viability of an alternative political system was achieved. Vietnam was so ruined by the war that it has been treated until recently as an economic basket case. The bombs ensured that Communism equals chaos.

The war haunts more than just the American psyche: the health of many veterans has been seriously jeopardized by their contact with Agent Orange. The American military were determined to prevent Viet Cong insurgency into South Vietnam, and believed that the lush jungle and mangrove forests gave the fighters cover. It was but a short imaginative step to decide that if the cover was eliminated, then the insurgents would be eliminated with it. Thus Operation Ranch Hand, the folksy name for the comprehensive chemical defoliation of South Vietnam between 1961 and 1973, was born. The issues that this strategy raised have never been addressed fully. Since Agent Orange was sprayed indiscriminately on jungle and farmland alike, in full knowledge that it would cause civilian suffering, was the spraying not a breach of the chemical weapons convention, even if its effect on the civilian population was not direct – i.e. if it deprived them of their livelihoods, not their health? Subsequent compelling evidence suggests that Agent Orange posed a direct and immediate threat to human health, but the question is whether, even without that knowledge, the use of the chemical was illegal. The relevance of this question in our times cannot be ignored: with war having been waged against Iraq partly on the grounds that it has historically deployed chemical weapons, and the continued use by the US of such methods in the so-called 'War on Drugs' in Colombia (ironically, again involving the world's favourite chemical company, Monsanto), the notion that the US deliberately deployed chemical weapons, and continues to do so, is not merely of academic interest.

Agent Orange, so called because its barrels were marked with an orange stripe, was manufactured by a number of companies – Dow, Diamond Shamrock, and Monsanto. It was a mixture of two herbicides, dichlorophenoxyacetic acid and trichlorophenoxyacetic acid. It has long been alleged that in the manufacturing process of Agent Orange a contaminant, TCDD, a type of dioxin, became concentrated to dangerously high levels, but this has never been accepted by Monsanto and others involved in its manufacture. Dioxins are the unintentional by-product of many other industrial processes involving chlorine such as waste incineration, chemical manufacturing, and pulp and paper bleaching. In the early 1980s the coffee industry was thrown into disarray when it was revealed that the chlorine bleaching process used for the production of coffee filters might lead to dioxin contamination. The International Agency for Research on Cancer (IARC), part of the World Health Organization, has considered since 1997 that the most potent dioxin, 2, 3, 7, 8-TCDD, is a Class 1 carcinogen, meaning a 'known human carcinogen'. Exposure to dioxin can also cause severe reproductive and developmental problems (at levels a hundred times lower than those associated with its cancer-causing effects) and immune system damage, and it can interfere with regulatory hormones. It is also remarkably persistent, breaking down very slowly in the environment and contaminating the entire food chain. Being fat soluble, it bio-accumulates, leading to very high levels in mammals such as fish, fowl, and cattle. Ducks, a favourite of the Vietnamese diet, are susceptible to the bio-accumulation of dioxins.

Monsanto went to great lengths to challenge the veracity of the scientific evidence proving the toxicity of dioxin. A class action brought against seven companies, including Monsanto, in respect of Agent Orange, was settled for a reported $180 million with the companies involved denying that Agent Orange was responsible for the health complaints that had been alleged to be connected with its use. The USA has a number of organizations dedicated to the dissemination of information about Agent Orange, offering also practical and financial assistance in those cases where a direct link can be shown between exposure to Agent Orange and the specific illness. By the terms of the settle-ment with the chemical companies, veterans can receive between $2,000 and $5,000 a month in compensation (the Vietnamese Government, by contrast, pays its damaged veterans $7 a month). However, the US military authorities still seek to suppress infor-mation concerning the number of veterans involved and, most importantly of all, deny that Agent Orange has caused or contin-ues to cause any health problems whatsoever for the Vietnamese in Vietnam. The subject is taboo in any diplomatic negotiations between the two countries aimed at normalizing trade relations: initial talks in the late 1980s were predicated on the sure knowl-edge that if the subject of Agent Orange were raised, the Americans would walk out. The Vietnamese, having been ravaged mercilessly during the war, now find themselves in the position of having to enter into a conspiracy of silence with their former persecutor in order to restore some semblance of economic order. Agent Orange is now as much a taboo subject for the Vietnamese as it is for the Americans. The reasons are easy to see, and have been hinted at widely in the press: with the country desperately trying to rebuild its economy, it is heavily reliant on the sales of agricultural produce and shellfish to the world. If there were any evidence of dioxin contamination of these exports, the country would be very hard hit again.

An estimated 5,700 tonnes, or 12 million gallons, of Agent Orange were sprayed on South Vietnam during the war, destroying as much as 14 per cent of the forest cover and 50 per cent of the mangrove swamp that had previously been a valuable source of lumber. Over 4.5 million acres of vegetation were wiped out, with devastating results for the wildlife and ecology, let alone any unfortunate Vietnamese who found themselves in the flight path of the sprayers. Inevitably farms and smallholdings were also sprayed, causing widespread poverty and starvation. It was ten years before crops could again be grown on land sprayed with Agent Orange. The health costs are still not fully understood, but some 400,000 deaths and serious cases of illness, and a further 500,000 birth defects in Vietnam have been attributed to the agent by the one in-depth study that has so far been conducted, by the Canadian Hatfield Consultancy Ltd. Dioxin enters the food chain through contaminated soil or water supplies, and the build-up in human tissue – revealed in one of the few 'hot spots' where it has been properly monitored – is rising, which suggests that the problem is increasing rather than fading away. It is one of the many vicious features of dioxin that it breaks down remarkably slowly.

Given that the problem is quietly recognized, it is not surprising that the coffee industry, which has traditionally prided itself on its scientific prowess, has examined the issue of possible dioxin residues in the same Vietnamese coffee that has flooded the world markets since the late 1990s. The industry was paralysed, albeit briefly, in the mid 1980s by the sudden scare involving chlorine-bleached coffee filter papers and possible dioxin residues therein. Dioxin has thus negatively impinged on coffee consciousness before, and it would be natural for industry professionals to have a

once-bitten-twice-shy level of paranoia on this issue. Indeed paranoia seems to be the order of the day, for information on the subject is very hard to gather. This is curious, because all the evidence
would suggest that, since dioxin is not water soluble, it cannot be
taken up by plants, including coffee. Nonetheless, the coffee trade
is very nervous about the subject. The PEC group of coffee scientists looked at the issue in 2002 and reported that no problems had
been found. Or rather they are rumoured to have reported this conclusion, because 'once it was established that there was no cause for
concern they didn't go public'. The report was unreported. This
guardedness may be in turn a result of the persistent scaremonger-
ing in the USA, where apparently – according to the National
Coffee Association of America – a group of people the NCAA are
unwilling to name have for unknown reasons been regularly feed-
ing the dioxin in coffee story to the press. At one stage they even
managed to start an entirely false rumour that the FDA had placed
an embargo on Vietnamese coffee. Whatever the motives of this
mysterious group, one thing is certain: if there were one sure way
to cure the current problems afflicting coffee producers, it would be
for the entire production of Vietnamese coffee to be taken off the
market. There would be an immediate and dramatic rise in world
coffee prices. There is thus an intriguing suggestion of commercial
terrorism in the existence of these shadowy figures: could it be that
a coffee-producing country devastated by low prices is making a
desperate attempt to influence the market? Or is some rogue syndi-
cate seeking to make a quick killing on the New York 'C' market?

Given the lessons that could have been learnt from the Agent
Orange débâcle, the cavalier way in which the US Government
repeats the errors of the past beggars belief. As we have seen,
in Colombia the 'War on Drugs' has led to the increasing use of
herbicides, raising similar environmental and public health issues
to those concerning Agent Orange. This carries on despite the
vociferous opposition of many scientists and advocacy groups in

the US, who charge that State Department reports made to Congress, which must be submitted by law before funding can be allocated, have been partial and inconclusive, and that the required reassurances that 'chemicals used in the aerial eradication of coca crops in Colombia do not pose unreasonable health or safety risks to humans or the environment' cannot be derived from the material presented in the reports. The inevitable conclusion must be that perceived geopolitical imperatives override all other concerns, and that in any case it will be the poor farmers of Colombia who will bear the brunt of any side effects. There are hints that contamination with Round-Up, the herbicide most widely used, may affect the coffee crop, in which case the State Department may in future be able to congratulate itself on having introduced poison from Latin America to its own citizens.

The way that other depressing historical patterns repeat themselves in the coffee industry is interesting. The botanical nature of coffee favours highland production: highlands in the tropics tend to be the last refuge of the virgin ecology, in the form of forest cover, wildlife, and indigenous peoples. Thus whenever coffee cultivation is increased, it tends to be at the expense of all three. Certainly the ethnic Cambodians, who until recently inhabited the areas of the central highlands of Vietnam where coffee production is being expanded, complain not only of being driven from their lands but also of being swamped by Vietnamese from the Red River and Mekong deltas who have been encouraged to move there. This is seen in some circles as a cynical political ploy to get them to leave for the areas nearer the Cambodian border where they would act as a 'security seal' against possible incursions from that country. As we have seen in Central America, the purging of indigenous Indians from their highland refuges is closely allied to the fortunes of the coffee industry, and it would seem that the Vietnamese are following in this lamentable tradition.

The enormous expansion of coffee production in Vietnam has been widely attributed to the World Bank, which has been at considerable pains to deny any involvement, producing fiercely worded press releases exonerating itself from any blame. As with Agent Orange, the veil of official secrecy is hard to tear aside, as the financial institutions as well as the Vietnamese Government itself are unwilling to shoulder the responsibility of having contributed substantially to the collapse in world coffee prices. If there had been a material improvement in the lot of the small coffee farmers to whom money was lent (by the government, with or without the cognizance of the World Bank) in order to plant coffee, that would be some consolation. However, as a result of their own 'success', these same farmers are currently being forced to sell their coffee at about 60 per cent of the cost of production, and are locked into having to repay loans taken out on the basis of wildly optimistic forecasts for potential revenues from coffee farming. Vietnamese coffee production, having boomed, is now falling rapidly as it is realized that the promised riches are chimerical. The larger cost, to the fragile highland environment, to its beleaguered wildlife, to the displaced indigenes, and to the migrant lowlanders left stranded without an income and deep in debt, is incalculable. It is not surprising that there is no one willing to take the blame.

Vietnam was the focus of well-meant development plans, of which coffee was a prominent feature, intended to pull it out of the chaos and devastation caused by the long war with America. Its chief asset, low labour costs, was a direct inheritance of that war. By deploying the promise of its cheap labour and factoring it into its projections, the government was able to attract development capital from institutions such as the World Bank, who foresaw a realistic route for the country into the global trading community. This is colonialism in our era: the exploitation of cheap labour by the deployment of capital from wealthy lenders for the benefit of First World consumers. The World Bank is of course controlled by its 51 per cent shareholder, the US Treasury. Along with the IMF and the WTO it is part of the unelected triumvirate of the Washington Consensus whose decisions affect the lives of millions. All three are ideologically motivated, infatuated with the American model of free market capitalism and the purported benefits it can bring. That the World Bank failed to act responsibly in the case of Vietnam and its coffee, bringing untold misery to millions around the globe, should come as no surprise to those who have followed the path it has charted over the last decade or so. The defection of its former chief economist, Joseph Stiglitz, who was ejected in 1999 for daring to suggest the Bank should soften its approach, provides the reassuring insight that everything that its worst enemies have said about the World Bank appears to be true: the one-size-fits-all economic prescriptions for countries seeking loans; the bribes to government ministers in return for the knock-down sale of public assets to Western corporate interests; the opening up of the financial markets to foreign investors that leads to runs on the local bank when confidence wavers; the anticipation of social unrest requiring strong measures to suppress it; the bailing out of local banks when their loans from Western banks are at risk; the constant reiteration of the free trade mantra despite the continuation of agricultural subsidies in the First World . . . The list is unrelenting. Stiglitz, an outspoken critic of the IMF, compares that organization's approach to a country's economic problems to high-altitude bombing: 'From one's luxury hotel, one can callously impose policies about which one would think twice if one knew the people whose lives one was destroying.' The bombing analogy is an apt expression of the way in which the wielders of power in global politics and economics are increasingly removed from the consequences of their actions. The deliberate killing of civilians – a war crime in any other context – has, by the curious circumlocutions of power politics, come to be regarded as unfortunate but wholly legitimate collateral damage resulting from aerial bombardment of strategic targets. Similarly, in the operations of the global economy, the wholesale destruction of lives and livelihoods of entire nations wrought by the financial institutions in pursuit of an ideology is not generally seen for the horror it is, but as the slightly misguided but fundamentally well-meant application of sound principles.

The reverberations in the coffee industry of these economic policies are manifold. Many coffee-producing countries used to have coffee marketing boards who bought up all the farmers' produce. Although these were frequently corrupt and overly bureaucratic, at least the farmers knew that they would sell their coffee, and that they would get paid. The structural adjustment programmes imposed by the IMF/World Bank in the 1980s and 1990s led to the abolition of many of these boards, allowing the market to be opened up to private traders. As these are frequently the transnationals that dominate the trade, the farmer rarely has much choice regarding whom to sell to and at what price, and there is no guarantee that they will come back for more. The effect has been shattering.

Coffee used to be a business in which, despite its manifest drawbacks, a man could think himself honourably employed. In common with many other businessmen, the coffee man as often as not now finds himself effectively a receiver of stolen goods and an enslaver of the Third World. The more conscientious may scratch their heads and wonder how on earth this came about. Most keep their conscience prisoner.

Number One World Trade Center, across from the building containing the Coffee Futures Exchange, used to house a restaurant on the top floor called 'Windows on the World', which commanded spectacular views over Manhattan and beyond. It was possible for the historian to peer down from these Olympian heights and hazard an informed guess as to where the fortifications stood on the Brooklyn Heights across the East River, to which George Washington withdrew his shattered army after the battle against the more numerous British troops on Long Island on 27 August 1776. A few days later 'Nine thousand (or more) disheartened soldiers, the last hope of their country, were penned up, with the sea behind them and a triumphant enemy in front . . .' From above, the ultimate armchair historian could sip Chablis and imagine how Washington had somehow arranged an orderly retreat back to Manhattan avoiding the English frigates, a miniature Dunkirk that not only saved the nation, but paved the way for the growth of American pre-eminence.

Now the restaurant, the Twin Towers, and our comforting illusion of historical perspective have collapsed like a telescope. Then, if you like, is now. The edifice of our modern Western cultural tradition, which allowed us to treat the past as something from which our own human narrative was somehow exempt, has been demolished. The stuff of history, that was supposed to have been consigned to history – empire, slavery, religious wars, oppression, famine and pestilence – is played out before our disbelieving eyes, and we can no longer patronize our past. 'We' now stand revealed as no better than 'they' were then: only the scale of the drama has changed.

CODA

Even the island's name carries the echoes of Empire. The original St Helena was the mother of the Emperor Constantine the Great, who discovered the remains of the True Cross on a pilgrimage to Jerusalem. In AD 306 Constantine was crowned in York, the northern English city after which New York was named. Although not himself a convert, Constantine made the Roman Empire safe for Christianity, and moved its capital to Constantinople, naming it 'New Rome', a title that quickly lapsed. Until it was sacked by the Ottomans in 1453, Constantinople was the centre of the Byzantine Empire, the rump of its predecessor, the Roman Empire, whose western territories were ravaged and invaded. The Ottomans, too, made Constantinople their capital, and it was here that coffee drinking first became a widespread phenomenon. The magnificent coffee houses on the banks of the Bosporus have made way for railway tracks and dual carriageways, but something like the traditional coffee house has made a comeback in the city recently. Ironically it is not coffee, but the *nargile*, the Turkish water pipe, that is the focus of the new trend, with groups of men and women meeting together and puffing away at a variety of Egyptian ultra-light flavoured tobaccos, including apple, strawberry, melon, and orange. Old men still favour strong, plain Turkish tobacco but are regarded as irredeemably unfashionable. Some of the more adventurous clientele have taken to using milk instead of water in the bowl of the pipe, and then drinking it after smoking. As one of the flavoured tobaccos is 'cappuccino', this raises the interesting possibility of drinking a cappuccino-flavoured post-smoke milk. The Turkish coffee served in such establishments would make their forbears blush: gone are the studied rituals of thrice boiling, scenting with ambergris, or lacing with opium. Instead the coffee is made by pouring already boiling water into an *ibrik* containing coffee grounds and sugar, stirring and cursorily boiling again. Fashion and fast-food culture thus blight the return of the coffee house of Constantinople.

St Helena suffered from the opening of the Suez Canal in 1869: the ships that had plied the Cape of Good Hope on their way to and from India no longer did so, and with them went the principal historic *raison d'être* of St Helena. From that time on, the island's remoteness, previously its main asset, weighed heavily against it, except when it came to prisoners. Another, more tractable, ruler was exiled to St Helena in 1890: the Zulu Chief Dinizulu. He came with several wives and a small retinue, and was charming to all he met, greatly impressing the bishop who succeeded in converting him to Christianity, a triumph of civilizing principles marred by the fact that only one of his wives could be officially recognized. He returned to Zululand in 1897, no doubt surprising his tribe with the spirited renditions in English of hymns he had learnt, accompanying himself on the piano. The Zulu party was followed by prisoners of the Boer War, including General Cronje: the prisoners eventually numbered six thousand, bringing a temporary measure of prosperity, rats, and typhoid in their train.

It is tempting to assume that the happy breed of coffee plant that had been imported to St Helena from Yemen had no rivals for the island's affection, but in the ensuing years a number of experimental plantings were conducted at the Botanical Gardens and elsewhere, and other varieties tried out. It says much for the original choice of blue-tipped Bourbon that no other variety has ever thrived on St Helena. When, in the 1950s, the flax industry threatened completely to dominate the island's economy, it was thought wise to look at alternatives such as coffee. A Mr Jones, an expert sent from the Kenya Coffee Research Station, thought it was remarkable that the island could produce any coffee at all, 'considering the strong winds, low rainfall and relative lack of sunshine'. The Yemeni stock should normally have found such conditions impossible, and so he recommended experimenting with some hardier strains, which all promptly died, leaving the delicate Bourbon variety the surprise survivor. Jones's report did nothing to encourage further investment in the industry, even when the flax industry collapsed overnight in 1966, the result of a decision by a civil servant in England to buy elastic bands rather than string.

St Helena has an air of fateful entropy about it, pervading both its inhabitants and its history. The soil slips into the sea, but no one thinks to cull the goats that destroy the trees that hold the soil. Peaches are infected by peach fly, which the peach growers cannot be bothered to cure by the simplest of measures. Sometimes it seems that even God has made the island an object of malicious trickery: when a wealthy philanthropist decided to build and equip a mackerel canning factory for the benefit of the island in 1909, as well as buying modern fishing boats, the seas that had teemed with mackerel up until that moment were suddenly, miraculously, empty, and the factory had to close within the year. The island, along with its dependencies of Ascension and Tristan da Cunha, relied increasingly on that most effete of post-colonial industries, postage stamps, the official mark of economic marginalization.

And then, much to the surprise of all, coffee started to make a comeback. A local shop owner invested in a small roaster and grinder and sold the local production on the local market. Although Saints are incorrigible tea-drinkers (at least those who don't drink beer are), gradually a small number started to buy their island's coffee, and a few packs in awful condition made their way back to the UK. In 1989 a London coffee broker heard of the coffee from the Agricultural Officer who was on leave in England and offered the whole crop of the island to me – I was the buying director of a coffee company at the time – which I bought sight unseen, as no samples were available. I was intrigued by the notion that I could have the entire production of an island, about which I then knew very little. The Government then leased the coffee-growing fields to David Henry, an Englishman whose father was a Saint and thus was able to gain the necessary permission to move to the island. He had first spent time there when a brief visit had been elongated as a result of the Falklands War, and had noted the island's coffee. Back in London, he researched its origins and decided that, if it could be developed properly, it could be a world-class coffee. He applied to the International Coffee Organization to have the coffee registered as a British product, so that it could freely be marketed, but his plans were stymied by the Government's uni-lateral decision prematurely to sell the coffee to me before he had had a chance to address the issues of husbandry, processing quality, and grading, all of which needed to be put on a proper footing.

In due course, and in inimitable St Helenan fashion, the Government found that it was unable to conjure up any enthusi-asm for coffee amongst the island's farmers, and leased the exper-imental plantations to David Henry. He has since developed these small estates and added several more, selling the coffee all over the world, either to roasters in Japan and the USA in green bean form, or over the Internet, sending individual parcels of roasted coffee to Hollywood and Honolulu. He is described by one visitor as the 'Heathcliff of the South Atlantic', but his satur-nine looks are allied to a passionate commitment to quality. As a result, St Helena coffee is the most expensive in the world.

Following his efforts, the other farmers on the island have real-ized that coffee, at least when it is as expensive as St Helena coffee is, can be a profitable business and have started to produce small quantities. However much the taste of St Helena coffee can be ascribed to its idiosyncratic history, soil, and microclimate, a considerable amount of skill and experience is required in the processing to bring out the optimum flavour. As each of the farmers on the island is doing his own processing, the results are variable and the expectations as to price that have been raised by the international success of David Henry's coffees have not been matched.

Television came to the island only a few years ago, a golden opportunity for sociologists to follow with intense interest the 'effect' that it was having on the population. As video recorders had been around for some time, many of the consequences of the television age were already in place: the popularity of weekly dances had dwindled, the cinema had closed, and people were staying at home more. Former studies had found that the island's children were amongst the best behaved and most well adjusted in the world. Nearly all become Girl Guides or Boy Scouts, and parades in uniform are a highlight of the social calendar. Since television was introduced, however, there has been an increase in petty crime, and the easy community in which every householder left his door unlocked when he went out has become more security conscious. The growth of St Helena's fledgling coffee industry makes an interesting case study likewise: 250 years of attempts to get started, then a sudden success positioning it as the world's most expensive coffee, then the rush to jump on the bandwagon and an increase in production, with all that might mean in terms of quality control, marketing, and distribution.

Following in the tradition of the Governors of the island for the last 350 years, the present incumbent shows a keen appreciation of the island's only success story. Plantation House, the original Governor's residence built by the East India Company in the 1790s, is reckoned by those who study such matters to be the most beautiful residence in Her Majesty's Diplomatic Service. It stands in lush gardens with distant views of the sea, built in the simple neoclassical style favoured by Empire's architects throughout the ages, with an elegant white portico and well-proportioned rooms. The lawns are grazed by a number of giant tortoises, originally natives of the Seychelles. One, a venerable and battered creature named Jonathan, is reputed to be over two hundred and twenty years old. He never met Napoleon as some have suggested – the Emperor did not visit Plantation House – but he breathed the same dank St Helenan air. History pervades the place, with the same silent, unassuming presence as that of Jonathan. The dining table stands beneath a chandelier cobbled together from two which used to hang over Napoleon at Longwood. On the sideboard is a splendid silver cloche emblazoned with the coat of arms of the East India Company. The servants' quarters have hardly changed in two hundred years. The stone-flagged larder has capacious cupboards stacked with the latest standard-issue diplomatic porcelain as determined by the Foreign Office. One cupboard reveals the depth of the present Governor's interest in the island's fledgling speciality coffee industry: two jars of instant coffee, trophies of a recent trip to England.

The weather, never St Helena's most endearing feature, is proving ever more unreliable. Torrential rains during the harvesting season have badly affected the coffee crop for the last two years and increased the soil erosion, which has stripped two-thirds of the island down to bare rock in five centuries. The population is decreasing, as those islanders equipped with qualifications, such as teachers and nurses, seek to ply their trade more lucratively elsewhere. If the trend continues, there will soon be less than four thousand islanders permanently living there, below the critical mass believed necessary to sustain a self-contained community. People complain, as they have done since 1659, about the Government and the impossibility of St Helena ever changing, whilst the ruling élite uphold the status quo from the fine Council Chamber in the Castle. The new Deputy Governor, parachuted in after an undistinguished career in English local government with the unlikely brief to encourage Private Finance Initiatives, has controversially been allowed to buy property on the island with his partner, where he intends to retire, his peace undisturbed by the host of ventures his presence was supposed to inspire. One of these is to build an airport and defray the cost by 'quality' housing developments and a championship golf course. The ageing RMS *St Helena* would be scrapped and the islanders would be forever fighting for seats on the aeroplane with Tiger Woods, according to this visionary proposal. A referendum was held, and the islanders voted in favour of the scheme. Supported by the UK Government, a team of twenty-five consultant engineers, surveyors, architects, and financiers had been scheduled to visit the island in spring 2002 finally to get down to negotiations with the island's notoriously intransigent Government. That Government cancelled the visit at the last moment, so that they could consult with the islanders once more. It will take more than a year for the same team to be reassembled.

St Helena is a peculiarly British anachronism, the one place left where, despite the government's corruption and ineptitude, there is a living flavour of what a cog in the machine of the Empire was like. The island has not succumbed to a nostalgic sense of itself, to the frustration of those who seek to preserve its heritage, and the relationship it has with England as a dependent colony is refreshingly at odds with the mantras of New Labour. Here can be found little sign of a burgeoning entrepreneurial culture; no dot-com wizards; and no one who could conceivably invest in business on the island is able to negotiate unmolested, whilst the coffee 'industry', which almost anywhere else would be the subject at least of some amazement and pride, is treated with the same indifference as any other of the island's foibles. Tourism consists of occasional passengers on the RMS, and the contents of the odd cruise boat, who emerge, blinking incredulously, on to what could be the set of an Agatha Christie film, except that the village shop is a Co-Op and the bar of the pretty, wrought-ironed Consulate Hotel is full of loud customers and yet louder Country and Western music. The Castle is the seat of power, and has been since the East India Company formally claimed the island in 1659. The records of the Company's administration exist in the form of the 'Consultations', well-preserved manuscript documents in 157 volumes covering the years 1678–1836, which still sit on open shelves in the cellars of the castle where they can be duly consulted – 'The meeting on Monday 8th December 1817 which was held at the Castle – Present Sir Hudson Lowe KCB Governor, William Weber Doveton Esq., Robert Leech Esq.' is minuted with the precise, unemotive language of a parish council meeting in rural England.

Unique in its isolation and its political status, St Helena is a curious mixture of dependency and self-containment. It thumbs its collective nose at its colonial masters, managing to beg proudly, but not to be too proud to beg. As Great Britain, the country that took possession of the island and to whose imperial power it contributed significantly, tries to reinvent itself as a fully modern country, St Helena has become something of an embarrassment, the unloved elderly relative who turns up at Christmas and quaffs too much sherry. However, because of its isolation the island rarely impinges on the national consciousness – even the celebrations in 2002 for the 500th anniversary of its discovery merited hardly a word in the British press.

This tiny, tired remnant of the British Empire contained the last years of the Napoleonic Empire, and the tricolour that flies at Longwood House expresses past French glories. The two countries, separated by the Channel and ancient enmities, meet on St Helena in a conspiracy of self-deception, to deny to themselves and each other that their time has passed, that they are but empires of anachronism.

APPENDIX

THE FIND AT KUSH

The discovery of two carbonized coffee beans in an archaeological dig at Kush in the United Arab Emirates may yet bring early coffee history into question. Kush was, for a thousand years until the end of the thirteenth century, a coastal trading port, and as a result of its strategic location near the mouth of the Persian Gulf seems to have attracted traders from all over the East. Pottery shards provide evidence of trade with India in the fourth century, China in the tenth century, and continuous activity with Persia and other local Arab traders.

In 1996, British archaeologists found a layer containing some Chinese pottery that could be dated with certainty to the early twelfth century. Significantly, the layer also contained shards of Yemeni yellow pottery of the same era, suggesting a contemporary trade with Yemen that had not been seen before. Amongst the detritus were the two carbonized coffee beans. These had been preserved only because they had fallen into a fire, charring them to a cinder, which meant they had contained no organic matter that would have caused them to rot away. By the use of a new palaeobotanical flotation machine, the carbonized matter was separated from the excavated soil and identified as *Coffea Arabica*. Dr Derek Kennet, the University of Durham archaeologist running the dig, believes that there is little chance of the coffee beans being 'intrusive' (i.e. later material that has found its way into the strata); but AMS carbon-14 dating has yet to be conducted on the beans to make certain.

The discovery, if it is found to be genuine, would require a significant rewriting of the history of coffee. Not only would it provide the first concrete evidence of the existence of coffee in the early 1100s, three hundred and fifty years before the first Haysi pottery shards suggest its ritual use amongst Sufis, but the fact that the beans were carbonized would put them in proximity with fire, indicating that they may have been being roasted before consumption. The presence of Yemeni pottery would also suggest that the coffee itself came from Yemen – the local region is far too dry for coffee cultivation – which in turn requires the re-dating of Yemen's coffee industry. Most significant, however, is the fact that the beans have survived at all, for this would imply that the scale of the coffee trade by the era in question was already significant enough to create the opportunity for the 'freak accident' by which the evidence survives. As the new techniques that allowed them to be identified have been used in very few archaeological digs in the region, it may be that there is a wealth of similar evidence waiting to be discovered.

There are two possible issues arising from the find that could destroy its validity. One would be if the carbon dating gives a different date, suggesting that the beans are intrusive. The other would be if the identification of the carbonized material as *Coffea Arabica* is disputed. Otherwise we have, for the first time, archaeological evidence of the trade in coffee more than three centuries before the date usually given by historians. Confirmation would lend credibility to the claims that the descriptions of the unknown substance in the works of Rhazes and Avicenna could be of coffee, bringing them from their rather isolated position, marooned chronologically in the ninth and tenth centuries, closer to the rest of coffee's historical narrative.

EPILOGUE

So once again I found myself on a long-haul flight in pursuit of coffee. Only in this case, I'd decided to track down the incinerated remains of two coffee beans found in the archaeological dig at Kush, rather than some rare current crop. But the principle remained the same: frequently you only really discover anything by going to the source. In the Appendix that you have just read, I wrote that if the find at Kush proves to be genuine, the whole early history of coffee will have to be rewritten – little thinking that I would turn out to be the one to rewrite it.

For clarity, Kush is a small, ruined ancient quarter close to the modern city of Ras Al Khaimah, the chief city of the eponymous Emirate, a former Trucial State under the British, now incorporated into the United Arab Emirates. Kush was a significant port on the ancient (pre-Islamic) and Islamic Arab maritime trade routes of the Indian Ocean, only to be superseded when it silted up by Old Julfar, another abandoned settlement. The discovery of coffee beans in Kush suggests that it is not likely to be a one-off, freak find in some trading backwater, but one right at the heart of the ancient Indian Ocean trade by sea.

A few months previously I'd contacted Khalid Al Mulla, founder of the Dubai Coffee Museum. We'd finally spoken on my mobile while I was walking in the shadow of the Eiffel Tower in Paris, and I began to discuss the find, assuming that he'd already know all about it – after all, Ras Al Khaimah is only a hundred kilometres up the Gulf coast from his hometown, Dubai. To our mutual astonishment, he hadn't.

In the few months following we'd conducted a frustrating twin-pronged research mission to find out more about the whereabouts of the elusive beans; I desperately wanted to visit the place to bring this aspect of coffee's history to a satisfying conclusion for this book. I dimly imagined the beans would be proudly displayed in some appropriately high-tech secure cabinet housed in the National Museum of Ras Al Khaimah, the Emir's historic former fort/palace in the town. I hoped they'd take pride of place, rather like the tiny test tube containing the invaluable smear of extraordinarily rare meteoric diamonds that you can find in the Treasury of the Natural History Museum in London (the obscure object of one of my former research desires). But if it were so displayed, the RAK authorities were keeping it very quiet. The day I left London for Dubai, a friend asked me what I hoped to find. I told her that I had no real idea.

But only a few days previously Khalid had managed to establish contact with Ahmed Obaid Al Tunaiji, the recently appointed General Manager of the Antiquities and Museums Department of the Government of Ras Al Khaimah. Khalid and I were both excited by this apparent progress, so when finally Khalid drove my companion and I to the National Museum of RAK (as it is called by those in the know . . .) we had a quick look around the nineteenth-century fort, rebuilt on the foundations of countless predecessors. It looked like a film set for a lavish remake of *Beau Geste* – unlike the drive from Dubai down the coastal highway, which, as befits the booming UAE economy, presents a vista of construction sites backed by the endless desert sands of Arabia, and the distant mountains bordering Oman.

Our contact wasn't to be found, nor was my eagerly anticipated display cabinet in the museum, or indeed any sign of objects from the find at Kush. Just as we were about to leave for our resort hotel (Ras Al Khaimah boasts a beach-strewn coastline bordering the sultry, salty waters of the Persian Gulf), Khalid managed to get through to Christian Velde, the Resident Archaeologist at the National Museum, who is originally from Germany but has been resident in RAK for more than twenty years (he'd assisted on the original dig, and had simply stayed on . . .) and arranged an appointment for early the next day.

When I showed up with my companion at an office building behind the museum, Dr Velde greeted us, along with his wife, Imke – also German, also an archaeologist. Having explained my presence there, and Khalid's absence (he had prior commitments), we chatted about the finding of the beans and some technical points. It emerged that the beans themselves had been microscopically identified as originating from a wild (i.e. undomesticated) coffee plant, which reinforced my initial thought that they could be of Ethiopian origin. Dr Velde, however, maintained that the process of plant domestication could take a long time, and they might have come from an early progenitor of the plants that eventually bedecked those fabulous Yemeni mountain terraces. I also discovered that the find itself was due to an almost miraculous concatenation of circumstance. A slight change of angle of the trowel, a marginally less vigilant use of the (then) relatively new technique of palaeobotantic flotation, and the whole discovery might have been missed. In Dr Velde's opinion it was extraordinarily unlikely for such a find to be replicated elsewhere.

I said I'd like to visit Kush itself, the site of this freak find. Although it was protected against the encroachments of developers, it was just an unprepossessing mound – 'a rubbish dump', I was told by Imke. The excavation trench had been refilled to protect possible future finds for posterity – a standard practice in the archaeological world – and the mound was being used as a mountain-bike playground by the local kids. Attempts to protect the site with fencing inevitably led to the fences being pilfered for use elsewhere. There was nothing to see there, Imke said firmly, and, as I was pressed for time, I gave in. It was now the moment for the big question: 'So where are the beans now? Can I see them?'

'They are in the UK with Dr Kennett,' Dr Velde said.

The UK. Where I had just come from.

I rang Khalid as soon as we got back to the hotel and, characteristically, he got on the case straight away and rang the archaeologist's boss, Ahmed Al Telije, fixing a meeting for 2pm the next day. Christian Velde would be there, too, he had been told, but Khalid had prior commitments again.

The government office of the Department of Antiquities and Museums is housed in an unprepossessing office building near the Old Fish Market. Introductions over, we were served the local-style coffee – very lightly roasted, fruity flavours to the fore. It reminded me of 'kisr', a drink made from husks of the coffee cherry that I'd had in Yemen many years previously. We got down to business. The fact was confirmed that the two carbonised beans were actually now back in England. Because of their very friable state, it had been decided that they were better off in the protective custody of Dr Kennett himself, who was busying himself finalising the official archaeological report, which, my hosts had been assured, would be available 'soon'. The dig had been twenty years earlier, but I was told that it was perfectly normal for archaeological reports to be concluded at geological speed. I can't say I wasn't disappointed about the beans: my dreams of cradling them like a fisherman with a prize salmon had been duly dashed. Likewise, the all-important Chinese and Yemeni pottery shards (not related to coffee consumption, apparently – another blow...) that had been found along with the beans were not available for viewing. Although the National

Museum had plans to display all the relevant material about their spectacular find, they were waiting for the official report, too. They were a bit concerned that there remained very little of the beans to see, and I told them the story I mentioned earlier of the microscopic meteoric diamonds at the Natural History Museum in London. 'They managed to make an almost invisible exhibit exciting,' I told them, which they seemed to find reassuring.

I also told Ahmed that, in my opinion, RAK could benefit substantially from any publicity surrounding the find. 'You're home to the oldest coffee beans ever found. That's unique.'

Ahmed said that he'd get an update for me from Dr Kennett, so that what you're reading here would be as up-to-date as could be. I duly received a copy of an email a few weeks later. It turned out that he'd had the beans re-examined by an internationally known expert in the field of palaeobotany, Professor Margareta Tengberg from the Museum of Natural History in Paris. Along with a PhD student of hers, she had recently confirmed the identification of one of the beans as coffee, but discounted the other. That's good news, but we're down to a single bean now. Carbon dating would mostly destroy the remaining bean, as I knew already. Nonetheless, Dr Kennett feels it would be the best idea to undertake it, after taking a photogrammetric image (3-D image), simply because it would remove any remaining uncertainty – as well as remove any remaining bean. So there's a tricky judgement call to be made, and ultimately the buck stops with the Sheikh of RAK, Ahmed's boss. The PhD student's report formally confirming the positive identification is due in early 2019. So that's where we're at right now.

In the meantime, I had other fish to fry. Khalid, he of the Dubai Coffee Museum, had managed to arrange a meeting with someone from DMCC, the China/Dubai coffee futures market idea that I will discuss later on. Yet again, a day later in a trendy Dubai coffee shop, I find myself in the strange position of introducing the existence of the find at Kush, and its significance, to an organisation with a special interest in coffee and based in the same country. I had no hand in the original discovery, of course, but increasingly I felt as if I had made the discovery myself . . .

This impression was confirmed early in the New Year of 2019 when Ahmed showed up in Southern Sri Lanka, where I was based while finishing up this book. He was on a family holiday, but it seemed pleasingly appropriate to be sitting on a hotel terrace looking across the wind-whipped Indian Ocean towards Arabia as we discussed the ancient bean. 'RAK has no oil, but at least it has a bean,' I joked. We met but briefly, but he was able to provide me with a few updates. The RAK authorities were now in touch directly with Professor Tengberg, and after much deliberation had decided to ask her to carbon date some of the other botanical material found alongside the bean, rather than the bean itself, thus preserving our (now) solitary specimen. It was a compromise, but it safeguarded the bean for who knows what technical advances that might come along eventually. Reports from Professor Tengberg and her PhD student are due imminently, but not imminently enough for me to include them here. Ahmed promised to ask Christian about his claim that the bean had been identified as coming from a wild coffee plant – he was unaware of this – but he did tell me that until I'd shown up the previous autumn, everybody in RAK had all but forgotten the find. He himself hadn't heard about it until Khalid called him. Plans for a refurbishment of the National Museum were well advanced, but this discovery had not been taken into account in the plans. The Tourist Ministry had submitted a ten-year plan with an emphasis on the cultural and archaeological significance of RAK, but the bean never got a mention. The head of the archaeology section dimly remembered something about it, and that he was still waiting for Dr Kennett's report to emerge from hibernation in his dusty office in distant Durham. There was even a question as to whether the ruler of RAK, Sheikh Saud bin Saqr Al Qasimi, knew about the find. Ahmed promised to take the next opportunity to ask him. So that's where we're at right *right* now.

I find it curious that, because in this book I'm often discussing events that are actually unfolding as I write, I'm becoming part of the story I'm telling. The tale of the ancient coffee bean is a case in point. If I hadn't picked up the thread of my researches from the first edition of this book, and persisted with them, going as far as to visit RAK uninvited, the authorities there would probably still be pretty much in their state of unknowingness. As it is, all sorts of things seem to be stirring. In quantum physics (so I'm told . . .) there's something known as the 'observer effect', whereby the very act of an observer taking a measurement changes the outcome of the measurement. That's the closest parallel I can find. Not so much a Dark History but a Pliable Present.

Meanwhile, the astonishing fact remains that the find is still largely unheralded in the coffee industry at large. Even though this remarkable discovery, at a stroke, pushes back the first proven sighting of coffee in history by some 300 years, most coffee company marketing material still blithely rehearses the Kaldi myth or its myriad variants that I sought to debunk in the first edition of this book. Dr Kennett wrote an article about the discovery in the US-based *Tea & Coffee Trade Journal* of 1 January 1998: other than that, there has been no trade coverage that I could find.

So what else does this unsung find reveal about coffee's history? In Dr Kennett's view, the beans are Arabica, ergo they must be of Yemeni origin. But as we have seen, the Yemeni coffee trade developed alongside the 'Abyssine' coffee mentioned in Francis Dickinson's letters from Mocha, so the beans themselves could have been of Ethiopian origin, even though they were found alongside Yemeni and Chinese pottery. In that case it would be rash to use the find to conclude that the cultivation of coffee in Yemen was developed earlier than previously thought, but it would be true to say that the *trade* in coffee (of Yemeni or Ethiopian origin) appeared to have been taking place in the late eleventh century. That's a long way back in history, much earlier than was previously thought, and a long way by sea – Ras al Khaimah lies 1,150 nautical miles from Mocha, the most likely port of origin. In turn, Mumbai lies that same distance away again.

Which brings us to another issue: how do we explain the presence of Chinese pottery in the same layer? That is more easily dealt with: a flourishing Indian Ocean maritime trading network had existed for at least a thousand years, dominated by Chinese and pre-Islamic, later Muslim Arab traders. This is amply documented in records from many different sources and countries.

Could coffee and its cultivation have been part of this trade? There is suggestive evidence. For example, it is known that in the early sixteenth century Muslims from Sumatra would make the *hajj* to Mecca, where coffee culture was already starting to establish itself. So it is likely that the inhabitants of the Indonesian islands would have been introduced to coffee drinking nearly two centuries before the Dutch introduced coffee plants to the neighbouring island of Java. Likewise, the word for coffee in the local language in Sulawesi (an Indonesian island in the east of the archipelago), '*kaa*', is thought ultimately to derive from the Arabic word '*quawah*', suggesting its origin with Arab traders rather than, as is more usually thought, the Dutch. This suggestion is reinforced by the discovery in the 1920s of 200–300-year-old coffee trees in the south of the island, pre-dating the supposed first arrival of coffee as being when the Dutch introduced it in 1830.

Certainly, the skills of the Arab mariners were especially appreciated by early European explorers when they first 'discovered' the Indian Ocean. Vasco da Gama would never have made his celebrated first landfall by a European in Calicut, in India, without the help and advice of the poet, mariner and, it so happens, Julfar local, Ahmed Bin, who was rumoured to have met him in Malindi, Kenya. Thus the presence of eleventh-century Chinese pottery in Kush should come as no surprise; the port was a significant link in the trade routes of the Indian Ocean long before it was first colonised by the Portuguese in the early sixteenth century.

The find also puts the known history of the worldwide spread of coffee cultivation in a totally new light. There has been a typically Eurocentric/colonial cast to this history, as we have seen. Generally speaking, it has largely concentrated on tales of derring-do involving intrepid Europeans breaking the jealously guarded Mocha monopoly on coffee, as if Arab traders had neither the nous nor the knowledge to seek pastures new for coffee cultivation (the exception is the myth of Babu Budan's introduction of coffee to India, a story that received short shrift earlier in this book). To find coffee over a thousand miles from its origin, evidently roasted, suggests that by the early 1100s both coffee consumption and trading was considerably more evolved than had previously been believed. And if that is the case, why should not the same be true of coffee *cultivation*? Evidence is very hard to find – plants don't survive long enough to be dated, and vegetable matter usually decays over a relatively short time. As we've seen, the very survival of the beans in the find at Kush is regarded as almost miraculous, indicating a very widespread trade, largely undiscovered and undiscoverable. But if we take the case of coffee cultivation on the island of Ceylon (now Sri Lanka), we can again see that documents and oral history can make an argument for the Arab cultivation of coffee long before 'pioneering' European initiatives.

The name Ceylon is so inextricably linked to tea cultivation in popular consciousness that it is hard to believe that by 1859 it was firmly placed amongst the big three world coffee producers, alongside Brazil and Indonesia, making fortunes for a few (both British and native Ceylonese) and substantially raising the island's GDP in general. It had arrived at this enviable position because of a long chain of circumstances. Its lowland littoral plantations of cinnamon had been variously under the control of the Portuguese from the 1500s to 1658, the Dutch East India Company (VOC) from 1658 to 1796, then a little-known period under the East India Company in 1796/8 (the result of a marvellously picaresque tale of treachery involving a counterfeit Scots professor, a mercenary Swiss aristocrat and an Edam cheese, but sadly, there's not enough room to tell it in this book), and finally the British Crown, which decided to make an honest colony of her.

Each colonial occupier has at some stage claimed responsibility for the introduction of coffee to Ceylon, but it seems that in reality there is general accord that the Arab traders on the coast were the guilty party. It's tempting to imagine our little band of merchants back in Kush sitting around a camp fire, enjoying their recently acquired – and addictive – habit of drinking roasted coffee, and wondering how they were going to be able to get hold of some to keep them going after their next long voyage east. It seems that at some stage they took some plants to Sri Lanka with them, not necessarily with an eye to commercial cultivation, but perhaps for personal consumption. The Portuguese later noted the plants' presence around some parts of the littoral, and that the native Sri Lankans used the leaves for flavouring their curries but seemed oblivious to their use as a beverage. The Dutch VOC, by the time they took over Ceylon, had decided that Java was to be their top coffee colony, and although they made some desultory efforts to cultivate the existing plants they found there on plantations, they realised that the lowlands around the Ceylonese coast were not of sufficient altitude for the production of top-quality coffee.

With the island finally in British hands after they had forcibly taken over from the Dutch in 1798, the last independent kingdom on the island, Kandy, was a thorn in the side of the new administration, and difficult to topple as its eponymous capital was located in the centre of the island, surrounded by remote, heavily forested mountains. Through a combination of British force, trade embargoes and diplomacy, the Kandyian kings finally kowtowed to their authority in 1815.

As they did an inventory of their new acquisition, the British administrators were surprised to come across a large tract of land at Hanguranketty, near Kandy, planted out to coffee. This was known as 'The King's Garden', and the coffee trees were for the production of flowers for garlands for temple ceremonies. Plants for the same use were found outside nearly every village in the kingdom. The sight of coffee plants seems to have struck a chord, because the first coffee estate was opened at Gampolla in 1824 by the brother of the commandant of Kandy, who did much to encourage others to follow suit in the remote forested mountains.

The Governor of Ceylon, Sir Edward Barnes, actively encouraged highland planting on the island as well, particularly after the abolition of slavery in the West Indies led to a supply squeeze back in Blighty for their previously very price-competitive coffees, and by 1840 the sound of tree chopping and forest clearance became an everyday feature of the highland soundscape, as a veritable 'coffee rush' ensued, with both the British and Sinhalese involved. The altitude, climate and soil conditions were found to be ideal for cultivating coffee and the end product was generally excellent. By 1859, Sir James Emerson Tennent commented in *Ceylon: An Account of the Island*:

> Although the plant had existed from time immemorial on the Island (having probably been introduced from Mocha by the Arabs), the natives were ignorant of the value of its berries, and only used its leaves to flavour their curries, and its flowers to decorate their temples.

The dreaded phrase 'time immemorial' is the bane of historians seeking precision, as it can be taken to mean anything from the time of the construction of the pyramids to last Saturday after breakfast. In general, though, it suggests some great age, and it chimed with Tennent's conviction that coffee was already established on the island before the Portuguese arrived. Certainly the plant type that was used for the frenzy of new planting was the same as that which was originally cultivated in Yemen, and by 1857 Ceylon was exporting 36 million tonnes a year – for comparison, Jamaica produces about 1.2 million tonnes today.

The fortunes made from this boom came at a price. The ecological devastation wrought in the highlands was only a part of the story. In their haste to cash in, planters adopted the practice of monoculture, using no shade trees, which made the new plantations particularly vulnerable to attacks by fungi, and as early as 1869 a devastating outbreak of the incurable *Hemileia vastatrix* (known locally, with suitably gallows humour, as 'Devastating Emily'), or 'coffee rust', brought the Coffee Rush to a juddering standstill, leading to a run of business and personal bankruptcies. From 1,700 planters at the boom's height, only

400 stayed on the island, and most only survived by turning to their saviour, tea. And the rest, as they say, is history.

And history, it is said, is written by the victors. So what war was fought that enabled European coffee traders to so thoroughly control coffee's historical narrative? The war in question was the centuries-long, mainly European fight to impose their will on the undeveloped, resource-rich parts of the planet. Generally it is known as colonialism. And generally victory was ultimately gained at the barrel of a gun.

In our supposedly more enlightened times, colonialism has become something of dirty word, and the countries that have achieved independence from it look back at the period with understandable disgust.

The buzzword in the trade in tropical commodities for some time has been 'vertical integration'. Its underlying principle seems to be a sort of justifiable revenge for colonialism. For centuries, Western colonial powers made fortunes from the sweat and blood of their colonial subjects (or using imported slave labour), producing sugar, coffee, tea and cocoa (to name but a few) on plantations frequently owned by themselves, hauling the produce off to the homeland at knock-down prices to 'add value' in the form of processing, packaging and marketing in the way that only Western know-how knows how. 'Why can't we add the value ourselves?' the argument runs in countries recently independent from their former colonial masters. Often it has been the sheer size of the capital outlay required that has been the biggest barrier to entry into these competitive markets. As a result of the technical problems involved in the coffee market, the cost of packaging machinery alone presents a grave obstacle. This is the reason why, as I observed earlier, one of the trials of a coffee buyer's life is to receive roasted and packed coffee from leading producing countries of quality green coffee that are almost invariably stale and virtually undrinkable.

Increasingly both (apparently) well-meaning Western compan-ies and native producers are seeking to solve this conundrum, some through having a direct stake in a producing plantation so that they are not dependent on middle-men or remote commodity markets. Alternatively, small producers at origin can make a reasonable stab at preserving the freshness of their coffee by, for example, buying individual pre-formed valve packs and filling them by hand. But there's no way they can compete with large roasters in the West who can churn out thousands of packs of coffee an hour, and plug into a distribution system which whizzes their branded product onto supermarket shelves across a nation within weeks, supported by an ample advertising budget so that, to consumers, their brand is already a familiar face. Imagine trying to do all that with, for example, Tanzania's finest Arabica grown on the slopes of Kilimanjaro, packed by hand in nearby Arusha, and you can get a sense of the size of the problem.

It's been a problem historically, not just for the coffee-producing countries, but for the tea-growing countries also, but with one big difference. Against all the odds, the sixth-largest tea company in the world was founded in 1986 by a native son of a tea-producing country, blended using exclusively his coun-try's teas, producing tea bags and packages to exacting international standards, and exporting to over a hundred coun-tries worldwide, making it the world's most successful vertically integrated tea company. Its name: Dilmah. The country? Sri Lanka – or, to give it its better-known tea name, Ceylon.

Had not disease laid waste to the island's coffee production, this enviable situation might never have arisen. The tea plant is hardier than the delicate Arabica, and it flourished mightily. Ceylon became the testing ground for new industrial plantation methods, producing high-quality CTC ('Cut, Torn and Curled') black teas on a previously unimaginable scale. The success of

Sir Thomas Lipton, who built his eponymous brand on these mass-produced teas, demonstrated that Western technology could not only create demand but satisfy it cheaply and effectively by the exploitation of colonial commodities, too. The paradigm was set, until Dilmah came along with a new one. There is no parallel in coffee. At least not yet.

But February 2019 will see the official opening of the coffee centre of the Dubai Multi Commodities Centre, an extremely ambitious venture that aims to reorientate world commodities and futures markets eastwards, with the best that the latest technology and infrastructure has to offer. Middle Eastern and Indian Ocean trade is very much on the agenda, as is the coffee centre, which has state-of-the-art coffee storage facilities, a roasting and packing complex and an online Exchange. The new centre is co-financed by the Dubai authorities – the modestly titled Mega Capital (a Hong Kong-based finance company) and the Yunnan State Farms Group Co. Ltd. This latter is the single largest state agricultural enterprise in China's subtropical Yunnan province, and produces 130,000 tonnes of coffee a year, the vast bulk of China's production. They will be using the DMCC to lighten the world's coffee future market dependence on the New York 'C' market and its vagaries, using Yunnan's Arabica coffee as the quality standard. There are no plans yet for the DMCC to produce their own branded coffee, but they will have all they need on site should they decide to do so. Then they will have fulfilled Sir Thomas Lipton's famous maxim 'from plantation to cup' – only under the control of the country that grows the coffee.

The heavy Chinese involvement in the DMCC initiative demonstrates vertical integration of a very high order indeed – not only Chinese direct involvement in the growing of their coffee, but complete control of the distribution network, including their own futures exchange, using their own coffee as the standard. The only flaw – if that's what it should be called – is that China may be many things, but by no stretch of the imagination is it a third-world country struggling to free itself from a former European colonial yoke.

In the face of the scale of ambition of this project, it's difficult to keep in mind that only a thousand years previously, a mere hour's drive up the coast from Dubai, a group of Arab traders were sitting around a camp fire in Kush, drinking coffee, surrounded by Chinese pottery. Were they discussing the opportunity 'to turn over a new chapter in global coffee trade', as Mega Capital's executive director put it when he announced their venture? Probably not, but in their own way it seems that the ancient traders were no less ambitious: they opened the Indian Ocean to coffee trading, consumption and cultivation long before it was generally thought of.

For this is the true significance of the find: it has finally provided us with hard evidence that enables us to have meaningful discussions about how coffee might have played an important role in the Indian Ocean trade before the era of European colonialism. In the example I have given of Ceylon/Sri Lanka, instead of being trapped in a cramped, artificial, largely mythical timeframe at Mocha before the arrival of European traders, the find of Kush has given us a far more expansive timeframe, in which even Tennent's use of the dread phrase 'time immemorial' assumes a greater degree of accuracy.

Q TESTING

When I was a young man, my entry into the world of coffee as the Taylors' buyer was enabled by proven wanderlust and unabashed nepotism – my family owned the company (and still does). I was sent to learn about the rituals of coffee 'cupping' at the side of a number of experienced coffee importers in the City of London. Then I returned to Yorkshire and put what I had learned to use. After a few years, I needed an assistant in turn. The problem in assessing the candidates was how to tell if one of them had the ability to taste and differentiate between tastes. (Only one candidate was a scion of the family, Frederick Belmont's grandson through his adopted daughter, and therefore presumably not genetically predisposed to it. And so it proved, much as I was willing him on to succeed.) I devised a rudimentary test, dissolving in a glass of water ever-diminishing amounts of sugar, salt, angostura bitters and vinegar (sweet, salty, bitter and sour). Umami (described as 'savoury', was then unrecognised by Western science, and not tested for. However crude, my test must have worked: the stand-out candidate I chose mainly on the basis of this test, Mike Riley, is now one of only two so-called Q Tasters (coffee tasters) qualified to train would-be Q Tasters in Europe. It's interesting to note that the crude tests that I had devised to assess his tasting capabilities bear some resemblance to ones that were evolved to put a trainee Q Taster through his or her paces, albeit infinitely more sophisticated. But I suppose that's because to assess the ability to detect graduated strength changes in certain flavours seemed to me the commonsense way to go, and the devisers of the Q Test must have felt the same.

The Q–Tasting qualification was almost unknown outside of the USA when I wrote the first edition of this book, but it has become such a force in the industry that it can't be ignored in this update. Run by the Coffee Quality Institute (CQI), an independent not-for-profit initiative set up in 1996 by the then Speciality Coffee Association of America (SCAA), it aimed to standardise the coffee vocabulary and methodology of the trade for the benefit of all. Some have called it the coffee equivalent of becoming a Master of Wine. It certainly seems to have done that – all the 'specialty' coffees that come to market worldwide have to achieve an aggregate score of 80+ from Q Tasters to qualify for the title – otherwise they're given the run-of-the-mill title 'commodity' coffee. And a qualified Q Taster has considerable career cachet in the trade today, which is not surprising considering the arduous nature of the exams, once memorably described as akin to trying to meditate in a traffic jam. Me? I've preferred to rest on my spurious genetic laurels rather than submit myself to the terrors of these tests.

Since the pupil has so outgrown his mentor (when it comes to coffee tasting, at least), we'll let Mike himself describe the complications of the Q. A note for the uninitiated: 'cupping' is the coffee taster's term for sampling set quantities of ground coffee brewed in boiling water via a spoon (appropriately, I always used the same 'Bettys' silver one, albeit plate, until it got irretrievably mangled in a waste disposal system while being washed up by – who else? – Mike. Make of that what you will, armchair psychologists . . .).

The Importance of Cupping Protocol
Mike Riley

A few years ago, I was in the Central Valley of Costa Rica on yet another coffee mission – looking for stand-out micro-lots. There was a day that had been particularly thrilling, when my hosts took me to some far-flung mountain farms where the focus had been entirely upon the production of top-quality coffee. The cherries were in full ripeness and the trees appeared to be in great health. I was struck by the enthusiasm of the farmers who seemed highly motivated to produce top-quality micro-lots. Many were working with local micro-mills which had been built exclusively for processing micro-lots of washed, honeyed and natural coffees. I remember feeling like I'd struck gold, and I was even more excited for the following day when we would visit the local exporter's offices and cupping lab to spend the entire morning cupping these potentially beautiful coffees.

The following day, my excitement quickly evaporated when I walked into the cupping lab and saw the coffees lined up – sixty cups or more – all ready for my assessment. Normally, of course, coffee people live for moments like these, but I was immediately drawn to the roast colour of the beans that appeared very close to second-crack. I could see oils on the surface of the beans and immediately knew that this would be a tough cupping session. And so it proved to be, with all the coffees displaying very little acidity and muted character other than that of dark chocolate, lots of full but stodgy body and hints of pub ashtrays. I could tell that there had been some great character in the samples, but this had long since disappeared up the roasting chimney.

Fast forward a few years to spring 2018 and I'm busy preparing to run a Q Grader course at Square Mile Coffee Roasters, in London. This will in fact (hopefully) be the final stage in my training and quest to become a Q Grader Instructor, and it is highly likely that I will share my Costa Rican story with the students because it represents the perfect example of why cupping protocols are so important when grading coffee. I will tell my students how I had taken several samples of the same coffees back to the Falcon Coffees cupping lab and roasted them to protocol: a roast between 8 and 12 minutes to achieve some nice colour development after first-crack but nowhere near second-crack. There would be no scorching or tipping and the coffee would be air cooled and cupped between 8 and 24 hours after roasting. The results had been incredible; beautiful caturra and catuai beans full of luscious, vibrant and complex citrus flavours with SCA scores ranging between 85 and 88.

It was the SCAA that initiated the protocols for the cupping of specialty coffee and the CQI that developed the Q Grader system for quality assessment and reporting. The success of such a system is almost immeasurable and I fail to see how it was ever possible to sensibly communicate cup quality in the absence of protocols. The need for a globally consistent approach to cupping preparation, cupping and reporting is paramount if we are to have an international language of coffee quality.

In the cupping lab there are just so many factors that influence a cup's profile, with roasting being the first step to a consistent approach to quality assessment. The water to coffee ratio is just as important, as is the setting at which the coffee is ground. Next comes the water. Temperature is crucial, but even greater impact on the coffee's profile is the hardness of the water itself and, of course, entire reference books have been written on this subject alone. The protocol's parameters are quite generous in my view. 'Ideal total dissolved solids are 125–175 ppm but should not be less than 100 ppm and no more than 250 ppm'. For newcomers to the coffee trade there is no better way of demonstrating water's impact on character than brewing a great Kenyan in London tap water and also in very soft water. The results are chalk and cheese (literally, in the case of the former). London's hard water will kill the cup with much of the complex citrus and blackcurrant notes lost in the soup of calcium carbonate. In a soft clean water that same coffee will shine and show off its beautiful nuances that might include lemon, rhubarb, blackcurrant, butter, etc. Again, this demonstrates the importance of protocol. A farmer's livelihood is often contained within our cupping spoons, so we are orally obliged to get this right!

And so it goes on – the way we stir, the way we skim, the temperatures we start to cup at and, of course, the way we report our findings. The SCA cupping form has been created to allow us to fully and objectively explore a coffee's potential: fragrance, aroma, flavour, after-taste, body, balance, uniformity, clean cups and sweetness. The numerical reward for each flavour attribute will produce a final score that must exceed 79.75 (so 80 and above) to be termed specialty coffee.

Perhaps it can be argued that the SCA and CQI's greatest achievement was not writing the cupping protocols (since a 10-page document of methods can't have been too demanding) but to create an army of professional cuppers – or Q graders – to uphold the protocols and use the common language of 'quality speak'. The road was a long one since 10 or even 100 Q Graders could only have limited global impact in the way specialty coffee is assessed. Nowadays there are more than 5,000 Q Graders around the world, with the programme being followed in virtually every coffee-producing and consuming country. The qualification is demanding – 19 blind-tasting tests – and the rules and regulations are rigorous and exacting. And rightly so, since the kudos of Q shouldn't ever be watered down by making it easy and tolerant of breaks in protocol.

I feel certain that if and when I return to that cupping lab in Costa Rica, I will see change. The specialty coffee world is moving on at a pace and it is highly likely that those cuppers will be using protocols that allow their valuable and delicious coffees to really show their true colours.

This description explains how Q Tasting 'cupping' is involved in the first, most vital, step in the long chain of events that leads from unroasted green beans derived from a tropical bush to a cup of coffee on your breakfast table. There are many other decisions to be made along the way – involving shipping, storage, roasting, grinding and packaging – but in none of these does coffee stand so naked, so exposed to scrutiny.

I'm glad that Mike's article also shows that some of the thrills of discovery in a coffee buyer's life still remain, despite the lineaments of cool professionalism. Mike had just started working with me at Taylors when I dropped everything and jumped on a plane to Yemen, having received a sample sack of beans with some Arabic written on it saying something like '2nd Bazaar stall on the left by the Golden Gate of the Old City, Sana'a'. The coffee world has moved on, Q tasting and all, but then so has the world. Yemen, a staggeringly beautiful country in both countryside and cities when I went, has been reduced to a famine-ridden rubble by the current war. That Golden Gate may well be no more.

Yemen, as we've seen, was the original home of coffee cultivation. You might think that the country's remaining coffee industry would be as wrecked as the rest of the nation, but despite all the formidable obstacles, a few enlightened entrepreneurs see artisanal coffee cultivation as a potential lifeline for beleaguered smallholder farmers. I've come across one such who sells micro-lots of Yemeni coffee on the London market, boasting Q-tasting scores of well over the 80+ necessary to qualify as a specialty coffee, greatly enhancing its marketability. There's no greater testimony to the success of the Q-tasting regime than that it is able to provide the tools for practical assistance in dragging a desperate, war-torn country's coffee trade from near total collapse.

SLAVERY

There was a good deal of discussion in this book about the role of slavery in the history of the coffee trade. When I wrote in the original foreword that 'dark history lifts lids and turns over stones', little did I know at the time that one of those secret stories that I would eventually reveal would be my family's – and my own – direct link to slavery, albeit in the unlikeliest of contexts: Switzerland.

I wrote earlier that I had been made the coffee buyer of Taylors by my family's connection to the business, and that this genetic accident apparently predisposed me to having the ability to taste properly. Perhaps, in the same way that the remaining hereditary peers in the British House of Lords know instinctively how to govern wisely and justly, that sort of thing. So how did the connection between coffee and my family come about? you may ask.

The simple answer to that is that my great-uncle, Fritz Butzer, was born in Switzerland, then migrated to England a few years before the First World War, and in 1919 started a successful café called Bettys in the elegant spa town of Harrogate, into which he installed my father, Victor, his sister's son, as his heir apparent. The business prospered, and by 1962, after Fritz's death, my father was able to buy the company's local tea and coffee supplier, C. E. Taylor and Co. of Leeds, later Taylors Tea and Coffee. That prospered even more, and when a post fell vacant for their coffee buyer, the company turned to Victor's 25-year-old son to fill the gap. Me.

I'd known from boyhood that my Swiss grandmother, Ida, had been orphaned at a young age, along with her younger brother Frederick, in a tragic fire in a mill in rural Switzerland. They had then been parted and raised by separate foster parents. Other than that, details were scant. Fostering, I dimly understood, was some sort of benign system of surrogate parenthood, much more like being brought up in a normal household than being placed in an orphanage. So it came as a total shock when, five years ago, a chance remark by my visiting Swiss cousin completely upended my Heidi-esque vision of rural Alpine bliss gleaned from numerous holidays – all pristine meadows, snowy peaks and great wheels of Gruyère.

We'd been talking over dinner about Great-Uncle Frederick (as he had Anglicised his name to Frederick Belmont), and how he'd come from Switzerland. I asked my father about the foster parents of Ida and Fritz, and he said Frederick had had to work for his keep on the farm where he lived from the age of five. 'Sounds tough,' I said.

'Have you heard about this petition they're getting together in Switzerland?' My cousin asked. 'They're wanting the government to pay compensation to the living victims of the Verdingkinder system.'

'Verdingkinder? What does that mean?'

'*Contract children,*' she translated for me.

'And what are they *victims* of?' I asked.

'Forced labour,' she said. 'Abuse. Forced sterilisation. Chemical castration. The kids were bought at auction. Like at a slave market.'

'*What? In Switzerland?*'

A few months later, and I'm working as the original researcher on a documentary for BBC World TV's *Our World* on Verdingkinder. The producer of the show, Diana Martin, was, I had learned, the woman who had worked on our programme on kopi luwak in Sumatra – not the faceless executive back in London who had decided upon our *Get-the-Hell-Out-of-Dodge* strategy back in Takengon, but working behind the scenes. I'd told her about the Swiss slave story, and she was interested enough to get the programme on the case. Kavita Puri, the well-known TV journalist, was persuaded to present it. On behalf of the BBC, I'd contacted various individuals and organisations in Switzerland concerned with the Verdingkind compensation petition – such petitions are the first step to a national referendum in the Swiss democratic process – and learned a lot about the world that Frederick had been unwittingly thrown into.

Obliged by law to look after its orphans and its destitute, cantons sought to rid themselves of much of this financial burden by literally auctioning these children and adults to the lowest bidder (usually a farmer in need of free labour) – that is, the one who demanded the least money from the canton for the food, clothes and shelter that the successful bidder was obliged to provide. The only other thing that they had to do was ensure that the children attended school. It was a situation ripe for abuse, which was duly delivered, with utter predictability, in spades.

The BBC name, despite the organisation's many detractors at home, still has a great cachet internationally. As the programme's official 'Original Researcher', I was free to bandy their name about during the research process, and I received a lot of help and information that might otherwise have languished in forgotten archives. One particularly vital item as far as I was concerned was a report that came to light, written by the then town clerk at Teuffenthal concerning my grandmother and Frederick. My father had the harrowing task of transcribing the manuscript from its flowery, old-fashioned Swiss German. Harrowing, because much of what he read was totally new to him. For instance, he discovered that his mother and her brother both 'had the appearance of being very hungry', that their dead father's meagre life insurance policy was used to subsidise their own servitude, and that they were kept under contract for about eight years.

Researching further, I found out the full extent of the Verdingkinder scandal. While it is impossible to determine the exact numbers involved, some historians estimate that as many as 5 per cent of all Swiss children were forced into farm labour from the nineteenth to the mid-twentieth century. According to one account from 1826, 'Who asked the least got the child despite its screaming and protests . . . The cheaper they had contracted the children, the better for the community.' While public auctions were phased out in some cantons, beginning in the mid-nineteenth century, a similar lowest-bid system is thought to have persisted until the 1930s in some rural districts, behind closed doors.

I ended up using some of this material for an article I wrote in an op-ed for the *International New York Times*, which they titled 'Slavery's Shadow on Switzerland'.

That shadow lengthened further when the BBC's *Our World* report came out, particularly as everything within the broadcaster is multi-channelled to heighten its impact. The BBC programme, *Switzerland: Stolen Childhoods*, aired in October 2014, on BBC World, and with radio versions on BBC Radio 4 and the World Service.

I had hoped that the unwelcome attention of articles and programmes in the international media would be an additional spur to action for the Swiss authorities. In the end they voted for a compensation scheme, albeit at a lower level than originally sought, of 25,000 SWF (about $26,500) for each of the over 8,000 former Verdingkinder that have applied. However, it seems that some have not come forward, being unwilling to rake over their traumatic past. The photographs of Verdingkinder you can find on the internet speak volumes about the hardships involved.

My Great-Uncle Fritz, now Frederick, apparently never talked about his own experiences, nor did he ever explain how he came to have a conspicuous childhood scar on his cheek. His childhood as an unpaid labourer for a Mr Schiffmann (the farmer who also happened to be a Teuffenthal town clerk) must have been harsh: his education at his village school had been frequently disrupted when he repeatedly ran away to find his sister at her place of work as an unpaid housemaid in a town nearly fifteen miles away. Quite a hike over the mountains for a young half-starving boy, who seems always to have been brought back kicking and screaming by the authorities that were sent to track him down.

My grandmother, Ida, died in 1949 and Fritz in 1952, both a few years before I was born, sadly, so I was never able to meet either of them. But I have – almost literally – seen the world through Fritz's eyes. When I was young I used to take his old beautiful brass and mahogany Zeiss microscope and its glass sample slides from the cupboard under the stairs at home and wonder at the minute marvels they revealed; then there was his Zeiss telescope, another heirloom, through which I gazed at the moon and into the heart of our galaxy. Despite never knowing my great-uncle, I could feel his burning, autodidactic curiosity, sparked by such little education as he had received, flare through me as these sublime instruments revealed these worlds unimaginably large and small. But how had he, a Verdingkind from rural Switzerland, acquired such costly treasures? The same autodidact trait had led him to teach himself the complex craft of baking and confectionery from books at the age of fifteen, when a costly Swiss apprenticeship was not possible for him. Secondary school – which was something he would have loved, my father told me – was also denied to him, this time by his widowed stepmother, who was lodging with him at her family's house.

Eventually he went to Marseille, getting himself a job at a French bakery where there was no need for formal qualifications, and then to Paris. And then somehow, almost by mistake, he made his way to Yorkshire, England. Bettys Café, founded by Fritz in 1919 with the financial help of his local wife's family, is now patronised by Prince Charles, David Beckham and a host of other celebrities, and has even played a cameo role in the planet's most popular period drama, *Downton Abbey*. Not as a result of canny product placement, I should add, but because the producers begged permission. And Bettys is still owned and run by my family, Fritz's descendants through his beloved sister, Ida. A lasting legacy. Bravo, Great-Uncle Frederick. And for me personally, he is the main reason I was able to enter into the coffee business, and the main reason I was in a position to write the original of this book, and the reason why I am writing these words now. I am the improbable, privileged, public-school-educated grandson of a slave.

Neither my grandmother nor her brother were able to benefit from the compensation scheme introduced recently by the Swiss government, obviously, but they would certainly have been eligible. They did not stand in need, but thousands of others did, many traumatised by their hardships, and deeply ashamed. Shame may have played a major part in Frederick Belmont's silence. He exhibited many other of the behaviours associated with childhood abuse – black moods, womanising, drinking, gambling, impulsive life-changing decisions, low self-esteem.

When the *New York Times* article appeared, I received a kind message from a friend, sympathising with me over the revelations it contained. At the time, I felt strangely detached from them – I didn't know my grandmother or Frederick, so what, ultimately, did it matter? But since then, I've been fascinated to read the latest research into the notion of inherited trauma, that our genes can contain information transmitted from our recent ancestors' life experiences. In my case, my grandmother's, not her brother's, of course. That set me thinking. What if the central idea of this 'Dark History' itself, the revelation of secrets, what I called 'the lifting of lids and the turning over of stones', were somehow impelled by some genetic inheritance, some unexplained desire to shine a light, almost avenge myself upon suppressed memories or hidden untruths?

Indulge me a moment here. Normally in this book, I have found myself driven to stick to the facts, but I need your forbearance now as I go a little off-piste and extrapolate a revenge scenario from the facts that I find utterly, humanly plausible, but I doubt will ever be verifiable by recorded testimony or some evidence emerging from dusty, long-forgotten archives.

After Frederick founded Bettys in 1919, it quickly prospered. The café brought a seemingly effortless continental atmosphere to Harrogate, the Yorkshire spa town then at the peak of its post-war fashion. As soon as the café opened its doors, the European aristocracy, reeling from the rigours of the Cure, flocked in – it seemed that the allure of sulphur water was no match for Frederick's cream hearts.

As little as three years later Frederick could afford to spend the summer in Switzerland visiting his sister Ida (my grandmother) and her children with his wife Claire, driving his brand-new American car, a 3-litre Willys-Knight. He also stayed in the luxurious Bellevue hotel in the capital, Bern. His diary of the time has some mysterious gaps, however. It seems that he particularly liked the company of my Aunt Hanni, my father's lively, chatterbox elder sister, and often used to go on driving trips with her, just the two of them.

What if, on one such outing, he drove to Teuffenthal, quite near Bern, to visit the Schiffmann farm where he had been a Verdingkind? The appearance of such a luxury car in the rural Switzerland of that time would have been almost unheard-of. What if he sounded the horn outside the farm, and Herr Schiffmann came out to see what was causing the commotion? And there was Fritz Butzer, his former abused charge, at the wheel? It might almost have given him a heart attack. Let's go back to the real facts. Herr Schiffmann died in September of that year, shortly after our putative visit. In fact, it was learning about the timing of his death that inspired me to reverse-engineer its possible cause. And let's face it, karmic payback makes a good story. I hope it's true. It's what I would have done if I'd been Frederick.

CENTRAL AMERICA

In the book you've just read, there's quite a lot of socio-political analysis relating to the coffee oligarchies' stranglehold over Central American politics in the seventies through to the nineties, and North American influence in support of the same. Globalisation has led to some diversification in such economies, meaning that no longer does one find such a major dependence on coffee as an income source. But in a grim blowback, the enormous strains placed on the administrative and justice systems during the political turmoil of that period have left many of these countries unable to cope with the new pressure they are under relating to gang violence, drug abuse, burgeoning populations and climate change. Under the current US administration we've seen an increasing desperation amongst the poor and disposed of those Central American countries, fleeing into the unwelcoming arms of their giant neighbour. What President Trump calls 'the bad guys' are to an extent the creation of his own country and its short-sighted Cold War policies in those earlier decades. While President Obama went some way to admitting that the policies were 'wrong', particularly in relation to El Salvador, his administration tacitly supported the brutal military overturn of a mildly reformist President in Honduras in 2009, Mel Zelaya. That substantially helped the capital, Tegucigalpa, to obtain the dubious honour of being named 'The Murder Capital of the World'. It appears recently to have lost its ranking in the Top Fifty list, according to *Business Insider*. All current ranking cities are to be found in the Western Hemisphere. One wonders why.

The Trump administration seems more at ease with the idea of demonising and dividing – in the latter case, literally, by splitting up refugee families, separating parents from children, and husbands from wives. Such cruelties are a vivid reminder of the times when paranoia about creeping Socialism underscored America's efforts to actively undermine the struggles of indigenous peasant populations of the region. It seems as if they were damned then by what they tried to do and are damned now by the result they flee. As I write, the might of the US military is being mobilised to prevent the entry of a rag-tag caravan of refugees marching north to seek asylum. Trump has said it includes unknown 'Middle Easterners' bent on invading America, an even more than usually preposterous assertion of its source. Meanwhile, back on planet Earth, a Honduran coffee farmer in the caravan spoke to the press. Years of drought and crop failure meant he had had to abandon the little land he had to try to find work in the capital. Gang violence and associated social problems there meant that in desperation he'd left his wife and kids behind and gone to seek work in America, so that at least he'd be able to feed them.

Meanwhile, even Nicaragua, which under the much-vaunted leadership of Sandinista Daniel Ortega had attracted so much attention from conscientious coffee buyers in the early eighties, is now accused of all sorts of human rights abuses, corruption and nepotism. Not unlike his predecessors, the Somoza dynasty, which his revolution had successfully overthrown . . . . *Plus ça change.*

COFFEE PODS

It's a sobering judgement on the coffee industry and the consumers it serves that at the moment in history when landfills are bulging with plastic bottles, riverbanks and motorway verges are strewn with plastic bags, and oceans are disfigured by gigantic gyres of plastic waste, the market should so wholeheartedly embrace a new method of serving coffee that requires up to 3 grams of plastic/aluminium packaging to contain 6 grams of actual coffee. It's the coffee market's (including both the trade and consumers) two fingers up to our fragile environment.

The domestic consumption of coffee has been revolutionised by the appearance on the market of the coffee pod. Also known as a capsule, the main characteristic of this relatively recent innovation is that it is single-serve, delivering a freshly brewed portion of coffee, individually, just for you. Compared with wrestling with an old-school espresso machine, filling and cleaning up after brewing in a cafetière or filter machine, or any one of the other myriad ways of making coffee in the home, the pod makes life deceptively simple, even resulting in an end product that bears more than a fleeting resemblance to the ubiquitous coffee-shop espresso coffee. Convenient home consumption that has captivated the consumer – allied to sleek engineering, A-list advertising and, in the case of Nespresso (the market leader), an upscale retail presence that seems to have consciously emulated the Apple Store – what's not to like? Your humble author is also an avid user, I should admit – if not actually an avid fan – when the opportunity arises. And there, in miniature, lies the nub of the problem: such is the compelling convenience of the capsule method that it seems to swat other judgements aside.

Consider the numbers for a moment: the market for coffee pods (largely known as K-capsules in the States) has grown pretty consistently at the phenomenal rate of nearly 20 per cent year on year since 2011, which means nowadays the world is producing nigh on 15 billion pods a year. The vast majority of these are non-recyclable, so they end up in landfill, but there is growing recognition, including at government level, of the waste problem, so there's a corresponding shift to 'hard', compostable and recycling pods. All these are technical fixes for what started life as a technical fix for the perceived inconvenience of coffee-making in the home. I suppose this is what is generally known as progress.

The scale of the plastic pollution problem is deeply scary and of recent making. As little ago as 1980, I sailed with some friends by rowing boat down the Indus River in Pakistan for three months. It's the eleventh-largest river in the world. We bathed in and drank its waters non-stop. Given that the human body is 75 per cent water, in due course I actually more or less *became* the river. And in all that time I didn't see so much as a single plastic bottle or bag. Now I read that, a mere forty years later, the Indus is the second-worst source of riverine plastic pollution in the world. As you can imagine, that's up against some pretty stiff competition. And there are hardly any coffee-pod users in Pakistan as yet . . .

News came in 2017 that the Swiss-based Ethical Coffee Company was ceasing production of its recyclable pods. The company was founded by Jean-Paul Gaillard, the former CEO of Nespresso from 1988 to 1997, directly to address the environmental problems created by its success. Despite having fought and won some serious – and seriously expensive – legal battles with Nestlé over their patent restrictions, Gaillard said that so many (he estimated 210 at the last count) manufacturers had jumped on board the capsule-manufacturing business competing solely on price that his alternative was simply no longer profitable. A no-frills, all-plastic, straight-to-landfill capsule is cheap to manufacture, as are the machines that make them. This carries on despite industry analysts trumpeting the arrival of a 'paradigm shift' in the capsule market, as manufacturers shift to 'soft pods', a refillable, biodegradable and compostable capsule.

There is some agreement, though, about the aluminium content of the original proprietary Nespresso capsules and some of its imitators. Whilst aluminium is of itself recyclable, most public recycling facilities aren't up to the task of separating it from the plastic that it is fused with. Nespresso makes a great play about offering to take the used pods off the consumers' hands, but the fact remains that the take-up of their kind offer is chronically underperforming. Their stated ambition is to achieve 100 per cent recycling by 2020. But even that would fail to satisfy those who think that we should avoid even producing products that require recycling. It's probably enough to salve the consciences of the producer and their clients, though, even if most Nespresso pods still end up in landfill. Whatever the company's intentions, recycling is seen as an inconvenience, especially in the context of a product whose very *raison d'être* is convenience.

The essential problem is the same as we've seen with coffee packaging throughout this book, namely how to keep the coffee fresh and flavoursome with a decent shelf life. Levels of residual oxygen still need to be at worst 1 per cent to fend off potential staling, and pod manufacturers often stand accused by vigilant consumer bodies of short-changing their customers in this respect. Nespresso pods pass this test with flying colours. That is why the company evolved their elaborate aluminium/plastic packaging solution in the first place: it's an excellent oxygen barrier. But those myriad cheap plastic pods, some with just a filter paper cover, that are a large part of the pod market – as Jean-Paul Gaillard noted – are prone to staleness. Some manufacturers seek to solve this problem by placing the pod in small, individual, gas-flushed foil sachets, creating yet more (in)disposable waste. Freshness, flavour and convenience come at a price paid for by the planet.

CLIMATE CHANGE

Coffee's dark history isn't all gloom and doom. Sometimes, it's *unrelenting* gloom and doom.

To give them credit, people in the coffee industry have been well aware of the threat that climate change poses to Arabica growers in particular for quite some time, and have invested heavily in potential solutions. The nub of the problem is that the conditions that make certain areas of the world suitable for quality coffee cultivation are fast disappearing. The combination of altitude and water availability that made the nurture of the delicate Arabica plant possible have been changing at an alarming rate, and the fact is that most cultivation is done by peasant farmers who are ill-equipped to deal with the increase in drought and pests that is the frequent result of higher temperatures. The industry has researched the matter extensively around the globe and concluded that as much as 50 per cent of the land that is, or until recently was, suitable for Arabica cultivation will no longer be so by 2050.

That number rises to as high as 88 per cent in Central America generally. So the caravans heading north to the United States are only going to get longer and more frequent.

Howard Schultz, founder and former chairman of Starbucks, can now be frequently found at the company's 600-acre coffee estate in Costa Rica where they are researching and developing varietals of plants that will be more resistant to water stress and diseases, and the loss of insects for pollination, especially bees, whilst retaining quality of flavour. They make their research freely available to the industry as a whole, on the basis that if the overall quality of coffee worldwide is threatened, it will be bad for everyone. There's no competitive advantage to be gained in not sharing important information regarding the threat, he says, which he perceives as existential. Separately, an industry-funded body, World Coffee Research, has a twenty-million-dollar coffee-monitoring programme across the world, involving over a thousand farms. Likewise, they share the results of their research openly.

Nearly all research points to the fundamental culprit being man-made carbon emissions, and many in the industry exhort politicians to stay with the Paris Accord. So what is going on here? While politicians dither, and often cite the lack of sufficient proof as a reason for not reacting, a major global industry (and coffee is not alone . . . tea is another) is not only sounding the alarm bells about global warming but is spending large sums trying to combat the problem. Indeed, Alessandro Illy, chairman of the celebrated Italian company of that name, goes further, saying that the coffee industry will need to spend over a billion dollars annually to deal with the problem. It's ironic that the coffee trade's recently discovered interest in specific varietals and artisanal coffees has effectively brought the major producers of coffee and its buyers closer together, through direct trading that cuts out the middle man, so that the effects of climate change are writ large for the major players in consumer markets to see. There are few climate-change denialists in the coffee world today.

In fact, the industry has become something of a bellwether for the need for political action on global warming. And in turn, some in the trade harbour political ambitions, as they see that politicians' intransigence towards the issue paves the way for global environmental disaster. Howard Schultz, for example, is said to be planning a presidential run on the Democratic ticket. It seems that the millions he earned from his company may be redeployed in pursuit of an agenda that would help save, among other things, the ultimate source of that fortune.

Unless he's too late.

The coffee industry has mapped the coming effects of climate change globally, and they are spread unevenly. In broad terms, Meso- and South America are amongst the most vulnerable, as we have seen, but there is also uneven regional distribution. While Nicaragua and El Salvador are set to be the worst-hit, Guatemala, Mexico, Honduras and Costa Rica have higher mountain areas that could possibly benefit. That they are frequently covered with virgin forest brings another future problem in its wake. Andean Arabica-growing areas likewise have the option of moving up the mountains (sounds so easy, doesn't it?), whereas Brazil doesn't.

Vietnam and India will also be under considerable pressure in the Asia Pacific region, whereas New Guinea and Indonesia have more scope to adapt, as will Uganda in Africa: Kenya is expected to not suffer much, and it may indeed benefit from new higher-altitude land becoming suitable. But the home of coffee, Ethiopia, is of particular concern. Despite what I wrote earlier about coffee being one of the most scientifically researched of foodstuffs, it turns out that one area has been relatively neglected, namely the genetic diversity of the Arabica coffee plant. Ethiopia is home to a wide variety of wild Arabica plants, a natural resource that is invaluable at a time when the industry is in urgent need of finding drought- and disease-resistant strains. But that stock of wild, native plants is precisely under great pressure from climate change, and unlike the coffee produced in the same areas, there is no possibility of relocating these wild plants. There is some encouragement to be found in the recent announcement that a genome can be sequenced of the Arabica plant, meaning that the genetic variants that might be found in Ethiopia's under-threat plants may be artificially created. However, there seems to be a cruel irony in the fact that what was once organically available through trial and error experiments on nature's own lab bench may have to be artificially manufactured using cutting-edge technology.

At the same time, people are increasingly turning to direct action, frustrated by the lack of meaningful political response. The coffee houses and their myriad customers remain relatively oblivious to the negative news that the coffee companies are, willy-nilly, forced to deal with. Perhaps there is too fundamental a disjunct between the need to extol the virtues about the particular discovery of a delicious new origin or varietal, and the fact that there may be a time, quite soon, when this new coffee, or others like it, may simply no longer be available. On the other hand, nowhere is better placed to inform and motivate their customers about the real and visceral threat posed by climate change. Perhaps it's time for the coffee house to actively seek to rekindle the revolutionary spirit that is so much a part of its heritage? Or perhaps they have decided that their customers can bear only so much reality.

One potential solution is longitudinal (or latitudinal) shift, a complex term for simply moving Arabica production to new areas of the country in question that are, or are deemed likely to be, better suited to its cultivation, if such exist. That this involves huge costs in terms of relocation and infrastructure is obvious. That is, without bringing in the human cost of the disruption, assuming that it is even possible. The vast numbers of those working worldwide at the sharp end of coffee production and their dependents are the least able to bear the cost of such a social breakdown. To take the example of Latin America, by the time the need for this scenario has arisen, not only are the caravan routes northwards looking more and more tempting, but the one billion dollars a year earmarked by Alessandro Illy is looking laughably inadequate. It's no coincidence that Starbucks have chosen Costa Rica as the site of their experimental coffee farm. The country has long been by far the most politically stable of its Central American neighbours. El Salvador, Honduras, Guatemala and Nicaragua are sliding into chaos, with powerful multinational companies doing deals with their governments that often, without consultation, literally dispossess the already figuratively dispossessed of their lands for mining or mineral extraction, and pollute vulnerable water supplies. Protesters or activists are intimidated or worse, and the judicial institutions that might offer some recourse are corrupt or non-existent. To attempt to introduce a countrywide coordinated response to climate change in such dire circumstances would seem nigh-on doomed to failure.

There's even talk of Arabica coffee becoming extinct by the end of the century. But the question is also whether there will be anyone left to witness this momentous event, as the possibility of human extinction is increasingly to be found on mainstream commentators' lips. Perhaps it would be a fitting end to this Dark History, to implode in some catastrophic digital meltdown, or to languish unread on a shelf marked '(Former) World History' in the library in an underground bunker in Paraguay built by a billionaire survivalist. I hope he's laid in adequate supplies of coffee. There'll be no more where that came from.

ACKNOWLEDGEMENTS

Thanks to Jordan Mulligan, my editor for his excellent advice and input, and all the team at 4th Estate.

And to Mike Riley, for his highly-qualified take on Q-Tasting, many thanks.

SELECTED FURTHER READING

Baigent, Christopher & Leigh, Richard *The Temple and the Lodge* (London: Jonathan Cape, 1989)

Battestin, Martin C. *Henry Fielding: A Life* (London: Routledge, 1989)

Ball, Daniella U. ed *Coffee in the Context of European Drinking Habits* (Zurich: Johann Jacobs Museum, 1991)

Barrett, David V. *Secret Societies* (London: Blandford, 1997)

Boxhall, Peter Diary of a Mocha Coffee Agent , in *Arabian Studies I,* Serjeant, R. and Bidwell, R. (eds) Cambridge-London, 1974

Chomsky, Noam *Rogue States* (London: Pluto Press, 2000)

Diamond, Jared *Guns, Germs and Steel* (London: Vintage, 1998)

Forrest, Denys *Tea for the British* (London: Chatto & Windus, 1973)

Gosse, Philip *St Helena 1502–1938* (Oswestry: Anthony Nelson, 1990)

Gribbin, John *In Search of Schrödinger's Cat : Quantum Physics and Reality* (New York: Bantam 1984)

Hall, Richard *Empires of the Monsoon* (London: HarperCollins*Publishers*, 1996)

Hardt, Michael & Negri, Antonio *Empire* (Cambridge, Mass: Harvard University Press 2001)

Hunersdorff, Richard von *Coffee: A Bibliography* (London: Hunersdorff, 2002)

Jacob, Heinrich Eduard *The Saga of Coffee* (London: George Allen & Unwin, 1935)

James, Jack 'Third Party" threats to research integrity in public-private partnerships *Addiction* 97, 1251–1255.

Jobin, Philippe *The Coffees Produced Throughout the World* (Le Havre: P. Jobin & Cie, 1982)

Jourdain, John *The Journal of John Jourdain,* ed.W. Foster (London: Hakluyt Society, 1905)

Jung, Carl *Jung on Alchemy* ed. Schwarz-Salant, N. (London: Routledge,1995)

Kauffman, Jean-Paul *The Dark Room at Longwood* (London: The Harvill Press, 1999)

Keay, John *The Honourable Company* (London: HarperCollins, 1991)

Levathes, Louise *When China ruled the Seas* (New York: Simon and Schuster, 1994)

Mackintosh-Smith, Tim *Yemen: Travels in Dictionary Land* (London: John Murray, 1997)

Martin. S. I. *Britain's Slave Trade* (London: Channel 4 Books, 1999)

Monbiot, George *Captive State* (London: Pan Books, 2001)

Multatuli *Max Havelaar or the Auctions of the Dutch Trading Company* (London: Penguin Classics, 1987)

Phillipson, David W. *Ancient Ethiopia* (London: British Museum Press, 1998)

Rimbaud, Arthur *Oevres Completes* ed. Antoine Adam (Paris: Gallimard, 1972)

Rushby, Kevin *Eating the Flowers of Paradise* (London: Flamingo 1999)

Ukers, William H. *All About Coffee* (New York: The Tea and Coffee Trade Journal Company,1922)

Said, Edward *Culture and Imperialism* (London: Vintage, 1994)

Schnyder-v.Waldkirch, Antoinette *Wie Europa den Kaffee Entdeckte* (Zurich: Jacob Suchard Museum, 1988)

Searight, Sarah *The British in the Middle East* (London: East West Publications, 1979)

Shah, Idries *The Sufis* (London: The Octagon Press, 1999)

Smith, Charlotte Fell *John Dee* (London: Constable and Company, 1909)

Stiglitz, Joseph *Globalisation and its Discontents* (London: Allen Lane, 2002)

Thomas, Hugh *The Slave Trade: The Story of the Atlantic Slave Trade 1440–1870* (London: Picador, 1997)

Tulard, Jean *Napoléon à Sainte-Hélène* (ParIs: Robert Laffont, 1981)

Turner, Anthony *Le Café* (Paris: Blusson Editeur, 2002)

Tuscherer, Michel ed. *Le Commerce de Café* (Paris: IFAO, 2001)

Vidal, Gore *Perpetual War for Perpetual Peace* (New York: Thunder's Mouth Press / Nation Books, 2002)

Weinberg, Bennett Alan & Bealer, Bonnie K. *The World of Caffeine* (New York: Routledge, 2001)

Williamson, George *A Reader's Guide to the Metaphysical Poets* (London: Thames and Hudson, 1968)

LIST OF ILLUSTRATIONS

p.1 author's collection; p.2 author's collection; p.3 courtesy of the British Library; p.4 wine bar by courtesy of Berry Brothers, Green Dragon courtesy of The Bostonian Society/Old State House; p.5 a Dutch Map of the East Indies © National Maritime Museum; p.6 map of Gulf of Mexico © National Maritime Museum, slave box © Julie Wilberforce; p.7 courtesy of the Louvre Museum © Photo RMN, Water Marc, Dining Room © Derry Brabbs; p.8 by kind permission of N.A.S.A.

All reasonable efforts have been made by the author and the publisher to trace the copyright holders of the images and material quoted in this book. In the event that the author or publisher are contacted by any of the untraceable copyright holders after publication, the author and the publisher will endeavour to rectify the position accordingly.

INDEX

value of coffee market 2
withdrawal of support from ICA and ICO 5, 253, 256
UTZ xxii

vacuum packaging 196–8, 199, 277
valve technology 198–9
Van den Brock, Pieter 82
van Linschoten, Jan Huygen 67
Vanderbilt Institute for Coffee Studies 218
Vanderbilt University Medical Center (Nashville) 218–19
Velde, Christian 311, 314
Velde, Imke 311
Venezuela 124, 125, 175
Venice 56–7
Verdingkinder 331–4, 335–6, 337
Vereenigde Ooste Indische Compagnie (VOC) *see* Dutch East India Company
Verlaine, Paul 184, 185
vertical integration 321–2
Vienna
  coffee houses 284
  Kolschitsky and coffee history of 60–3
  Siege of (1683) 59–61, 63
Vietnam xvi, 21, 264, 269, 285–95, 344
  coffee industry 285, 292, 293
  expansion of coffee production 6–7, 294–5
  French rule 285–6
  history 285–8
  spraying of Agent Orange and impact of 249, 250, 285, 289–92
Vietnam War 249, 250, 288–9

Wall Street Journal 1
Warren, Joseph 131, 132, 133
Washington Consensus 295
Washington, George 135, 137, 298
Washington, George (Belgian) 199
Wellington, Duke of 154
Wellstone, Paul 248–9
West Indies 122, 228

Western hemisphere 228–32, 255
Wilberforce, William 230
wild coffee 101–2
Wild, Victor 331
Wilkins, Dr John 89, 90
Wilks, Governor 152, 153, 159
Will's Coffee House 94
'Women's Petition Against Coffee' 91
World Animal Protection xxii
World Bank 1, 2, 6, 7, 9, 226, 285, 294, 295–6, 297
World Coffee Research 343
World Health organization (WHO) 220
World trade Organization (WTO) 296
Wyld, Dr Frederico Lehnoff 199

Yemen ix, x, xiii, 13, 26, 29, 31–3, 69, 99, 310, 312, 316, 329–30
  arrival of coffee in 31–2
  drinking of coffee by Sufis and conjecture over inroduction of 31, 34, 45–7
  landscape 72
  and Mocha *see* Mocha
  and *qat* 24, 40
  settling of by Mamelukes 49
  spread of coffee from ritual to domestic consumption 48
  switch of principal source of coffee production from Ethiopia to 71–3
  terrace guilding project 72
  ways of maintaining monopoly on coffee production 75–6, 107
Yemeni Mocha Matari xv
York, Duke of 123
YouTube xix
Yunnan State Farms Group Co. Ltd. 323

Zapatista movement 236–7
Zaydis 32
Zelaya, Mel 338
Zen Buddhism 37
Zheng He, Admiral 38–9, 40
Zhu Di 38–9
Zhu Zhanj, Emperor 40

P.S.

Ideas,
interviews
& features ...

Q & A

You were trained as a coffee taster and worked as a buyer. How did that affect your writing of this book?

Obviously fifteen years in the trade gave me a thorough grounding in the subject which no amount of research could match. But more importantly, it was through coffee that I started my writing career, gradually expanding from articles in trade and consumer magazines to small books on various commodities. As I was heavily involved in establishing the speciality coffee market in the UK, one of the ways in which my weird and wonderful discoveries could be marketed was through provenance, and this meant that I had to research in depth the historical origins of each one. This in turn led to my interest in European colonialism, and to my first significant book, *The East India Company: Trade and Conquest from 1600*, in 1999.

How did you get involved in the coffee trade?

Through my family's company, Bettys & Taylors of Harrogate. From my childhood I was immersed in tea and coffee, and in later years, having travelled a lot for personal pleasure, it seemed a natural development to travel for business, whether on the ground or in the imagination.

Coffee has become very fashionable. Why is that?

The consumer world, particularly at the luxury level, is intensely snobbish: expense, obscurity and exoticism are *de rigueur*.

Nowadays nearly all coffee companies with any pretensions to the quality end of the market trumpet their particular expertise, exemplified by the rarity of the coffee selections and the exclusivity attached to their relationships with their suppliers. Nonetheless most of the coffee that they sell – and that consumers buy – is still relatively ordinary. However, as with couture fashion, the press and public interest in the highly specialized coffees mainly supports the bread-and-butter blends – the *prêt à porter* coffees, to continue the parallel.

Why is the book subtitled 'A Dark History of Coffee'?
Coffee is a dark liquid, and its history is intimately connected with mankind's darker side – slavery, colonization and exploitation. Coffee farmers are currently in acute crisis, a situation which nonetheless is arguably business as usual from a historical perspective. In addition there is an esoteric aspect to coffee's influence on mankind which interests me. The title is also in part a reaction to what I think is a tendency among historians to write about the past as if it were somehow removed from the present, as if our own times were exempt from the continuum of the human narrative. I sometimes like to think that 'Dark History' will become a genre in itself.

Is that why there is more of an analysis of the present-day state of the coffee trade than might usually be expected in a history?
Exactly. I've tried to bridge the gap between ▶

> ❝ The consumer world, particularly at the luxury level, is intensely snobbish: expense, obscurity and exoticism are *de rigueur*. ❞

BORN
....
1955, Harrogate, Yorkshire

EDUCATED
....
Sedbergh School,
Cumbria; Bristol
University

CAREER
....
Coffee Director of Bettys
& Taylors of Harrogate
until 1995. Since then has
written seven books and a
screenplay.

Q & A *(continued)*

◀ the past and the present and at the same
time between two literary genres: the 'single-
subject history' and what for want of a better
word could be called the 'anti-globalization'
genre. Writers in the former category tend to
ignore the present while the latter frequently
resort to concepts such as 'neo-colonialism'
or 'Empire' without necessarily subjecting
them to proper analysis. The book allowed
me to develop ideas about how the current
state of the market is the extension of long-
standing historical trends. Just because the
slave trade which led to the huge expansion of
coffee production has been abolished, that
doesn't mean that we in the West haven't con-
nived in the creation of its successor in kind.

**Do you think that the Fair Trade
movement in coffee represents a
sustainable alternative?**
There are many sides to this question. The
fact that there is a trade mechanism that
allows coffee farmers a fair deal would
seem laudable. But if this only exists in
parallel with a much larger system which is
inherently unfair, then I would prefer to see
political change at that level – what I refer to
as the creation of a 'Fair Trade nation'. This
would in turn create a strong argument for a
'Fair Trade world'. All of which seems highly
unlikely – the last such attempt crashed with
the Berlin Wall. There is also the issue of the
environment: shipping coffee around the
planet, whether Fair Trade or not, is hardly
'sustainable' if the cumulative effects of the
damage caused by international trade are
accounted for.

Do you think your book will offend the people you know in the trade?
I think that many of the issues I raise might be considered highly controversial, whether it be Fair Trade, pseudo-science or neo-colonialism. Coffee people would probably rather not think about them, and my book is doing them no favours. However, I think we are at a stage in the affairs of mankind where the head-in-the-sand approach appears increasingly dysfunctional, and I suspect that many are beginning to see the necessity for an honest appraisal of our condition.

You also write extensively about the religious and cultural aspects of coffee drinking. Why is this?
One of the fundamental features of coffee is that it contains a mind-altering drug, caffeine. Thus its wholesale adoption, initially by Islam and later by the emerging mercantile nations of Europe, carries with it the intriguing suggestion that it was actually affecting the state of mind of entire populations, and with it the evolution of national cultures.

Why do people say that coffee affects them differently from tea?
I have concluded, reluctantly, that this is cultural. As an Englishman of a certain age I found it inconceivable that anyone would offer a cup of coffee to console the recipient of bad news. When I found out through a straw poll of my acquaintances that this is precisely what happens in Germany, Italy ▶

Q & A (continued)

◀ and most of the western hemisphere, and indeed is something that the younger generation in England might do, I realized then that what I perceived as a difference was mainly the result of my own cultural prejudice.

What coffee do you like most?

I once wrote that coffee is 'liquid history and geography', and for me the best coffees are inextricably mixed up with my own memories of visiting the countries which produced them. Thus I have to nominate St Helena for my top three, because I helped to establish its coffee industry and finally visited the island for the purpose of writing this book. I'd also have to nominate Yemeni coffee, because that country is probably the most beautiful that I have ever visited, and its coffee is so wonderfully artisanal and full of history. Then I'd have to mention Cuba, probably the world's only surviving example of a 'Fair Trade nation', and producer of some fine coffee to boot. If I had ever visited Ethiopia, the country of origin of coffee, it would probably feature too – certainly Harar Longberry and Sidamo coffees are sublime.

And what coffee do you actually drink?

I was hoping you'd forget to ask that. For the most part, good standard branded supermarket fare, well packaged, and often from Guatemala, spiritual home of political incorrectness. ■

❝ As an Englishman of a certain age I found it inconceivable that anyone would offer a cup of coffee to console the recipient of bad news. ❞

Serendipities:
November 2003

Music:
Matthew Herbert and
Plat du Jour

ONE FEATURE OF coffee tasting which inevitably causes embarrassed giggles amongst onlookers is the taster's 'slurp and spit' routine, whereby the hot liquid is taken into the mouth via a soup spoon with a loud slurp, which sprays it onto the palate, and then spat out, hopefully into the spittoon. It is a particularly uncompromising process, not known for its mass appeal, so it was strange to find myself in the audience of the Grande Salle of the Pompidou Centre in Paris on a cold December night listening to a recording of my own slurp and spit routine hugely amplified through a public-address system as part of a musical performance. The slurp came across as particularly gruesome, sounding like some space alien disposing of its unfortunate enemy. However, the sell-out crowd did not appear to be the slightest discomfited.

It came about as follows. Shortly after the hardback of this book was published I received an e-mail out of the blue from Matthew Herbert, a record producer who was interested in turning my book into a track on his new album about food. To be subjected to the scrutiny of one's literary peers is one thing: to be the inspiration of an artist in another medium is altogether more amusing. Particularly when I found out a ▶

7

Music: Matthew Herbert (*continued*)

◀ little more about his work, which ranged from big band jazz albums of his own compositions to free downloads of tracks built from audio samples of crushed styrofoam McDonald's packs and the like. These latter seemed to me a considered artistic response to the perils of corporatism, interesting in conception, and deep-felt.

We talked, and he asked for my suggestions, which I made on the basis of the elements from my book which I thought would be most powerful and suggestive in audio terms, as well as corresponding to the underlying theme of his up-and-coming album, *Plat du Jour*, which is concerned with the iniquities of food production and distribution. We settled on a few ideas, and a few weeks later I found myself in his small studio in Brixton where the initial writing and recording were taking place. The fact that he had committed himself to a live première of the album at the Queen Elizabeth Hall a couple of weeks later added a frisson of urgency to the occasion.

How does one turn a book into a record? I'll describe how Matthew does it. I'd suggested that sixty coffee beans was an interesting number, as it was the number used in the average espresso today, as well as the number that Beethoven used to count out for his preferred brew. A musical connection, as well as a topical one, I thought.

I sent him some unroasted Vietnamese robusta coffee beans, as it is those that have flooded the market and caused rock-bottom prices – a catastrophe that earns its chapter in the book, in which I also describe the

> ❝ How does one turn a book into a record? ❞

toxic residue of the use of Agent Orange in America's war on that country. I suggested that he recorded the dropping of sixty of the unroasted beans onto a barrel of Agent Orange. This seemed like an apt metaphor for the match of imperialism and its tropical handmaiden, coffee.

Matthew had meticulously set the beats per minute of the emerging track at 79.93, because that is how many million people live in Vietnam. He had also picked up on the theme of Islam in the book, and in particular the fact that the croissant was in effect invented by a baker in Vienna to celebrate the lifting of the siege of the city in 1683 and the subsequent rout of the Ottoman army, which left behind its coffee supplies, leading to the introduction of that beverage to the West. In the book I suggested that the consumption of coffee and croissants was in a sense a kind of anti-communion, representing the triumph of Christendom over Islam. Thus Matthew had recorded the sound created by two Sara Lee ready-mix croissant tins connected by string as another feature of the track. Then he had recorded a teaspoon hitting a Nescafé jar. The three audio elements were then used to represent what Matthew saw as the three central themes of the book – the caffeinated masses portrayed by the sixty robusta beans hitting a can of Monsanto's Roundup (Agent Orange, a former product of the company, unfortunately – if that's the word – not being available), the onward march of Western Imperialism represented by the Sara Lee cans, and the plight of the coffee producers represented by the sound of the teaspoon ▶

❝ One feature of coffee tasting which inevitably causes embarrassed giggles amongst onlookers is the taster's "slurp and spit" routine. ❞

Music: Matthew Herbert *(continued)*

◄ on the Nescafé jar. These he had turned into the composition which he invited me to his studio to listen to. And the result was remarkable.

Most remarkable. As Matthew says, it is hard to make the sound of green coffee beans hitting a plastic container 'chirpy', and it isn't. Like some latter-day audio alchemist Matthew believes that the sound of a thing says something about the nature of the thing itself – a version perhaps of Goethe's concept of enchereisis, the interconnectedness of all things. This is one of the underlying themes of my book as well – how this thing that we call coffee has woven a web around the planet and its effects are inextricably connected with its nature. Whether this is materially expressed in the notion that coffee is the chosen drug of capitalism, or more spiritually in the uses that Sufis made of it for connecting with God, there is something satisfactory in the fact that the 'music' Matthew created from the objects I had suggested seemed to ring the same cosmic bells as the book itself. Indeed I'm tempted to think that the very fact of Matthew picking up on the book and interpreting it in this way is a symptom of the same enchereisis. Hence the title of this section, 'Serendipities'. The fact that our times are so troubled, and that materialism seems to have triumphed, makes the reminder of the presence of these nerves running through all our lives both reassuring and disturbing. Mostly they remain buried beneath the thick skin of our rampant consumerism, but occasionally they are exposed, sore, aggravated but beautiful, and necessary too.

> ❛ This thing that we call coffee has woven a web around the planet and its effects are inextricably connected with its nature. ❜

There was still some work to be done before Matthew would be ready for the live première. I told him about the audio qualities of the professional coffee taster's slurp and spit routine, and as a result his assistant recorded me at a friend's flat tasting a variety of coffees which I'd chosen – Yemeni, St Helena, Colombia (where Roundup is increasingly being sprayed in the 'War on Drugs') and the Nestlé instant which he had featured before. I haven't heard the playback, but it seemed to me that there was little to distinguish the genuine coffees, whereas the instant actually managed to sound quite different. We also recorded the sound of the sixty beans being roasted – when they are just about cooked coffee beans make some explosive sounds like a less than enthusiastic popcorn.

Matthew's approach is inspiringly honest: he doesn't fake sounds simply to take a shortcut, and believes that by in effect educating people to recognize things with which they are already subconsciously familiar, then a whole world is potentially opened up to them. As the inventor of the first microscope might have done, he points his microphone at everyday objects and says, 'Listen! This is how it sounds! Isn't it extraordinary?' Then he allies this minute attention to detail with his compositional talents, creating something of peculiar grace. One may not 'like' the result, but you can't ignore its intensity. ■

www.youtube.com/watch?v=9aCNTacPdMg

❛ Coffee is a dark liquid, and its history is intimately connected with mankind's darker side – slavery, colonization and exploitation. ❜

Film: The Francis Brothers and *Black Gold*

ANOTHER RESPONSE TO the book has proved equally interesting, albeit in a different way. A few months after publication I received a call from Nick Francis, who, with his brother Marc, was in the midst of editing a film about coffee when he came across the review of the book in *Time Out* and bought it. He felt that it reflected in part the point of view that their film, *Black Gold*, was trying to portray, and soon I had a rough-cut VHS to watch. I could see his point: starting with the plight of coffee farmers in Ethiopia, lately out of work and dependent on aid, they had followed the attempts of an official from a co-operative to realize a higher price from coffee merchants in the UK than strict market logic would dictate. I was intrigued to see that this kind of unilateral Fair Trade effort was met with a genuinely receptive attitude by the British coffee merchants seen in the film: certainly when I was active in the business up until ten years ago there would have been a far less informed and sympathetic response.

The film then takes us to Cancun where a World Trade Organization meeting founders on the rocks of Western intransigence with regard to their agricultural subsidies, although the Western delegates would have us believe that it was the failure of the developing countries to live up to their responsibilities and to free their markets. The film gives a fascinating insight into the workings of this monolithic organization which makes (or should that be 'imposes'?) decisions affecting millions of lives in pursuit of corporate agendas masquerading as global interests. It reminded me of something I read once by an economist proselytizing the virtues of globalization, who maintained how marvellous it would be for their local economies if African villagers were able to raise credit against their mud huts. This is what the globalized world boils down to: the unstoppable pursuit of unbridled capitalism.

I made a few suggestions regarding the film and eventually helped a little with the script. The opening paragraphs of my book concern the lack of agreement about the number of coffee farmers and their dependants that are affected by the current crisis, and this suddenly became an issue – the film-makers wanted a single figure for the opening line of the commentary. In the end they decided to plump for an average of the wildly diverging figures which I had quoted. As the reason I had quoted all these figures was to show how enormous the scale of the crisis was, in which tens of millions of people could be included in – or excluded from – its monstrous embrace depending on whether one reads Christian Aid reports or the *Wall Street Journal*, this necessary averaging caused me some amusement. But that in part is the difference between a film and a book. Whereas I was able to dwell on this aspect of the coffee trade for a few paragraphs, I could never hope to convey the dignity in the ▶

‘ This is what the globalized world boils down to: the unstoppable pursuit of unbridled capitalism. ’

Film: The Francis Brothers *(continued)*

◀ face of despair of the Ethiopian coffee farmers which the film revealed in simple, telling images. I was aware while writing that this human face was possibly a missing feature of my book – the true life stories of those embroiled in the coffee catastrophe – but in the end decided that there were plenty of people working to bring those stories to public attention and that my efforts might appear at best contrived. Seeing the footage in the film made me realize that my decision had been the right one.

I arranged to meet up with the Francis brothers on a trip to London. Young (late twenties), articulate and highly motivated, they have an attitude and modus operandi in relation to film-making which is distinctly their own. The funding of documentaries is evidently dominated by TV commissions, so the idea of self-financing a project ought to have been hopelessly unrealistic, but somehow they have contrived to do just that without compromising the quality of the end product. New technologies – digital cameras, desktop editing and so on – have undoubtedly helped, but theirs has essentially been an exercise in the clever management of cash flow, underpinned by serious talent. Instead of seeking to raise the £300,000 necessary to fund the film from a TV company all in one gulp, they have raised it in fits and starts, each completed stage further increasing the money-raising potential of the project. Many favours have been asked, and many favours have been forthcoming, mainly as a result of the strength of feeling about the issues raised by

❝ Shipping coffee around the planet, whether Fair Trade or not, is hardly "sustainable" if the cumulative effects of the damage caused by international trade are accounted for. ❞

the documentary. But editors, composers and other film professionals trapped in the drudgery of serving the dumbed-down reality of modern television have also responded to the opportunity that the Francis brothers have given them to work with a passion for the medium.

Owning their film also means that the brothers are in a position to be far more strategic in the marketing of it than a TV monolith would be. The film documentary has become flavour of the month since the success of *Fahrenheit 9/11* – indeed, it would seem that it is only in the cinema that one can see the kind of critical works which previously might have been found on TV – and that creates one avenue of distribution. But the brothers are also looking at alliances with charities and NGOs working in the area, and are creating a DVD to be sold from the film's website. The broadcast of the film on TV, which conventional wisdom would suggest was the only way to get it made, may actually be relegated to the lowest priority. This subversion of the commercial norms is inspiring, and the fact that the subject matter is effectively concerned with the failure of those commercial norms in relation to the coffee trade makes it even more so. The poet Don Patterson has written, 'Poetry is the paradox of language turned against its own declared purpose, that of nailing down the human dream', and the fact that *Black Gold* is also a product of a new way of film-making makes its message more poetic – and powerful.

Given the nature of the project, ▶

> Coffee farmers are currently in acute crisis, a situation which nonetheless is arguably business as usual from a historical perspective.

Film: The Francis Brothers *(continued)*

◄ inevitably the Francis brothers and I started to have conversations about how the film and this paperback might work together, whether Matthew's track could feature on the film, the DVD or the CD of the DVD, and which website could link what to what. Once one enters that path, the potential for a kind of explosive, exponential multi-mediacrity is intoxicating.

The convergence of the technical means of production of media on the desktop and the corresponding divergence of distribution channels creates many exciting opportunities, and is itself a consequence of globalization. The rough cut of this film critique of globalization can be sent in edited form over the internet to a distant studio so that the composers can work on the music, then forward it with that music to the editor in another location for his or her input. An electronic spider's web of connectivity has freed a team of creators from the necessity of being together in one place at one time, allowing a new generation of 'live/work' spaces to develop to suit the operational demands of the new media artist. Globalization mobilized to defeat itself: one has to revel in the paradox. ■

www.speak-it.org